A Short Introduction to World Religions

A Short Introduction to World Religions

Updated and revised by Tim Dowley

General Editor: Christopher Partridge

Fortress Press

Minneapolis

Contents

PART 1
UNDERSTANDING RELIGION

PART 2
INDIGENOUS RELIGIONS

PART 3
HINDUISM

PART 4
BUDDHISM

PART 5
CHINESE, KOREAN, AND JAPANESE RELIGIONS

PART 6
JAINISM

PART 7
JUDAISM

PART 8
CHRISTIANITY

PART 9
ISLAM

PART 10
SIKHISM

PART 11
RELIGIONS IN TODAY'S WORLD

Contributors

The late Sir Norman Anderson, formerly Director of the Institute of Advanced Legal Studies, University of London, UK: *The Law of Islam*

David Arnold: *I am a Jew*

Dr John H. Berthrong, Associate Professor of Comparative Theology, Boston University School of Theology, MA, USA: *Chinese Religions*

Resham Singh Bhogal: *I am a Sikh*

Dr Barbara M. Boal, formerly Lecturer in Primal Religions, Selly Oak Colleges, Birmingham, UK: *Indigenous Religions in Asia*

Dr Fiona Bowie, Honorary Research Fellow, Department of Archaeology and Anthropology, University of Bristol, UK: *The Anthropology of Religion, Ritual and Performance*

Rt Revd Colin Buchanan, previously Bishop of Woolwich, London, UK: *Christianity: Worship and Festivals*

John Mohammed Butt, Islamic scholar and broadcaster, Muslim chaplain at Cambridge University: Consultant on Islam

Dr Eric S. Christianson, formerly Senior Lecturer in Biblical Studies, University College Chester, UK: *Judaism: Sacred Writings*

Dr George Chryssides, Research Fellow, University of Birmingham, UK: *New Religious Movements*

Dr Dan Cohn-Sherbok, Professor Emeritus of Judaism, University of Wales, UK: *Judaism: Beliefs*

The late Harvie M. Conn, Professor of Missions, Westminster Theological Seminary, Philadelphia PA, USA: *Sinkyo*

Dr Geoffrey Cowling, formerly Senior Lecturer in History, Macquarie University, New South Wales, Australia: *Judaism: A Historical Overview*

Dr James L. Cox, Professor of Religious Studies, University of Edinburgh, Scotland: *Inuit, African Indigenous Religions*

Dr Douglas Davies, Professor in the Study of Religion, Department of Theology and Religion, University of Durham, UK: *Myths and Symbols*

Dr Andrew Dawson, Senior Lecturer in Religion, Lancaster University, UK: *South American Indigenous Religions*

The late Dr Richard T. France, formerly Principal, Wycliffe Hall, Oxford, UK: *Jesus, Christianity: Sacred Writings*

Dr Theodore Gabriel, Honorary Research Fellow, Department of Religious Studies, University of Gloucestershire, UK: *Hinduism: Sacred Writings, Hinduism in the Modern World*

Daniel Guy, MA, University of Cambridge, UK: *Summaries*

Dr Malcolm Hamilton, Senior Lecturer, Department of Sociology, University of Reading, UK: *The Sociology of Religion*

Dr Elizabeth J. Harris, Senior Lecturer, Comparative Study of Religions, Liverpool Hope University, UK: *Buddhism: Beliefs, Family and Society, Buddhism in the Modern World*

Dr Graham Harvey, Reader in Religious Studies, The Open University, UK: *Understanding Indigenous Religions*

Dr Paul Hedges, Senior Lecturer in Theology and Religious Studies: *Theological Approaches to the Study of Religion*

Jason Hood: *I am a Christian*

Dr Lynne Hume, Associate Professor in the School of History, Philosophy, Religion and Classics, University of Queensland, Australia: *Australian Aboriginal Religions*

Dr Edward A. Irons, Director of the Hong Kong Institute for Culture, Commerce and Religion, Hong Kong: *Christianity in Contemporary China*

Dr Sewa Singh Kalsi, Lecturer in Sikh Studies, University of Leeds, UK: *Sikhism: Sacred Writings, Beliefs, Worship and Festivals*

Mohammed A. Khan: *I am a Muslim*

The late Dr David Kerr, formerly Professor in Missiology and Ecumenics at the Centre for Theology and Religious Studies at Lund University, Sweden: *The Unity and Variety of Islam, Islam: Worship and Festivals*

Dr Anna S. King, Reader in Theology and Religious Studies, University of Winchester, UK: *Hinduism: Beliefs*

Magdalen Lambkin, PhD student at the University of Glasgow, Scotland: Consultant, *Understanding Religion, Women and Religion*

Dr David Lyon, Professor of Sociology, Queen's University, Kingston, Canada: *Religion and Globalization*

Dr Russell T. McCutcheon, Professor of Sociology of Religion, University of Alabama, USA: *What is Religion?*

Dr Alister McGrath, Professor of Theology, Ministry, and Education at Kings College London, UK: *Christianity: A Historical Overview*

Dr I. Howard Marshall, Professor Emeritus of New Testament Exegesis, University of Aberdeen, UK: *Christianity: Beliefs*

The late Dr J. W. E. Newbery, formerly Professor Emeritus (Native Studies), University of Sudbury, Canada: *South American Indigenous Religions*

Dr Christopher Partridge, Professor of Religious Studies, University of Lancaster, UK: *Rapid Fact-finder*

Naren Patel: *I am a Hindu*

Dr Robert Pope, Reader in Theology, University of Wales, Trinity St David, UK: *Religion and Politics*

Samani Charitra Prajna: *I am a Jain*

Dr Michael Pye, formerly Professor of the Study of Religions, University of Marburg (Philipps-Universität), Germany: *Japanese Religions*

Dr Elizabeth Ramsey, Lecturer, Liverpool Hope University College, UK: *Judaism: Worship and Festivals, Judaism in the Modern World*

Dr Peter G. Riddell, Professorial Dean of the BCV Centre for the Study of Islam and Other Faiths, Melbourne, Australia: *Islam: Sacred Writings, Beliefs*

Very Revd Michael Sadgrove, Dean of Durham Cathedral, UK: *Branches of the Church*

Dr Emma Salter, Course leader, Religion and Education, University of Huddersfield, UK: *Jainism: A Historical Overview, Sacred Writings, Beliefs, Family and Society, Worship and Festivals, Jainism in the Modern World*

Paul Seto: *I am a Buddhist*

Helen Serdiville: *I am a spiritual seeker*

Dr Christopher Shackle, Emeritus Professor of Modern Languages of South Asia, University of London, UK: *Sikhism: A Historical Overview, Sikhism Today*

Revd Dr David Smith, Senior Research Fellow, International Christian College, Glasgow, UK: *Contemporary Christianity*

Revd Angela Tilby, Diocesan Canon, Christ Church, Oxford, UK: *Rapid Fact-finder*

Dr Alana Vincent, Lecturer in Jewish Studies, University of Chester, UK: Consultant, *Judaism*

Dr David Waines, Professor of Islamic Studies, University of Lancaster, UK: *Islam in the Modern World*

Dr Maya Warrier, Lecturer on Hinduism, University of Wales, Trinity St David, UK: *Hinduism: A Historical Overview, Worship and Festivals*

The late Revd Dr William Montgomery Watt, former Professor of Arabic and Islamic Studies, University of Edinburgh, UK: *Islam: A Historical Overview*

Dr Paul Williams, Emeritus Professor of Indian and Tibetan Philosophy, University of Bristol, UK: *Buddhism: A Historical Overview, Sacred Writings*

Revd Dr Marvin R. Wilson, Harold J. Ockenga
Professor of Biblical and Theological Studies,
Gordon College, Wenham, MA, USA: *Branches of Judaism*

Dr Linda Woodhead, Professor of Sociology of
Religion, Lancaster University, UK: Christianity:
Family and Society, Secularization and Sacralization

Revd Dr John-David Yule, Incumbent of the
United Benefice of Fen Drayton with Conington,
Lolworth, and Swavesey, Cambridge, UK: *Rapid Fact-finder*

Benjamin Zephaniah, poet, Lincolnshire, UK:
I am a Rastafarian

List of Maps

List of Time Charts

List of Festival Charts

List of Illustrations

Preface

A Short Introduction to World Religions is an abridged version of *Introduction to World Religions*, Third Edition. This original version of this textbook was first published by Lion Hudson and Christopher Partridge served as the general editor. The first Fortress Press edition (2005) featured significant changes in style and substance. It was further updated, revised, and refreshed in the second edition (2013) by editor Tim Dowley. This abridged version, also edited and revised by Tim Dowley, includes all the key features of the main textbook, including the full color maps, images, charts, and timelines, as well as suggestions for future reading and discussion questions at the conclusion of each major section. The volume's shortened length was achieved by eliminating sections from the unabridged Third Edition.

PART I
UNDERSTANDING RELIGION

SUMMARY

Belief in something that exists beyond or outside our understanding – whether spirits, gods, or simply a particular order to the world – has been present at every stage in the development of human society, and has been a major factor in shaping much of that development. Unsurprisingly, many have devoted themselves to the study of religion, whether to understand a particular set of beliefs, or to explain why humans seem instinctively drawn to religion. While biologists, for example, may seek to understand what purpose religion served in our evolutionary descent, we are concerned here with the beliefs, rituals, and speculation about existence that we – with some reservation – call religion.

The question of what 'religion' actually is is more fraught than might be expected. Problems can arise when we try to define the boundaries between religion and philosophy when speculation about existence is involved, or between religion and politics when moral teaching or social structure are at issue. In particular, once we depart from looking at the traditions of the West, many contend that such apparently obvious distinctions should not be applied automatically.

While there have always been people interested in the religious traditions of others, such 'comparative' approaches are surprisingly new. Theology faculties are among the oldest in European universities, but, while the systematic internal exploration of a religion provides considerable insights, many scholars insisted that the examination of religions more generally should be conducted instead by objective observers. This phenomenological approach was central to the establishment of the study of religion as a discipline in its own right. Others, concerned with the nature of society, or the workings of the human mind, for example, were inevitably drawn to the study of religion to expand their respective areas. More recently, many have attempted to utilise the work of these disparate approaches. In particular, many now suggest that – because no student can ever be entirely objective – theological studies are valuable because of their ability to define a religion in its own terms: by engaging with this alongside other, more detached, approaches, a student may gain a more accurate view of a particular religion.

CHAPTER I

What Is Religion?

Although no one is certain of the word's origins, we know that 'religion' derives from Latin, and that languages influenced by Latin have equivalents to the English word 'religion'. In Germany, the systematic study of religion is known as *Religionswissenschaft*, and in France as *les sciences religieuses*. Although the ancient words to which we trace 'religion' have nothing to do with today's meanings — it may have come from the Latin word that meant to tie something tightly (*religare*) — it is today commonly used to refer to those beliefs, behaviours, and social institutions which have something to do with speculations on any, and all, of the following: the origin, end, and significance of the universe; what happens after death; the existence and wishes of powerful, non-human beings such as spirits, ancestors, angels, demons, and gods; and the manner in which all of this shapes human behaviour.

Because each of these makes reference to an invisible (that is, non-empirical) world that somehow lies outside of, or beyond, human history, the things we name as 'religious' are commonly thought to be opposed to those institutions which we label as 'political'. In the West today we generally operate under the assumption that, whereas religion is a matter of personal belief that can never be settled by rational debate, such things as politics are observable, public, and thus open to rational debate.

THE ESSENCE OF 'RELIGION'

Although this commonsense distinction between private and public, sentiment and action, is itself a historical development — it is around the seventeenth century that we first see evidence that words that once referred to one's behaviour, public standing, and social rank (such as piety and reverence) became sentimentalized as matters of private feeling — today the assumption that religion involves an inner core of belief that is somehow expressed publicly in ritual is so widespread that to question it appears counterintuitive. It is just this assumption that inspires a number of people who, collectively, we could term 'essentialists'. They are 'essentialists' because they maintain that 'religion' names the outward behaviours that are inspired by the inner thing they call 'faith'. Hence, one can imagine someone saying, 'I'm not religious, but I'm spiritual.' Implicit here is the assumption that the institutions associated with religions — hierarchies, regulations, rituals, and so on — are merely secondary and inessential; the important thing is the inner faith, the inner 'essence' of religion. Although the essence of religion — the thing without which someone is thought to be non-religious — is known by various names (faith, belief, the Sacred, the Holy, and so on), essentialists are in general agreement that the essence of religion is real and non-empirical (that is, it cannot itself be seen, heard, touched, and so on); it defies study and must be experienced first-hand.

THE FUNCTION OF 'RELIGION'

Apart from an approach that assumes an inner experience, which underlies religious behaviour, scholars have used the term 'religion' for what they consider to be curious areas of observable human behaviour which require an explanation. Such people form theories to account for why it is people think, for example, that an invisible part of their body, usually called 'the soul', outlives that body; that powerful beings control the universe; and that there is more to existence than what is observable. These theories are largely functionalist; that is, they seek to determine the social, psychological, or political role played by the things we refer to as 'religious'. Such functionalists include historically:

- Karl Marx (1818–83), whose work in political economy understood religion to be a pacifier that deadened oppressed people's sense of pain and alienation, while simultaneously preventing them from doing something about their lot in life, since ultimate responsibility was thought to reside in a being who existed outside history.

Karl Marx (1818–83).

- Émile Durkheim (1858–1917), whose sociology defined religious as sets of beliefs and practices to enable individuals who engaged in them to form a shared, social identity.
- Sigmund Freud (1856–1939), whose psychological studies prompted him to liken religious behaviour to the role that dreams play in helping people to vent antisocial anxieties in a manner that does not threaten their place within the group.

Although these classic approaches are all rather different, each can be understood as *functionalist* insomuch as religion names an institution that has a role to play in helping individuals and communities to reproduce themselves.

THE FAMILY RESEMBLANCE APPROACH

Apart from the *essentialist* way of defining religion (i.e. there is some non-empirical, core feature without which something is not religious) and the *functionalist* (i.e. that religions help to satisfy human needs), there is a third approach: the *family resemblance* definition. Associated with the philosophy of Ludwig Wittgenstein (1889–1951), a family resemblance approach assumes that nothing is defined by merely one essence or function. Rather, just as members of a family more or less share a series of traits, and just as all things we call 'games' more or less share a series of traits – none of which is distributed evenly across all members of those groups we call 'family' or 'games' – so all things – including religion – are defined insomuch as they more or less share a series of delimited traits. Ninian Smart (1927–2001), who identified seven dimensions of religion that are present in religious traditions with varying degrees of emphasis, is perhaps the best known proponent of this view.

'RELIGION' AS CLASSIFIER

Our conclusion is that the word 'religion' likely tells us more about the user of the word (i.e. the classifier) than it does about the thing being classified. For instance, a Freudian psychologist will not conclude that religion functions to oppress the masses, since the Freudian theory precludes coming up with this Marxist conclusion. On the other hand, a scholar who adopts Wittgenstein's approach will sooner or later come up with a case in which something seems to share some traits, but perhaps not enough to count as 'a religion'. If, say, soccer matches satisfy many of the criteria of a religion, what might not also be called religion if soccer is? And what does such a broad usage do to the specificity, and thus utility, of the word 'religion'? As for those who adopt an essentialist approach, it is likely no coincidence that only those institutions with which one agrees are thought to be expressions of some authentic inner experience, sentiment, or emotion, whilst the traditions of others are criticized as being shallow and derivative.

So what is religion? As with any other item in our lexicon, 'religion' is a historical artefact that different social actors use for different purposes: to classify certain parts of their social world in order to celebrate, degrade, or theorize about them. Whatever else it may or may not be, religion is at least an item of rhetoric that group members use to sort out their group identities.

RUSSELL T. MCCUTCHEON

CHAPTER 2

The Anthropology of Religion

Anthropology approaches religion as an aspect of culture. Religious beliefs and practices are important because they are central to the ways in which we organize our social lives. They shape our understanding of our place in the world, and determine how we relate to one another and to the rest of the natural, and supernatural, order. The truth or falsity of religious beliefs, or the authenticity or moral worth of religious practices, are seldom an issue for anthropologists, whose main concern is to document what people think and do, rather than determine what they ought to believe, or how they should behave.

RELIGION AND SOCIAL STRUCTURE

An early observation in the anthropology of religion was the extent to which religion and social structure mirror one another. Both the French historian Fustel de Coulanges (1830–89), drawing on Classical sources, and the Scottish biblical scholar William Robertson Smith (1846–94), who studied Semitic religions, demonstrated this coincidence in form. For example, nomadic peoples such as the Bedouin conceive of God in terms

> *The belief in a supreme God or a single God is no mere philosophical speculation; it is a great practical idea.*
>
> Maurice Hocart

of a father, and use familial and pastoral imagery to describe their relationship with God. A settled, hierarchical society, by contrast, will depict God as a monarch to whom tribute is due, with imagery of servants and subjects honouring a supreme ruler. These early studies influenced the French sociologist Émile Durkheim (1858–1917), whose book *The Elementary Forms of the Religious Life* (1912) was foundational for later anthropological studies of religion. Rather than seeing religion as determining social structure, Durkheim argued that religion is a projection of society's highest values and goals. The realm of the sacred is separated from the profane world and made to seem both natural and obligatory. Through collective rituals people both reaffirm their belief in supernatural beings and reinforce their bonds with one another.

The totemism of Australian Aboriginals, which links human groups with particular forms of animal or other natural phenomena in relations of prohibition and prescription, was regarded by many nineteenth-century scholars as the earliest form of religion, and as such was of interest to both Durkheim and the anthropologist Edward Burnett Tylor

(1832–1917), who postulated an evolutionary movement from animism to polytheism and then monotheism. However, as evolutionary arguments are essentially unprovable, later work built not on these foundations, but on the more sociological insights of Durkheim and anthropologists such as Alfred Radcliffe-Brown (1881–1955) and Sir Edward Evan Evans-Pritchard (1902–73).

Evans-Pritchard sought to retain the historical perspective of his predecessors, while replacing speculation concerning origins with data based on first-hand observations and participation in the life of a people. His classic 1937 ethnography of witchcraft, oracles, and magic among the Azande in Central Africa demonstrated that beliefs which, from a Western perspective, appear irrational and unscientific – such as the existence of witches and magic – are perfectly logical, once one understands the ideational system on which a society is based.

SYMBOLISM

While Durkheim was avowedly atheist, some of the most influential anthropologists of the later twentieth century, including Evans-Pritchard, were or became practising Roman Catholics. This is true of Mary Douglas (1921–2007) and Victor Turner (1920–83), both of whom were particularly interested in the symbolic aspects of religion. They were influenced not only by Durkheim and Evans-Pritchard, but more particularly by Durkheim's gifted pupils Marcel Mauss (1872–1950) and Henri Hubert (1864–1925), who wrote on ceremonial exchange, sacrifice, and magic.

> *Man is an animal suspended in webs of significance he himself has spun. I take culture to be those webs.*
>
> Clifford Geertz, *The Interpretation of Cultures: Selected Essays* (New York, 1973)

In her influential collection of essays *Purity and Danger* (1966), Douglas looked at the ways in which the human body is used as a symbol system in which meanings are encoded. The body is seen as a microcosm of the powers and dangers attributed to society at large. Thus, a group that is concerned to maintain its social boundaries, such as members of the Brahman caste in India, pays great attention to notions of purity and pollution as they affect the individual body. In examining purity rules, Douglas was primarily concerned with systems of classification. In her study of the Hebrew purity rules in the book of Leviticus, for example, Douglas argued that dietary proscriptions were not the result of medical or hygiene concerns, but followed the logic of a system of classification that divided animals into clean and unclean species according to whether they conformed to certain rules – such as being cloven-hooved and chewing cud – or were anomalous, and therefore unclean and prohibited. Like Robertson Smith, Douglas observed that rituals can retain their form over many generations, notwithstanding changes in their interpretation, and that meaning is preserved in the form itself, as well as in explanations for a particular ritual action.

In the work of Mary Douglas we see a fruitful combination of the sociological and symbolist tradition of the Durkheimians and the structuralism of Claude Lévi-Strauss (1908–2009). Lévi-Strauss carried out some fieldwork in the Amazonian region of Brazil, but it is as a theoretician that he has been most influential, looking not at the meaning or semantics of social structure, but at its syntax or formal aspects. In his four-volume study of mythology (1970–81), he sought to demonstrate the universality of certain cultural themes, often expressed as binary oppositions, such as the transformation of food from raw to cooked, or the opposition between culture and nature. The structuralism of Lévi-Strauss both looks back to Russian formalism and the linguistics of the Swiss Ferdinand de Saussure (1857–1913), and forwards to more recent psychoanalytic studies of religion, both of which see themselves as belonging more to a scientific than to a humanist tradition.

RITUAL AND SYMBOL

On the symbolist and interpretive side, Victor Turner (1920–83) produced a series of sensitive, detailed studies of ritual and symbols, focusing on the processual nature of ritual and its theatrical, dramatic aspects, based on extensive fieldwork among the Ndembu of Zambia carried out in the 1950s. Clifford Geertz (1926–2006) was equally concerned with meaning and interpretation, and following a German-American tradition he looked more at culture than at social structure. Geertz saw religion as essentially that which gives meaning to human society, and religious symbols as codifying an ethos or world view. Their power lies in their ability both to reflect and to shape society.

Recently, important changes have stemmed from postmodernism and postcolonial thinking, globalization and multiculturalism. Anthropologists now often incorporate a critique of their own position and interests into their studies, and are no longer preoccupied exclusively with 'exotic' small-scale societies; for instance, there is a lot of research into global Pentecostalism and its local forms. The impact of new forms of media in the religious sphere has also become a significant area of study.

FIONA BOWIE

MYTHS AND SYMBOLS

One dimension of religions which has received particular attention by scholars has been that of myths and symbols. If we had just heard a moving piece of music, we would find it strange if someone asked us whether the music were true or false. Music, we might reply, is neither true nor false; to ask such a question is inappropriate. Most people know that music can, as it were, speak to them, even though no words are used.

As with music so with people. The question of what someone 'means' to you cannot fully be answered by saying that he is your husband or she is your wife, because there are always unspoken levels of intuition, feeling, and emotion built into relationships. The question of 'meaning' must always be seen to concern these dimensions, as well as the more obviously factual ones.

Myths

Myths take many forms, depending on the culture in which they are found. But their function is always that of pinpointing vital issues and values in the life of the society concerned. They often dramatize those profound issues of life and death, of how humanity came into being, and of what life means, of how we should conduct ourselves as a citizen or spouse, as a creature of God or as a farmer, and so on.

Myths are not scientific or sociological theories about these issues; they are the outcome of the way a nation or group has pondered the great questions. Their function is not merely to provide a theory of life that can be taken or left at will; they serve to compel a response from humanity. We might speak of myths as bridges between the intellect and emotion, between the mind and heart – and in this, myths are like music. They express an idea and trigger our response to it.

Sometimes myths form an extensive series, interlinking with each other and encompassing many aspects of life, as has been shown for the Dogon people of the River Niger in West Africa. On the other hand, they may serve merely as partial accounts of problems, such as the hatred between people and snakes, or the reason for the particular shape of a mountain.

One problem in our understanding of myths lies in the fact that the so-called Western religions – Judaism, Christianity, and Islam – are strongly concerned with history. They have founders, and see their history as God's own doing. This strong emphasis upon actual events differs from the Eastern approaches to religion, which emphasize the consciousness of the individual. Believing in the cyclical nature of time, Hinduism and Buddhism possess a different approach to history, and hence also to science.

In the West, the search for facts in science is like the search for facts in history, but both these endeavours differ from the search for religious experience in the present. In the West, history and science have come to function as a framework within which religious experiences are found and interpreted, one consequence of which is that myths are often no longer appreciated for their power to evoke human responses to religious ideas.

The eminent historian of religion Mircea Eliade (1907–86) sought to restore this missing sense of the sacred by helping people to understand the true nature of myths. The secularized Westerner has lost the sense of the sacred, and is trying to compensate, as Eliade saw it, by means of science fiction, supernatural literature, and films. One may, of course, keep a firm sense of history and science without seeking to destroy the mythical appreciation of ideas and beliefs.

Symbols

Religious symbols help believers to understand their faith in quite profound ways. Like myths, they serve to unite the intellect and the emotions. Symbols also integrate the social and personal dimensions of religion, enabling individuals to share certain commonly held beliefs expressed by symbols, while also giving freedom to read private meaning into them.

We live the whole of our life in a world of symbols. The daily smiles and grimaces, handshakes and greetings, as well as the more readily acknowledged status symbols of large cars or houses – all these communicate messages about ourselves to others.

To clarify the meaning of symbols, it will help if we distinguish between the terms 'symbol' and 'sign'. There is a certain arbitrariness about signs, so that the word 'table', which signifies an object of furniture with a flat top supported on legs, could be swapped for another sound without any difficulty. Thus the Germans call it *tisch* and the Welsh *bwrdd*.

A symbol, by contrast, is more intimately involved in that to which it refers. It participates in what it symbolizes, and cannot easily be swapped for another symbol. Nor can it be explained in words and still carry the same power. For example, a kiss is a symbol of affection and love; it not only signifies these feelings in some abstract way; it actually demonstrates them. In this sense a symbol can be a thought in action.

Religious symbols share these general characteristics, but are often even more intensely powerful, because they enshrine and express the highest values and relationships of life. The cross of Christ, the sacred books of Muslims and Sikhs, the sacred cow of Hindus, or the silent, seated Buddha – all these command the allegiance of millions of religious men and women. If such symbols are attacked or desecrated, an intense reaction is felt by the faithful, which shows us how deeply symbols are embedded in the emotional life of believers.

The power of symbols lies in this ability to unite fellow-believers into a community. It provides a focal point of faith and action, while also making possible a degree of personal understanding which those outside may not share.

In many societies the shared aspect of symbols is important as a unifying principle of life. Blood, for example, may be symbolic of life, strength, parenthood, or of the family and kinship group itself. In Christianity it expresses life poured out in death, the self-sacrificial love of Christ who died for human sin. It may even be true that the colour red can so easily serve as a symbol of

The cross is the central symbol of Christianity.

danger because of its deeper biological association with life and death.

Symbols serve as triggers of commitment in religions. They enshrine the teachings and express them in a tangible way. So the sacraments of baptism and the Lord's Supper in Christianity bring the believer into a practical relationship with otherwise abstract ideas, such as repentance and forgiveness. People can hardly live without symbols because they always need something to motivate life; it is as though abstract ideas need to be set within a symbol before individuals can be impelled to act upon them. When any attempt is made to turn symbols into bare statements of truth, this vital trigger of the emotions can easily be lost.

Douglas Davies

CHAPTER 3

The Sociology of Religion

The sociological study of religion has its roots in the seventeenth- and eighteenth-century Enlightenment, when a number of influential thinkers sought not only to question religious belief, but also to understand it as a natural phenomenon, a human product rather than the result of divine revelation or revealed truth. While contemporary sociology of religion has largely abandoned the overtly critical stance of early theoretical approaches to the truth claims of religion, the discipline retains the essential principle that an understanding of religion must acknowledge that it is, to some degree at least, socially constructed, and that social processes are fundamentally involved in the emergence, development, and dissemination of religious beliefs and practices.

METHODOLOGICAL AGNOSTICISM

While some sociologists consider that some religious beliefs are false, and that recognition of this is crucial to a sociological understanding of them, the dominant position in the sociology of religion today is that of 'methodological agnosticism'. This method states that it is neither possible, nor necessary, to decide whether beliefs are true or false in order to study them sociologically. Theology and philosophy of religion, not sociology, discuss questions of religious truth. The conditions which promote the acceptance or rejection of religious beliefs and practices, which govern their dissemination and the impact they have on behaviour and on society, can all be investigated without prior determination of their truth or falsity.

ROOTS IN INDIVIDUAL NEEDS

Theoretical approaches in the sociology of religion can usefully – if a little crudely – be divided into those which perceive the roots of religion to lie in individual needs and propensities, and those which perceive its roots to lie in social processes and to stem from the characteristics of society and social groups. The former may be further divided into those which emphasize cognitive processes – intellectualism – and those which emphasize various feelings and emotions – emotionalism.

In the nineteenth century, intellectualist theorists such as Auguste Comte (1798–1857), Edward Burnett Tylor (1832–1917), James G. Frazer (1854–1941), and Herbert Spencer (1820–1903) analyzed religious belief as essentially a pre-scientific attempt to understand the world and human experience, which would increasingly be supplanted by sound scientific knowledge. The future would thus be entirely secular, with no place for religion.

Emotionalist theorists, such as Robert Ranulph Marett (1866–1943), Bronislaw Malinowski (1884–1942), and Sigmund Freud (1856–1939), saw religions as stemming from human emotions such as fear, uncertainty, ambivalence, and awe. They were not attempts to explain and understand, but to cope with intense emotional experience.

ROOTS IN SOCIAL PROCESSES

The most influential sociological approaches that consider the roots of religion lie in society and social processes, not in the individual, are those of Karl Marx (1818–83) and Émile Durkheim (1858–1917).

For Marx, religion was both a form of ideology supported by ruling classes in order to control the masses, and at the same time an expression of protest against such oppression – 'the sigh of the oppressed creature'. As a protest, however, it changed nothing, promoting only resignation, and promising resolution of problems in the afterlife. Religion is 'the opium of the people', in the sense that it dulls the pain of the oppressed and thereby stops them from revolting. Hence, the oppressed turn to religion to help them get through life; the ruling classes promote it to keep them in check. It will simply disappear when the social conditions that cause it are removed.

> Religion is the sigh of the oppressed creature and the opium of the people.
>
> Karl Marx, A Contribution to the Critique of Hegel's Philosophy of Right (Deutsch-Französische Jahrbücher, 1844).

Durkheim saw religion as an essential, integrating social force, which fulfilled basic functions in society. It was the expression of human subordination, not to a ruling class, as Marx had argued, but rather to the requirements of society itself, and to social pressures which overrule individual preferences. In his famous work *The Elementary Forms of the Religious Life* (1912), Durkheim argued that 'Religion is society worshipping itself.' God may not exist, but society does; rather than God exerting pressure on the individual to conform, society itself exerts the pressure. Individuals, who do not understand the nature of society and social groups, use the language of religion to explain the social forces they experience. Although people misinterpret social forces as religious forces, what they experience is real. Moreover, for Durkheim, religion fulfils a positive role, in that it binds society together as a moral community.

MAX WEBER AND MEANING THEORY

Later theoretical approaches in the sociology of religion have all drawn extensively on this earlier work, attempting to synthesize its insights into more nuanced approaches, in which the various strands of intellectual, emotional, and social factors are woven together. A notable example is the work of Max Weber (1864–1920), probably the most significant contributor to the sociology of religion to this day. His work included one of the best-known treatises in the sub-discipline, *The Protestant Ethic and the Spirit of Capitalism* (1904–05), and three major studies of world religions.

Weber's approach to religion was the forerunner of what has become known as 'meaning theory', which emphasizes the way in which religion gives meaning to human life and society, in the face of apparently arbitrary suffering and injustice. Religion offers explanation and justification of good and of bad fortune, by locating them within a broader picture of a reality which may go beyond the world of immediate everyday perception, thereby helping to make sense of what always threatens to appear senseless. So those who suffer undeservedly in this life may have offended in a previous one; or they will receive their just deserts in the next life, or in heaven. Those who prosper through wickedness will ultimately be judged and duly punished.

RATIONAL CHOICE THEORY

The most recent, general theoretical approach in the sociology of religion, which synthesizes many previous insights, is that of 'rational choice theory'. Drawing upon economic theory, this treats religions as rival products offered in a market by religious organizations – which are compared to commercial firms – and leaders, to consumers, who choose by assessing which best meets their needs, which is most reliable, and so on. This approach promises to provide many insights. However, it has been subjected to trenchant criticism by those who question whether religion can be treated as something chosen in the way that products such as cars or soap-powders are chosen, rather than something into which people are socialized, and which forms an important part of their identity that cannot easily be set aside or changed. Furthermore, if religious beliefs are a matter of preference and convenience, why do their followers accept the uncongenial demands and constraints they usually impose, and the threat of punishments for failure to comply?

SECULARIZATION AND NEW MOVEMENTS

The sociology of religion was for many decades regarded as an insignificant branch of sociology. This situation has changed in recent years, especially in the USA. Substantive empirical inquiry has been dominated by two areas: secularization and religious sects, cults, and movements. It had been widely assumed that religion was declining in modern industrial societies and losing its social significance – the secularization thesis. This has

Hare Krishna Festival of Chariots in Trafalgar Square, London. Hare Krishna is one of many New Religious Movements.

been questioned and found by many — especially rational choice theorists — to be wanting. The result has been intense debate. The dominant position now, though not unchallenged, is that the secularization thesis was a myth.

Central to this debate is the claim that — while religion in its traditional forms may be declining in some modern, Western industrial societies — it is not declining in all of them, the USA being a notable exception; and that novel forms of religion are continuously emerging to meet inherent spiritual needs. Some new forms are clearly religious in character. Others, it is claimed, are quite unlike religion as commonly understood, and include alternative and complementary forms of healing, psychotherapies, techniques for the development of human potential, deep ecology, holistic spirituality, New Age, the cult of celebrity, nationalist movements, and even sport. Whether such things can be considered forms of religion depends upon how religion is defined, a matter much disputed.

A second crucial element in the secularization debate is the rise of a diversity of sects and cults – the New Religious Movements – which have proliferated since the 1960s and 1970s. For the anti-secularization – or 'sacralization' – theorists, this flourishing of novel religiosity gives the lie to the thesis; while for pro-secularization theorists, such movements fall far short of making up for the decline of mainstream churches and denominations. Whatever their significance for the secularization thesis, the New Religious Movements – and sects and cults in general – have fascinated sociologists, whose extensive studies of them form a major part of the subject.

Heavy concentration on New Religious Movements has been balanced more recently by studies of more mainstream religious churches and communities, and by studies of the religious life of ethnic minorities and immigrant communities, among whom religion is often particularly significant and an important element of identity. Added to the interest in new forms of religion and quasi-religion, such studies make the contemporary sociology of religion more diverse and varied than ever.

MALCOLM HAMILTON

CHAPTER 4

Theological Approaches to the Study of Religion

During the development of the study of religion as a new discipline in the twentieth century, the pioneers of the field were often at pains to stress that what they did was different from theology. As such, it might be asked whether a theological approach even belongs within the study of religion. Many scholars today, who emphasize it as a scientific or historical discipline, distance themselves from any notion that theology, in any form, has a place within the study of religion. For others, the relationship is more ambiguous, while some scholars even argue that theological approaches are essential to understanding, and so truly studying, religion.

WHAT DO WE MEAN BY 'THEOLOGY'?

It is best to start by defining what we mean by 'theology' in relation to the study of religion. We will begin with some negatives. First, it does not mean a confessional approach, where the teachings of one school, tradition, or sect within a religion are taught as the true, or correct, understanding of that religion. Second, theology does not imply that there is any need for a belief, or faith content, within the person studying in that idiom. It is not, therefore, under the classic definition of the medieval Christian Anselm of Canterbury (1033–1109), an act of 'faith seeking understanding'.

We come now to the positives. First, it is about understanding the internal terms within which a religion will seek to explain itself, its teachings, and its formulations. We must be clear here that 'theology' is used loosely, because while it makes sense as a Christian term – literally it is the study of God – and can be fairly clearly applied to other theistic traditions, it is also used elsewhere to talk about broadly philosophical traditions related to transcendence. Accordingly, people use the term 'Buddhist theology' – although others question whether this usage is appropriate, but space does not permit us to engage in such disputes here. Second, it means engaging with empathy with questions of meaning as they would make sense within the religious worldview, and so goes beyond reasoning and relates to a way of life. Here, we see clear resonances with phenomenological approaches, where we seek to understand a religion on its own terms.

Anselm of Canterbury (1033–1109).

Indeed, without a theological viewpoint, it can be argued that the study of religions fails, because on the one hand it is either simply reductionist, that is to say it explains via some chosen system why the religion exists, what it does, and what it means — as tends to be the case with some parts of the sociology or psychology of religion. Or, on the other hand, it becomes merely descriptive, telling us what rituals are performed, what the ethics are, what the teachings are, how it is lived out, and so on — a simply phenomenological approach. A theological approach looks into the religion, and seeks to understand what it means to believers within its own terms, and how that system works as a rational worldview to those within it.

INSIDER AND OUTSIDER

Two important pairs of distinctions are useful to consider how theological approaches are applied. The first, developed by the anthropologist Kenneth Pike (1912–2000), and often applied to religion, concerns what are called 'emic' and 'etic' approaches. An emic approach attempts to explain things within the cultural world of the believer. An etic approach is the way an external observer would try and make sense of the behaviours and beliefs of a society or group in some form of scientific sense. Within anthropology, these basic distinctions are seen as part of the tools of the trade. Unless she enters into the thought-world of a group, culture, and society, the anthropologist will remain forever exterior, and will not understand what things mean to those in that group. Moreover, emic understandings can help inspire etic description, and assess its appropriateness. Clearly, in the study of religion, this originally anthropological distinction suggests that an emic, or theological, approach is justified.

Our second pair of distinctions is the notion of 'Insider' and 'Outsider' perspectives. These are, respectively, concepts from somebody who is a believer (an Insider), and a non-believer, that is, the scholar (an Outsider). This differs from the emic/etic distinction, because they are always perspectives of the Outsider: the scholar. As such, an emic theological approach is different from the confessional theology of an Insider. However, this distinction is often blurred. Field anthropologists speak of spending so much time within the group or society they study that they often almost become part of that group, and part of good fieldwork is about entering the life world of those studied. This applies equally to scholars of religion, especially those engaged in fieldwork.

Another issue is that scholars may be believers within a religion, and so may inhabit both Insider and Outsider worlds. This raises many interesting questions, but here we will note simply that the notion of the detached, impartial, and objective scholar is increasingly questioned. Issues raised by critical theory have suggested that every standpoint will always have a bias, and some have argued further – notably the Hindu scholar, Gavin Flood – that a religious point of view, if openly acknowledged, can form part of the broader study of religions. Moreover, religious groups are often affected by what scholars of religion say about them. Therefore, Insider worldviews and Outsider descriptions – etic or emic – become intertwined in a dance that affects each other. As such, the question of how a theological approach fits into, or works within, religious studies is far from simple.

ALWAYS 'TAINTED'?

Scholars such as Timothy Fitzgerald, Tomoko Masuzawa, and Tala Asad have argued that the supposedly secular study of religion has always been 'tainted', because it developed in a world where Christianity dominated – often with a particular kind of liberal theology – so that no study of religion is entirely free from theology. Certainly, some foundational figures, such as Mircea Eliade, had a religious worldview, and a lot of mid-twentieth century work developing the phenomenology of religion, or comparative religion, made assumptions about a religious realm that underlay all traditions. However, it is arguable whether all scholars of religion then and since are affected in this way, while a case can be made that it was not solely Christian assumptions that affected the study of religion, but that such assumptions were shaped by the encounter with various religious traditions. As such, while we must be suspicious of some categories within the study of religion, we do not need to assume that everything has a Christian basis. Indeed, Frank Whaling argues we must also not forget that many religions have a lot to say about other religions, and this leads into theorizing on comparative religion, comparative theology, and the theology of religions within a confessional standpoint which is not entirely separate from understanding a religion and its worldview.

The relationship of the study of religions and theology varies in different countries. For instance, in Germany the two tend to be starkly polarized, with theology departments being – at least traditionally – strictly confessional, normally Roman Catholic or Protestant, and the study of religions – understood as a primarily reductionist secular discipline – is always separate from theology. In the UK, the ancient universities started to admit non-Anglican Christian denominations from the nineteenth century, and so lost their confessional stance, with seminaries for training priests becoming separate or linked institutions. For this reason, it was easier to start teaching theology from a generic standpoint, which could integrate other religions as part of the curriculum, and so there are many combined departments for theology and the study of religion. The USA tends to have a more separate system, although there are places where an active study of religion discipline exists within a theology department. Obviously, such regional differences affect the way a theological approach to the study of religion is accepted or understood.

PAUL HEDGES

CHAPTER 5

Ritual and Performance

Like myths and symbols, ritual and performance is an area that has particularly interested religious studies scholars. Ritual is patterned, formal, symbolic action. Religious ritual is usually seen as having reference to divine or transcendent beings, or perhaps ancestors, whom the participants invoke, propitiate, feed – through offering or sacrifice – worship, or otherwise communicate with. Rituals attempt to enact and deal with the central dilemmas of human existence: continuity and stability, growth and fertility, morality and immortality or transcendence. They have the potential to transform people and situations, creating a fierce warrior or docile wife, a loving servant or imperious tyrant. The ambiguity of ritual symbols, and the invocation of supernatural power, magnifies and disguises human needs and emotions. Because rituals are sometimes performed in terrifying circumstances – as in certain initiation rituals – the messages they carry act at a psycho-biological level that includes, but also exceeds, the rational mind. Symbols and sacred objects are manipulated within ritual to enhance performance and communicate ideological messages concerning the nature of the individual, society, and cosmos. Rituals are fundamental to human culture, and can be used to control, subvert, stabilize, enhance, or terrorize individuals and groups. Studying them gives us a key to an understanding and interpretation of culture.

Anthropologists and religious studies scholars sometimes look at rituals in terms of what they do. For instance, Catherine Bell (b. 1953) distinguishes between:

- rites of passage or 'life crisis' rituals
- calendrical rituals and commemorative rites
- rites of exchange or communication
- rites of affliction
- rites of feasting, fasting, festivals
- political rituals

Another approach is to focus on their explanatory value. Mircea Eliade (1907–86) was interested in ritual as a re-enactment of a primal, cosmogonic myth, bringing the past continually into the present. Robin Horton emphasizes the reality of the religious beliefs behind ritual actions. Using the Kalabari of Nigeria as an example, he insists that religious rituals have the power to move and transform participants because they express beliefs that have meaning and coherence for their adherents. Taking a lead from Durkheim (1858–1917), other scholars claim that rituals are effective because they make statements about social phenomena. Maurice Bloch, writing about circumcision rituals in Madagascar, makes the interesting observation that because a ritual is not fully a statement and not fully an action it allows its message to be simultaneously communicated and disguised. In some cases ritual symbols may be full of resonance, as Victor Turner demonstrated for Ndembu heali ng, chiefly installation, and initiation rituals in Central Africa. In other cases the performance of the ritual itself may be what matters, the content or symbolism having become redundant or forgotten over time, as Fritz Staal has argued for Vedic rituals in India.

> *No experience is too lowly to be taken up in ritual and given a lofty meaning.*
>
> Mary Douglas

PATTERNS IN RITUAL

A key figure in the study of ritual is Arnold van Gennep (1873–1957), who discerned an underlying patterning beneath a wide range of rituals. Whether we look at seasonal festivals such as Christmas, midsummer, or harvest, or 'life crisis' rituals that mark a change in status from one stage of life to another, such as birth, puberty, marriage, or mortuary rituals, we see beneath them all the threefold pattern of separation, transition, and reintegration. Van Gennep also noted that there is generally a physical passage in ritual as well as a social movement, and that the first time a ritual is celebrated it is usually more elaborate than on subsequent occasions, as it bears the weight of change of status.

Victor Turner took up van Gennep's schema, emphasizing the movement from social structure to an anti-structural position in the middle, liminal, stage of a rite of passage. In the middle stage, initiands often share certain characteristics. There is a levelling process – they may be stripped, or dressed in such a way as to erase individuality, hair may be shaved or allowed to grow long. Neophytes are often isolated from the everyday world, and may undergo certain ordeals that bind them to one another and to those initiating them. Turner coined the term 'communitas' to describe a spontaneous, immediate, and concrete relatedness that is typical of people in the liminal stage of a rite of passage. Liminality can also be institutionalized and extended almost indefinitely, as for instance in the military, monastic communities, hospitals, or asylums.

MALE AND FEMALE INITIATION

Bruce Lincoln has criticized both van Gennep and Turner's models as more relevant to male than female initiations, pointing out that women have little status in the social hierarchy, and therefore the middle stage of a woman's initiation is less likely to stress anti-structural elements. Rather than being brought low as a prelude to being elevated, her lowlier place within society is reinforced. A woman is more likely than her male counterparts to be initiated singly, and to be enclosed within a domestic space. Women are generally adorned rather than stripped, and the nature of the knowledge

passed on during initiation is likely to be mundane rather than esoteric. Rather than separation, liminality, and reintegration, Lincoln proposes that for women initiation is more likely to involve enclosure, metamorphosis or magnification, and emergence.

Malagasy children, Madagascar.

A ritual is a type of performance, but not all performances are rituals. Richard Schechner (b. 1934) has pointed out that whether a performance is to be classified as ritual or theatre depends on the context. If the purpose of a performance is to be efficacious, it is a ritual. If its purpose is to entertain, it is theatre. These are not absolute distinctions, and most performances contain elements of both efficacious intention and entertainment. At the ritual end of the continuum we are likely to have an active 'audience', who share the aims and intentions of the main actors. Time and space are sacred, and symbolically marked, and it is the end result of the action that matters — to heal, initiate, aid the deceased, or whatever it may be. In a theatrical performance, the audience is more likely to observe than participate, and the event is an end in itself. It is performed for those watching, and not for, or in the presence of, a higher power or absent other.

FIONA BOWIE

TIMELINE OF WORLD RELIGIONS

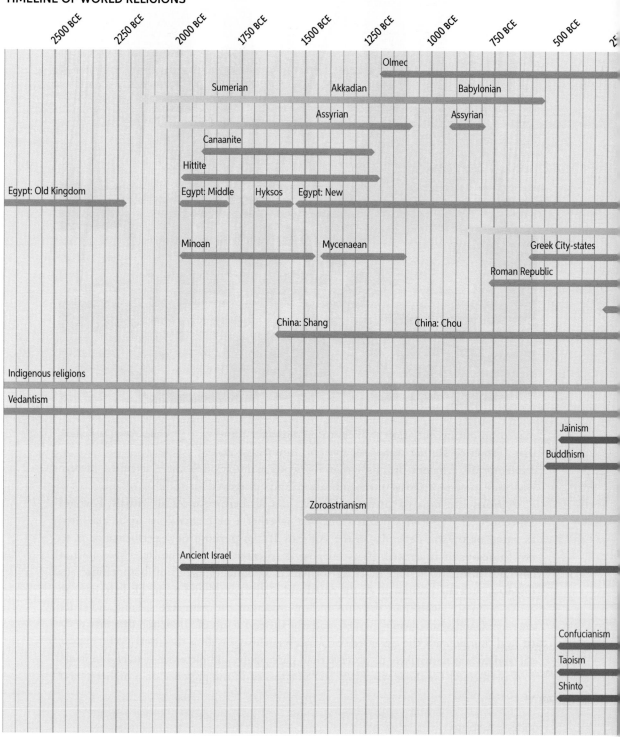

2500 BCE · 2250 BCE · 2000 BCE · 1750 BCE · 1500 BCE · 1250 BCE · 1000 BCE · 750 BCE · 500 BCE · 25...

Olmec

Sumerian · Akkadian · Babylonian

Assyrian · Assyrian

Canaanite

Hittite

Egypt: Old Kingdom · Egypt: Middle · Hyksos · Egypt: New

Minoan · Mycenaean · Greek City-states

Roman Republic

China: Shang · China: Chou

Indigenous religions

Vedantism

Jainism

Buddhism

Zoroastrianism

Ancient Israel

Confucianism

Taoism

Shinto

A SHORT INTRODUCTION TO WORLD RELIGIONS

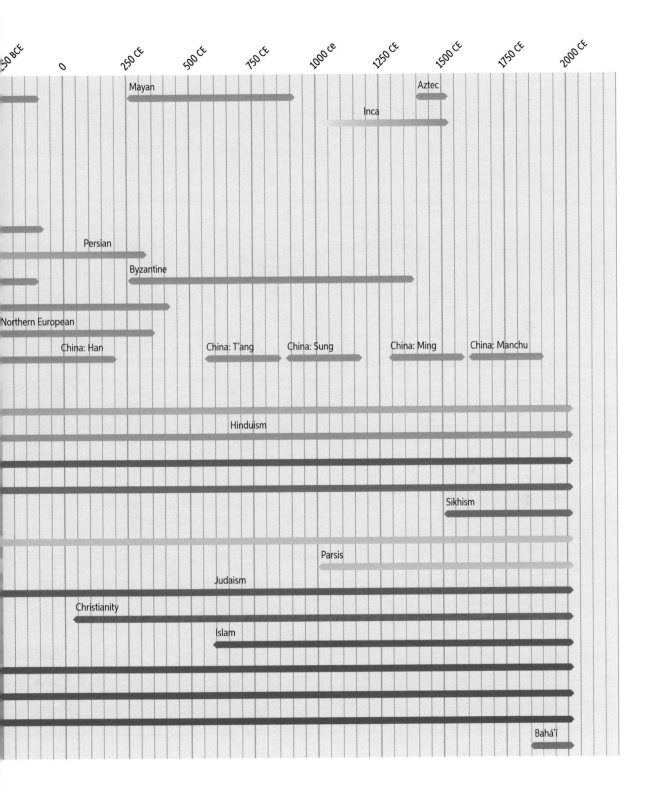

250 BCE | 0 | 250 CE | 500 CE | 750 CE | 1000 ce | 1250 CE | 1500 CE | 1750 CE | 2000 CE

Mayan

Aztec

Inca

Persian

Byzantine

Northern European

China: Han

China: T'ang

China: Sung

China: Ming

China: Manchu

Hinduism

Sikhism

Parsis

Judaism

Christianity

Islam

Bahá'í

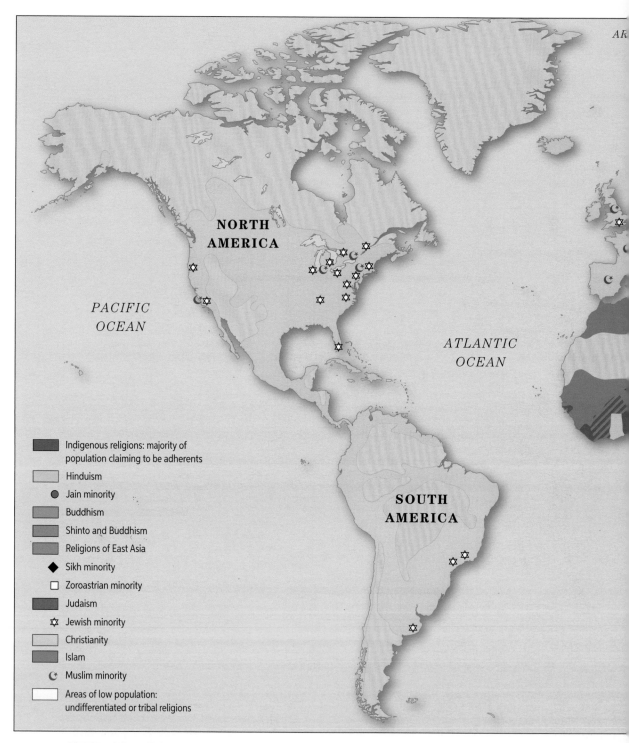

The World's Religions

Legend:

- Indigenous religions: majority of population claiming to be adherents
- Hinduism
- Jain minority
- Buddhism
- Shinto and Buddhism
- Religions of East Asia
- Sikh minority
- Zoroastrian minority
- Judaism
- Jewish minority
- Christianity
- Islam
- Muslim minority
- Areas of low population: undifferentiated or tribal religions

NORTH AMERICA

SOUTH AMERICA

PACIFIC OCEAN

ATLANTIC OCEAN

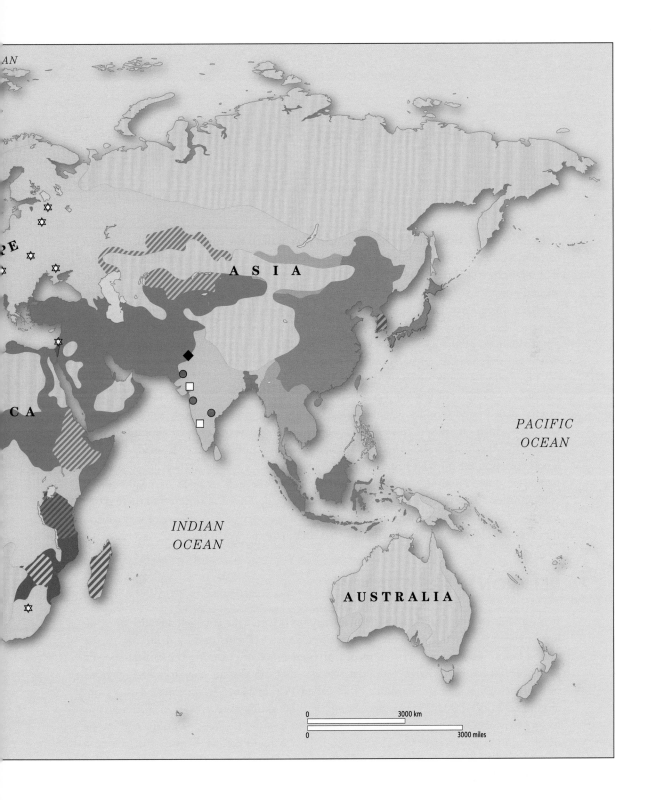

PACIFIC
OCEAN

INDIAN
OCEAN

ASIA

AUSTRALIA

0   3000 km

0   3000 miles

CHAPTER 6

Religions of Antiquity

Evidence suggests that, for as long as humans have walked the earth, we have been drawn to religious belief of some kind. While some scholars have hypothesized that behaviour that might be called religious is evident even in the animal community, it seems clear that we and our ancestors have engaged in forms of ritual for at least the half a million years. Evidence from early *Homo sapiens*, such as widely distributed 'Venus' figurines, suggests that the basic needs of these hunter-gatherer communities, such as fertility, were the chief preoccupations of their religions. As humankind developed more advanced tools, settled down, farmed the land, and – above all – wrote, religion became more complex.

The civilizations of antiquity developed belief systems in which – with a few notable exceptions – families of gods and goddesses, often hierarchical, were served by professional priests in dedicated temples. Unlike many modern religions, these were not missionary faiths, to which one might convert, and which required a very personal commitment to God, but rather religions of the state, part of the fabric of the state. In many cultures, it was common for popular folk beliefs to coexist with the official state religion, and for people of one community to respect, and even fear, the god or gods of neighbouring communities. There was considerable diversity in the religions of antiquity, but there is one thing they almost all share: with the exception of a few survivors, such as Zoroastrianism, they were displaced by the new religions that dominate the world today.

RELIGION IN PREHISTORY

It is difficult to state exactly when human religion began. This is largely because most of our knowledge of religion comes from written sources. Prehistory, by definition, is the period before we have any written record of human activity. Among the earliest specific evidence that has been used to support the idea that our distant ancestors had religious or supernatural beliefs are the skulls of so-called 'Peking Man' (*Homo erectus*), dating from around 600,000–700,000 years ago. Some of these skulls were broken in such a way as to give easy access to the brain, which appears to have been eaten, probably as a means of absorbing the power of the dead person. This is hypothetical, because the lack of a written record makes it almost impossible to understand any prehistoric religion fully. Nevertheless, important inferences can be drawn from evidence such as stone figures or cave paintings; without these, a key stage in the development of human belief systems of considerable significance to the later development of formal religion is missed.

Neanderthals, who lived alongside *Homo sapiens* for some time before their extinction around 40,000 years ago, almost certainly had religious beliefs and appear to have had some form of belief in life after death. They buried their dead with ceremony, and offered grave gifts, while there is also evidence that in some communities bears or other animals were worshipped. Burials of early *Homo sapiens*, in France and Russia for example, are very similar, with valuable possessions being buried with bodies, suggesting that our species has always had some form of belief that can be identified as religious. Likewise, it has been hypothesized that the famous cave paintings in southern France and northern Spain (c. 30,000 to 40,000 BCE) had a religious function, on the basis that more recent societies have considered the depiction of an animal (for example the buffalo dances of Plains Indians in North America) as likely to increase the chances of a successful hunt.

By around 10,000 BCE (usually identified as the start of the Neolithic period, or New Stone Age), humans had begun to settle in villages and to use their new polished tools as they became farmers. With the shift from hunter-gatherers to farmers came subtle changes in religion. Inhumation (burial underground in cemeteries as we would understand them today) became the norm, and small figurines, often supposed to be servants for an afterlife, were left with bodies. The development of farming also led to specialization, as the settled lifestyle it created allowed some to perform new roles. Crucially, it is clear from the remains of temple sites across Europe and Asia that a priesthood began to emerge at this time. In one example from Russia a sophisticated form of sacrificial worship took place: a large altar was at the centre of the temple structure, and there was a large clay chair, presumably for the priest. Megalithic monuments, of which Stonehenge in Wiltshire, England (c. 3100 BCE), is the best-known example, shows a later level of development in Neolithic temples. The exact purpose of these structures remains unknown, but many have evident links with nearby burial sites, and were almost certainly places of worship. Many, including Stonehenge, appear to have had an astronomical purpose and may have been significant in the early development of a religious or ritual calendar.

THE ANCIENT NEAR EAST

The development of writing – at different times in different parts of the world – marks one of the most significant stages of human development. With it came the shift from prehistory to the historical era: the world for which we have written sources of evidence. One ancient civilization that illustrates well this shift is the collection of communities that emerged in ancient Mesopotamia (the Greek name for the lands of the Tigris and Euphrates rivers, that is, modern Iraq and Syria), regarded by many as a key 'cradle of civilization' and, therefore, of formal religion. The Sumerians, in the south of this region, were among the first in the world to have a system of writing (cuneiform), developed because of the need to organize their communities, farming, and irrigation. This gives us crucial insights into the religious belief and practices of these communities in a way that is not possible for earlier societies. The Sumerians developed a strong temple culture based around their two major deities, Anu, the supreme god, and Inanna, the 'great mother' and fertility goddess. Each of these was the object of one of the two most significant temples in the city of Uruk. The temples, in common with many later religious institutions, became significant economic interests, owning vast estates that employed thousands of people to farm the land or serve as craftsmen making sacred objects or vestments.

The Sumerians had a clear sense of the relationship between the different deities, and there was a cadre of theologians whose role it was to define this. There were official poets, too, who told stories about the gods, many of which were probably set to music. Mythology developed across Mesopotamia, and the different civilizations of the region shared each other's myths. One of the best known of these is the Epic of Gilgamesh, the story of a legendary king, now thought to have lived around 2700 BCE, which largely

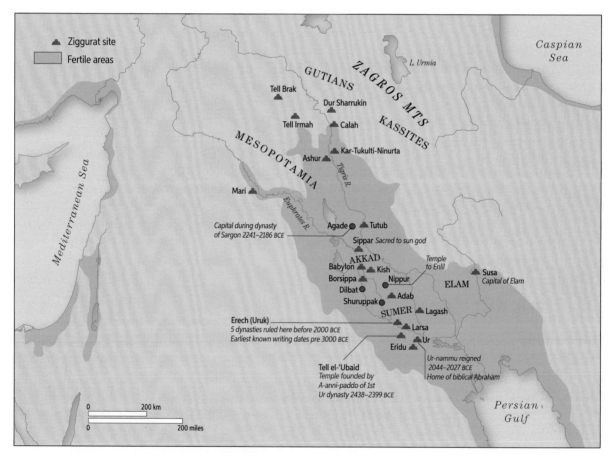

Religious Sites of Ancient Mesopotamia

concerns his quest for immortality and eternal youth. During his quest, Gilgamesh meets an ancient man, Ut-napishtim, who recounts the story of a great flood sent by the gods to destroy humanity. Enki, the creator god, warned Ut-napishtim of this, and told him to build a large boat on which he, his family, and a variety of animals could survive until the floods receded. This part of the story is one of a number of ancient myths concerning a flood sent by a deity to destroy humankind, including the biblical story of Noah.

The gods of Mesopotamia were unpredictable, so a special class of priests emerged whose job it was to read omens. These men would be consulted on a wide range of questions, such as whether a king should go to war, or whether a marriage should take place. The will and intentions of the gods could be understood through a number of different methods, including the movements of animals, the shapes of cracks in a wall, or close examination of the liver of a sacrificed animal. These priests also studied the stars closely, and are thought to be some of the earliest to tell fortunes by astrology.

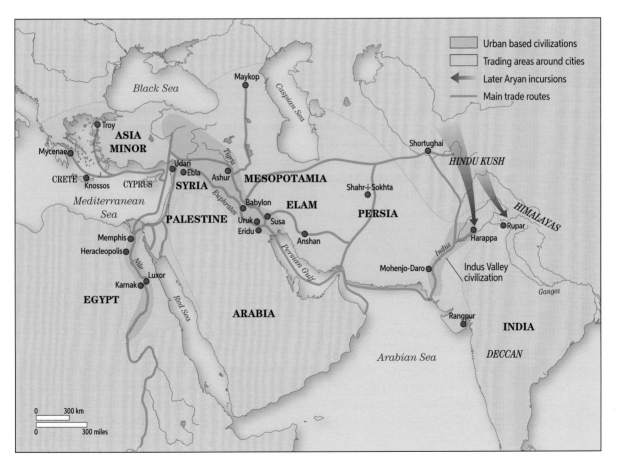

The Fertile Crescent and the Rise of City Religions

PRE-COLUMBIAN CENTRAL AMERICA

On the other side of the world, a number of civilizations developed in Central and South America from around 1200 BCE. Like most religions of antiquity, the religions of this region were in large measure a reflection of the specific needs of the societies they served. As elsewhere, the formal state religions here often existed alongside the local religion of the common people, without tension necessarily arising between them.

Among the earliest Central American civilizations we know of were the Olmecs, who lived on the Gulf Coast of Mexico between around 1200 and 500 BCE. The religion of the Olmecs appears to have centred on veneration of the jaguar. Various artefacts have been found depicting the jaguar in different forms, including part bird and part snake. One carving shows the jaguar in union with a woman, an act the Olmecs believed led to the creation of a race of human-jaguar hybrids, who were probably gods of fertility. It has been suggested that this jaguar-god may later have been believed to be the ancestor of Quetzalcoatl, a god significant to a number of Mesoamerican communities. The idea that different animals combined to form one god was crucial to Central American religion in the pre-Columbian era.

From around 200 BCE the Maya, who succeeded the Olmecs, developed an elaborate state religion around temple cities. At the core of Mayan religion was a form of bargain, or contract, between humans and gods. The gods provided food and humans provided payment – usually in advance – through sacrifice, which could be donated human blood, animals, or produce such as maize. One form, of course, was human sacrifice, which involved the extraction of the heart while the live victim was held down. The most significant of the Maya temple cities is Teotihuacan, which flourished between around 300 and 700 CE. The size and scale of the complex at Teotihuacan gives a sense of the importance of the state religion in Mayan society. As in a number of ancient civilizations, the temples dominated their communities, leading to the conclusion that the state and its religion were utterly inseparable. The Maya state was, in effect, a theocracy.

The Aztecs, who migrated into the Valley of Mexico in the late twelfth century, believed in two primordial beings: Ometecuhtli ('Lord of the Duality') and Omecihuatl ('Lady of the Duality'). Together, these two were the originators of a number of other gods who created the earth. One god created the sun through an act of self-sacrifice, and his example was copied by a number of other gods in order to start the sun on its course across the sky. Taking these gods as their example, the Aztecs believed that daily human sacrifice was needed to prevent the sun from ceasing to rise and set. It has been estimated that around 20,000 people – mostly captives of war – were killed annually for this purpose. By 1470 CE, the Inca, whose society coexisted with that of the Aztecs, controlled most of modern Peru. In Inca religion, the god most revered was Inti, the male sun god, who protected and matured the crops. Sacrifice was as important to the Inca as to other pre-Columbian societies, though the offering was generally of maize beer, food, or llamas, rather than human flesh.

Within fifty years of the Spanish invasion of 1532, almost all these ancient societies were destroyed by war, famine, and disease. Aspects of the belief systems of these communities lingered on, however, and continue to coexist with Catholic Christianity in indigenous religion, as well as in what might be defined as local culture, rather than religion, such as the Day of the Dead festival in Mexico (though this too is a blend of Aztec remnants with the Christian holy day of All Souls). The study of Pre-Columbian religion is of considerable importance in understanding the nature of religion in ancient communities because the survival of Mesoamerica up to the European Early Modern period meant that forms of religion that have much in common with those that existed in Europe and the Middle East in the distant past can be understood more readily.

ANCIENT EGYPT

The religion of ancient Egypt, by which we mean the civilization of the lower reaches of the Nile Valley, emerged around 3100 BCE, with the development of writing, and the introduction of a single central government. From the outset, Egyptian religion was an arm of the emerging state. As elsewhere, many of the gods of Ancient Egypt were derived from the forces of the natural world, and were frequently portrayed in animal form. The sun, for example, was crucial as a deity, and was represented by a hawk, probably on account of their both flying across the sky. In general, people in Egypt were free to worship different gods at different times for different purposes and in different places, depending on their needs. Ancient Egyptians are also known for their belief in the sacredness of animals. While the practice varied from century to century, vast numbers of animals were mummified for burial, including baboons, crocodiles, ibises, cats, and dogs. In some cases, whole species were considered as sacred, while in others, an individual animal might be singled out as the incarnation of a god.

The extent to which religion and state were intertwined in Egypt is shown by the fact that, in theory, the king carried out all religious ceremonies in Egypt. In reality, priests acting as his deputies generally undertook such ceremonies. The priests and their temples became – as in so many other societies – a powerful vested interest that could exert considerable authority. Amenophis IV attempted to expand the cult of Aten (to the extent that he changed his own name to Akhenaten – 'the one who is beneficial to Aten') and suppress other gods, in an attempt to create a form of monotheism. The ultimate failure of this project can perhaps in part be put down to the resistance of the priests as a vested interest. The temple buildings themselves were, perhaps surprisingly, rather plain when viewed from outside. They were concerned less with expressing the power and majesty of a god (as with, say, a Gothic cathedral) than with the intricacy and detail of the ritual that took place inside.

There were a number of different creation myths in Ancient Egypt, the most common of which focused on the idea of a universe of water from which a hill arose and life began. The Egyptians seem always to have believed in an afterlife, as even the earliest tombs uncovered contain food and other items to help the dead on their journey. The journey to the afterlife was believed to be incredibly difficult, with obstacles and demons blocking the route. For this reason food, tools, weapons, and scrolls containing ritual incantations were left in tombs with the deceased. The purpose of mummification was also to aid the dead on their journey: the departing spirit still needed the body as a base, so its preservation was essential.

ZOROASTRIANISM

Zoroastrianism, the state religion of the Persian Empire, differs markedly from most of the religions labelled as 'ancient'. While most belief systems in the ancient world were polytheistic, often deriving their gods and goddesses from aspects of the natural world, Zoroastrianism is monotheistic, recognizing one God only. The other important way in which Zoroastrianism differs from most ancient religions is that it is still practised by a significant number of people today. Perhaps the best way to think of Zoroastrianism, then, is as the most ancient of the modern religions. The religion originates in the teachings of the ancient Persian prophet Zarathustra (often known in the West as Zoroaster), who probably lived around 1200 BCE, at the time when Persia was emerging from the Stone Age, making him the first of the great prophets of world religion. At the age of thirty, Zarathustra had the first of a series of visions, which led him to preach a new message.

The key aspect of Zarathustra's teaching was the emphasis he placed on personal religion, as opposed to the community bargain more typical of ancient religions elsewhere. In Zoroastrianism, all men and women were required to choose personally between good and evil. Those whose good thoughts, deeds, and words outweighed the evil would go to heaven at the first judgment, while those for whom the reverse was true would be sent to hell. Hell was seen as a corrective measure rather than a place of eternal damnation. A cruel ruler, for example, who tortured and starved his people, would be tortured and starved in hell before having the opportunity to go to heaven at his second judgment. The Zoroastrian universe is dominated by an on-going battle between good and evil. God (Ahura Mazda, or Ohrmazd, 'Wise Lord') created the world, but it was subsequently defiled and polluted by the devil (Ahriman), who was not of God's creation. When Ahriman emerged apparently victorious, the first human couple were created, to help God in the battle of good and evil. Zoroastrians are required to direct their lives toward the maintenance and expansion of God's creation, through agriculture and by raising a family.

Zoroastrianism spread through the Achaemenid Empire (c. 550 – 330 BCE) largely as a result of the missionary work of the Magi, a priestly tribe. The Magi acted as royal chaplains, travelling with military or diplomatic delegations (Christians will be aware of the Magi visiting the infant Jesus in Matthew's Gospel), highlighting the sense that Zoroastrianism was very much a state religion in Persia.

As Islam began to dominate Persia after 633 CE, the status of Zoroastrianism became precarious. Gradually, the religion retreated to the periphery of Persia and encountered persecution in towns. Yet Zoroastrianism survived under these conditions for 1,400 years into modern Iran, where it is estimated that 25,000 followers remain. Today, there are around 115,000 Zoroastrians in the world, mostly in India, but with communities in the West (particularly the United States) and elsewhere.

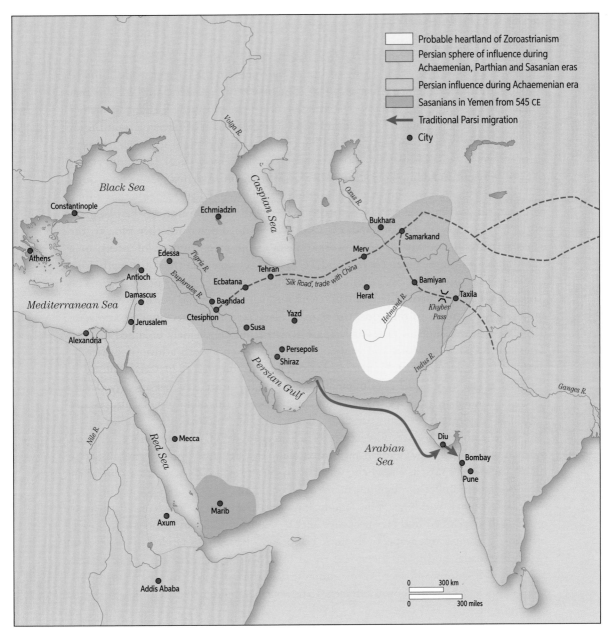

Legend:
- Probable heartland of Zoroastrianism
- Persian sphere of influence during Achaemenian, Parthian and Sasanian eras
- Persian influence during Achaemenian era
- Sasanians in Yemen from 545 CE
- Traditional Parsi migration
- City

Zoroastrianism

GREECE AND ROME

The religion followed in ancient Greece has a history covering a period of around 6,000 years, the earliest of which was – like so much else in the ancient world – linked closely with the development of agriculture. The first literate society, however, was that of the Myceneans, whose system of writing – the so-called Linear B script – was not deciphered until 1952, when it was found to be an archaic form of Greek. Extant Linear B tablets, while mostly concerned with administrative detail, contain some references to ritual offerings made, the roles of priests, and, crucially, some gods of later importance to Greek society, including Poseidon, Athena, Hermes, and Artemis.

Following the destruction of the Mycenean world around 1100 BCE, there is a long period during which little is known about Greece, with the exception of the two great works of epic poetry, *The Iliad* and *The Odyssey*. It is not known whether Homer, the name given to the author of these works, was a single man, a group of poets, or a tradition built up over time. *The Iliad* and *The Odyssey* set down much of the mythology central to the culture of classical Greece, including accounts of many of the gods. The gods of Homer are portrayed in human terms, but neither grow old nor die. By praising and making sacrifices to the gods, the human characters in Homer hoped to appease them, though this did not necessarily spare a man from his divinely ordained destiny. They can be gods of wrath and vengeance as much as gods with a love of justice or decency. The epic poetry of Homer, aside from being a foundation of Greek culture, is regarded as key stage in the development of Western literature. *The Iliad* and *The Odyssey* have a continued significance that extends down through the literature of Europe, and remain an inspiration for many novelists, playwrights, and filmmakers.

By the sixth century BCE, Greece consisted of around 160 independent city states, most of which had a population no greater than 10,000. The political and religious life of these cities was, as elsewhere, very closely bound up, and there was a significant growth in the number of temples, many of which acted as treasuries for the state as much as religious buildings. The temple buildings themselves, which were generally quite small, developed in three successive 'orders' – Doric, Ionic and Corinthian – each of whose columns were respectively more elaborate. The temples tended to be devoted to one particular god or goddess, and ritual was focused on offerings, including the pouring of libations and sacrifice of animals. Examples of vase painting, a major art form in ancient Greece, show altar scenes and sacrifice more often than other aspects of temple life.

Greek religion spread throughout the Mediterranean world with many other aspects of Greek culture, particularly following the conquests of Alexander the Great (356–323 BCE). While Greece influenced much of the ancient world, including Egypt, it was its influence on the rising power of Rome that was most significant.

For the Romans, whose empire grew to cover most of Europe and the Mediterranean world by the time of Christ, religion was a fundamental part of their identity. The Romans often liked to think of theirs as a practical religion, lacking in superstition. Their gods were functional. Irrespective of any particular mythology attached to a particular

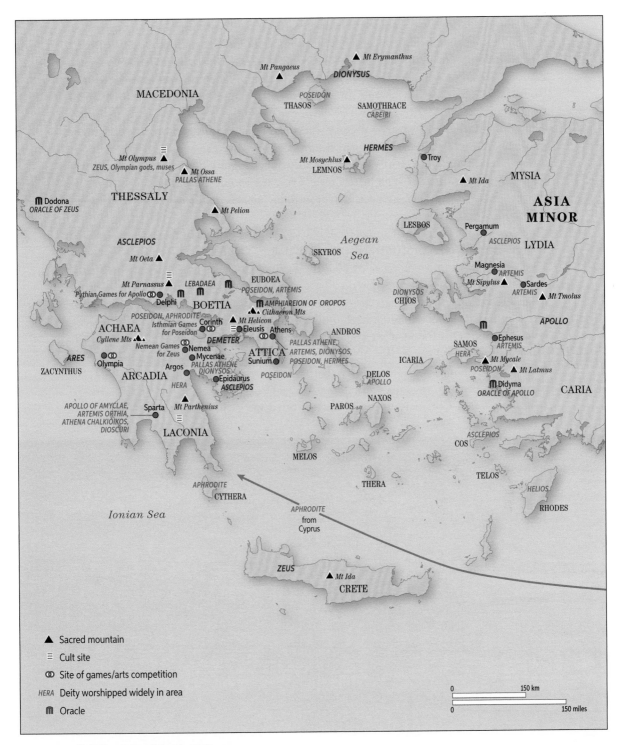

Cult Centres of Ancient Greece

Map content:

MACEDONIA

Mt Erymanthus ▲

Mt Pangaeus ▲

DIONYSUS

POSEIDON
THASOS

SAMOTHRACE
CABEIRI

HERMES

Mt Olympus ≡ ▲
ZEUS, Olympian gods, muses

Mt Ossa ▲
PALLAS ATHENE

Mt Mosychlus ▲
LEMNOS

Troy ●

Mt Ida ▲

MYSIA

THESSALY

Dodona ⋔
ORACLE OF ZEUS

Mt Pelion ▲

*Aegean
Sea*

LESBOS

Pergamum ●

ASIA
MINOR

ASCLEPIOS LYDIA

ASCLEPIOS

SKYROS

Mt Oeta ▲

Magnesia
ARTEMIS

Mt Sipylus ▲

Sardes ●
ARTEMIS

Mt Tmolus ▲

Mt Parnassus ≡ ▲
Pythian Games for Apollo ◎ ●
Delphi

LEBADAEA ⋔

⋔

BOETIA

EUBOEA
POSEIDON, ARTEMIS

DIONYSOS
CHIOS

APOLLO

POSEIDON, APHRODITE

⋔ *AMPHIAREION OF OROPOS*
▲ ▲ *Cithaeron Mts*

Ephesus ●
ARTEMIS

ACHAEA
*Isthmian Games
for Poseidon*
Corinth ●

◎◎ Eleusis
Mt Helicon ▲

Athens ●

SAMOS
HERA ⋔

Mt Mycale ▲

Cyllene Mts ▲▲

DEMETER

*PALLAS ATHENE,
ARTEMIS, DIONYSOS,
POSEIDON, HERMES*

POSEIDON

Mt Latmus ▲

ARES

*Nemean Games
for Zeus*
Olympia ●

◎◎
Nemea
● Mycenae

ANDROS

ICARIA

Didyma ⋔
ORACLE OF APOLLO

CARIA

ZACYNTHUS

ARCADIA

Argos ●

*PALLAS ATHENE
DIONYSOS*

Epidaurus ●
ASCLEPIOS

HERA

Sunium ●

ATTICA

POSEIDON

DELOS
APOLLO

DELOS

ASCLEPIOS

COS

*APOLLO OF AMYCLAE,
ARTEMIS ORTHIA,
ATHENA CHALKIOIKOS,
DIOSCURI*

Sparta ●

Mt Parthenius ▲

≡

LACONIA

PAROS

NAXOS

TELOS

HELIOS

RHODES

Ionian Sea

APHRODITE
CYTHERA

MELOS

THERA

APHRODITE
from
Cyprus

ZEUS

Mt Ida ▲

CRETE

Legend:
▲ Sacred mountain
≡ Cult site
◎◎ Site of games/arts competition
HERA Deity worshipped widely in area
⋔ Oracle

0 ___ 150 km
0 ___ 150 miles

deity, the Romans were concerned above all to assign a precise office for the purpose of worship, rather than being concerned about the personification of that god. While the Romans adopted many foreign gods – especially Greek – they adapted them to meet Roman needs. For example, the Greek god of healing, Asklepios, was introduced into Roman mythology, as Aesculapius, only in 293–291 BCE, in order to help overcome a major epidemic.

In Roman religion, the forces of conservatism and change worked alongside each other in a managed way. Conservatism, which aimed to preserve the status of the old gods (above all the 'Capitoline Triad' of the most ancient gods: Jupiter, Juno, and Minerva) was represented in the office of high priest (*pontifex maximus*); while innovation was fostered by the *viri sacrisfaciundis*, officials responsible for introducing new deities when they considered it appropriate.

Following the fall of the Roman Republic (27 BCE), the imperial dynasty increasingly used religion as a means of furthering its own power. The Emperor Augustus (63 BCE–14 CE) took on the ancient office of *pontifex maximus* as a means of enhancing his status, while oaths show he was considered to be 'son of a god'. During the imperial period, Rome's traditional deities (with the exception of the Capitoline Triad) were supplanted by the cult of the imperial house itself. Following Julius Caesar's assassination in 44 BCE, he was deified. This founded a tradition that led to the deification of many emperors, often while they still lived. By the start of the fourth century CE, traditional religion faced serious competition from a new faith: Christianity. The Edict of Milan (313), permitted Christian worship throughout the empire, and the last non-Christian emperor, Julian, ended his

Temples on the Capitoline Hill, Rome.

A SHORT INTRODUCTION TO WORLD RELIGIONS

reign in 363. A few elements of traditional Roman religion lingered on, not least in the status of Rome itself, which became the premier city of Western Christianity. Perhaps the most obvious remnant of this survival was the adoption of the ancient office of *pontifex maximus* ('supreme pontiff') by Rome's bishop, Pope Leo the Great (reigned 440–61), to enhance the power of the papacy.

DISPLACEMENT AND SURVIVAL

The religions discussed above almost all have one common characteristic: they have disappeared. However, it is important to note that aspects of many religions of antiquity live on. We have seen the example of Zoroastrianism, a religion that dominated a long extinct state, and yet which managed – against the odds perhaps – to survive into the modern world. Similarly, a few parts of Europe retained their traditional religions until surprisingly recently. Lithuania did not become a Christian state until the fifteenth century, while the cult of Perkons (a thunder god) remained dominant in Latvia until 1750, and was still followed in a few places until the nineteenth century.

The religions of ancient societies continue to appeal to some in an era in which many have turned away from the established religions of the West yet still seek a faith. Since the 1960s, many in the New Age movements have looked to traditional folk beliefs, or the gods and goddesses of Norse, Egyptian, Greek, or Mesopotamian religions, for inspiration.

Other fragments of ancient religion also live on today. We have already seen that the early Church adopted some of the trappings of Roman imperial power; but some European folk and Roman traditions were also incorporated into Western Christianity. One well-known example is the link between the Anglo-Saxon festival devoted to the god Eostre and the Christian celebration of Christ's resurrection as Easter. Other fragments of ancient religious belief also survive in literary and popular culture. The prominence of Norse and Germanic mythology in the operas of Wagner, for example, or even gods such as Thor in comic book stories and films, show the continuing appeal of some of these stories. Darker aspects of ancient mythology are also significant in much the same way. The Slavic folk legends of vampires and werewolves, which were an important aspect of local belief, are now better known as ingredients of Gothic literature and horror cinema.

QUESTIONS

1. What is a religion, and why can the term be problematic?

2. Why did many phenomenologists reject theological approaches to religion?

3. An atheist will always be a more objective student of religion than a believer. How far do you agree or disagree with this statement?

4. What problems might you encounter in studying a religion as an outsider?

5. What did Marx mean when he referred to religion as 'the sigh of the oppressed creature'?

6. How do Marx and Weber differ in their perceptions of religion?

7. Explain Durkheim's view of the role of religion in society.

8. Why has there been renewed interest in the sociology of religion in recent years?

FURTHER READING

Connolly, Peter (ed.), *Approaches to the Study of Religion*. London: Continuum, 2001.

Eliade, Mircea, *The Sacred and the Profane: The Nature of Religion*. New York: Harcourt, Brace, 1959.

Fitzgerald, Timothy, *The Ideology of Religious Studies*. Oxford: Oxford University Press, 2000.

Flood, Gavin, *Beyond Phenomenology: Rethinking the Study of Religion*. London: Cassell, 1999.

Geertz, Clifford, 'Religion as a Cultural System', in Michael Banton, ed., *Anthropological Approaches to the Study of Religion*, pp. 1–46. London: Tavistock, 1966.

Kunin, Seth D., *Religion: The Modern Theories*. Baltimore: Johns Hopkins University Press, 2003.

Levi-Strauss, Claude, *Myth and Meaning*. Toronto: University of Toronto Press, 1978.

McCutcheon, Russell T. ed., *The Insider/Outsider Problem in the Study of Religion*. London: Cassell, 1999.

Otto, Rudolf, *The Idea of the Holy*. London: Oxford University Press, 1923.

Pals, Daniel L., *Eight Theories of Religion*. New York: Oxford University Press, 2006.

Van der Leeuw, Gerardus, *Religion in Essence and Manifestation*. London: Allen & Unwin, 1938.

PART 2
INDIGENOUS RELIGIONS

SUMMARY

The prominence today of a handful of religions with a huge number of followers throughout the world can easily blind us to the existence of the huge number of religions which exist only in small communities, whether in a particular region or even a single village. Unsurprisingly, diversity abounds among indigenous religions, meaning it is inappropriate to generalize when considering their features, or to imagine it is possible to use them to outline a supposed evolution of religious types, as many scholars in the past did. Many have raised concerns about considering indigenous religions as 'religions' at all, especially because local languages often have no concept of 'religion' as it is understood in the West.

Nevertheless, commonalities are to be found. One concept that permeates many indigenous societies is that of respect for others, for one's elders, or ancestors. Many native North American communities, for example, place great value on their ancient wisdom, and consider living elders as a link to this. Many indigenous communities have highly-developed conceptions of sacred and profane space. Australian aborigines, for instance, consider the landscape to have been shaped by their ancestors. Commonly, the life and wellbeing of the community is the primary concern of religious life, and the purpose of ritual reflects this. Equally, shamans are often valued for their role in preventing the subversion of the common good by means such as witchcraft.

Today, of course, many small indigenous religions have been wiped out, as a result of the growth of religions such as Christianity; but in many places they have adapted to this challenge, or even adopted some aspects of the incomers. This reflects the strength of some local religions: far from being stuck in time, many have – throughout their history – adapted to new challenges facing the communities they serve.

CHAPTER 7

Understanding Indigenous Religions

Indigenous religions make up the majority of the world's religions. They are as diverse as the languages spoken, the music made, and the means of subsistence employed by the many and various people who find them meaningful and satisfying. The number of people who might be counted as members of indigenous religions may not form the majority of the world's religious people – some of these religions exist only in one small village – but they are far from insignificant when considered altogether.

This overview is intended to improve approaches to, and understanding of, indigenous religions such as those discussed in the 'case studies' in this section. It is important to note that not all indigenous religions are the same. Just as there are hundreds of indigenous languages in North America or in Papua New Guinea, so there are many different ways of being religious.

Few indigenous languages have a word like 'religion', and some people have drawn the conclusion that it is inappropriate to speak of 'religion' with reference to indigenous cultures. But if we think of religions as particular ways of living in, and particular ways of seeing, the world, then we can find religion in the ordinary, everyday lives of many people who do not use the word. In fact, it is unusual for adherents of any religion to separate their religious beliefs and practices from their everyday lives – so indigenous people are not so very different. It is also noteworthy that religions are not all about seemingly strange ideas and peculiar practices, although these are often the things that stand out when we encounter something new to us. There is nothing wrong with noticing 'strange things', as long as we also pay attention to the more everyday ways in which people speak of what makes their lives meaningful and interesting.

TRADITION AND CHANGE

As a result of the spread of transcultural or global religions – for example Buddhism, Christianity, and Islam – some indigenous religions have been destroyed, rejected, or abandoned. Some indigenous people have accepted the arriving religion on their own terms, and slotted it into an indigenous understanding. Many indigenous religions have been adapted to the presence of more powerful, or dominating, religions and continued with considerable vitality and creativity. While many people are returning to their 'traditional ways', others are engaging in both an indigenous and another, newer, religion.

Such processes, which keep religions continuously relevant, are not only interesting in themselves, but provide the most recent example of the quite ordinary fact that all religions continuously change. 'Tradition' does not mean nothing ever changes; rather, it means one generation sets standards by which the next might judge the value of an idea or practice before changing. Indigenous religions are not the fossilized remains of the earliest, or first, religions. They are rarely simple or simplistic, and should not be mistaken for the basic building blocks from which 'more advanced' religions were built or evolved. Hence, earlier terms – such as 'primitive religion' or 'primal religion' – detract from a proper, and respectful, understanding of the vibrant ways in which people understand, and engage with, the world. Similarly, it is unhelpful to speak of groups that might include millions of people as 'tribes', and of their religions as 'tribal religions'. Indigenous religions are not stuck in the past, nor do they make sense only when practised in their original homelands. Although indigenous religions are severely affected by colonialism, they continue to provide resources for people surviving and thriving in the new, globalized world.

RESPECT

The notion of respect is important in discussing indigenous religions. Elders continuously encourage younger people to show respect in particular ways to those who deserve it. Asking who is respected, and how respect is shown, can be quite revealing about what is of central importance. In many parts of Africa, for example, beer is offered to those one respects. Native Americans did not traditionally use alcohol, and continue to give gifts of tobacco or sage to respected people. In some cultures it is appropriate to be reserved when first meeting another person; in others it is permissible to act quite intimately. Knowing whether to touch someone else at all, and in what way, is important. Do you shake hands or press noses? Do you hand people gifts – or place them on the ground in front of them?

WHO IS A PERSON?

Important as these questions are, the more radical question is 'Who is a person?' Most cultures understand humans are not the only kind of person. Christians, Jews, and Muslims, for example, consider God and angels to be persons of considerable importance. Of course, this nicely illustrates the point that not all persons are the same, and that there are different ways to approach particular persons. There are indigenous religions in which teachings about a God who created the world are significant. There are many more in which everything we see is the result of the creative activities of many other persons. Perhaps a single creator, or a creative process, started it all, but then life developed as each living being, or person, played their part. Trees separated sky and land, mountains arose to shape the land, coyote or jaguar or a robin tamed fire, corn taught planting cycles and ceremonies, humans built towns, and so the world became the way it is. And similar processes continue to change the world, making it important that people learn to act responsibly and respectfully. All this is commonplace in a great variety of indigenous religions.

What needs more careful thought is the implication that there is a great variety of creative persons. Some of these might be recognized as being like the God monotheists acknowledge, others are more polytheistic deities, often encountered in the kind of intimate, everyday matters for which some academics use the word 'immanence' – the divine within the world and everyday experience. Many significant persons are humans: elders, priests, shamans, grandparents, rulers, and so on. Although ancestors are important, it is important to note that among indigenous people this word typically refers to those from whom a particular person or family is descended, and rarely means 'all those who have died'. This can cause difficulties, because some museum scientists consider that all human remains belong to 'humanity' universally. The difference between these 'scientific' and indigenous ways of speaking – and the resulting confusion – is illustrated in references to 'our ancestors' by those museum officials who reject requests for the return of particular remains to their places of origin. Such misunderstandings also illustrate tensions familiar from wider concerns about globalization.

If ancestors are pre-eminent among the community of human persons in many indigenous cultures, and deserve appropriate displays of respect, they are far from alone in being categorized as 'persons'. In many, but not all, indigenous cultures, words equivalent to 'person' can refer to animals, plants, rocks, clouds, and more. Having learned from Ojibwe people in southern-central Canada, Irving Hallowell (1892–1974) coined the influential term 'other-than-human persons'. That is, in Ojibwe understanding, the world is inhabited by a vast community of persons, only some of whom are human. There are human-persons, tree-persons, rock-persons, cloud-persons, and so on. From a rock-person's perspective there might be 'other-than-rock persons', such as some humans, with whom it is possible – and even desirable – to communicate. Many indigenous peoples have similar understandings of the nature of life and personhood.

EXCHANGING GIFTS

Children brought up in particular indigenous religions may have to be taught to distinguish between persons and objects, but religious education is rarely presented as lectures and lists. More commonly, children are taught how to act towards other persons. Just as they receive gifts from, and give gifts to, older relatives, they learn that the process of giving and receiving is a vitally important element of the relationships that mark people as different from mere 'things'. Gifts are given as signs of respect and love to those more powerful, or more esteemed, than us. Gifts are received as signs of support, help, and compassion from those more powerful, or esteemed, than us. Gifts initiate, maintain, and further relationships between people. Gifts carry obligations and create ongoing relationships. Just as Ojibwe children might offer respected elders gifts of tobacco, elders might offer tobacco to respected rocks or eagles, or to sage plants from which they wish to cut leaves. Gift processes thus demonstrate who are considered to be persons, who is expected to act personally towards other persons.

POWER DYNAMICS

Gift is also central to the dynamics of power. Understandings of power are also a common theme in discussions of indigenous religions. Although the history of Western scholarship contains misunderstandings of indigenous ideas about power, the theme is an important one. Some scholars have claimed that many indigenous people have 'primitive' and mistaken notions about mystical powers being something like electricity. Often these scholars have not listened attentively to their hosts, who have been explaining the social dynamics by which people interact. For example, social – not mystical – powers are usually at stake in Polynesian references to *mana* and Ojibwe references to *manitou*. Again, this usage is not alien to Westerners, who are familiar with the language of 'empowerment'. There are more and less powerful persons. More power manifests itself as more ability to perform certain roles – for example, making pots or speeches – and brings with it the responsibility to act respectfully and to the benefit of others.

> Mau e ki mai, he aha te mea nui?
>
> Maku e ki atu,
>
> he tangata, he tangata, he tangata.
>
> *If you ask what is the greatest thing*
>
> *I will tell you*
>
> *it is people, people, people.*
>
> Taitokerau Whakatauki – Maori

SHAMANS AND WITCHES

Person, gift, and power are also central to common problems to which indigenous religions proffer solutions. For example, some indigenous people understand it is possible to cause harm by performing particular rituals, such as witchcraft and sorcery. Solutions might be found among some people by recourse to diviners, while others employ shamans. For the indigenous people, these specialists are adept at finding knowledge unavailable to others, and require careful – and sometimes frightening – training for their role. In response to questions about whether such practices are superstitious, indigenous people might point to the fact that rather different questions are important in indigenous communities. The interesting question for them is not why a grain store collapsed: everybody knows that grain stores collapse because termites eat their supports away. The important

> 'A ńlọ wá ìmò, òtító, àti òdodo.
>
> *We are going in search of knowledge, truth, and justice.*
>
> A line of Ifa divination text – Yoruba

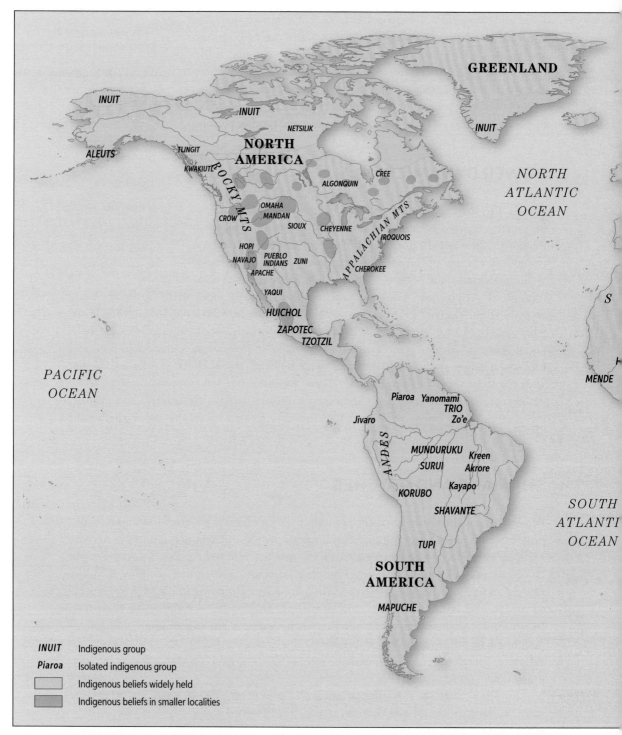

Indigenous Religions Worldwide

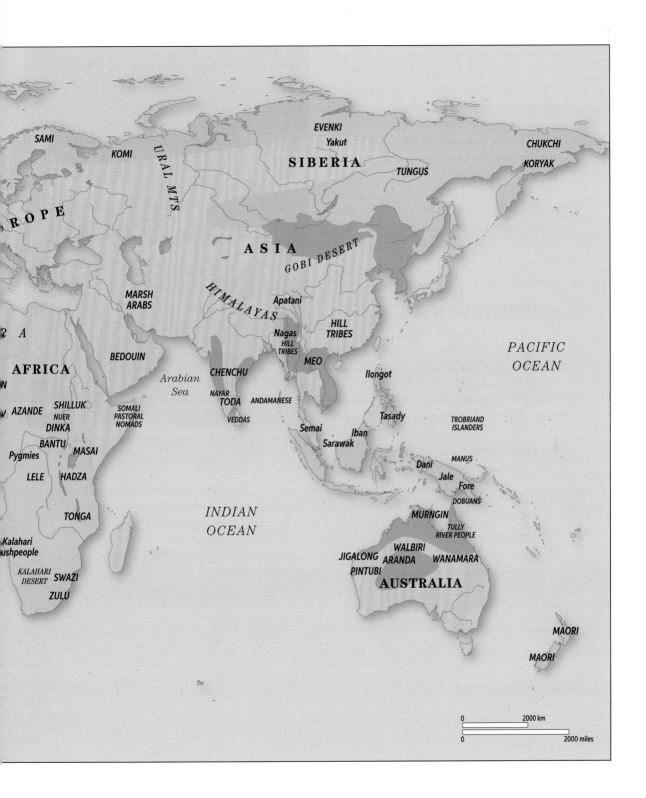

question, as they see it, is why it collapsed when this person sheltered beneath it, rather than earlier or later. In indigenous religions, talk of witchcraft arises in a personal and relational world, where the person who shelters beneath a grain store may previously have insulted an ancestor or a witch, and made himself or herself liable to disaster. Alternatively, a person aware of having incurred another's wrath might offer the kind of gifts commonly identified as 'sacrifices' to restore a more positive relationship.

INDIGENOUS RELIGIONS

Indigenous religions, like all other religions, may be considered to be ways in which particular groups of people seek the means of improving health, happiness, and even wealth for themselves, their families, and communities. Finding out what a particular group means by health, wealth, and happiness, and how they go about

1831 painting by George Catlin of native American Ojibwe Chief of the Plains.

improving these, will greatly enhance understanding of that group's culture. Indigenous religions have been of considerable importance in the study of religions and anthropology, and their adherents are now participants in rich and significant dialogues with members of other religions or none. The recognition that religion may be largely about the etiquette by which people relate to one another can be seen as one of the most significant gifts of indigenous people to understanding what it means to be human.

GRAHAM HARVEY

CHAPTER 8

Indigenous Religions in Asia

CASE-STUDY I

Asian tribal peoples do not separate the sacred and secular. Their religious concepts are expressed in ritualized activities involving the community. These concepts and actions do not result from verbal 'beliefs'. In this they differ from 'religion' as we know it in the world's major faiths.

The key to understanding Asian tribal worldviews is 'relationship': with gods and spirits; with fellow human beings; with nature. These cannot be separated: they form one whole. Each group has religious practices appropriate to themselves and their environment, most often seeking to restore the good order that was created 'in the beginning'. So the practices of tribal groups stretching across Asia and the neighbouring islands vary widely.

SHAMANS

Shamans dominate religion in Siberia, where people believe in a high god, beyond all good and evil. Chosen by the spirits from certain families, male and female shamans enter rigorous training. Their souls leave the body by ecstatic trances to communicate with the spirits. They bring back instructions to correct the erring and restore harmony between people, the spirit world, and everything created. This harmony is fundamental to their beliefs. Similar beliefs are held by the Ainus of northern Japan, the mountain peoples of Taiwan and, to some extent, the Hakka of China.

NOMADIC GROUPS

Many people think the nomadic groups are descendants of Asia's ancient peoples who have preserved traditional ways down the ages. Today they live in small bands in remote, forested hill-country, where they were probably pushed long ago by more highly organized immigrants. They include very small tribes in west-central and south India and in Chota Nagpur, and they are also found on the Andaman Islands, and scattered in remote forest and swamp areas of coastal Cambodia. Better known, perhaps, are the small groups of Semang-Negritoes and their neighbours, the Senoi, inhabiting the jungle hills of northern and central peninsular Malaysia; also the Aëtas-Negritoes of Luzon, Mindanao, and Mindoro in the Philippines. Other hunter-gatherer groups can be found wandering in central Kalimantang, the Celebes, and eastern Sumatra.

Such groups may be made up of one elder and his family, or several families. Scarcity of food dictates size. However much they roam, they usually keep within their own boundaries. Food is always shared equally — roots, tubers, leaves, and fruits from the forest, possibly fish speared or trapped. Small game is hunted by bow-and-arrow, except on the Malaysian peninsula, where Senoi blowgun and poisoned dart have also been adopted by the Semang.

The Mah Meri people belong to the Senoi sub-group of Malaysia, and most live along the coast of South Selangor.

A SHORT INTRODUCTION TO WORLD RELIGIONS

LAND AND RITUAL

Their home area of land and its produce has great religious significance. However far they wander, they return repeatedly to the place they regard as their own. Many, such as the Malaysian Senoi hill-people — widely known as *Sakai*, 'slave' — have changed to slash-and-burn cultivation for part of each year. They still live in very temporary shelters during food-collecting expeditions, but cultivation demands settled base-camps at some seasons, which changes their religious attitude to the land and to the spirits.

The Senoi, like other hill-cultivators, are surrounded by taboos and work restrictions as soon as they choose which trees to fell and fire to prepare a hill-plot. Through a series of rituals, they seek the spirits' help in securing a good crop, until the final harvest celebration. These rituals are performed by the whole community; for instance, all are in 'quarantine' on the first day of planting. Similarly, one person's sickness involves everybody; for the person's soul has wandered out of the group and must be brought back. The shaman employs the power of certain herbs and plants disliked by the spirit world to drive away the evil and call back the wandering soul.

TABOO

In cases of serious illness the whole group is involved in taboos and ritual observances, perhaps in days and nights of music and spirit-possessed dance. Finally, when blood sacrifice has been offered, the spirit is driven out. If the patient dies, another set of pollution observances begins. Deaths, like births, are full of danger, and the group must isolate itself, both for its own safety and that of its neighbours. If any member breaks the taboo, terrifying tropical storms will follow. These come from a supreme god, but the Senoi have little idea of a hierarchy of spirit beings. To them, the presence of ancestor-spirits is vague and unwelcome. Safety and well-being depend on the unity and harmony of the living community.

Tribes with more complex social structures, and more settled and advanced economic patterns, develop a stronger pattern of rituals, which demands ritual specialists for proper celebration. Though certain rites may be performed for the individual, they still involve the wider community. The Kondhs provide an example.

> *The elements of the taboo ... are always the same: certain things, or persons, or places belong in some way to a different order of being, and therefore contact with them will produce an upheaval at the ontological level which might well prove fatal.*
>
> Mircea Eliade, *Patterns in Comparative Religion* (1958).

THE KONDHS

The Kondhs — or Kui, as they call themselves — live in the jungle-covered Eastern Ghats of Orissa, India, and number more than a million. Traditionally, they supported themselves by slash-and-burn hill-plots, and by hunting and gathering during the dry 'hungry season'. Paddy-cultivation has now steadily increased.

In 1835 the British East India Company first encountered the Kondhs' constant human sacrifices to satisfy the earth's demands. Kondh myths taught that only in return for this costliest form of sacrifice would the earth deity grant them fertility of crops, animals, and healthy children.

The creator-god, Bura, formed the earth-goddess, Tari, as his companion, but found her sadly lacking in wifely attentions. She tried in vain to prevent his creating the world and humankind. All was paradise in the created world, except for her growing jealousy, which led to a fierce conflict between the two. All the Kondhs, except a small minority, believed the earth-goddess had won, although she let the creator keep second place. She taught the arts of hunting, war, and cultivation only in return for human blood, her 'proper food'.

Buffalo now replace human victims, and – though declining – this ritual continues. Strips of flesh are hacked from the victim and buried in the village and in neighbouring villages, to release her gift of fertility. Many villages were formerly at war. Brief, strict peace-pacts are therefore made for each annual stage of this three- or four-year ritual, ensuring cooperation for the set few days. In some areas, this ritual is still annually celebrated in each district, also at certain farming seasons, or when the health of the people or its livestock is affected. This binds the people together as Kondhs, when otherwise the strongest unit is the lineage group.

A number of myths and dialogues show how the Kondhs tried to avoid the earth-goddess's demands: 'We will die rather than give you human beings!' But breaking the relationship with her also involved breaking the relationship with the land – bringing drought and famine – and with humankind, bringing pestilence and death. Hence she always made them submit, as the means of recreating harmony and well-being.

KONDH RITUALS

The Kondhs try to use mystical powers in many other rituals, to increase or restore relationship – thus strength and well-being – in the district, village, kin-group, or household:

- Rituals between the high god, humankind, and the land. These follow the farming calendar, from ground preparation and sowing, to reaping and threshing; also taboo-lifting rituals on hunting and gathering wild produce.
- Rituals to seek the blessing and help of the ancestors. These may involve other clans: such as marriage or the taking of a second wife, or the removal of an entire village with its ancestors, if problems and pestilences show the need.
- Rituals to guard against loss of well-being through pollution. Ritual impurity runs the full gamut from small household avoidances to incest, which pollutes the earth and everybody in the area. All births and deaths pollute, but most serious for the Kondhs are deaths before due time, by tiger-mauling, in childbirth, or by hanging, falling from a tree, or drowning. These place the entire village in 'quarantine', traditionally for a month, but nowadays for a shorter period, while priest and people undergo daily purification rites.
- Rituals to safeguard life. The danger may come from high-ranking spirits: gods of the hill, of smallpox, of boundaries, of iron (war), or hunting. These are stronger than spirits of springs, trees, and lesser hills. Offence against them rapidly brings disaster. Also life-destroying is an overpowering belief in evil eye, sorcery, and witchcraft. These powers – neutral in themselves – become evil and deeply feared when someone uses them against their fellow, for this reverses Kondh beliefs about community well-being. Counter-rituals by 'witch-detectives' may return the evil to its originator, but the victim may nevertheless fall sick or die.

Seers communicate with the spirits through trances or divination, to find out who caused the problem and why. Priests perform the rituals, sacrificing cocks, goats, pigs, or buffalo. A spirit-chosen keeper of the village's shrine-stones performs many annual purification rituals. Many villages also have groves sacred to the hill-god or guardian spirit. The household head is priest for ancestor rites, and some look after bronze emblems of animals, reptiles, or other household spirits.

ONE COMMUNITY

The ancestors, the unborn, and the living all form one community; the same daily activities continue in the shade-world. Death in old age with a full funeral gives the best hope of passing peacefully to the ancestors. The dead are also rehabilitated into the bereaved home in the form of a spider, found near the funeral pyre. Sudden death in the feared forms mentioned earlier rules out being accepted by the ancestors. This results in unbearable loneliness for the now dangerous spirit. For the Kondhs, it is as necessary to live in community after death as before it. The manner of death – not good or evil behaviour in this life – decides the future life.

BARBARA BOAL

CHAPTER 9

Australian Aboriginal Religions

CASE-STUDY 2

Australia is a vast continent that was peopled sparsely by its indigenous inhabitants before the advent of Europeans. When Europeans did arrive, they found a very different land from the one they had left, and an indigenous population that held religious views and lifestyles they found almost impossible to comprehend. The archaeological record of human life on the continent reaches back at least 40,000 years, white colonization little more than 200 years.

LAND AND CREATION

Central to Aboriginal beliefs are stories that tell of their relationship to the land, of totemic ancestors that once lay beneath the land and who, in the creative period, or founding drama, gave form to the formless and instituted unchangeable laws that humans were to follow for all time. The ancestors gave shape to an existing, yet formless world; they were self-created and creative, possessing special powers that could be used for good or harm. When they rose up from beneath the land, they journeyed across, under, or over it, leaving tangible expressions of their essence, or power, in the land itself. Where they stopped to urinate, for example, one might find a waterhole; where they sat, one might find a shallow depression; where they slept might be a rock; where they bled, ochre deposits were left; where they dug in the ground, water flowed and springs formed; where they cut down trees, valleys were formed. These primordial beings, the ancestors of living Aborigines, instituted tribal laws for their progeny to follow, and, when they completed their travels, they returned into the land whence they had come. Because all things share a common ancestral life force that is sacred, everything is interconnected, the living to the non-living, the sentient to the non-sentient, within a sacred geography that provides visual evidence of ancestral presence.

Aboriginal beliefs about the origins of the universe, and the place of humans in that universe, are conveyed in stories to do with the ancestors, and relayed through ceremonial performance, art, dance, and song. Songlines consist of a number of songs that follow

Aboriginal rock painting in Kakadu National Park, Northern Territory, Australia.

tracts of land pertaining to particular ancestors and their associated journeying, and those areas of land are associated with particular species of animals, birds, and other phenomena, and their connections to humans. Everything is linked, in an all-encompassing system of interrelatedness, and a network of tracks that cover the continent.

THE DREAMING

When Frank Gillen and Baldwin Spencer encountered the Arrernte Aborigines in central Australia in the late nineteenth century, they tried to understand what they referred to as their *Altyerrenge/Alcheringa* — the fundamental religious concepts that permeated every aspect of Aboriginal life and death. The closest translation these two white men could arrive at was 'Dream times', because it seemed to them that the Arrernte were talking about a past period of a vague and 'dreamy' nature, yet one that was still present. They realized that the *Altyerrenge* was of great importance to Aboriginal culture, but also that 'Dream times' — which later became 'the Dreaming' or 'Dreamtime' — did not adequately convey the meaning of the Aboriginal term. W. E. H. Stanner described the Dreaming as 'everywhen', to convey the sense of a non-linear, ever-present aspect to the Dreaming. Other Aboriginal language groups throughout Australia use similar concepts, and so the term 'Dreaming' came to have a universal application. Aborigines are more likely to give specific language names to the concept, or to call it their 'Law'. T. G. H. Strehlow aptly described it as 'eternal, uncreated, sprung out of itself'.

Since different parts of the landscape were created by particular ancestral beings, there is a plurality of Dreamings. Access to the Dreaming can come about through various means: participation in ceremonial performance, song, dance, or ritual, and via dreams and other methods. The significance of Dreaming stories is conveyed through these means, and according to an individual's position in the scheme of sacred knowledge. For example, a song might have several layers of meaning: at the basic level, men, women, and children have access to the public nature of a story conveyed in the song; at another level, a sacred meaning would be conveyed; and at a secret-sacred level, only those who have undertaken a specific initiation in either 'men's business' — knowledge about the Dreaming pertaining to men — or 'women's business' — knowledge about the Dreaming pertaining to women — would be privy to the deepest levels of meaning. Similarly, paintings also have layers of meaning, from public to esoteric knowledge, held by only a few senior people. The most secret, restricted knowledge is owned, or known, by senior men who are experts in 'men's business' and by senior women who are experts in 'women's business'.

> *I am not painting just for my pleasure; there is the meaning, knowledge, and power. This is the earthly painting for the creation and for the land story. The land is not empty, the land is full of knowledge, full of story, full of goodness, full of energy.*
>
> Marika, quoted in Wally Caruana and Nigel Lendon, *The Painters of the Wagilag Sisters' Story* 1937–97 (National Gallery of Australia, Canberra, 1997).

OWNERSHIP

The concept of 'ownership' has relevance only to knowledge, not to ownership of land. Ownership of knowledge extends to everything that is non-material: the right of someone to paint certain designs, to sing a song, or to tell a story. The expression 'keeping up country' means that the people who come from a specific area, or 'country', and are associated with it through the Dreaming, must look after it in the form of stewardship or custodianship – by continuing the rituals, following the songlines, and maintaining a proper relationship with the ancestors of that 'place'.

Legal recognition of traditional ownership is an ongoing concern for Aboriginal people, many of whom were displaced from their original lands after colonization. This is a major issue for Aboriginal people, still under debate in courts of law throughout Australia.

ABORIGINES AND CHRISTIANITY

After 200 years of colonization and Christianization through missionary influences, a great many Aboriginal people are now Christian, or combine tenets of Christianity with indigenous beliefs and practices. Their stories of the Dreaming, their displacement, and their sometimes traumatic experiences as a result of European presence, are all depicted in their distinctive art – which now consists of traditional methods such as dot paintings and abstract designs – Christian influences, and political statements about their lived experiences.

LYNNE HUME

CHAPTER 10

South American Indigenous Religions

CASE-STUDY 3

This overview concerns the religious world views of the indigenous peoples of Central and South America, focusing upon those disparate and diverse communities whose tribal practices and geographical remoteness have until relatively recently helped to preserve much of a cultural heritage that very substantially predates European 'conquest' (1492–). Because of the linguistic and cultural diversity of these communities, examples have been introduced from as many different contexts as possible, with indigenous sources cited regarding their most popular name. The majority of examples relate to peoples inhabiting the forested highlands and lowlands of northern/central South America, with broader representation gained by referring to assorted groups in Tierra del Fuego and Patagonia in the south and the Central American isthmus to the north. A proper appreciation of the practices and belief systems of these indigenous groups requires an awareness of an overarching worldview, consisting of an enormously complex interaction of situated socio-cultural processes and localized economico-political dynamics.

TIME AND SPACE

Conceiving time as linear rather than cyclical, these indigenous peoples make sense of the present with reference to the foundational events of a primordial past. Here, a mythical period of momentous upheavals engenders an increasingly variegated world, in which flood, fire, and violence mould and reshape the cosmos. Indigenous mythologies represent the world as the intended product of pre-existent deities, such as Temáukel of the Ona, or as an unintended result caused by their godly and semi-divine offspring, as with Kumai of the Baniwa. The transition from mythical pre-history to human time is often effected through the foundational practices of mythical cultural heroes, such as Elal of the Tehuelche. Within this period of momentous change and unfolding differentiation, tribal traditions are established, and classificatory systems formulated – the ambiguities, contradictions, and maladies of which continue to find their basis in the primeval period. The recalcitrant disorder of the present is framed by the ambivalent discontinuities of a mythic past.

The indigenous cosmos is spatially divided into a series of overlapping tiers, some of which are further subdivided. The number of strata differs from culture to culture, with the Kógi having as many as nine divisions, the Siona and Waiwai five, the Tapirapé and Baniwa four, and the Toba, Matsigenka, and Pemón three. At its simplest, the universe has the earth sandwiched between the heavenly terrain of the gods above, and the subterranean world below. With the Baniwa, the heavenly realm comprises a lower 'Other World', adjacent to the earth, and a more distant 'Other Sky'. The underworld can also be layered, as with the Campa's partition of it into two. Although any particular stratum may be divided laterally, the earthly tier is most commonly subjected to such treatment, with prominent environmental features, such as mountains, lakes, and dense parts of the forest, and mythical places, such as the Avá-Chiripá's 'land without evil', accorded extra-special status.

THE PHYSICAL MIRRORS THE SUPERNATURAL

The physical space and moral environment of indigenous peoples is ordered to reflect mythico-cosmic space-time. The Kayopó village, for example, both in its design and external orientation to the surrounding forest, exemplifies physical space as a microcosm upon which temporal heritage and spatial hierarchy write themselves, through individual lives and social processes. As with the village, so too the human individual is held to mirror the cosmic order of things. The indigenous self is seen in a wide variety of ways. The Waiwai, certain Guaraní groups, and the Toba talk of the self as having two principal elements, rendered 'souls' by most scholars. The Avá-Chiripá, Matsigenka, and other Guaraní groups understand the self as comprised of three primary components. Whatever the structure, indigenous conceptions of the self and its constituent parts serve at least two basic functions:

- As within many other mythico-religious systems, they allow for continuity in the face of spatio-temporal change. Whether awake or asleep, as with the nocturnal roamings of the Matsigenka 'free soul' and the Toba 'image soul'; alive or dead, as with the post-mortem ascension of the Waiwai 'eye-soul' to Kapu; in this world or another, as with the 'soul flight' of shamanic ecstasy, partitioned conceptions of the self help to preserve a continuity of personal identity.
- They help to situate the individual amidst a multiple configuration of mythical, temporal, and spatial reality. Whether unified, dualistic, or tripartite, these views of the self serve generally to articulate an understanding of the individual as constituted through the continuous interplay of its divine origins, base corporeality, and personal-social processes. They thereby allow for relations with other spheres of existence both in this life and the next, ground the individual in the corruptible materiality of this world, and preserve a personal identity which is derived from more than its heavenly-physical origins. The indigenous self exists as a nodal point at which mythical, spatial, and temporal dynamics intersect.

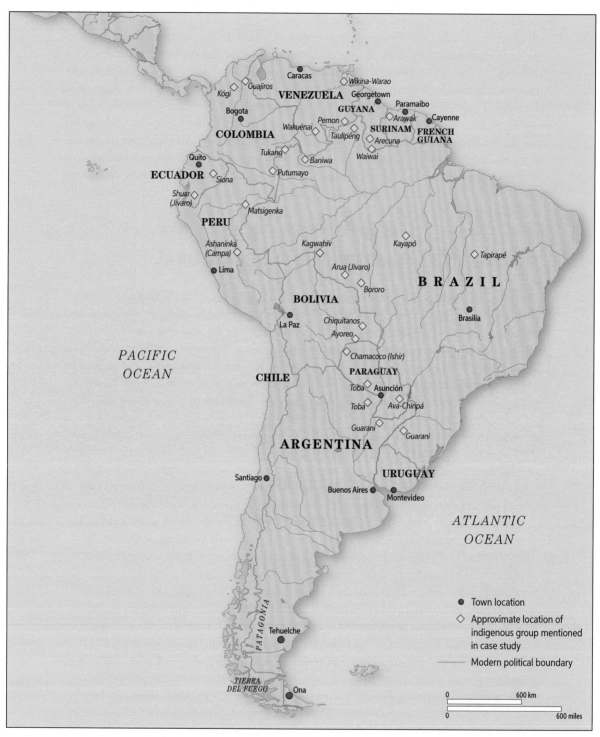

Indigenous Groups of South America

A SHORT INTRODUCTION TO WORLD RELIGIONS

SUPERNATURAL BEINGS

Alongside humankind and the flora and fauna surrounding it, the indigenous universe is populated by a broad array of supernatural beings. Whilst taxonomy differs from people to people, the following categories are generally representative:

- Inhabiting the higher strata of the cosmologies, often remote from everyday human activity, are – for some tribes – uncreated/pre-existent deities such as Kóoch of the Tehuelche, Ñanderuvusú of the Guaraní, and Nanderú Guazù of the Avá-Chiripá.

- These divine beings are accompanied by a pantheon of lesser deities, whose origins and characteristics are usually connected with celestial, climatic, totemic, and otherwise routine phenomena – as with Gidosíde, the Ayoreo moon goddess; Karuten, the Tehuelche god of thunder; the black monkey of the Arawak or the tiger of the Goajiros; and Pel'ek of the Toba, the owner of the night.

- Although indigenous deities involve themselves in the general ordering of human affairs, and are at times difficult to differentiate from the more numerous category of 'spirits', it is the latter who most directly influence day-to-day affairs. Usually occupying the lower strata of the cosmos, the spirits of animals, plants, and elementals – for example, of water – along with those of deceased human beings, are regarded as primary causal forces, potentially influencing every facet of personal well-being, interpersonal relations, and social reproduction.

- Experienced through dreams or visions, encountered at night in the village or by day in the forest, the spirits of the indigenous world view are central to the dynamics of a human world which is, after all, nothing but a pale imitation of the 'real world' they inhabit. Whilst benevolent and malevolent forms exist, within the indigenous mindset spirits are, by and large, morally ambivalent in their dealings with humans. However, with adequate inducements and the appropriate opportunities they are quick to make their ubiquitous presence felt. The prevalence of widespread supernatural causality demands constant and careful handling, and most indigenous peoples turn to ritualized activity, managed by the local shaman, to limit or coordinate the impact of the spiritual upon the material.

THE SHAMAN

Although intended – as opposed to accidental and undesired – engagement with indigenous spirits is not restricted to formal shamanic activity, the shaman is the primary agent in human-supernatural interaction. Selected by way of heredity, as with the Putumayo, or shamanic preference, as with the Avá-Chiripá, shamans undergo rigorous and prolonged training. Lasting anywhere from less than five years – as with the Matsigenka, Siona, and Chiquitano – to more than ten – as with the Kógi, Arecuna, and Taulipáng – shamanic apprenticeship comprises an extended period of isolation and instruction, coupled with numerous ordeals and disciplinary regimes. In effect, literal marginalization, sexual abstinence, emetically induced purgation, and narcotically managed disruption to sleep and hygiene patterns reconstitute the shamanic novice as one who is to live and function at the personal and spiritual margins of everyday life. Yet the shaman is an 'outsider within', for the overwhelming role accorded supernatural causality entails that the shaman's place is thoroughly intertwined within the warp and woof of daily routine.

The Tapirapé, for example, hold shamanic activity to be central to biological reproduction, believing the shaman to be responsible for the safe transit from other realms of the souls of those newly conceived. Like many other indigenous communities, the Baniwa regard serious illness as a direct result of spirit assault. Whether induced at the behest of other – usually shamanic – human beings, or resulting from the breaking of any number of food, hygiene, and social taboos, an attack by spirits can only be properly dealt with through recourse to one trained in the arts of the supernatural spheres. In addition to the almost daily routine of preventing, diagnosing, or curing serious illness, the shaman is a focal point of communal festivals, such as harvest; rites of passage, such as female menarche and male coming of age; socio-economic reproduction, such as successful hunting; and political processes, such as assuaging internal discord or inter-tribal dispute.

Differentiation of shamanic specialisms is a varying phenomenon among indigenous peoples. The Jívaro and Wakuénai distinguish two classes of shaman, whereas the Ishír, Winikina-Warao, and Desana have three types. The grounds for such differentiation differ from tribe to tribe, with the most popular distinctions related to abilities to heal or injure, the frequenting of different supernatural realms, or the relationship with particular spirits, often relative to the use of specific hallucinogenic agents.

Whatever his – and the indigenous shaman is overwhelmingly male – title, role, or place in society, the shaman executes his responsibilities by drawing upon a vast range of knowledge acquired through initiation, apprenticeship, and practice. In addition to memorizing the structures of the numerous cosmic realms, the shaman must master the techniques of ecstasy, dream, and vision through which other worlds are visited, and the services of their supernatural inhabitants engaged. The shaman thereby provides a heavily ritualized service, the execution of which demands combining a vast cosmological knowledge with gruelling physical regimes, diagnostic lore with curative techniques, and socio-economic practices with religious performance.

Central to successful shamanic practice are the alliances forged by the indigenous shaman with spiritual forces from other worlds. Generally occupying the higher strata of the cosmos, 'guardian spirits' serve as powerful allies to the shaman, offering protection from supernatural assault, and information as to the probable causes of individual malady and social disturbance. Visiting their domains in person, a shaman communicates with his guardian spirits by transporting his soul through the media of naturally occurring, ritually induced, and narcotically stimulated dreams, trances, and visions. Complementing the overarching support of a particular shaman's set of guardian spirits may be any number of auxiliary spirits, principally of animals and plants. Resident within the shaman himself, auxiliary spirits play a diagnostic role, but come into their own as active agents in the curative techniques called upon in shamanic practice. The principal relationship between a shaman and his auxiliary spirits is one of mutually beneficial exchange. Here, the resident spirits get to enjoy whatever hallucinogenic agents are used in ritualized shamanic activity, in return for their aid in resolving problems. In this instance narcotics, such as tobacco and ayahuasca — *Banisteriopsis caapi* — are not simple hallucinogens, but commodities of a highly ritualized exchange forming the central component by and around which other forms of shamanic performance, such as chant and dance, are ordered.

The shaman's ability to persuade, co-opt, suborn, and manipulate agents of the spirit world, subsequently exploiting these alliances and relationships for the betterment of his community, furnishes a practical corollary to indigenous belief in widespread supernatural causality. Triadic in nature, shamanic activity is:

- mimetic, in that its recapitulation of received tradition reappropriates for the present the powerful forces of primordial times;
- restorative, in that these forces align current practices with primeval order;
- creative, in that the correlation of past and present staves off disorder and assures futurity.

Integral to the indigenous worldview, shamanic practice exemplifies indigenous existence as a nodal point through which a multiple configuration of mythico-religious forces write themselves upon human space-time.

ANDREW DAWSON

CHAPTER 11

Native North Americans

CASE-STUDY 4

Contrary to popular belief, indigenous religions are today reviving in many parts of the world. The superior attitude which spread European civilization over the globe, spurred on by Western Christianity and materialism, was discredited in the twentieth century. Native faith-ways – scorned, forbidden, almost destroyed – reached their lowest point at the end of the nineteenth century.

Today disregard for the earth, for community, and for spirituality have brought the whole human enterprise into jeopardy. Arising like the phoenix from the ashes, tribal peoples are gathering again in their ceremonial circles, remembering discarded teachings, renewing the traditional ways. As they do so, perhaps they are laying the foundations for what they themselves are calling 'the fourth world', and a hope for a new beginning on the earth.

Wisdom, for such people, is found in the past, in the long experience of the race, in tradition. A very frequent expression in their ceremonies is, 'it is said ...', by which is meant the teaching of the ancients. The teachers are the Elders, who are closest to those things of the past that are important. For tribal people, life is one. The sacred is very real – and specially real in some times and places. But the sacred is not divided off from times and places called secular; all life is sacred. All things are 'indwelt' to some degree. The whole range of life is open to spirit.

ONE GREAT SPIRIT

The tribal peoples of North America proclaim the One Great Spirit. Their thought and action is governed by the circle, which they see as basic in nature: the shape of moon and sun, the wheeling stars above them, the rotating seasons, the actions of birds and animals. 'Everything tries to be round.' This form is evident in everything they do – in myth, ceremony, art, and community organization. Essential to the circle is its centre, from which it is created. This is the symbol of the Great Spirit, reflected in all the dances around the fire, drum, or pole, and in ceremonies such as the sacred pipe.

TWO-NESS

Tribal people also reflect upon the two-ness of life and nature. Native North Americans symbolize this by a divided circle, as in the Plains shields, and in many forms of art and craft. Nature presents itself in pairs: dark and light, cold and hot, male and female, good and bad, and so on. These are not contradictory, but complementary. This twoness is expressed in the myths, such as that of the two sons of Mother Earth; in the totems of the west coast, such as Sisutl of the Kwakiutl, the two-headed serpent which punishes and protects; in the Thunderbird, threatening and caring; and in ceremonies, such as the forked pole of the Sundance.

But the two are always seen as aspects of the one, the circle. They are different, but they appear in balance, in harmony – the overriding virtue. Contentment is found not by conflict, but by coming to terms. An example of this is the native Arctic-dwellers, the Inuit. Intruding whites complain about a harsh, cruel environment, and when they go north take with them all manner of technologies to beat the climate. The Inuit, on the other hand, live face to face with nature, and, when untouched by the intruder, are happy. They have found harmony with their surroundings, and treat the ice and snow as friends, not enemies.

TRIANGLE ON CIRCLE

Give and take is the basis of all healthy relationships, and can be symbolized as a triangle on a circle. Tribal people search for support that will make their ventures succeed. This help is obtained in ceremonies whose action is three-sided. For example, a Mohawk community is threatened by drought, and corn withers in the fields. Help lies with the Thunderbeings; the rain must be sought with their aid by means of the rain dance. The community gathers in the fields, the drum and shaker sound, the dance begins, prayer is sung, water is sprinkled, and the rains come. The same give and take, between human need, heavenly power, and particular action, is found in all ceremonies for healing, guidance, and power.

> *When we killed a buffalo, we knew what we were doing. We apologized to his spirit, tried to make him understand why we did it, honouring with a prayer the bones of those who gave their flesh to keep us alive, praying for their return, praying for the life of our brothers, the buffalo nation, as well as for our own people.*
>
> John Lame Deer, twentieth-century Sioux shaman

THE FOUR POWERS

Native peoples in North America, as elsewhere, tended to see the structure of the world, and of the powers that control it, as four-sided. The symbol they used for this is a circle, with four points on the circumference.

Lame Deer, a present-day Sioux, explains:

> *Four is the number that is most sacred [wakan]. Four stands for the four quarters of the earth … the four winds … seasons … colours … four things of*

which the universe is made – earth, air, water, fire. There are four virtues which a man should possess … We Sioux do everything by fours …

Into this structure of fours is gathered and classified all life's variety. It is made one – the circle – through the 'great law of sacrifice', in which each part depends upon, and contributes to, all the others. 'One dies that another may live.' The 'wheel' is the pattern of all ceremonies, because it symbolizes the variety of life in the wholeness of life. This concept of unity in variety, and variety within unity, is basic to the goal of harmony and balance in life, seen by tribal people as the foundation of all health, peace, and well-being in the world.

> *Every object in the world has a spirit and that spirit is* wakan. *Thus the spirits of the tree or things of that kind, while not like the spirit of man, are also* wakan. Wakan *comes from the* wakan *beings. These* wakan *beings are greater than mankind in the same way that mankind is greater than animals. They are never born and never die … Mankind can pray to the* wakan *beings for help … The word* Wakan Tanka *means all of the* wakan *beings, because they are all as if one.* Wakan Tanka Kin *signifies the chief or leading* wakan *being, which is the Sun. However, the most powerful of the* wakan *beings is* Nagh Tanka, *the great Spirit who is also* Taku Skanskan.
>
> Sword, *Wakan*, trans. Burt Means

MYSTERY OF SEVENS

A 'mystery of sevens' lies at the root of ancient wisdom, and is found among indigenous cultures in all parts of the world, including the tribal people of North America. We hear of the seven sacred rites of the Sioux, the seven prophecies, or fires, of the Ojibwa Midewiwin, and the seven stopping-places in their ages-long migration westward. We hear of cycles of seven years and seven-times-seven years, and we hear of the seven Grandfathers.

The seven Grandfathers, found in Ojibwa mythology, are symbolized in the teaching staff, hung in the centre of the ceremonial circle, and made up of three straight sticks bound together at their centres. These sticks have six points, standing for the four directions plus the 'above' power – sky – and the 'below' power – earth, with a seventh at the crossing-point. It is the 'here' place of power, the self, the power within. This is not to say that the individual is the centre of all, but that all the powers are available to, and are flowing through, individuals. The powers come to them in visions and dreams, and are working through them in teachings and ceremonies.

Finally, there is the simple quartered circle, the symbol of wholeness. When taking part in the ceremonies, as the sweet grass is burned, the water drunk, the pipe smoked, one hears from each worshipper the words 'All my relations'. All are related to each, and each to all. Participants are conscious that the whole universe is around them, sharing in their need and their prayer.

J. W. E. NEWBERY

CHAPTER 12

African Indigenous Religions

CASE-STUDY 5

The continent of Africa covers more than 11.5 million square miles/30 million square kilometres and has a population of more than 1000 million. The diversity of religions in such a vast region is immense and extremely complex. Islam has been present in most of North Africa since the seventh and eighth centuries CE and, following the spread of European colonialism in the eighteenth and nineteenth centuries, Christianity has been growing rapidly throughout the sub-Saharan regions. As a result, it is accurate to say that no 'indigenous' religion exists in Africa today, if we mean by the term 'indigenous' that which is original, archaic, or unchanging.

In fact, the religious expressions of African peoples have always been dynamic, changing just as societies have changed, and taking different forms as contact is made with other African peoples, and as economic modes and power structures have evolved. Indigenous, therefore, is not a term referring to some original African religiosity: it designates what we are able to know historically about the religious life and practices of particular African societies prior and subsequent to extensive encounters with Islam and the colonial West, and through a study of those practices which persist among contemporary African peoples. The indigenous religions of Africa thus are known through a wide combination of methodologies, including the study of historic documents, analysis of oral traditions, archaeological evidence, phenomenological classifications, and anthropological fieldwork.

> *The African is notoriously religious.*
>
> J. S. Mbiti, Kenyan theologian

CHARACTERISTICS

Although wide variations exist, most scholars of African indigenous religions identify eight characteristics that practitioners hold in common, particularly those living in the sub-Saharan regions.

- Because African indigenous religions are coextensive with their societies, and based largely on kinship relationships, religion cannot be separated from other cultural practices. Society, in its widest sense, is thought to include not only the living, but what the community understands to be a variety of spiritual forces, foremost among which are the ancestors.

- The impossibility of segregating the religious from the social means that – to outsiders – the visibility of African indigenous religions is low. What people in the West typically regard as secular, such as planting and harvesting crops, is connected closely to religious understandings in Africa.

- The multi-stranded nature of thought that is used to explain the misfortunes, illnesses, and catastrophes which commonly afflict communities can appear unsystematic and unanalytical to an outsider. For example, if the remedy prescribed by a traditional healer or diviner fails, other diviners are consulted, who may offer quite different solutions. Sometimes explanations relate to violations of social norms that occurred long before the present generation was alive, and thus cannot be remembered by the living. These ways of resolving human crises are not thought by the participants to be irrational, since the multi-stranded nature of thought means many apparently contradictory explanations are believed and acted on at the same time.

- Rituals are performed primarily to guarantee tangible benefits in this life only. African indigenous religions are pragmatic, concerning themselves with securing and maintaining largely material advantages, which promote the well-being of the community as a whole. Communication with a variety of spirits in rituals is intended to achieve this end.

- Reciprocity between the community and the spirits defines the primary way that such tangible benefits are acquired and maintained. Generally this means the community must provide gifts to the spirits, usually in the form of sacrificed animals, as a sign of respect and remembrance; in return the spirits provide protection and material gains for the community.

- Beliefs are not articulated, but remain implicit. Hence, there are no doctrines, theologies, claims to truth, or factional disputes between sects. African indigenous religions are non-missionary in their intent.

- African indigenous religions readily adopt ideas, beliefs, and practices from other religions. They have an open mind, importing their deities and rituals readily, and integrating them into their own complex systems.

- African indigenous religions are adaptive: they are able to accommodate to new factors, including modernization. In the modern religious scene in Africa, most believers have expanded their original religious perspectives to include that of an imported religion, usually Christianity or Islam. The widespread popularity of African-founded churches, often referred to as African Independent or African-initiated Churches, confirms the process of adaptation of traditional beliefs and practices to missionary religions.

CONTENT

Although it is possible to outline the substantive features or general content of the religiosity of African peoples, summarized in the following six points, it must be kept in mind that these do not constitute a coherent doctrinal system, or a kind of 'African systematic theology'.

- Reality is regarded as dynamic: centres of power are located in natural phenomena, animals, and humans. Some societies may acknowledge one source of power behind these, but the overriding concern is to ensure that such power enhances the quality of human life, rather than diminishing it. An example of the positive use of power is when ancestors provide ample rain to ensure the abundance of crops and the health of the cattle. Witchcraft is always identified with a power that diminishes the quality of a community's life.
- African indigenous religions can be called a form of humanism, because religious activity focuses on how positive benefits for society can be enhanced. Forces seen as spiritual — whether deities, ancestor spirits, or nature spirits — are understood primarily in connection with their ability to guarantee human well-being.
- This humanism is communal and not individualistic. Fulfilment comes for individuals as they participate in family and community relationships.
- Because religion focuses on communal well-being, Africans are concerned with the present moment and not with a future existence after death. There is no sense of the past moving through the present to some future event; the past and the future find their meaning in the present. Hence, distance from the present is more important than the direction time takes.
- Maintaining good health defines a dominant concern for African societies. When good health fails, methods for healing must be identified and employed. Healing has to do with the preservation and/or restoration of human vitality in the context of the community as a whole. Ultimately, health depends on right human relationships and harmony with the spirit world, particularly the ancestors.
- The fundamental concerns of African societies with health and well-being are expressed primarily through ritual activity. Festivals, feasts, dances, and artistic expressions celebrate communal existence, both of the living and the dead.

Taken together, the characteristics of African indigenous religions and the basic content within the African way of life lead to the following core definition: African indigenous religions are localized, kinship-based, non-missionary religions with inarticulate, multi-stranded, and pragmatic beliefs aimed at securing optimal material health for the community, primarily through ritual activity.

INTERVIEW WITH A DINER

This definition is exemplified vividly by an interview the present author conducted in Zimbabwe in 1992 with a traditional healer and diviner, or *n'anga*, a woman of about fifty, who was the chosen medium of the spirit of her deceased father. When the interview began, the *n'anga* was seated outside her hut with her daughter and granddaughter, wearing a simple dress and a sweater. She explained that the people in the region come to her with many different problems, such as sickness, poor crops, death, infertility, and problems at school. She indicated that her deceased father speaks to these people through her, and tells them why they are having problems, and what to do about it. She started doing this about three years earlier, following a long illness no one had been able to cure. During a special ritual prescribed by a *n'anga*, she became possessed by her father, and then recovered completely. Since then, she has helped other people.

The present author's questions seemed to confuse her. When asked how her father takes control of her, she replied simply: 'He does.' Asked if her father — as an ancestor spirit — has special knowledge that he did not have when he was alive, and whether he was in communication with other ancestors, she began to appear uncomfortable, turning away and shaking a little. Further questions followed: 'Does your father carry messages to higher ancestor spirits, even to God? Do any people come to you who are victims of witchcraft?' The woman muttered something to her daughter, let out a very loud belch, and began to shake. Her daughter announced she was now possessed and needed to put on her clothes. They then entered the nearby hut, from which a deep voice could be heard asking, 'Who are these people? Why are they asking my daughter such hard questions?'

The *n'anga* returned from the hut, no longer dressed in simple village attire, but wearing a skirt of animal skins, a hat of eagle feathers, a black cloth over her shoulders and around her waist, and with rattles tied on the side of her legs. She was holding a dark walking stick, about three feet [one metre] in length, with designs on the top. She walked with heavy steps, like a man, and spoke in a deep voice. She was then asked the same questions that had been posed earlier. The reply was, 'These are questions that cannot be answered.' Then a practical problem was raised, and the atmosphere suddenly became quite relaxed. The present writer indicated he had lost his wallet somewhere in his travels around the region. He asked if the woman, now possessed and acting as the medium for her father's spirit, could help retrieve it.

What followed was a dramatic presentation and explanation. The medium said that, on the way to the Chief's home, at a local shop, someone in the crowd spotted the wallet and said to himself, 'Ah, *murungu* (white person)! I will be rich.' He slipped the wallet out of the back pocket and left the shop. When he looked in the wallet, however, he was disappointed, because there was very little money in it. He threw it in some red soil beside the road. Another person came along and spotted it. He also thought, 'Ah, I will be rich!' When he found no money in it, he threw it back into the red soil. That is what happened, said the spirit medium, and the wallet will never be found. During the whole time she was telling this story, she was acting it out. She showed how the man had slipped the wallet out of the back pocket, how he hurriedly left the shop, how he opened it, and expressed disappointment before throwing it by the road. When the medium finished, she sat down again, with her legs crossed like a man. She then stood up and announced: 'I am returning to a mountain near Great Zimbabwe.' At that, the woman re-entered the hut, appearing shortly after in her simple dress and sweater. When asked if she remembered being possessed by her father, she said she did not remember anything.

For the spirit medium, the possession had nothing to do with revealing knowledge of the other world, nor with constructing a systematic diagram of the relationships between ancestor spirits. Its purpose was entirely practical, to alter the enquirer's experience, if possible, in favour of health and well-being. This does not mean her reactions to the analytical questions posed were simplistic; indeed, she illustrated the type of rationality characteristic of the indigenous religions of Zimbabwe. Her responses were pragmatic, concerned with the present — never speculative in a cosmological sense — and employed the spirit world only to influence experience in the here-and-now material existence.

CONCLUSION

If the definition of African indigenous religions presented and exemplified in this article accurately captures their essence, we would expect to detect these emphases, to a lesser or greater extent, in all forms of African religions, including Christianity and Islam. By identifying these central characteristics and core elements, therefore, the student of religions in Africa is provided with key concepts for analysing the multiple, complex, and often bewildering expressions of religion found throughout this immense and culturally diverse continent.

JAMES COX

QUESTIONS

1. Why is interpreting indigenous religions as 'primitive religions' from which 'more advanced' examples later emerge so problematic?

2. Why is the concept of respect so pervasive in indigenous religions?

3. Why do so many indigenous religions regard witchcraft and sorcery as problematic?

4. Why might it be more appropriate to refer to 'beliefs' rather than 'religion' when considering indigenous traditions?

5. Explain why land is so important to Australian aborigines.

6. Why do African religions often lack a distinction between the sacred and the secular?

7. Compare and contrast the beliefs of three indigenous religions.

8. Why is the pairing of opposites in nature so important to native North Americans?

FURTHER READING

Burridge, Kenelm, *New Heaven, New Earth: A Study of Millenarian Activities*. Oxford: Basil Blackwell, 1986.

Durkheim, E., *The Elementary Forms of the Religious Life*. New York: Free Press, 1965 (1915).

Evans-Pritchard, E. E., *Nuer Religion*. London: Oxford University Press, 1956.

Harvey, Graham, *Shamanism: A Reader*. New York: Routledge, 2002.

Herdt, Gilbert H., ed., *Rituals of Manhood: Male Initiation in Papua New Guinea*. Berkeley: University of California Press, 1982.

Martin, Joel W., *The Land Looks After Us: A History of Native American Religion*. New York: Oxford University Press, 2001.

Ray, Benjamin, *African Religions*, 2nd ed. Englewood Cliffs, NJ: Prentice-Hall, 1999.

Turner, Victor, *The Ritual Process*. Ithaca: Cornell University Press, 1969.

PART 3
HINDUISM

SUMMARY

The religion today known as Hinduism may be almost as old as Indian civilization itself: archaeological evidence suggests continuities between the religion of the Indus Valley society of 2500–1500 BCE and the Hinduism of today. The Vedic texts, from the period that followed, provide the basis for some of the central themes of Hindu belief, including *samsara*, the doctrine that all creatures are reborn repeatedly unless the cycle can be broken through liberation (*moksha*), and *karma*, the notion that actions in one life are rewarded or punished in the next. The Vedic religion was hierarchical, and centred around sacrificial offerings. In time, sacrifice was largely replaced by *puja*, the personal devotion of an individual to a particular deity.

Hinduism has a vast body of sacred texts, from the early Vedas onward, and generally is divided into the more authoritative *Sruti* – revealed scripture – and the less authoritative *Smriti* – which includes Epics such as the *Mahabharata* (including the *Bhagavad Gita*) and the *Ramayana*. A hierarchy of sorts also exists amongst the many gods of India, with Vishnu and Shiva enjoying a privileged position – although there is no consensus as to whether there are in fact many gods, or whether the many are merely different representations of the one God, *Brahman*.

Today, like so many religions, Hinduism has a following throughout the world, largely because of the many Indian diaspora communities. Despite this, the subcontinent remains hugely important for Hindus, in part because of the value placed on the many sacred sites in the country, such as the River Ganges, and in part because of the strong ties that bind the wider community. Within India itself – now a secular democracy – there exists something of a division between those at ease with recent developments, such as secularization and the changing role of women, and the emergent Hindu nationalists – often deeply hostile to other religions in the region, particularly Islam – who seek a stronger role for religion in public life.

CHAPTER 13

A Historical Overview

The term 'Hinduism' as we understand it today refers to the majority religion of the Indian subcontinent. The present understanding of Hinduism as a 'world religion' has come about only since the nineteenth century, when Hindu reformers and Western orientalists came to refer to the diverse beliefs and practices characterizing religious life in South Asia as 'Hinduism'. Yet this classification is problematic, as Hinduism possesses many features characteristic of 'indigenous religions': it has no single historical founder, no central revelation, no creed or unified system of belief, no single doctrine of salvation, and no centralized authority. In this sense, it is different from other 'world religions'. Huge diversity and variety of religious movements, systems, beliefs, and practices are all characteristic features of 'Hinduism'. Also, there is no clear division between the 'sacred' and 'profane' – or natural and supernatural: religion and social life are inseparable and intertwined. Nevertheless, most scholars would agree there are unifying strands that run through the diverse traditions that constitute it. Although the term Hinduism is recent, the diverse traditions that it encompasses have very ancient origins that extend back beyond the second millennium BCE.

> *Hinduism is a living organism liable to growth and decay and subject to the laws of nature. One and indivisible at the root, it has grown into a vast tree with innumerable branches.*
>
> Mahatma Gandhi, *Hindu Dharma* (New Delhi: Orient Paperbacks, 1987).

THE INDUS VALLEY CIVILIZATION

The earliest traces of Hinduism can be found in the Indus Valley civilization which flourished from 2500 to about 1500 BCE along the banks of the River Indus, which flows through present-day Pakistan. Archaeological excavations in this area have revealed evidence of what appears to be a highly developed urban culture with sophisticated water distribution, drainage and garbage disposal technologies and well-developed systems of farming, grain-storage and pottery. Little is known about the religion of this civilization. The large number of terracotta figurines unearthed through excavations suggest a continuity between the iconographic features of these images and those of such later Hindu deities as Shiva and the mother goddess. Given the lack of systematic evidence for such continuity, however,

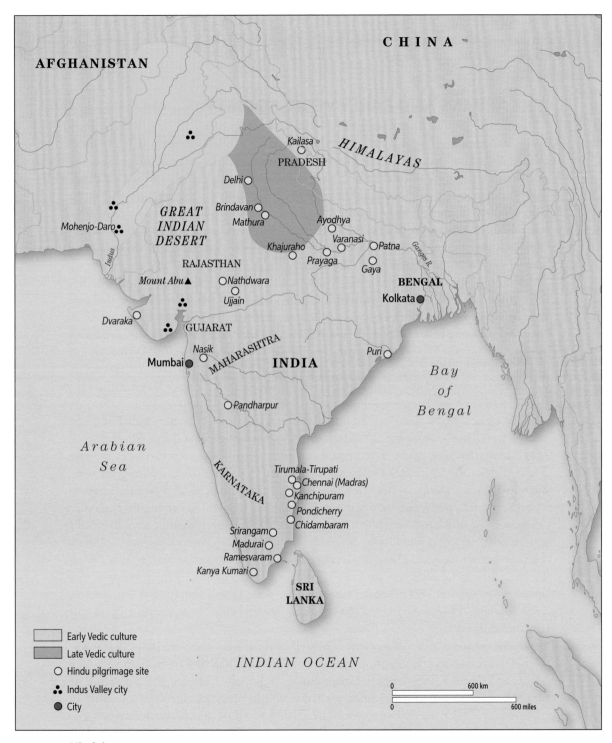

AFGHANISTAN

CHINA

Kailasa
PRADESH

HIMALAYAS

Delhi

Brindavan
Mathura

Ayodhya

Varanasi

Patna

Ganges R.

GREAT
INDIAN
DESERT

Khajuraho

Prayaga

Gaya

BENGAL

Mohenjo-Daro

Indus

Kolkata

RAJASTHAN

Mount Abu ▲

Nathdwara

Ujjain

Dvaraka

GUJARAT

Nasik

Mumbai

MAHARASHTRA

INDIA

Puri

Bay
of
Bengal

Pandharpur

Arabian
Sea

KARNATAKA

Tirumala-Tirupati

Chennai (Madras)

Kanchipuram

Pondicherry

Chidambaram

Srirangam

Madurai

Ramesvaram

Kanya Kumari

SRI
LANKA

INDIAN OCEAN

0   600 km

0   600 miles

Early Vedic culture

Late Vedic culture

○ Hindu pilgrimage site

⣿ Indus Valley city

● City

Hinduism

scholars are inclined to be cautious. Archaeological evidence suggests that the Indus Valley civilization declined rather suddenly between 1800 and 1700 BCE, perhaps because of flooding or inadequate rainfall.

THE ARYANS AND EARLY VEDIC SOCIETY

What followed is a matter of considerable controversy. Some maintain that the Indus Valley civilization came to be replaced by the culture of the Aryans, Indo-European invaders, or migrants from the Caucasus region, who moved south and settled in the Indian subcontinent. Others believe the Aryan civilization developed from within the Indus Valley culture and was not introduced from outside. Whether Aryans came from outside the subcontinent or not, the history of Hinduism as we understand it today is the history of the next 2000 years of Aryan culture, often interacting with, but always dominating, non-Aryan cultures in the area.

The language of the Aryans was Sanskrit. Knowledge of the early Aryans derives primarily from early Sanskrit compositions, the Vedas, a corpus of texts compiled over hundreds of years. It is important to note that the Vedas were oral for thousands of years before being written down. In South India, the oral performances of the Vedas are still important; the Vedas are articulated, embodied, and performed, rather than simply read. Many Hindus today regard the Vedas as timeless revelation and the repository of all knowledge, and as a crucial marker of Hindu identity. The Vedas constitute the foundation for most later developments in Hinduism.

The earliest Vedas were mainly liturgical texts, used primarily in ritual. The Vedic rituals were rituals of sacrifice, addressed to such early gods as Agni (the fire god) and Soma (the plant god). The central act was the offering of substances – often animals, but also such items as milk, clarified butter, grain, and the hallucinogenic soma plant – into the sacrificial fire. The ritual was usually initiated by a wealthy sponsor (*yajamana*), and conducted by ritual specialists, who were the most highly ranked in Vedic society, which followed a fourfold system of hierarchical classification. Below the priests or ritual specialists (Brahmans) came the warriors or rulers (*Kshatriyas*), followed by the traders (*Vaishyas*). These three classes (*varna*) were known as 'twice-born' (*dvija*), because their male members underwent initiation that confirmed their status as full members of society. This initiation rite separated them from a fourth class, the servants (*Shudras*), who – because of their 'low' status – were debarred from perpetuating Vedic ritual traditions.

In due course, Aryan culture came to be well established in northern India. Brahmanic ideology became central to social and political life, and was concerned with the ritual status and duties of the king, the maintaining of social order, and the regulation of individual behaviour in accordance with the all-encompassing ideology of duty, or righteousness (*dharma*). Dharmic ideology related to ritual and moral behaviour, and defined good conduct according to such factors as one's class (*varna*) and one's stage of life (*ashrama*). It operated simultaneously at several levels: the transcendental, and therefore eternal (*sanatana dharma*), the everyday (*sadharana dharma*), and the individual and personal (*svadharma*). Neglecting *dharma* was believed to lead to undesirable social, as well as personal, consequences.

THE LATER VEDIC PERIOD

Alongside the performance of Vedic ritual, speculation arose about its meaning and purpose. These speculations were developed in the later Vedic texts – the *Aranyakas* and *Upanishads* – which tended to see the observance of ritual action as secondary to the gaining of spiritual knowledge. Central to this approach was the *karma-samsara-moksha* doctrine:

• all beings are reincarnated into the world (*samsara*) over and over again;
• the results of action (*karma*) are reaped in future lives;
• this process of endless rebirth is characterized by suffering (*dukkha*);
• liberation (*moksha*) from this suffering can be obtained by gaining spiritual knowledge.

Gaining spiritual knowledge thus came to assume central importance, and the self-disciplining and methods of asceticism necessary for gaining it were developed in Hinduism's traditions of yoga and world renunciation. Ascetic groups known as strivers (*sramanas*) were formed during this period, seeking liberation through austerity. Buddhism and Jainism, both of which rejected the authority of the Vedas, originated in these groups. Whereas monastic institutions developed in Buddhism from its inception, similar institutions appeared within the Hindu pale only later, possibly in the eighth and ninth centuries CE, when – according to Hindu belief – the theologian Shankara (c. 788–820 CE) founded monastic centres in the four corners of India, and instituted the first renunciatory order of the Dasanamis.

Alongside early Hinduism's elaboration of systems of ritual, and its teachings about liberation/salvation involving yoga and meditation, there developed highly sophisticated philosophical systems, the *darshanas*, comprising mainly Samkhya and Yoga, Mimamsa and Vedanta, and Nyaya and Vaisheshika. These in turn generated a multitude of metaphysical positions, and traditions of rigorous philosophical debate, within the parameters of Vedic revelation and the doctrine of liberation. One of the most important of these Indian philosophical traditions today is the philosophy of non-dualism (*advaita vedanta*), propounded by Shankara, the most famous of Indian philosopher-theologians.

SECTARIAN WORSHIP

Through much of the first millennium CE, sectarian worship of particular deities grew and flourished in India. Vedic sacrifice came to be increasingly marginalized, giving way – though never disappearing completely – to devotional worship or *puja*. *Puja* is a ritual expression of love or devotion (*bhakti*) to a deity, often a personal god or goddess, with whom the devotee establishes an intense and intimate relationship. Corresponding to the growth of Hindu theism and devotionalism, Sanskrit narrative traditions grew and flourished, the most important of which were the Hindu epics or *itihasas* – the *Ramayana* and the *Mahabharata* – the Puranas – devotional texts containing, among other things, mythological stories about the gods and goddesses, and treatises on ritual worship – and devotional poetry in several Indian regional languages, most notably Tamil. One of the most important developments at this time was the composition of the *Bhagavad Gita*, the 'Song of the Lord', contained in the *Mahabharata*. This work, perhaps the most famous of the Hindu scriptures, expresses in narrative form the concerns of Hinduism: the importance of *dharma*, responsible action, and the maintenance of social order and stability, combined with the importance of devotion to the transcendent as a personal god.

Temple cities grew and flourished in this period, serving not only as commercial and administrative hubs of kingdoms, but as ritual centres, with the temple located at the heart of the town and, therefore, of the kingdom. Kings sought to derive legitimacy for their rule through their royal patronage of these ritual sites, dedicated to one or the other of the major Puranic deities. Large temple complexes stood testimony to a king's dharmic rule over his kingdom, which was often modelled on the ideal of divine kingship symbolized by the great god Vishnu. Sectarian devotional groups emerged, dedicated to the worship of Vishnu (*Vaishnavas*), Shiva (*Shaivas*), and the goddess Devi (*Shaktas*).

HINDUISM DURING BRITISH COLONIAL RULE

These theistic traditions continued to flourish, to lesser or greater degrees, through much of the following period, when large sections of the Indian subcontinent were conquered and ruled by Muslim rulers. The rule of the last Muslim emperor in India came to an end in the eighteenth century, and British forces, initially in the form of the East India Company, and later the British crown, stepped in to assume power. By the middle of the eighteenth century, British power was at its peak. Hindu traditions, which had tended to be relatively insular in the intervening period, now responded actively to the British and, more importantly, Christian presence in their midst. Hindu reform movements arose, led by such figures as Ram Mohan Roy (1772–1883), Dayananda Sarasvati (1824–83), and Vivekananda (1863–1902), all seeking to restore the perceived glory of Hinduism's ancient past. It was at this time that Hinduism came to be defined in the terms by which we understand it today – a world religion, with a distinct identity. These reform movements, often collectively referred to as the Hindu renaissance, absorbed Christianity's rationalist elements, and paid particular attention to social and ethical concerns. Most of these movements were closely linked with the increasingly vocal Indian nationalist movement, which brought about the end of British colonial rule, and established India as an independent nation state in 1947.

RELIGIOUS NATIONALISM IN CONTEMPORARY INDIA

Though India defined itself as a secular state on gaining independence, it has experienced a resurgence of religious nationalism, particularly since the 1980s, expressed in *Hindutva* ('Hinduness'), the ideology of Hindu nationalists who call for a state in which civic rights, nationhood, and national culture would be defined by Hinduism. Their politicized, activist religious nationalism has precedents in various movements of organized Hinduism that arose in British India. Today the Sangh Parivar, a 'family' of social and political organizations, works to propagate *Hindutva*, with its political wing, the Bharatiya Janata Party (BJP, 'Indian People's Party'), winning enough support to head a coalition government between 1998 and 2004.

A significant act of religious violence in recent times was the destruction of the Mughal Babri mosque in Ayodhya in 1992, by supporters of *Hindutva* demanding the setting up of a temple dedicated to the Hindu deity Rama at the site, which they believe to be Rama's birthplace. Several violent incidents between Hindus and Muslims have been precipitated by this temple/mosque controversy.

BEYOND INDIA'S FRONTIERS

Yet many Hindus are not greatly concerned, as 'Hindu-ness' is not something they explicitly think about. Running counter to these chauvinist and violently exclusivist forms of Hinduism, other forms of Hindu belief and practice adopt a more inclusive, universal orientation, emphasizing values such as social justice, peace, and the spiritual transformation of humanity – though Hinduism has in fact always been inclusive, encompassing many traditions and practices. Some recent manifestations of Hinduism, especially in the form of Indian gurus addressing Western and/or multicultural audiences, have transcended nationalistic boundaries in their teaching and philosophy.

Hinduism has also transcended national boundaries in another sense. While Hinduism has long flourished beyond the Indian subcontinent, in places such as Java and Bali, in the twentieth century the Hindu diaspora spread markedly, establishing communities in host cultures across the globe. This geographical transcendence of boundaries does not always parallel ideological dispositions and orientations, however. Religious nationalism often strikes deep roots in diaspora communities, such that India as a geographical entity comes to be perceived, in the imagination of Hindus abroad, as their sacred, or holy, land, which they identify with conceptions of a Hindu religious polity, and therefore a Hindu nation state.

MAYA WARRIER

HINDUISM TIMELINE

3000 BCE	2500 BCE	2000 BCE	1500 BCE	1000 BCE	500 BCE	0	500 CE	1000 CE	1500 CE	2000 CE

c. 2700 BCE Evidence of Harappa culture in Indus Valley

c. 1500 BCE Aryan invasion of northern India

c. 800 BCE Oral *Vedas* collected

c. 600 BCE *Upanishads* created

326 BCE Alexander the Great enters India

c. 272 BCE King Ashoka accedes to throne

c. 200 BCE–200 CE *Bhagavad Gita* composed

c. 200 BCE Hinduism makes first contacts with South-east Asia

c. 200 BCE Compilation of Laws of Manu and Natya Sastra completed

c. 50 Beginnings of tantric tradition

c. 800 Shankara's Advaita Vedanta

1000–1150 Angkor Wat built in Cambodia

1017–1137 Ramanuja, Vaishnava philosopher

c. 1200 Muslims enter northern India

1486–1583 Chaitanya, Bengali Vaishnava bhakti leader

1498 Portuguese enter India

1757 British rule established in Calcutta

1828 Ram Mohan Roy founds Brahmo Samaj

1836–86 Ramakrishna Paramahamsa

1875 Dayanand Sarasvati founds Arya Samaj

1893 Vivekananda at World's Parliament of Religions, Chicago

1926–2011 Satya Sai Baba

1948 Mahatma Gandhi assassinated

1998 Hindu nationalist party BJP wins Indian national election

CHAPTER 14

Sacred Writings

Hindu scriptures comprise a vast corpus of literature, dating from 1300 BCE to modern times. Most of the scriptures are in Sanskrit — a word meaning 'refined' — a classical Indian language now used only by scholars and for ritual purposes. There is also a considerable amount of religious literature in regional Indian languages, and variants of the original texts, which emphasize a particular aspect of Hindu belief. For example, the *Adhyatma Ramayana* is a version of the popular epic *Ramayana* that stresses devotion (*bhakti*). What follows does not exhaust the many diverse categories of Hindu sacred writings, but outlines the major elements of a vast array of texts, dealing with various aspects of belief, ritual, and tradition in Hindu society.

Hindus generally divide their scriptures into two categories: heard or revealed (*Sruti*) and remembered (*Smriti*). *Sruti* scriptures are believed to be communicated directly by God to ancient Indian sages; *Smriti* scriptures are less authoritative, and consist of texts such as the Hindu epics —the *Ramayana*, and the *Mahabharata*; the *Dharma Sutras* — books of law, concerned with customs and correct conduct — and *Puranas* — mythology.

THE VEDAS

The Hindu canon is usually termed Veda, from the root *vid*, meaning 'knowledge'. The Vedas comprise four main types: The Vedic *Samhitas*, *Brahmanas*, *Aranyakas*, and *Upanishads*.

1. The Vedic *Samhitas*, classified as the *Rig, Sama, Yajur* and *Atharva* Vedas, are the earliest known Hindu religious literature (1300–200 BCE), consisting mainly of praises to various deities of ancient Hinduism, led by Indra, king of the gods.
2. The *Brahmanas* stipulate the details of, and explain the significance of, rituals (*yaga* or *yajna*), especially the fire ritual, in which oblations were poured out, or cast into fire, to be conveyed to the gods. The prominence of Agni, the god of fire, and of the Brahman priest in these texts indicates the growing importance and complexity of the fire ritual in early Indian religion.
3. The *Aranyakas* ('forest books') provide analysis and interpretation of the fire ritual, whereby a correspondence is drawn between the ritual and the cosmos. The ritual, moreover, is understood to have an intrinsic power, by which the gods are to some extent bypassed. Indeed, the *Aranyakas* also represent a transition from the

ritualistic *Brahmanas* to the far more contemplative and philosophical themes of the *Upanishads*, tending to move away from the polytheism of the *Samhitas* towards a more philosophical, monistic, or pantheistic understanding of reality, in which despite appearances all is one. Hence, the *Aranyakas* and the *Upanishads* mark a growing resistance to the ritualism of the fire sacrifice, and a preference for more contemplative and spiritual forms of worship.

4. The *Upanishads* (*upa* = alongside, *nishad* = set) are commentaries and elaborations of the ideas encountered in the Vedic *Samhitas* and *Brahmanas*. Four major themes can be identified: internal sacrifice, the idea of the *atman* (similar to 'soul' or 'self'), *Brahman* (non-personal divine being), and monistic theology, which equates the *atman*, and indeed the whole cosmos, with *Brahman* — everything is *Brahman*. The previous emphasis on the importance and intricacy of the fire ritual is overshadowed by an emphasis on personal spiritual development. In religious terminology, *tapas* or *pranagnihotra* — sometimes described as the oblation of one's body in the fire of one's breath — is shown as much more efficacious and powerful than the external *yajna*. The *atman-Brahman* identification has tremendous implications for the Hindu's understanding of the nature of God, the cosmos, and the liberation — or 'salvation' — of the individual.

> *Then was not non-existence nor existence: there was no realm of air, no sky beyond it. What stirred, and where? What gave shelter? Was water there, unfathomed depth of water?*
>
> *Death was not then, nor was there anything immortal: no sign was there of the day's and night's divider. That One, breathless, breathed by its own nature: apart from it was nothing whatsoever.*
>
> *Darkness there was: at first concealed in darkness this. All was indiscriminate chaos. All that existed then was void and formless: by the great power of heat was born that One.*
>
> *Thereafter rose Desire in the beginning, Desire, the primal seed and germ of Spirit. Sages who searched with their heart's thought discovered the bond of existence in the non-existent . . .*
>
> *Who truly knows and who can here declare it, whence it was born and whence comes this creation? The gods came later than this world's creation. Who knows then whence it first came into being?*
>
> *He, the first origin of this creation, whether he formed it all or did not form it, Whose eye controls this world in highest heaven, he verily knows it, or perhaps he knows not.*
>
> The Creation Hymn, *Rig Veda* 10.129, transl. Ralph T. H. Griffith, 1896, adapted

DHARMA SUTRAS

Of the *Dharma Sutras* (literally, aphorisms relating to duties), the most important is the compendium of law known as *Manava Dharma Shastra* (The laws of Manu), which stipulate the duties, laws, and regulations binding on all categories of Hindus, whatever their caste (*varna*), stage of life (*ashrama*), or gender. Because ideas of salvation in Hinduism involve adherence to these laws, regulations, and duties, it is vital for Hindus to know and understand them. In other words, devout Hindus seeking release from *samsara* – the cycle of lives, deaths, and reincarnations – need to obey the *Dharma Sutras*.

THE EPICS

Perusal of the two epics of Hinduism, the *Ramayana* and the *Mahabharata*, is deemed a sacred duty, and helpful in progressing towards liberation/salvation (*moksha*) from the cycle of worldly life. These epics, allegedly written by the ancient sages Valmiki and Vyasa, are deemed by scholars to be compilations of folk-tales, songs sung by minstrels, and heroic stories composed in honour of kings. However, the editing of these scriptures was highly skilful and, despite their complexity and bewildering multiplicity of themes, they seem to point to a central theme of salvation of the world, and the continual war between good and evil in the universe. The stories are threaded into a central theme of a world slowly, but inexorably, declining to an age of destruction. The Battle of Kurukshetra is a climactic event in the *Mahabharata*, for instance, marking the beginning of the age of evil (*Kaliyuga*), and witnessing the gradual decline of honour, compassion, and chivalry during its denouement. In the *Ramayana*, the war between Rama and Ravana symbolizes the confrontation between the forces of good and evil in the world. In both, the principal characters are either gods or demi-gods and demons. Although the gods ultimately win, they have to compromise, and often resort to devious stratagems to achieve their victory. The end result is a tainted world, in which even the gods are not entirely free from unethical actions.

Both epics have common features: a righteous prince excluded from kingship and exiled; a climactic battle between forces of good and evil; the intervention of God on behalf of the good; in spite of many reverses, the ultimate triumph of good over evil. The epics present many ideals and heroic role models to Hindus, and are generally Vaishnavite, extolling the god Vishnu.

THE *BHAGAVAD GITA*

The *Bhagavad Gita* ('song of the Lord') is a small part of the epic *Mahabharata*. Nevertheless, it is a highly influential scripture within Hinduism, and has acquired almost an independent standing of its own. It is a discourse between Krishna, the incarnation (*avatar*) of the god Vishnu, and his devotee Prince Arjuna, the greatest warrior in the *Mahabharata*. The discussion is obviously an insertion into the epic, and many scholars consider it to be an *Upanishad*.

Above all, the *Bhagavad Gita* is an irenic scripture, which seeks to unite the major theological strands of Hinduism. It says that all ways to salvation are equally valid: the way of enlightenment (*jnana marga*), the way of altruistic righteous action and progression through the caste hierarchy (*nishkama karma marga*), the way of meditation (*yoga marga*), and the way of devotion (*bhakti marga*). However, it argues that the way of devotion (*bhakti*) is the highest of all paths and — for the first time in Hinduism — it reveals that the devotee is greatly loved by a gracious God. Consequently, it also proposes a radical rethinking of traditional Hindu concepts of salvation (*moksha*), in that it argues that it is open to all castes, and to men and women.

THE *PURANAS*

The *Puranas* — 'ancient stories' — are, again, a vast body of literature. Traditionally, there are eighteen *Puranas* which have been classified as associated with the gods Vishnu, Brahma, and Shiva, as well as many associated with minor deities and with holy places, such as particular temples or sacred sites. The contents are wide-ranging, including, for example, genealogies, law codes, descriptions of rituals, and pilgrimages to holy places. They are not merely a collection of old tales, as the name *Purana* seems to suggest, but narratives that highlight a theistic stance and vision.

THEODORE GABRIEL

CHAPTER 15

Beliefs

What we now know as Hinduism has developed into a rich, pluralist religious culture, with a great variety of customs, forms of worship, gods and goddesses, theologies, philosophies, stories, art, and music. Many Hindus believe its essential teachings remain the same down the centuries; however, diversity within Hinduism has led some scholars to talk of Hindu religions rather than a single Hindu religion, 'Hinduisms' rather than 'Hinduism', and even to abandon the term 'Hinduism' altogether. Moreover, many different Hindu voices and traditions compete globally to define the essential beliefs of Hinduism.

Hindus generally accept that they share common beliefs, principles, and structures. For many, however, Hinduism is not so much a system of beliefs as a way of life, a religious culture, a spiritual and intellectual quest, and an intense identification with the myriad ways in which the sacred is present in India. If asked about their beliefs, they often begin by talking about ethical teachings: kindness and truth; hospitality to the guest; respect for the family – and particularly for elders and parents. They may go on to consider beliefs in particular gods or goddesses, the authority of important sacred texts, the merit of pilgrimage, or the doctrine of *karma*. Some – not all – may accept the social hierarchy of the four *varnas* (caste system) and certain principles of purity and pollution. Any study of popular Hindu beliefs begins with the gods and goddesses of Hinduism.

GOD, GODS, AND GODDESSES

Hindus may be polytheistic, monotheistic, or monistic – believing that all reality is actually one. There are even orthodox Hindus who are atheistic. Many Hindus believe there is one God (*Brahman*) who can be worshipped in many forms. God can, for example, appear as a baby, a friend, a king, a mother, or a lover. God can manifest as male or female, or in non-human form; be worshipped as without form (*nirguna Brahman*) or with form (*saguna Brahman*); appear through icons and images (*murti*), or in human shape as a living saint or *guru*. Some Hindu gurus, such as Vivekananda (1863–1902), have even taught that God is embodied in the form of the universe, and in all sentient beings: hence, in serving others we are – quite literally – serving God.

Statue of Ganesha, the elephant-headed god.

God is sometimes understood in a threefold way, as *Trimurti*. The *Trimurti* consists of Brahma (the creator), Vishnu (the sustainer), and Shiva (the destroyer). However, not only is Brahma seldom worshipped, but nowadays the *Trimurti* is often replaced by a group of five gods: Vishnu, Shiva, Devi, Surya, and Ganesha.

The two pre-eminent gods, worshipped by Hindus everywhere, are Shiva and Vishnu. Vishnu is principally associated with the preservation of the cosmos and its proper order. He is, therefore, linked to kingship, and to the maintenance of *dharma* – law, order, righteousness. He is probably most frequently worshipped in his incarnations (*avatar*) as Rama and Krishna.

Shiva, 'the auspicious', is both the lord of *yogis* (ascetics) – depicted with matted hair, a body smeared with ashes, and meditating in a cremation ground – and also the divine lover. He is worshipped most commonly in the form of the phallus (*linga*). He has two sons: Ganesha, the elephant-headed god, and Skanda, or Murugan. Shiva reveals the ultimate nature of reality, the polarities of life and death, creation and destruction, the ascetic and the erotic, on whose interrelationship the whole of life depends.

Vaishnavism (devotion to Vishnu), Shaivism (devotion to Shiva), and Shaktism (devotion to the Goddess, or Devi) are the best-known traditions within Hinduism. However, Hindus often have a chosen deity (*ishtadev*) who, for the devotee, can take on the aspects of the ultimate god. Such gods and goddesses are worshipped both as distinct beings with their own stories and iconography, and as forms of the one ultimate reality (*Brahman*). Hindus may worship many gods, but they also believe all gods are one.

GODDESS WORSHIP

Goddess worship is one of the most distinctive traditions of Hinduism, going back to prehistoric times. *Shakti* (power, strength, force) is a term used to refer to the power of any deity, and is also the activating energy incarnated in goddesses. All goddesses can be seen as distinct deities, or as diverse forms of (Maha)devi, the (Great) Goddess. The Goddess (*Adyashakti*) is worshipped as the Supreme Being, but also as the consort of a male god.

Detail of a statue of Shiva, displaying the dynamic feminine aspect of the supreme Divine, Shakti.

The consorts of the three great gods are Lakshmi, Sarasvati, and Parvati.

Sometimes scholars draw a distinction between independent goddesses, who are dangerous and 'hot', and wifely goddesses, who are restrained and 'cool'. For many Hindu women Sita, the wife of Rama, is the model Hindu wife, whose resolute integrity and courage are today emphasized by the Indian women's movement.

The land of India itself is worshipped as 'Divine Mother' (*Bharat Mata*), and is further sanctified by *Shaktipithas* (centres of Goddess worship), and by great rivers like the Ganges, which are worshipped as bestowers of prosperity and liberation.

AVATARS

Avatars are manifestations (literally 'descents') of God. They periodically intervene to fight evil, and ensure that the universe functions in accordance with *dharma*. The best loved are Krishna and Rama (*avatars* of Vishnu).

Krishna is worshipped as a child, as the god of erotic mystical love, and as the hero of the epic *Mahabharata*. While the youthful Krishna with his flute entrances the world with his play (*Krishna-lila*), in the *Bhagavad Gita* Krishna reveals himself as the great teacher and supreme god (Vishnu).

Rama is worshipped as the ideal ruler and the restorer of *dharma*. Always popular in northern India, Rama, has latterly become the principal god of Hindu nationalism. His reign (*Ram Rajya*) is invoked as a golden period of justice, harmony, and prosperity.

IMAGE WORSHIP

While many Hindus acknowledge that *Brahman* is the ultimate reality, the vast majority also worship divine beings and images. Many believe that the power (*shakti*) of a deity is actually present in that deity's image (*murti*). Therefore, in worshipping before an image, worship is offered to the deity whose power is in the image, and also to the deity as an image. When an image is consecrated, the ceremony transforms images of stone, metal, and wood into embodiments of God. Hindus go to the temple for *darshana*, the 'sight' or 'vision' of the deities. It is believed that *darshana* brings good fortune, grace, and spiritual merit. It also makes possible an intimate, loving relationship between deities and their devotees. During ritual worship (*puja*), the gods are served and cared for as honoured guests by the offerings made to their images.

DHARMA

Hindus today often refer to Hindu beliefs and practices as *sanatana dharma* (eternal religion), or Vedic *dharma* (Vedic religion). *Dharma* may mean the social order, or the cosmic order, but equally it can refer to personal behaviour and attitudes. At the simplest level, it means the individual's religious and social duties, according to status and stage of life. The *Bhagavad Gita*, for example, teaches that it is better to do one's own duty imperfectly than that of another well.

SAMSARA

Many Hindus, particularly those in the higher castes, believe in the endless cycle of rebirth (*samsara*). Efforts to bring the cycle to an end are at the core of many Hindu religious practices. The picture of a world as a place where the eternal soul is perpetually reincarnated has dominated the Indian imagination for over three millennia.

KARMA

Central to the teaching about reincarnation, *karma* is the taken-for-granted belief that one's actions determine one's condition in this life and rebirth in the next. Every action has its inevitable fruit or consequence. *Karma* is thus inseparable from *dharma* and *samsara*. To summarize the belief: good deeds result in good *karma*, which produces good fortune in this life and a good birth in the next life; bad deeds result in bad *karma*, which may lead to much less desirable rebirths in the next life, as a human lower down the social hierarchy, as an animal, or even as an unfortunate soul suffering the torments of one of the many hells.

> *To see the universal and all-pervading Spirit of Truth face to face one must be able to love the meanest of creation as oneself.*
>
> Mahatma Gandhi, *An Autobiography* (Harmondsworth: Penguin, 1982).

There are ways in which *karma* may be overridden. Devotion to a deity is perhaps the most potent, whilst religious rituals and meritorious action may also cancel past sins. Some Hindus withdraw from the world and practise non-engagement. However, the *Bhagavad Gita* teaches that adherence to one's duty, combined with internal renunciation of attachment to, or desire for, the results of one's actions, can lead to liberation (*moksha*) from the cycle of *samsara*.

Karma can lead to either fatalism or ethical activism. It can be seen as an uncontrollable, impersonal determinant of the human condition; or can encourage people to feel responsible for their own fate, and promote a dynamic view of action in the world.

THE THREE PATHS

The three paths — *margas* or *yogas* — to spiritual fulfilment are: *jnana* (knowledge, insight, wisdom), *karma* (action) and *bhakti* (ecstatic devotion). Some Hindus consider each of the three paths requires exclusive concentration, and is sufficient for liberation. However, many modern teachers and gurus teach a *yoga* of synthesis, arguing that the three paths are linked, and liberating knowledge may be obtained through all.

Jnanayoga – the path of wisdom/knowledge – liberates from *karma* and rebirth, and indeed from sickness, old age, and death. It leads to the overcoming of ignorance and the realization of *Brahman*. The pursuit of wisdom implies religious practice, meditation, self-purification, and above all study of the scriptures. The Vedas, and particularly the *Upanishads*, provide knowledge of *Brahman,* and of our true condition. Indeed, the famous teaching of the *Upanishads* is that in soul (*atman*) humans are identical with *Brahman*. According to some Hindu schools, if humans realize this truth, they can be liberated-in-life (*jivan-mukta*).

Karmayoga – the path of work – enables ordinary people everywhere to give spiritual meaning to their everyday lives. It is associated for many with the *Bhagavad Gita's* teaching that action can be a positive means of personal transformation, if people perform their duty selflessly, and act without the desire for status or reward. Gandhi reinterpreted *karmayoga,* by equating

A Hindu pilgrim sits beside the River Ganges, Varanasi, India.

it with social commitment and struggle, and found in the *Gita* authority for his philosophy of non-violence and peaceful resistance to British rule.

Bhaktiyoga – the path of loving devotion – is characterized by an intense personal relationship between the deity and devotee. Selfless love of God consumes past *karma,* and results in a state of intimate, blissful, and loving communion with the deity. Vaishnavas often speak of *prapatti* – complete self-surrender in love – to Vishnu. God-intoxicated saints are depicted as immersed in blissful devotion. Today many busy Hindus follow the path of *bhakti*: their spiritual discipline (*sadhana*) may vary, but is broadly characterized by selfless service and loving devotion to God.

THE FOUR GOALS

Hinduism offers four legitimate goals (*purusartha*) for human beings which, taken together, are believed to ensure spiritual and social harmony:

1. *Artha* – worldly wealth and success – is a proper goal, if pursued without desire, anger, and greed. Kautilya's *Artha Shastra*, written in the third to fourth century BCE, argues that prosperity is the basis of a well-ordered state, and people need *artha* if

A SHORT INTRODUCTION TO WORLD RELIGIONS

they are to practise religion. Thus pursuing an occupation, accumulating wealth, governing and so on are justified if they do not violate *dharma*.

2. *Kama* – pleasure, desire – is also a legitimate goal, if it accords with *dharma*. This is the pursuit of pleasurable activities, including sexuality, play, recreation, the arts, and literature. The *Kama Sutra*, written in the third or fourth centuries CE, deals at length with erotic techniques, the arts of pleasure, and seduction.

3. *Dharma* – virtue, morality – has two levels: it is both one's own particular set of duties (*svadharma*) and the absolute morality, valid universally. When profit and pleasure are pursued for themselves, outside of *dharma*, they lead to social chaos.

4. *Moksha* – spiritual liberation – is the ultimate Hindu quest: release from the bondage of suffering and rebirth (*samsara*).

Some Hindus believe these goals are interconnected and that no goal is primary. Others believe they form an ascending hierarchy, with *moksha* transcending – even opposing – the other three. Whatever one's understanding, this system of the four goals implicitly recognizes the complexity of human drives and aspirations.

> *Just as a person casts off worn-out garments and puts on others that are new, even so the embodied soul casts off worn-out bodies and takes on others that are new. Weapons do not cleave the Self, fire does not burn the Self. Waters do not drench the Self, winds do not parch the Self. The Self is the same forever: unmanifest, unthinkable, still.*
>
> Bhagavad Gita II, 22–25

DEATH AND THE AFTERLIFE

Hindu beliefs about the afterlife are complex. Most Hindus believe they will be reborn into another body, according to their *karma*. However, *moksha* – salvation or ultimate spiritual fulfilment – may be understood in different ways: as final union with *Brahman*; as a perfectly blissful state; as communion with God; or as liberation in some heavenly realm or paradise. Many Hindus may find the concept of salvation, or liberation after death, a very distant ideal.

Moreover, ancient understandings of the afterlife persist, and Vedic views are implied in the death ritual. Funerary rites of passage, and memorial rituals for the dead, indicate a belief in the continued existence of ancestors (*pitr*), who are benefited and pleased by offerings made by their descendants. There are also popular beliefs about the journey of the soul after death; the multiplicity of heavens and hells, and the role of the god of death (Yamraj or Dharmaraj) as judge; and restless or malicious ghosts (*pret*, *bhuta*) who may possess or disturb the living.

TIME

Hindu, Buddhist, and Jain beliefs about the vastness of time, and the age of the universe, in some senses coincide with modern scientific understanding. The classical Hindu view is of gradually deteriorating conditions, until finally the world is destroyed by fire and returns to chaos. The world itself perpetually undergoes cycles of evolution, from a state of non-differentiation, through a series of ages, to its dissolution (*pralaya*) back into the unevolved state, from which the cycle starts again. This process of evolution and dissolution is a 'day of Brahma': each day of Brahma divides into the fourteen 'periods of the Manu'; each of the fourteen periods of Manu divides into four great ages; each of the four great ages divides into four *yugas*. The passing of the *yugas* is marked by progressive moral and physical deterioration. We are now in the middle of the last, and worst, age: the *Kaliyuga*. Hence, that there is apparent moral decline, suffering, famine, and war is no surprise to Hindus; indeed, the orthodox view is that life will get worse as we progress through the *yuga*.

GURUS

The *guru* – spiritual teacher – is a figure of the greatest importance in Hinduism, the object of *darshan* and worship, and comes in all shapes and sizes, traditions and orders. Some may assert their status by virtue of their charisma, others are initiated into a long-established lineage (*sampradaya*). Many have carried their spiritual message to the West, helping to extend the bounds of Hinduism. One of the best known gurus was Sathya Sai Baba, worshipped as an *avatara* of Sirdi Sai Baba, and of Shiva and Shakti. There have also been women gurus, such as Sarada Devi (1853–1920), widow of Ramakrishna, Mira Alfassa (1878–1973), Mother of the Aurobindo organization, Ananda Mayi Ma (1896–1982), and Mata Amritanandamayi (b. 1953).

ANNA S. KING

CHAPTER 16

Worship and Festivals

YAJNA

In early Vedic times, worship usually took the form of a sacrificial ritual (*yajna*), addressed to nature gods such as the sun god, Surya; the rain god, Indra; the god of fire, Agni; or the Soma god, believed to reside in a probably hallucinogenic plant of the same name. These rituals involved the sacrifice of animals such as goats and cows, or the pouring of oblations of such items as clarified butter, honey, and milk into a sacrificial fire, accompanied by the chanting of Vedic hymns and prayers. The early Vedas are liturgical texts, which set out in great detail the method of ritual observance. These rituals were intended to please the gods through worship, and to ensure the well-being of the sponsor or patron of the sacrifice — the *yajamana* — and his family.

PUJA

Yajnas are something of a rarity in the contemporary Hindu world; far more commonly observed is *puja*, a ritual of devotional worship regularly conducted at temples, usually by Brahman priests, and often observed privately at household shrines. *Puja* may be addressed to any of the manifold gods and goddesses in the Hindu pantheon, important among whom are the great gods Vishnu and Shiva, and the goddess Shakti, all of whom appear in myriad forms and aspects in Hindu mythology, and across the contemporary Hindu sacred landscape.

> *Whatever you do, or eat, or give, or offer in adoration, let it be an offering to me; and whatever you suffer, suffer it for me.*
>
> Bhagavad Gita 9.26

Temples dedicated to the different Hindu gods and goddesses usually contain a sanctified image of the deity, and to this image the ritual of *puja* is addressed. During *puja*, the priest ritually purifies himself and the shrine, invokes the presence of the deity in the image, and then worships the image by ritually bathing and adorning it, feeding it symbolically, and waving a flaming lamp in a circle around it in a ritual of light. This is usually accompanied by the chanting of Sanskrit mantras, the blowing of conches, and the ringing of bells. In Hindu households, the family usually observes an abbreviated form of this ritual.

The relationship between the image and the divine presence is, in the Hindu world, often a complex one. For most Hindus, the image is symbolic of the divine presence; but for many, it is also the divine presence, manifesting itself in tangible form. Moreover, Hindus seldom agree on the importance of *puja*. While some see it as an act of great religious significance, others see it as a largely unnecessary, outward expression of religious piety, and prefer instead a more inward-oriented mode of spiritual development. Besides *puja*, other modes of worship commonly practised in Hindu society include *bhajana* – the singing of hymns – and the recitation of the *sahasranama*, the thousand names of the gods and goddesses.

Part of the huge Hindu temple complex at Angkor Wat, Cambodia – the world's largest religious monument – built by the Tamil king Suryavarnman II in the twelfth century CE.

I am the same to all beings, and my love is ever the same; but those who worship me with devotion, they are in me and I am in them.

Bhagavad Gita 9.29

A SHORT INTRODUCTION TO WORLD RELIGIONS

Festivals of Hinduism

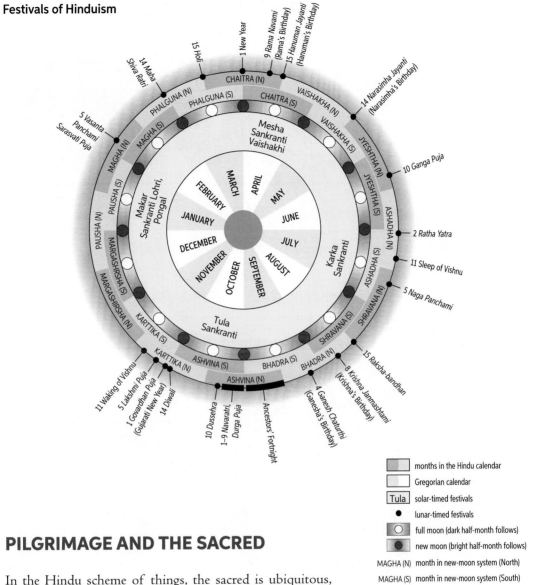

Chart labels (outer ring, clockwise from top):

1 New Year
9 Rama Navami (Rama's Birthday)
15 Hanuman Jayanti (Hanuman's Birthday)
14 Narasimha Jayanti (Narasimha's Birthday)
10 Ganga Puja
2 Ratha Yatra
11 Sleep of Vishnu
5 Naga Panchami
15 Raksha-bandhan
8 Krishna Janmashtami (Krishna's Birthday)
4 Ganesh Chaturthi (Ganesha's Birthday)
Ancestors' Fortnight
1–9 Navaratri, Durga Puja
10 Dussehra
14 Diwali
1 Govardhan Puja (Gujarati New Year)
5 Lakshmi Puja
11 Waking of Vishnu
15 Holi
14 Maha Shiva Ratri
5 Vasanta Panchami Sarasvati Puja

Month labels (Hindu calendar ring):

CHAITRA (N), CHAITRA (S), VAISHAKHA (N), VAISHAKHA (S), JYESHTHA (N), JYESHTHA (S), ASHADHA (N), ASHADHA (S), SHRAVANA (N), SHRAVANA (S), BHADRA (S), BHADRA, ASHVINA (N), ASHVINA (S), KARTTIKA (N), KARTTIKA (S), MARGASHIRSHA (N), MARGASHIRSHA (S), PAUSHA (N), PAUSHA (S), MAGHA (N), MAGHA (S), PHALGUNA (S), PHALGUNA (N)

Solar-timed labels (inner):

Mesha Sankranti Vaishakhi
Karka Sankranti
Tula Sankranti
Makar Sankranti Lohri, Pongal

Gregorian months (centre):

JANUARY, FEBRUARY, MARCH, APRIL, MAY, JUNE, JULY, AUGUST, SEPTEMBER, OCTOBER, NOVEMBER, DECEMBER

Legend:

- months in the Hindu calendar
- Gregorian calendar
- Tula — solar-timed festivals
- ● lunar-timed festivals
- ○ full moon (dark half-month follows)
- ◐ new moon (bright half-month follows)
- MAGHA (N) — month in new-moon system (North)
- MAGHA (S) — month in new-moon system (South)

PILGRIMAGE AND THE SACRED

In the Hindu scheme of things, the sacred is ubiquitous, contained not only in temples and sacred images, but also in nature — in stones, trees, mountains, and rivers. Every once in a while the sacred 'manifests' itself in the form of a mysterious rock, stream, or spring, and the site of such manifestation becomes a place of worship. Pilgrims flock to such places during auspicious months of the Hindu calendar, and mythological stories grow about the miraculous nature of the pilgrimage site. Particularly important in the Hindu cosmology are sacred rivers, and holy towns and cities situated along their banks, which are seen as places of crossing (*tirtha*) between the mundane and the sacred, and between the worlds of the living and the dead. The water of the Ganges in North

Hindu pilgrims gather on the banks of the holy River Ganges at Varanasi, India, to perform their morning religious rituals.

A SHORT INTRODUCTION TO WORLD RELIGIONS

India is believed to be especially potent in this respect, and a single dip in the river is believed to earn for the worshipper untold spiritual merit.

The sacred often manifests itself in living things too. The cow, the monkey, and – in some parts of India – even the snake and the rat are believed to be sacred and therefore worshipped. Yet more common is the worship of men and women believed to be holy, and therefore capable of performing miracles that can transform the lives of devotees, and ensure their well-being. Many such holy figures attract an extensive following, and head vast spiritual empires extending across regional and national boundaries.

FESTIVALS

The Hindu (lunar) calendar year is punctuated by a series of religious festivals. Temple festivals are usually marked by processions, when worshippers carry the deity's image through the temple town or village, offering devotees a chance to glimpse it in all its glory. Other festivals – which celebrate landmark events in Hindu mythology – include:

Image of Durga, a popular fierce form of the Hindu goddess, depicted with up to eighteen arms.

- *Janmashtami* (July–August): the celebration of the birthday of the popular Hindu god, Krishna.
- *Ganesh Chaturthi* (August–September): a festival dedicated to the elephant-headed god, Ganesh, the remover of obstacles.
- *Dussehra* (September–October, towards the end of the monsoon): marking the victory of Rama and his monkey army over the demon-king Ravana. It encompasses *Navaratri* – also known as 'the festival of nine nights' – which in Bengal culminates in a grand celebration dedicated to the worship of the goddess Durga.
- *Diwali* (October–November): the festival of lights, following shortly after *Dussehra*. Hindus throughout the world illuminate their homes with lamps and exchange gifts.

I AM A HINDU

I was born a few years after India gained independence, in a village in Gujarat, India, just outside the town of Dandi – famous for Gandhi's Salt March protest against the British colonial government. I came to England when I was eleven, because my father was employed in a car factory in Coventry. Although I attended school in India from the age of five, I found schooling in England difficult, mainly because I knew little English. However, I quickly learned the new language and settled in.

At sixteen, I joined a local engineering company, and began an apprenticeship. After five years, I successfully concluded it, and was encouraged to apply to Sussex University. After being awarded a degree in Mechanical Engineering, I returned to the company, and worked my way up to become one of their chief engineers, which has led to my travelling to various parts of the world.

As a Hindu, I believe in one God who has many incarnations (*avatars*). I believe in all these gods, but – like many Hindus – focus on a particular god who has become special to me: Krishna, a very popular god within Hinduism. I am particularly moved and helped by the many stories about Krishna. My belief in God has encouraged me to be a helpful, contributing member of society. For instance, I assisted in starting a cricket club for young people, and I have been its secretary for thirty years. I did this because, as a Hindu, I wanted to put something back into the community from which I have benefited so much. I believe that, if I lead a good life, helping others, and worshipping God, as a result of reincarnation I will be reborn into a better life.

I do not believe it is necessary to visit the temple every day to keep in touch with God. God is with me every hour of the day. I pray to God in my thoughts wherever I am, and reflect on my beliefs, and whether what I'm doing is good for me or for other people. I do this, not only because they are good things to do, but also because they will contribute to a good reincarnation. That said, I like to be in the temple whenever I can, serving my community. I find that regular attendance helps my religious life, by expanding my thoughts, and helping to make me less selfish and to see the best in others. This is what faith means to me. It is a faith I learned particularly from my mother, a traditional Hindu; she has been the greatest influence on my religious upbringing.

When we moved to Cheltenham, we were the first Hindu family, and there was no temple. We had a shrine in our house, but had to return to Coventry for important festivals, celebrating there as we had done in India, if on a smaller scale. Finally, in 1975, the growing Hindu community in Cheltenham established their own temple, an occasion of much rejoicing and celebration.

In 1976 I returned to India, where I met my wife, a traditional Hindu from Gujarat. Already a devout Hindu, after our marriage I became more involved in the activities of the temple, as its secretary and now its treasurer. Because of my work, I do not participate in worship in the temple every day, but attend at least three times a week. When I retire, I will attend worship in the temple far more regularly.

In our home, we have a temple-like shrine, at which my mother and my wife perform *puja* every day. After bathing in the morning, I also pray there for a short time. I observe fasting on special occasions, but am not too particular about my diet. My wife and my mother are far more traditionally Hindu in this respect. My faith is more interior than exterior: I am less concerned about outward symbols, such as dress, than I am about what I think and do. That said, I do often wear traditional Indian dress for *puja* and other religious functions.

I do not have time to attend scripture study

regularly. Once or twice a year I attend scripture reading and exposition in Coventry. I would like to go regularly to a local reading of Hindu sacred texts, but none is available, although scholars from the Hare Krishna temple in Watford are sometimes invited to explain Hindu texts locally.

I visit India most years, and whenever I go I make a point of visiting places of pilgrimage or particular temples. My aspiration is to visit most of the temples and sacred places in South India, which I believe are the original Hindu temples. My goal, when I retire, is to devote my life to seeking inner peace through prayer and meditation.

My wife is more devout than I am, and observes all the Hindu calendar events, and my family life is firmly based on Hindu religion and culture. My faith has helped strengthen my relationship with my wife, mother, and sisters. Together we observe all the Hindu festivals and celebrations, such as *Navaratri* and *Janmashtami*, and key ceremonies (*samskars*) such as cyclical funerary rites (*sraddha*). I took my father's ashes to India to scatter in rivers and on the land, especially in our hometown.

As a Hindu community we are very close-knit. We all get to know about the sickness, death, and other problems faced by other Hindu families. The close friendships we have mean we are always ready to support each other in times of need.

Naren Patel

- *Shivaratri* (January–February): a festival during which Shiva is worshipped.
- *Holi* (February–March): a spring festival, during which people drench one another in water and coloured powder.

Besides these, there are several localized festivals observed in different parts of the Hindu world. The *Kumbh Mela*, perhaps the most popular of these, attracts pilgrims in vast numbers to its four sites in North India — Hardwar, Nasik, Ujjain, and Allahabad — where it is celebrated on a rotational basis once every three years. The *Purna Kumbha Mela* takes place once every twelve years in the holy town of Allahabad. Billed as the 'biggest gathering on earth', in 2001 more than 40 million people gathered on its busiest days.

MAYA WARRIER

CHAPTER 17

Hinduism in the Modern World

Hinduism, the most ancient world religion, has been subject to many changes in the course of its long history. The rise and fall in prominence of some ancient gods, such as Indra, King of gods, and Varuna, god of the sea; the decline in importance of the fire sacrifice; the rise in popularity of the *bhakti* (devotional) tradition in the sixth century CE are all instances of this. In the nineteenth and early twentieth centuries Hindu reformers such as Vivekananda (1863–1902), Ram Mohan Roy (1772–1833), Mohandas (Mahatma) Gandhi (1869–1948), and Sarvepalli Radhakrishnan (1888–1975) advocated an ethical form of Hinduism, which campaigned against social practices such as *sati* – the self-immolation of widows on their husbands' funeral pyres – and child marriage, and displayed the influence of Western values. In modern times, Hinduism has moved away from this puritanical type of religion, which decried many ancient beliefs as superstitious, and has returned with full vigour to traditional Hinduism.

ASTROLOGERS AND GURUS

A large number of Hindus now defend traditional Hindu mores and practices. Contemporary Hindus are not worried about being labelled 'superstitious', and openly consult astrologers and gurus. The increased veneration of gurus has given rise to the cult phenomenon in modern Hinduism. Some prominent gurus, such as Swami Prabhupada, Bhagavan Rajneesh, and Satya Sai Baba, established popular new religious movements that have spread beyond India, attracting a considerable following from Westerners, although, technically, conversion into Hinduism is impossible, because Hindus are – as a result of their *karma* – those born into Hindu families and into a particular caste. Non-Hindus do not have a caste identity; hence, traditionally Hindu missionary activity was aimed at recovering Hindus who had lapsed into Christianity or Islam, and required a purification ritual, or *shuddi*. However, in the modern world, new cults and movements have emulated Christians, by engaging in mission to non-Hindus. Many of these new Hindu movements have been successful in recruiting Westerners.

POLITICIZATION

One of the most striking modern developments has been the politicization of Hinduism, and the rising militancy among some factions, perhaps a natural consequence of the emergence of Hindu nationalism in a country so long under the yoke of Muslim and Christian powers. Independence for India in August 1947 ended around 400 years of such rule and, although the Indian leaders opted for a secular, or religiously neutral, nation, the vast majority of the population is Hindu. With the passing of time, the secular ideals of Jawaharlal Nehru (1889–1964) – first Prime Minister of India – and Gandhi have become less valued, and today many view India as a Hindu, rather than a secular, multi-religious, nation.

This shift toward Hindu nationalism should be seen in the context of the rise of Muslim nationalism in the subcontinent, and the perennial dispute over Kashmir, the Muslim-majority state located between India and Pakistan. Hindu nationalistic parties such as the RSS (Rashtriya Swayam Sevak Sangh/National Self-Service Association), the VHP (Vishwa Hindu Parishad/World Hindu Organization) and BJP (Bharatiya Janatha Party/Indian People's Party) promote India as a Hindu state, and believe Hindu religion, ideology, and values should predominate. This has increased pressure on the religious minorities and created division. The actions and claims of more militant sections of Hindu nationalist organizations, such as the Bajrang Dal, have been denounced by Hindu intellectuals as uncharacteristic of Hindu religion and culture, with its image of tolerance, and willingness to absorb beliefs and practices from other religions and philosophies. The militants have an ideology based on *Hindutva* ('Hindu-ness'), which raises problems for the religious minorities, and raises the possibility of a Hindu theocratic state, alienating the millions of non-Hindus in the nation.

The Birla Mandir, or Laxmi Narayan, Hindu Temple, Delhi, India, built between 1933 and 1939.

The appeal of the Hindu nationalistic ideology is more evident among the less literate and rural sections of the Hindu community, who constitute the majority of the Indian populace. This combination of political power and militant religious nationalism has led to tension in some areas of India where several faith communities live alongside each other. The massacre of Muslims in Gujarat in 2002 was allegedly condoned, and even abetted, by the Hindu nationalist state government. Hindu nationalists seek the Hinduization of Indian polity, culture, and education. This trend, often termed 'saffronization' – saffron being a colour associated with Hinduism – is growing stronger, although opposed by the Indian intelligentsia, who argue against the politicization of religion, its identification with the nation and growing hostility to other faiths.

THE HINDU DIASPORA

A significant development in Hinduism has resulted from the migration of many Hindus to the West. Because these diaspora communities are minorities, a defensive, more fervent type of Hinduism has emerged. For example, in southern states of the USA, where there is a strong conservative Christian culture, Hindus have challenged what they see as the misrepresentation of Hindu concepts and practices in school textbooks.

Westernized Hindu ideas, when imported back to India, have been responsible for an increased awareness of mystical traditions, sacred sites, and some esoteric forms of Hindu spirituality. There has been a burgeoning interest in pilgrimage to sacred shrines, such as the Sabarimala Temple in Kerala, and great festivals, such as the *Kumbh Mela*. There has also been an increase in pilgrims visiting gurus in search of miracles.

THE CASTE SYSTEM

Modern Hinduism has also seen a strengthening of the caste system. At the turn of the twentieth century, a campaign by Hindu reformers such as Dayananda Sarasvati (1824–83), Vivekananda, and Gandhi sought to reform what they saw as the chauvinism and discrimination of the caste system. Caste did not disappear, but it was felt to be out of date and incompatible with modern egalitarian ideals. For some, the conversion of 'untouchables' to Christianity, Islam, or Buddhism seemed to threaten the predominance of Hinduism in the subcontinent. Under Gandhi's influence, the Indian constitution and laws guaranteed privileges to the untouchables in education and employment. In recent years this has faced opposition by 'forward communities', who claim positive discrimination policies have undermined the economic status of their own communities. In some areas there have been caste wars between the *savarnas* – those belonging to the *varna* or caste system – and the *avarnas* – the untouchables. Both the untouchables and the *savarnas* have now organized into vote banks to achieve political influence.

Revisionist thinking now emphasizes the positive side of the caste system. Even practices such as *sati* have been praised by fundamentalists, despite a growing feminist movement within

Hinduism. On the other hand, there is a phenomenon termed '*sanskritization*', which has seen untouchables and tribal peoples of India attempting to Hinduize their religious practices. Some untouchable and tribal groups are beginning to abandon their traditional deities and practices to build temples and worship Hindu deities, such as Vishnu and Shiva, possibly in an attempt to enter the Hindu fold, or gain higher status for their community. The Indian constitution has made the restriction of entry of untouchables to Hindu temples illegal, and some untouchables have undertaken Hindu theological training and demanded entry to the priesthood, even at *savarna* temples.

Meanwhile, other untouchable and tribal groups have retained their traditional pantheon and ritual praxis, but attempted to identify their deities and practices with Hindu gods and worship, by reinterpreting their mythology and ritual proceedings. The leaders of the Muthappan cult of northern Kerala, for example, have reinterpreted the Muthappan deities as Vishnu and Shiva, although originally tribal gods of the forest dwellers of the region.

WOMEN IN MODERN HINDUISM

Nineteenth-century and twentieth-century social reformers spearheaded efforts to achieve the liberation of women, at considerable risk. Ram Mohan Roy's campaign resulted in the banning of *sati*. Ishwar Chandra Vidyasagar married a widow, to set an example of improving the lot of people treated as virtually dead — widows lived in seclusion, were not allowed to remarry, had to forgo all adornments, and were looked on as inauspicious. Gandhi, for the first time in modern India, brought Indian women into the public arena, in his campaign for independence. Women took part in public demonstrations and in the civil disobedience movement. The momentum gained has not been lost: the traditional image of the Hindu woman — domesticated and subservient to father and husband — is changing rapidly. Women are well represented in the employment sector and in government, and there has been a move to set quotas for women members of the *Lok Sabha* (parliament).

Traditionally, the role of the woman was in the home, serving her husband and nurturing her children. Hindu mythology often emphasized this image. Female figures such as Sita, the virtuous and long suffering wife of Rama, and Savithri, who pleaded successfully to Yama, the god of death, for the life of her husband, were held up as paradigms of womanly behaviour. Modern Hindu women do not adhere to these norms; they are out in public, competing against men in all fields, even in occupations traditionally viewed as exclusively male, such as law, engineering, and the police and armed forces. Feminist groups such as the Working Woman's Forum are active in trying to achieve equality. Film directors such as Mira Nair and Deepa Mehta have made films highlighting the aspirations of Indian women and the problems they face, such as *Fire* (1996) and *Monsoon Wedding* (2001), provoking controversy among right-wing Hindu groups.

THEODORE GABRIEL

QUESTIONS

1. What continuities are there between early Vedic religion and modern Hinduism?

2. Explain the different views of the role of *Brahman* in Hinduism.

3. Explain the different views of the nature of human existence held by the three main Vedantic schools (*Advaita*, *Vishishtadvaita*, and *Dvaita*).

4. What role do the *Ramayana* and *Mahabarata* play in helping to attain liberation?

5. Explain why some believe the term 'Hinduisms' to be more appropriate than 'Hinduism'.

6. Why are Shiva and Vishnu considered to be so important?

7. Why do Hindus understand *moksha* (liberation) in a variety of different ways?

8. Explain some of the different roles of the guru in Hinduism.

9. Why are some geographical sites seen as sacred in Hinduism?

10. Why has the caste system been so important in Hinduism and Indian society?

FURTHER READING

Biardeau, Madeleine, *Hinduism: The Anthropology of a Civilization.* Delhi: Oxford University Press, 1989.

Blurton, T. Richard, *Hindu Art*. Cambridge: Harvard University Press, 1992.

Hiriyanna, Mysore, *The Essentials of Indian Philosophy*. London: Allen and Unwin, 1985.

Kinsley, David R., *Hindu Goddesses: Visions of the Divine Feminine in the Hindu Religious Tradition*. Berkeley: University of California Press, 1988.

Lopez, Donald S. Jr., ed., *Religions of India in Practice*. Princeton: Princeton University Press, 1995.

Mittal, S., and G. Thursby, eds., *The Hindu World*. New York: Routledge, 2004.

Narayan, R. K., *Ramayana: A Shortened Modern Prose Version of the Indian Epic*. New York: Viking, 1972.

Swami Prabhavananda and Frederick Manchester, trans., *The Upanishads*. New York: Signet, 2002.

Swami Prabhavananda and Christopher Isherwood, trans., *Bhagavad-Gita: The Song of God*. New York: Signet, 2002.

von Stietencron, Heinrich, 'Hinduism: On the Proper Use of a Deceptive Term', in Gunther D. Sontheimer and Hermann Kulke, eds., *Hinduism Reconsidered*, pp. 11–27. New Delhi: Manohar, 1989.

Williams, Raymond Brady, ed., *A Sacred Thread: Modern Transmission of Hindu Traditions in India and Abroad*. Chambersburg, PA: Anima, 1992.

PART 4
BUDDHISM

SUMMARY

Buddhism, it is now generally believed, emerged into the world sometime around the fifth century BCE, in northern India, and is derived from the teachings of one man – Siddhartha Gautama – known to his followers by the title Buddha. Central to the Buddha's teachings was the idea that one had to experience dissatisfaction or suffering in order to understand that these have a cause: the egocentric desire for satisfaction, pleasure, or even life itself. Once this understanding is reached, followers of the *Dharma*, 'the teaching', can begin their quest for enlightenment, *nirvana*, by following the Buddhist moral code, and by meditating in order to purify the mind. As a non-theistic religion, Buddhism does not concern itself with the existence of a creator, in the Western sense at least, teaching that attainment of *nirvana* is a person's route out of the endless cycle of death and rebirth.

A variety of different schools and monastic traditions emerged within Buddhism, from *Theravada*, the earliest surviving monastic school, to *Tantra*, which advocates the use of ritual magic to control hidden forces or aid the path to *nirvana*. One of the most important traditions is *Mahayana*, through which some seek not only to achieve *nirvana* but actually to become a Buddha. Regional variations also emerged, as Buddhism spread outward from India across much of eastern Asia. In many cases, these variations are closely related to local religious traditions, or are even the product of wider syncretism, such as the Cao Dai in Vietnam, which has roots not only in Buddhism but also Catholic Christianity, Confucianism, and Taoism. In recent decades, Buddhism has faced suppression in many Asian countries, perhaps most notably in Tibet, where rule by Maoist China led to severe repression of the local traditions. Alongside this, though, Buddhism has experienced growth elsewhere, buoyed both by migration and Western interest in the religion.

CHAPTER 18

A Historical Overview

Buddhism is the '-ism' that is named after the Buddha. 'Buddha' is not a personal name, but a title meaning 'the one who has awakened'. The Buddha was a historical individual who lived and died some centuries BCE, although it is difficult to be precise about his exact dates. The common traditional date for the Buddha's birth is 563 BCE, and the sources agree he lived in North India for eighty years. However, modern scholarship questions the reliability of this date, and most historians place his birth eighty to a hundred years later, and his death around 400 BCE. The Buddha's clan-name was Gautama, but later tradition called him Siddhartha in Sanskrit, or Siddhattha in the Pali language, in which many early Buddhist works were written.

'Buddhism' is an English name for a religion that its followers often simply refer to as the *Dharma* (Pali, *Dhamma*), which can be taken here as meaning both 'the teaching' and 'the way things are'. It was discovering this, and teaching it, that made Siddhartha Gautama 'the Buddha'. Whereas Western discussions tend to stress the importance of its founder (Buddha + ism, no doubt on the model of Christ + ianity), Buddhists prefer to emphasize not him, but rather what he taught; for them the obvious place to start is the teaching. This teaching, they say, leads people to understand how things truly are, and thence to a radical reassessment of their lives. The Buddha simply awakened to this truth and taught it. In this he was not unique, for — it is said — others had awakened before him, and there will be many, many after him too.

> *Hatred is never quenched by hatred; by non-hatred alone is hatred quenched. This is an Eternal Law.*
>
> *Dhammapada*, v. 5

WHO WAS THE BUDDHA?

To start with the life story of the Buddha is the Western tradition. Even if we start with it here too, this life story should not be read as historical fact, though we can reasonably take it that Siddhartha Gautama lived and died. He was considered by his followers to have achieved the fullest possible understanding of reality, an understanding that is true freedom. The historicity of the rest is difficult to assess. Some of it we know is very unlikely to have happened, but Buddhism has always been more interested in the ways in which the life story illustrates Buddhist teachings than in its literal historical truth.

The legendary account of the Buddha's life developed gradually in the centuries after his demise. In that account, he is a prince who is protected from all knowledge of the nasty things of life. However, in the Pali sources he is simply a highborn Shakyan who had little awareness of suffering as he grew up, but the shock of discovering old age, sickness, and death led him to renounce worldly pursuits. He had married and had a son, but left his family and took to the life – not uncommon in India then as now – of a wandering seeker. He sought the final truth that would lead to complete freedom from suffering – a harsh life of meditation, study, and asceticism. Food – and very little of it – came from asking for alms. But eventually Siddhartha, looking within, in deep meditation, reached the truth he sought. He came to 'see it the way it really is', and this truth set him free. He was now the awakened one, the Buddha. The Buddha gathered around him a group of disciples and wandered northern India, teaching all who would listen. Eventually, in old age, the Buddha died. But for him death was nothing; for he was now free from death, as he was free from all other forms of unpleasantness, imperfection, and frustration. After death, there is nothing more to say.

Chinese Buddha figurine.

WHAT DID HE TEACH?

The life story of the Buddha is all about things appearing one way and really being another. The Buddha taught that 'seeing things the way they really are' is the way to overcome every sort of unpleasantness, imperfection, and frustration. These are all classed under the expression *dukkha* (Pali), a term which in the everyday context of the time meant literally 'pain' or 'suffering'. He taught that, when we look deeply, we can see that all our lives are, one way or another, at root simply *dukkha*. The Buddha was uninterested in the question of God; and Buddhist tradition has been unanimous that a creator-God, in the sense in which he is thought to exist by Christians, for example, simply does not exist. Suffering, for Buddhists, is the result of our ignorance, not understanding the way things really are, and we all live our lives in the light of that failure in understanding. The central dimension of such misunderstanding lies in our not appreciating that everything in our experience is by its very nature impermanent. Alongside impermanence – in fact, logically and doctrinally prior to it – is conditionality: the teaching that things arise and pass away in dependence upon conditions. Suffering results from holding on, trying in our experiences and in our lives to 'fix things' so they do not break up and cease to be. Clearly we are doomed to failure. We need to learn to let go let go of attachment and a fixed sense of selfhood; but this letting go has to occur at a very deep level indeed, since we have been confused and suffering in this manner for infinite lifetimes.

For Buddhists, human experience consists of a flow of consciousness, with associated mental contents such as feelings and intentions, and a body that is ever changing too. Any further unchanging element, called a 'self' (Pali, *atta*; Sanskrit, *atman*), would appear to be unnecessary. Indeed, it could lead to a dangerous form of self-grasping, the very opposite of letting go. Rather, Buddhist tradition teaches 'not-self' (Pali, *anatta*; Sanskrit, *anatman*). At death the body ceases, but the ever-flowing continuum of consciousness and its mental accompaniments continues and 'spins', as it were, another body in accordance with one's good or bad deeds (*karma*). Such 'rebirth' means that one is yet again subject to suffering – old age, sickness, death and so on. This process ceases only with letting go at the deepest possible level, attained through meditation. It is a letting go that springs from seeing things as they truly are, and completely reversing one's almost instinctive and frantic patterns of grasping after things. This cessation Buddhists call 'enlightenment' (Pali, *nibbana*; Sanskrit, *nirvana*).

MONASTIC TRADITIONS AND DOCTRINAL SCHOOLS

Central to the Buddha's vision of the way forward was an order of monks and nuns – known as the *Sangha* – living on alms, and expressing in their state of renunciation their commitment to the radical transformation we all need. In time, monasteries were established, together with a monastic rule, to regulate the conduct of the *Sangha*, and promote the peace and harmony necessary in order to follow the Buddha's path. The Buddha did not appoint a successor, reportedly declaring that the teaching – the *Dharma* – should be his successor. But after his death, with time, disagreements occurred, initially over the monastic rules. Where disputes over the rule could not be reconciled, monks in the minority were required to depart, forming their own groups based on variants of the monastic rule. Eventually, a number of different monastic traditions were formed. The best known of these – and the only one of the early Indian Buddhist monastic traditions to survive to the present day – is the 'Way of the Elders' (*Theravada*), found nowadays in, for example, Sri Lanka, Thailand, Cambodia, and Myanmar (Burma).

In Buddhism, 'schism' (*sanghabheda*) technically concerns monastic rule, not doctrinal disagreement, which is relatively less serious. Nevertheless, as time passed, different doctrinal positions also evolved, sometimes followed by identifiable schools – for example the school known as *Pudgalavada* ('Teaching the *pudgala*'). The point of contention here was that of the 'person' (*pudgala*). Advocates urged that, although the Buddha taught 'not-self', there still exists something – albeit difficult to specify what – called the *pudgala*, as something in some sense really there 'in' us. Others viewed this *pudgala* as just a self in disguise, and an abandonment

> Let none deceive another, not despise any person whatsoever in any place. Let one not wish any harm to another out of anger or ill-will …
>
> Let thoughts of boundless love pervade the whole world: above, below and across, without any obstruction, without any hatred, any enmity.
>
> From the *Metta Sutta*, The Discourse on Loving Kindness, *Sutta Nipata*, verses 6 and 8

of a central part of the Buddha's teaching. Further issues of debate involved who or what the Buddha himself was. Some urged that a Buddha is really much more extraordinary than people realize. For example, although he seems to teach, really he is permanently in meditation. He has no need to sleep, to defecate, or even to eat, but only does these things in order to act in accordance with the expectations of the world. Many such topics were debated in early – and even later – Buddhism, as the Buddha's followers sought to put his teaching into practice, and to explain it clearly to others. Indeed, also discussed was the relative importance of practising the *Dharma* for one's own freedom from all suffering, as opposed to compassionately teaching it to others.

WHAT IS MAHAYANA BUDDHISM?

To understand early Buddhist history it is thus necessary to distinguish doctrinal dispute and debate – that is, doctrinal schools – from behavioural disharmony and schism – monastic traditions. Different again, and appearing in the literature from about the first century CE, is the greatest internal development within Buddhism, the growth of the *Mahayana*: the 'Great Vehicle' or perhaps 'the Vehicle that leads to the Great'. Mahayana Buddhism is not a doctrinal school; within the Mahayana there are many doctrinal schools. Moreover the Mahayana is to be distinguished from a monastic tradition. There is no such thing as a distinct set of Mahayana monastic rules (*vinaya*). For example, monks in India holding to the Mahayana perspective would be ordained and live in accordance with any one of the sets of monastic rules that had already developed, and were sometimes to be found in monasteries with others who did not hold to the Mahayana perspective.

Hence it makes no sense to speak of two 'schools' of Buddhism, Theravada and Mahayana. Theravada is a monastic tradition; Mahayana is not. They are not comparable phenomena: there could in theory be a Theravada follower of Mahayana. However, in their practice Mahayana and Theravada are very different phenomena, with different scriptures and practices. Mahayana can best be thought of as a vision of what Buddhism is really, finally, all about. Mahayana appears first in texts – writings known as *Mahayana sutras* – claiming, controversially, to be the word of the Buddha himself. Crucially, what gradually emerges in these writings is a distinction between simply being free from all suffering – in other words, enlightened – and actually being a Buddha. A Buddha is spiritually more than just free from his own suffering; a Buddha is also perfectly compassionate. Thus to be a Buddha is better than simply being enlightened. This is not only because of a Buddha's great compassion, but also because of the many marvellous – indeed miraculous – abilities a Buddha possesses in order to help others. But it takes many, many lifetimes of spiritual striving to become a Buddha. Thus, those who aim for the highest goal should seek not just their own freedom from suffering and rebirth, but should also vow to follow the long path to Buddhahood. This path is to be followed over very many rebirths, willingly taking on their attendant sufferings, in order eventually as a Buddha better to be able to help others.

The Mahayana, in a nutshell, is the way of those who aspire to become perfect Buddhas, which is said to be for the benefit of all sentient beings – all those with consciousness. Those who vow to do this are known as *bodhisattvas*, perhaps originally meaning 'one who is capable of awakening'. Mahayana sources go into great detail about the stages of the path that a *bodhisattva* must follow in order to become a Buddha.

With time, the Mahayana also elaborated on the ways in which a Buddha is superior to someone who has simply put an end to his or her own suffering, developing further the idea that a Buddha is really much more than he appears to be. Even his death was just a show, put on in order to give a 'skilful teaching' of impermanence. For the Mahayana, the Buddha – indeed infinite Buddhas – are still around, living on higher planes – 'Pure Lands' – from which, through their great compassion and with miraculous powers, they are available and willing to help those who have need of them. With them are advanced *bodhisattvas*, who are also full of compassion and able to help others. Some of these Buddhas and 'celestial' *bodhisattvas* are named, such as Avalokiteshvara, a *bodhisattva* who is said to be the very incarnation of compassion, or Mañjushri, likewise the very incarnation of wisdom and insight.

Stone Buddha in Buddhist temple, Bangkok, Thailand.

BUDDHISM BEYOND INDIA

Significant to the history of Buddhism in India was the conversion of the great Emperor Ashoka (third century BCE), which gave the religion important imperial patronage – although scholars now discount the view that he attempted to make Buddhism the state religion. From the time of Ashoka, Buddhism began to migrate further afield, according to tradition reaching Sri Lanka at this time. It subsequently spread into South-East Asia, reaching China along the Central Asian trade routes during the early centuries CE, spreading to Korea and other countries of East Asia, and reaching Japan in the sixth century CE. Buddhism came to Tibet from various directions – including India and China – probably from about the seventh century. In India, however, for various reasons not yet fully understood, but possibly partly related to the rise of devotional theistic forms of Hinduism, as well as the impact of Islam on India, Buddhism declined, almost ceasing to exist from about the fourteenth

BUDDHISM TIMELINE

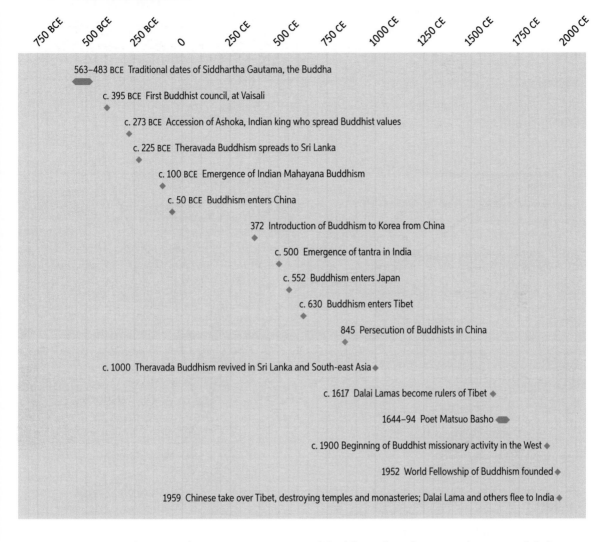

750 BCE 500 BCE 250 BCE 0 250 CE 500 CE 750 CE 1000 CE 1250 CE 1500 CE 1750 CE 2000 CE

563–483 BCE Traditional dates of Siddhartha Gautama, the Buddha

c. 395 BCE First Buddhist council, at Vaisali

c. 273 BCE Accession of Ashoka, Indian king who spread Buddhist values

c. 225 BCE Theravada Buddhism spreads to Sri Lanka

c. 100 BCE Emergence of Indian Mahayana Buddhism

c. 50 BCE Buddhism enters China

372 Introduction of Buddhism to Korea from China

c. 500 Emergence of tantra in India

c. 552 Buddhism enters Japan

c. 630 Buddhism enters Tibet

845 Persecution of Buddhists in China

c. 1000 Theravada Buddhism revived in Sri Lanka and South-east Asia

c. 1617 Dalai Lamas become rulers of Tibet

1644–94 Poet Matsuo Basho

c. 1900 Beginning of Buddhist missionary activity in the West

1952 World Fellowship of Buddhism founded

1959 Chinese take over Tibet, destroying temples and monasteries; Dalai Lama and others flee to India

century. It has revived in recent centuries, and Buddhism has also now taken on a global dimension. Perhaps the most well known modern Buddhist is the Dalai Lama of Tibet (1935–), a former winner of the Nobel Peace Prize.

It is common, although misleading, to speak of the Buddhism of, for example, China, Japan, and Tibet as Mahayana, as opposed to the Theravada Buddhism of, for example, South-East Asia. As we have seen, these are not comparable phenomena. Nevertheless, many Mahayana scriptures were transmitted to, and usually given unquestioning authority in, China, Japan, and Tibet. Unlike in South-East Asia, Buddhists in those countries could be expected to express adherence, in one way or another, to the Mahayana vision as embracing their highest and final aspirations.

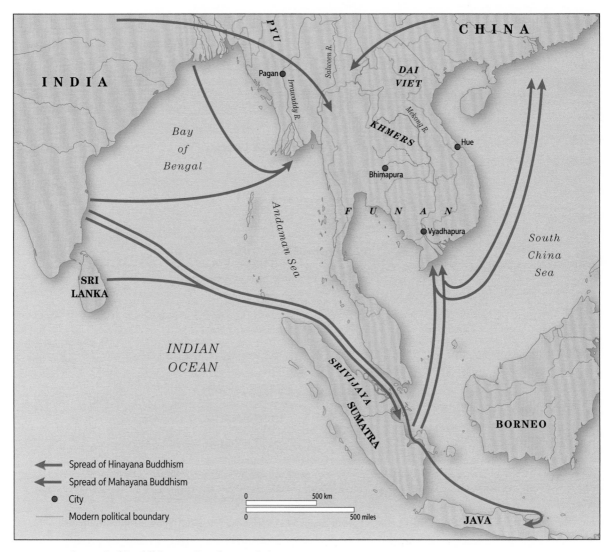

Spread of Buddhism to South-east Asia

ZEN

Particularly characteristic of East Asian Buddhism is the tradition known in Japan as *Zen*. Zen – the word itself is related to 'meditation' – is known for stressing direct, non-verbal, intuitive insight, expressed through arts such as painting, but sometimes also employing humour and shock tactics to bring about awakening. This awakened 'Buddha-nature', it is urged, is already present within all of us, if we did but realize it. Also important in, for example, Japanese Buddhism is the tradition of Shinran (thirteenth century CE). For Shinran, the awakening of a Buddha is quite beyond unenlightened capabilities; only by completely letting go of reliance on ourselves, and trusting in the Buddha's salvific ability, can the already-enlightened nature of the Buddha (a Buddha known here as *Amida*) shine forth. According to this teaching, humans have to let go completely of even the subtle egoism that encourages them to think they can achieve anything spiritually worthwhile – including enlightenment – through their own efforts. Being a monk or nun, or even meditating, is finally irrelevant, a distraction, and a possible source of egoistic attachment.

TANTRA AND VAJRAYANA

The final important development to mention is *Tantra*. From the beginning Buddhists, in common with their peers, accepted magic – bringing about desired results through manipulation of hidden forces, usually by ritual means such as sacred circles (*mandalas*), utterances of power (*mantras*), visualizations and so on. In addition to teaching, among the services Buddhist monks and nuns might be required to perform for the lay communities that supported them would be magical rituals – for crops, for health, for children and so on. Although this was not their main interest as Buddhists, its appropriateness, as an act of caring, and efficacy was not questioned. From quite early on, Buddhist ritual texts were produced, and in some circles such texts were – again controversially – attributed to the Buddha himself, and often called *tantras*.

Also controversial was the development, from perhaps the seventh century CE or earlier, of certain *tantras* claiming one could actually become a Buddha through the use of such magical means. Secret initiations were required, with unquestioning devotion to the teacher (*guru*), in order to learn their use. Even more controversial were *tantras* that explained the possibility of this supreme attainment through the employment and manipulation of a sort of subtle, psycho-physical body that everyone is said to possess within them. In this, the ritual use of sexual intercourse was held to be a particularly powerful technique – a practice reserved for advanced practitioners who do not respond to sexual stimuli with craving or attachment. Since an awakened Buddha is beyond all worldly entanglements and confusions, also recommended – expressing humanity's awakened nature – are not only sexual activity – in ways, and with partners, usually considered outside the socially accepted norm – but also other behaviour surprising to the unenlightened. These developments – often linked with the expression *Vajrayana* (Way of the Thunderbolt, Way of the Diamond), which followers used to distinguish their approach from the *Mahayana* (the Great Way), and the early schools, which they disparagingly termed '*Hinayana*' (lesser vehicle) – also produced a genre of literature detailing the unexpected exploits of certain awakened tantric 'persons of magical power' (*siddhas*).

Not surprisingly, such developments within Buddhism were – and still are – highly controversial. With time, and subjected to orthodox, and particularly monastic, control, the more controversial dimensions of Tantric Buddhism were 'tamed' and absorbed into the wider Mahayana spiritual context of great compassion and wisdom. It is in this form that one finds today the widest and most well known presence of *tantra*, in the Buddhism of Tibet.

PAUL WILLIAMS

CHAPTER 19

Sacred Writings

The Buddha himself wrote nothing; he simply taught. He sometimes taught his vision of the world, humanity's place within it, and the spiritual and moral way to freedom — eventually complete freedom — from incompleteness, frustration, and suffering. At other times he settled disputes among his followers, or legislated for the best sort of life to live to attain this complete freedom. According to Buddhist tradition, soon after the Buddha's death those monks who had achieved the goal — enlightenment (Pali, *nibbana*; Sanskrit, *nirvana*) — met to recite what they remembered of the Buddha's discourses at the First Buddhist Council. (It is often stated there were three such councils in classical times, although only two are accepted by all Buddhist traditions.)

ORAL TRANSMISSION

The emphasis from the beginning was on memory and recitation. For the first few centuries, the Buddhist scriptures were handed down orally — which partly explains the importance in Buddhism of the oral transmission from teacher to pupil — rather than in written form. Different groups of monks specialized in preserving different texts, or collections of scriptures; and transmission through oral recitation in groups proved to be a very effective way of preserving the Buddha's words — at least as accurate as writing, since interpolation of additional — and perhaps controversial — material or omission is much more difficult, as it would immediately be noticed. According to one Buddhist tradition, the scriptures were not written down until the first century BCE. The decision to resort to writing was perhaps partly due to fear in time of social and political stress that the teachings might become lost through the death of significant numbers of important reciters by disease, war, or famine — something that seems to have happened, for example, with some of the scriptures of Jainism.

THE BUDDHIST CANON

The texts recited at the First Council form the basis of the Buddhist scriptural canon. They are divided into:

sutras (Pali, *sutta*) – the general discourses of the Buddha and, sometimes, the teachings of his authorized followers

vinaya – texts relating to the structure and discipline of the monastic order.

With time, a further section of the canon was added, the *abhidharma* (Pali, *abhidhamma*): perhaps 'higher [or 'more precise'] teaching'. This section consists mainly of works that develop an elaborate description of how the psycho-physical world looks when seen 'as things really are' by an enlightened person, rather than through everyday unenlightened vision. The canonical *abhidharma* texts probably date from after the death of the Buddha, but all claim direct origin from him.

These three sections together form the 'Three Baskets' (Pali, *Tipitaka*; Sanskrit, *Tripitaka*), which are themselves subdivided. For example, in the Pali Canon, the *sutra* 'basket' is divided into four sections – plus one supplementary section – known as *Nikayas*. Perhaps the best known of these is the 'Collection of Long Discourses' (*Digha Nikaya*).

It was some centuries before the canon became more or less closed, such that – at least in theory – no more works could be added to it and given the prestige of 'coming directly from the Buddha himself'. Some scholars think the *Sutta Pitaka* was closed 150 years after the Buddha, while the other sections were closed later. There are also some Buddhist texts which have all the authority of canonical scriptures, but are not technically part of the canon at all – for example the monastic rule, still recited regularly by monks and nuns.

DIFFERENT VERSIONS

There is a tradition that the Buddha recommended preserving and transmitting his teachings in local languages rather than Sanskrit, the pan-Indian language of education. Hence, from quite early times, Buddhist scriptures were in a number of languages and also underwent translation. Moreover, as the various Buddhist monastic traditions and doctrinal schools were formed, different versions of the canon began to appear, often in different Indian languages. Nowadays, the comparative study of different canonical versions of recognizably the same text forms a fruitful area of scholarly research.

Scriptures require some sort of authoritative body to preserve and transmit them down the ages. In Buddhism, particularly in the Indian world, this has always been the monastic order, the *Sangha*. The only Buddhist monastic tradition to have survived from the early centuries to the present day is the 'Way of the Elders' (*Theravada*); the canon preserved by the *Theravada* – the sole version to have survived in its entirety and in its ancient Indian language – is the 'Pali Canon', written in the *Pali* language. Although old – and of inestimable importance for the study of Buddhism – the Pali Canon is only one of a number of Buddhist canons that existed in ancient times. Other individual canonical works, or collections, have survived, either in other Indian languages, or in ancient translations, for example into Chinese or Tibetan, made as part of Buddhist missionary activity.

With time, and with greater reliance on writing than on oral transmission, certain Buddhist traditions and schools in India started to preserve their scriptures in Sanskrit, which is why Buddhist terms are often given in both their Sanskrit and Pali forms — usually very similar: for example, *nibbana* (Pali), *nirvana* (Sanskrit). As Buddhism spread across India, using just one language made sense, rather than relying on different translations in different areas. Educated people would be familiar with Sanskrit, and a monk with a Sanskrit text could take it anywhere, without needing to have it translated, explaining in the vernacular what the text meant to less educated people as part of his teaching mission. This change to the use of Sanskrit can be seen occurring in the greatest post-canonical scriptural development in Indian Buddhism, the appearance of the Mahayana *sutras*. A number of the early Mahayana *sutras* show signs of having been translated into Sanskrit out of other Indian languages, in which, presumably, they were originally composed.

APOCRYPHAL SCRIPTURES

The earliest form in which we know Mahayana Buddhism is in its scriptures. Indeed, for followers of Mahayana, scriptural support appears to be older by some centuries than archaeological evidence. Mahayana *sutras* are apocryphal, and their ideas often seemingly new and radical. As apocryphal *sutras*, although they claim to be the words of the Buddha himself, this claim is hotly disputed within Buddhism, and the extant versions of these *sutras* cannot possibly be that old. Elements of at least some early Mahayana *sutras* may have originated in inspiring, meditative visions and revelations, held to be from a Buddha, who was thus thought to be still accessible to us on some 'higher plane'. Although there may have been attempts to add such *sutras*, they are not included in any official canon preserved by any known Indian monastic tradition.

Apocryphal *sutras* were not created in India alone. For example, many Mahayana apocryphal *sutras* were composed in China, and unknown in India in classical times. Even today, outside areas usually associated with Mahayana — for example, the monastically Theravada world of Sri Lanka — apocryphal Buddhist *sutras* are still produced, claiming to spring from some sort of special revelation, but not accepted as canonical by the mainstream, local Buddhist monastic order.

It has been suggested that the origin and survival of Mahayana as a movement required the existence of writing. Religions often produce controversial texts claiming to be the words of, or in some sense inspired by, their founder; but such works disappear unless taken up and preserved by enthusiasts down the ages. In traditional Buddhism, canonical works have been preserved and transmitted to future generations by the monastic *Sangha*. But the *Sangha* was unlikely to preserve apocryphal texts, and certainly not texts such as the early Mahayana *sutras*, which inclined sometimes to be critical of

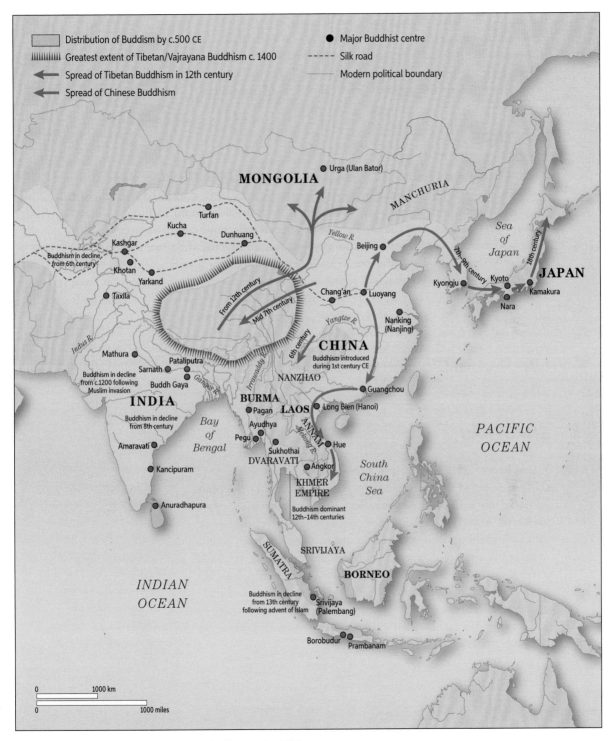

Map legend:

Distribution of Buddism by c.500 CE
Greatest extent of Tibetan/Vajrayana Buddhism c. 1400
Spread of Tibetan Buddhism in 12th century
Spread of Chinese Buddhism

● Major Buddhist centre
- - - - Silk road
——— Modern political boundary

MONGOLIA
● Urga (Ulan Bator)
MANCHURIA
● Turfan
Kucha
Kashgar
Dunhuang
Khotan
Yarkand
Buddhism in decline from 6th century
Taxila
Yellow R.
Beijing
Sea of Japan
JAPAN
7th–9th century
Kyongju
Kyoto
Kamakura
Nara
18th century
From 12th century
Mid 7th century
Chang'an
Luoyang
Nanking (Nanjing)
6th century
Yangtze R.
CHINA
Buddhism introduced during 1st century CE
Mathura
Pataliputra
Sarnath
Buddh Gaya
Buddhism in decline from c.1200 following Muslim invasion
Ganges R.
NANZHAO
INDIA
Irrawaddy R.
BURMA
Pagan
LAOS
Guangchou
Long Bien (Hanoi)
Buddhism in decline from 8th century
Bay of Bengal
Ayudhya
Pegu
ANNAM
Hue
Amaravati
Sukhothai
Mekong R.
DVARAVATI
Angkor
South China Sea
PACIFIC OCEAN
Kancipuram
KHMER EMPIRE
Buddhism dominant 12th–14th centuries
Anuradhapura
SUMATRA
SRIVIJAYA
BORNEO
INDIAN OCEAN
Buddhism in decline from 13th century following advent of Islam
Srivijaya (Palembang)
Borobudur
Prambanam

0   1000 km
0   1000 miles

The Spread of Chinese and Tibetan Buddhism

the existing monastic hierarchy. Hence, so long as the canon was transmitted orally, the preservation of significant new perspectives – such as that of Mahayana, claiming the authority of the Buddha – was all but impossible. However, the writing down of the scriptures made possible the preservation and transmission of apocryphal works and perspectives. A written text could survive, providing someone was willing to preserve it.

TANTRAS

The other major corpus of apocryphal, scriptural literature in Buddhism claiming the authority of the Buddha himself consists of the *Tantras*, texts associated with the use of ritual magic. Their origins in Buddhism – they are also found in Hinduism and Jainism – are obscure, and the earliest *Tantras* are certainly some centuries later than the earliest Mahayana *sutras*. This literature is very large. To practise the ritual prescriptions of these texts, which in time came to include techniques for attaining enlightenment as well as more mundane magical activities, requires initiation, close instruction from a teacher (*guru*), and vows of secrecy. Tantric texts involve the use of such methods as magical diagrams, utterances (*mantras*), and visualizations. *Tantras* have become linked with, and in places such as Tibet assimilated into, Mahayana; but recent research has also found tantric literature in Myanmar (Burma) and Cambodia, countries not normally associated with Mahayana perspectives.

SHASTRAS

In addition to scriptures – those accepted by all as canonical, and those of disputed authority, held by some as apocryphal – Buddhist literature also includes a vast number of exegetical treatises, often known as *shastras*. These have been produced by great scholars of various Buddhist traditions and schools, to clarify difficult points of interpretation, to defend their understanding against rivals and alternatives, or, like the 'Treasury of Abhidharma' (*Abhidharmakosha*), to serve as critical compendia of the Buddhist doctrine and path. Such exegetical treatises have been produced in each country in which Buddhism has been established, and are very important for the study of Buddhist doctrinal history.

PAUL WILLIAMS

Asked by some citizens of Kalama for guidance, the Buddha said: 'Be not led by reports or tradition or hearsay. Be not led by the authority of religious texts, nor by mere logic or inference, nor by considering appearances … But, O Kalamas, when you know for yourselves that certain things are unwholesome (akusala) and wrong and bad, then give them up … And when you know for yourselves that certain things are wholesome (kusala) and good, then accept them and follow them.'

Anguttara Nikaya 3.65 (i 188).

A SHORT INTRODUCTION TO WORLD RELIGIONS

CHAPTER 20

Beliefs

A disciple of the Buddha, Malunkyaputta, complained that the Buddha had not answered some of the most important questions of life – Is the world eternal? Is the soul the same as the body? and so on. The Buddha replied with a story.

> *A man is wounded by an arrow thickly smeared with poison. His friends and relatives brought a surgeon to him. The man said, 'I will not let the surgeon pull out this arrow until I know whether the man who wounded me was a noble, a brahman, a merchant or a worker. I will not let the surgeon pull out the arrow until I know the name and clan of the man who wounded me … until I know whether the he was tall or short or of middle height … until I know whether the bow that wounded me was a longbow or a crossbow … until I know whether the bowstring that wounded me was fibre or reed or sinew or bark …*
>
> *All this would not be known to the man and he would die.*

Abridged from the *Culamalunkya Sutta, Majjhima Nikaya 63 (I, 246)*.

So, the Buddha added, will those die who insist they must know the answers to speculative questions about the nature of reality before starting to live the holy life. For such questions are not beneficial to the real task, the cessation of suffering.

This story points to the heart of what Buddhism is about. Buddhism is less a set of beliefs than a path, leading from suffering to the cessation of suffering, from ignorance to compassion and wisdom. The Buddha's first invitation to those who wished to follow him as monks or nuns in the fifth century BCE was: 'Come, live the holy life, in order that you make an end of suffering.' The only credal statement in Buddhism, therefore, is:

> *I go to the Buddha for refuge;*
> *I go to the Dhamma for refuge;*
> *I go to the Sangha [the Buddhist community] for refuge.*

These are the 'Three Jewels' or 'Three Gems': anyone who places them at the centre of life, by 'going for refuge' to them, is a Buddhist. The *Dhamma* (Pali; Sanskrit, *Dharma*) – literally, 'that which constitutes', or 'the way things are' – is what the Buddha 'awoke to' at his enlightenment, and what he taught for forty years after. For Buddhists, it is the truth about the nature of existence; the truth that upholds the cosmos; the truth that all Buddhas have taught. Across the different schools of Buddhism, the *Dhamma* is expressed in a variety of ways; however, there are elements that all schools hold in common.

LIVING THE HOLY LIFE

Living the holy life involves a way of seeing reality and a way of acting. The way of seeing begins with experience rather than metaphysics: the experience that something in life is dislocated, flawed, unsatisfactory, and full of suffering, and the realization that one reason for this is that everything is impermanent. We are separated from loved ones. We lose our strength. We grow old, sicken, and die. Everything we cherish – youth, strength, possessions, relationships – passes away. Buddhism speaks of three defining characteristics of existence: impermanence (Pali, *anicca*; Sanskrit, *anitya*), unsatisfactoriness (Pali, *dukkha*; Sanskrit, *duhkha*), and not-self (Pali, *anatta*; Sanskrit, *anatman*). The characteristic of not-self arises when the concept of impermanence is applied to the self. As with all external phenomena, everything in our bodies and minds is changing, everything is conditioned. There is no unchanging 'self', 'soul', or ego. Mahayana Buddhists use the word 'emptiness'. All things – the self included – are 'empty' of their own nature.

> *Whatever harm an enemy may do to an enemy, or a hater to a hater, an ill-directed mind inflicts on oneself a greater harm.*
>
> Dhammapada, v. 42

This is the start of the Buddhist view of existence, but not the end. The message of the Buddha was that the suffering or unsatisfactoriness of life is not haphazard, random, or immovable. It has a cause, as all other phenomena have a cause, and if this cause is eradicated, suffering will not arise. The cause abides within the mind, and the Buddha identified it as 'craving': self-centred desire for sensual pleasures and life itself. Remove this craving, and suffering will cease, giving way to the liberation of *nibbana* (Sanskrit, *nirvana*). It is this 'view' that forms the first three of the Four Noble Truths:

- The Noble Truth of *Dukkha*: that there is an incompleteness and unsatisfactoriness at the heart of existence;
- The Noble Truth of the Origin of *Dukkha*: that the cause is craving or thirst (Pali, *tanha*; Sanskrit, *trsna*), the thirst for sensual pleasures, the thirst for continued existence, and the thirst for annihilation;
- The Noble Truth of the Cessation of *Dukkha*: that there is an end, based on the law of cause and effect – that is, if craving is destroyed, *dukkha* cannot arise;
- The Noble Truth of the Path to the Cessation of *Dukkha*: the Eightfold Path (see below).

The Buddhist view of the world is, therefore, of a world dis-eased (that is, ill at ease), a world entrapped in craving, where *dukkha* reigns supreme because people have not seen the *dhamma*, the truth about existence. It is a world where people are trapped in mental prisons of their own making. But it is a world where liberation awaits all who can change the way they look at the world and work towards freedom from the craving that is rooted in ignorance and expressed through greed and hatred.

THE WAY TO LIBERATION

The Noble Truths are the 'house' into which everything else fits in Buddhism.

The Fourth Noble Truth is the Noble Eightfold Path, the way to the ending of suffering:
- right view
- right resolve
- right speech
- right action
- right livelihood
- right effort
- right mindfulness
- right concentration or meditation

This is often reduced to just three categories: morality (Pali/Sanskrit, *sila*); concentration or meditation (Pali/Sanskrit, *samadhi*); and wisdom (Pali, *panna*; Sanskrit, *prajna*). Sometimes the following verse from the *Dhammapada*, a text known and loved throughout the Buddhist world, is quoted:

> *The avoidance of evil, the undertaking of good, the cleansing of one's mind;*
> *this is the teaching of the awakened ones.*

Dhammapada, v. 183

MORALITY

Morality is the bedrock of the Buddhist path. It involves 'the avoidance of evil, the undertaking of good'. Without moral discipline, the holy life cannot be lived. Most lay Buddhists place the following five precepts at the centre of their life:
- to abstain from harming any living being
- to abstain from taking what is not given
- to abstain from sexual misconduct
- to abstain from false speech
- to abstain from anything that clouds or intoxicates the mind, such as drugs and alcohol.

The Golden Buddha, Phra Phuttha Maha Suwan Patimakon, is the world's largest solid gold statue, and sited at the Temple of Wat Traimit, Bangkok, Thailand. It was created roughly 700 years ago.

Many would insist that these precepts involve not only abstention, but cultivation. A commitment not to harm involves the development of loving-kindness and compassion. The commitment to abstaining from taking what is not given involves recognizing the dignity and worth of other people, as does abstaining from sexual misconduct. Abstaining from false speech involves cultivating honesty and integrity.

An ancient text in the Theravada tradition, the *Karaniyametta Sutta*, describes loving-kindness in the following way: 'Just as a mother would protect her only child at the risk of her own life, even so cultivate a boundless heart towards all beings.' One way to do this is to meditate on loving-kindness (*metta*). The first step is to imagine oneself surrounded by loving-kindness. Then this loving-kindness — sometimes imagined as a white, warm light — is thrown further and further outwards into the world. First of all those dear to the meditator are brought to mind. Then the radius widens, eventually reaching those who are disliked, or even hated. It is a transformative practice that spills into everyday conduct.

Morality, for many Buddhists, is also linked with the law of action, the law of *karma* (Sanskrit; Pali, *kamma*), that moral action will produce good fruit, and unwholesome action bad fruit. This does not mean Buddhist morality is essentially selfish. Rather, self and other are seen to be interconnected. What is good for others is good for self; what would not be done to oneself would not be done to another.

MEDITATION

The task of meditation is to cleanse the mind. It ties in with the heart of the Buddha's message: that the cause of our dis-ease lies in our craving, in the three unwholesome roots of greed, hatred, and delusion. Since it is our minds and hearts that generate this craving, according to Buddhism, the only way to uproot craving is to work on the mind and heart. Buddhism offers numerous meditation methods, but these can be reduced to two main practices: tranquillity meditation (Pali/ Sanskrit, *samatha*) and insight meditation (Pali, *vipassana*; Sanskrit, *vipasyana*).

Tranquillity meditation is not unique to Buddhism. It is a method through which an object of meditation is used to concentrate the mind and gain one-pointedness. The most popular object is the breath: some Buddhists pay attention to the breath as it enters and leaves the nostrils; others watch the rise and fall of the abdomen. The meditator sits with the back upright; in some traditions the eyes are closed, in others they remain partly open. When the mind wanders away from the object, it is brought back, gently and non-judgmentally, to the breath. Traditionally, forty other meditation objects can be chosen, under the direction of a teacher. This kind of meditation may lead to what Buddhists call 'meditative absorptions' or *jhanas* (Pali; Sanskrit, *dhyanas*), states of intense absorption and mental refinement.

Vipassana means 'seeing clearly' – seeing the body and the mind clearly – and is unique to Buddhism, and distinct from altered states of consciousness. Its aim is direct verification of the *Dhamma* through observation of the body and the mind. Many exercises have been developed within the Buddhist tradition to aid this. One method used widely is 'bare attention', or 'choiceless awareness', a form of mindfulness that emphasizes the present moment. Whatever arises in the mind and the body becomes the object of meditation, of awareness. It may be a reaction of attraction or aversion to an external noise, a feeling of pain in the legs, or thoughts of hatred, jealousy, or love. Nothing is judged good or bad, nothing clung to. Everything is watched, noted, and allowed to pass; its impermanence and not-self seen. The

The Pure Mind

All that we are is the result of what we have thought: it is founded on our thoughts, it is made up of our thoughts. If a man speaks or acts with an evil thought, pain follows him, as the wheel follows the foot of the ox that draws the carriage.

All that we are is the result of what we have thought: it is founded on our thoughts, it is made up of our thoughts. If a man speaks or acts with a pure thought, happiness follows him, like a shadow that never leaves him.

'He abused me, he beat me, he defeated me, he robbed me' – in those who harbour such thoughts hatred will never cease.

'He abused me, he beat me, he defeated me, he robbed me,' – in those who do not harbour such thoughts hatred will cease.

For hatred does not cease by hatred at any time: hatred ceases by love, this is an old rule.

The world does not know that we must all come to an end here: but those who know it, their quarrels cease at once.

He who lives looking for pleasures only, his senses uncontrolled, immoderate in his food, idle, and weak, Mara (death) will certainly overthrow him, as the wind throws down a weak tree.

He who lives without looking for pleasures, his senses well controlled, moderate in his food, faithful and strong, him Mara will certainly not overthrow, any more than the wind throws down a rocky mountain.

The Dhammapada 1.1–8, transl. by Max Müller and Max Fausböll, 1881, adapted.

greed, hatred, and delusion in everything is seen, as well as what   Thai Buddhist temple.
triggers them. Each period of meditation becomes a voyage of
discovery into the way the mind and body function. Other methods include noticing the
impermanent or insubstantial nature of experience, and dismantling the experience of
selfhood by examining it in the light of Buddhist teachings.

Buddhists believe meditation is the principal means through which greed, hatred,
and delusion or ignorance can be uprooted and transcended. Central to 'delusion'
(Pali, *moha*) is the belief that we have an unchanging 'I' or ego that has to be placed at
the centre of all things, to be protected, promoted, and pampered. Meditation shows
that the things we believe to be 'self' – our feelings, our thoughts, our pain – are
impermanent and empty.

REBIRTH

Buddhists stress that there is continuity after death, but that the ultimate goal of religious
practice is not an after-death state. The term most often used is 'rebirth', which most
Buddhists prefer to 'reincarnation', since they do not believe there is an unchanging soul

to reincarnate, but rather an ever-changing process of cause and effect. Death is believed to lead continually to rebirth after rebirth, until greed, hatred, and delusion are eradicated. For the Theravada Buddhist, one can be reborn into any of five realms:

1. the hells;
2. the animal world;
3. the realm of the hungry ghosts;
4. the realm of humans; and
5. the realm of the gods.

Mahayana Buddhists have added another heavenly realm:

6. that of the demi-gods.

> *Monks, there are to be seen beings who can admit freedom from suffering from bodily disease for one year, for two years, for three, four, five, ten, twenty, thirty, forty, fifty years; who can admit freedom from bodily disease for even a hundred years. But, monks, those beings are hard to find in the world who can admit freedom from mental disease even for one moment, save only those in whom the asavas ('corruptions' such as ignorance) are destroyed.*
>
> Anguttara Nikaya Text ii, 143.

Each realm is linked to a particular emotion or characteristic, and they are states of mind as well as states of being. So one who is in the grip of hatred and anger is, in one sense, already in the hell realm.

The goal of the Buddhist path is to go beyond all of these realms by attaining *nirvana*, through eradicating greed, hatred, and delusion. Some Buddhists see this as a well-nigh impossible immediate goal. For them, rebirth in a heavenly realm, through following the five precepts and developing loving kindness, is goal enough. Others insist that *nirvana* is possible in this very life. Whether it is seen as possible now, or in the distant future, all Buddhists speak of it with joy and wonder. *Nirvana* is the end of suffering and rebirth, attained when the fire of craving is put out. It is the highest ethical state, but also beyond all human ethical constructs. It is defined by wisdom and compassion, yet beyond anything that the unenlightened person can conceive. It is absolute security and bliss. It is liberation. Some Mahayana Buddhists link it with realizing one's Buddha nature. Theravada Buddhists speak of reaching the state of the *arahat*. What happens after death to those who have realized their Buddha nature, or reached the state of the *arahat*, is left open. The message of the texts is that it is beyond all human concepts.

Some Buddhists in the Mahayana tradition have an additional goal: the liberation of all beings. They take what is known as the *bodhisattva* vow, an aspiration to achieve enlightenment not for oneself alone, but for the sake of all beings. This is sometimes envisaged as a commitment to stay within the realm of birth and rebirth until all beings have been liberated.

ELIZABETH J. HARRIS

I AM A BUDDHIST

I was born in Brisbane, Australia, into a Roman Catholic family, and have Japanese, Irish, and English ancestry. For seventeen years I strove to be a good Catholic boy, until the time of the Vietnam War. All the Christian religious teaching I had received included as a central premise the commandment, 'Thou shall not kill.' I was therefore confused when I learned that Australia had introduced conscription for seventeen-year-old boys. This seemed to me to be hypocrisy and made me question the religion I had taken for granted. Eventually, I decided to explore my Japanese heritage.

I had already become interested in the martial arts of judo and karate. However, as I pursued my interest, I learnt that *karate* means 'empty hand' and *judo* means 'the gentle way'; that it is not violence and coercion that lead to success, but rather becoming so developed and aware that one cannot be hurt. However, much training is required to remain focused and alert. There is a saying concerning being attacked by a sword, 'The beginner can only see where the sword is, and cannot move. The master sees everywhere that the sword is not, and quietly moves there.'

Later I discovered the calm, smiling, accepting faces of the Buddha statues, which attracted me strongly. Here, in front of them, was a place where I could sit, and no one was going to criticize me; where I could let my guard down and just be a boy – relaxed and happy. Over the years, the Buddha faces became more real, as I began to meet Buddhist monks and nuns, people who could explain in great detail why and how they looked so peaceful. In essence, it was because they had given up worrying. 'If something can be done, then do it. Do not worry. If something cannot be done, then it cannot be done. Do not worry.'

This is one of the most valuable things I have discovered as a Buddhist. It is always possible to do something useful in every situation. No matter how difficult or impossible something might seem, there is always an explanation, and always something to do next. For example, if I fail at a task and feel awful, Buddhist teaching instructs me to examine who I think I am. Am I just a collection of other people's judgments, good or bad? Or do I truly have a reality and an essence that is already complete and whole, yet is at the same time developing with everything – good or bad – that I do? This deep understanding helps me to move forward in life. If suddenly there is a mountain in front of me – whether literally or figuratively – I can either sit down defeated or start climbing upwards step by step. It is only by climbing a mountain that one becomes a good mountain climber. The same is true of every human situation. I can only become a more compassionate person by acting compassionately, a good leader by leading well, a good follower by learning to give loyalty to those who have been appointed to lead.

My Buddhist teacher tells me I must learn to love problems like chocolate! He means that problems provide opportunities to develop the wisdom to see the best way forward in every situation. Although the experience of happiness should be fully enjoyed, it is impermanent and constantly changing – just like problems. Nothing lasts forever.

After many years, I have learnt that, if my heart and my mind are truly in a compassionately wise state, the results will usually be effective and useful to myself and other people. To this end, I start each day with prayers and readings from the Buddhist lineage that I follow – the Tibetan Gelugpa lineage of His Holiness the Dalai Lama. I try, as my teacher advises, to sit in formal meditation for at least forty-five minutes each day. In this way, I can set my motivation and focus for the coming day, which on a 'normal' day is full of competing demands on my time, energy, and attention. Although I have a formal time of meditation, I seek to stay in a 'meditative state of mind' all day, which is the goal of all spiritual practice: to live the faith in the 'real world' and thereby show that it is alive and well.

In the evening, I briefly review what has happened during the day, and determine to try to be even more mindful the following day. Also, I pray that the Buddhas and gurus will watch over me throughout the night, and teach me in my dreams. This is a way of reaching through the limited conceptual mind into the core being of who I really am, and why I am really here – not the collection of public facades that I have to wear for my various roles and positions.

There are four special days of the Buddhist year on which I fast:

1. *Wesak*,
2. The Descent to teach in this world,
3. The day of the Buddha's first teaching – the Four Noble Truths,
4. Tibetan New Year.

I also try to fast on all full moon days – many Buddhists still use a lunar calendar. During the two weeks when the moon is waning, I practise reducing my negative activities; and in the two weeks of the waxing moon, I practise developing my positive qualities.

Over Christmas, I often go on a retreat and fast for forty-eight hours, drinking just a little fruit juice or black tea. I find it relatively easy, especially if I do it in a Buddhist centre, with no television, radio, or music to distract me. I am not a strict vegetarian, although some Buddhists are. As one who follows a Tibetan tradition, I am not required to be. The Tibetans, because of their environment, are not vegetarian: not many crops grow above the snow line, and yak meat is very warming in a stew. That said, the overall emphasis in Buddhism is always to try to reduce harm with every thought, word and deed.

Every week I go to my local temple to hear my teacher discuss his views on the scriptures and how to apply them in modern life. This keeps me in touch with 'real reality', rather than the reality of the newspapers and television.

Paul Seto

CHAPTER 21

Buddhism in the Modern World

What can Buddhism offer to the contemporary world? In what ways is it challenging society? In what ways is it reinforcing the traditional? To answer these questions it is first necessary to look at some of the forces that have influenced the development of Buddhism in the last two hundred years.

EUROPEAN COLONIALISM

Sri Lanka (Ceylon) was the first predominantly Buddhist country to be affected by European colonialism. When the British occupied Colombo in 1796, Sri Lanka had already known two colonial powers: the Portuguese and the Dutch, though both ruled only part of the island. The British brought the whole under foreign rule, by bringing down the previously independent Kandyan Kingdom in 1815. Myanmar (Burma) was the second Buddhist country to be affected by European colonialism. In 1795, the Burmese authorities allowed a British Resident in Yangon (Rangoon). Three Anglo-Burmese wars followed, until in 1885 all of Myanmar came under British rule. Independence for both Sri Lanka and Myanmar came in 1948. Cambodia, Laos and Vietnam were the third Buddhist areas, coming under French rule. For Cambodia, the process began in 1864, and by the 1890s the French had almost complete control over the internal running of the country. Significant also was Western penetration into China: between 1839 and 1865 the West, through military action and forced treaties, gained rights of residence and, in some parts of the country, jurisdiction.

This imperialistic movement affected Buddhism in two main ways. Firstly, Western visitors to these countries started to study Buddhism and interpret it to the West, working in tandem with European-based orientalists. In the early years of the nineteenth century, some drew on oral sources in Asia, but, as the century progressed, the texts took precedence, leading to an increasingly textualized interpretation of Buddhism in the West. Secondly, Asian Buddhism itself underwent revival, as it attempted to resist the Christian missionary activity that accompanied colonialism. In Sri Lanka, for instance, archival records suggest that Buddhists at first sought coexistence with Christians; they were willing to procure Buddhist texts for them and teach them the language of the texts, Pali. When they discovered, however, that the missionaries would use their knowledge to undermine Buddhism, hospitality turned to confrontation, and to the development of 'Protestant Buddhism' – a form of Buddhism that both 'protested' against Christianity and borrowed elements from it, from the Young Man's Buddhist Association and hymns to Protestant Christianity's emphasis on texts and devaluing of ritual. Myanmar witnessed a similar revivalist development, influenced by Sri Lanka, and in both countries revival movements and independence movements gave strength to each other. At the beginning of the twentieth century, Chinese Buddhism also underwent revival, again in response to the impact of the West, although its impact was lessened by the growth of secular ideologies.

SECULAR IDEOLOGIES AND AUTHORITARIANISM

In the middle years of the twentieth century, Buddhism in Cambodia, China, Korea, Laos, Tibet, and Vietnam was adversely affected by secular ideologies, Communism in particular. Communist leaders in China, after the establishment of the Chinese People's Republic in 1949,

Buddhist prayer flags on the mountainside, Nepal.

simply expected Buddhism to die away. When it did not, particularly from 1966–76, the years of the Cultural Revolution, there were violent attacks on Buddhist leaders and religious buildings.

It was the British withdrawal from India that gave Communist China the opportunity to invade Tibet. The process began in 1950 and culminated in 1959, when China imposed direct rule on the country and the Dalai Lama fled. Systematic suppression of Tibet's Buddhist heritage followed: the looting of monasteries; the destruction of libraries and religious images; the execution of some monks; and the torture and imprisonment of others. In the late 1970s, there was some relaxation of this policy, leading to a limited renewal of Buddhism in the country.

Cambodia gained its independence from the French in 1953. In 1975, Phnom Penh fell to the Khmer Rouge under Saloth Sar (Pol Pot, 1925–98). Although before victory the Khmer Rouge had seemed to praise Buddhism, after 1975 Buddhism was systematically dismantled, together with everything else that evoked Cambodia's former culture. Almost all Buddhist temples were razed, Buddhist monks were killed or given degrading labour, and Buddhist libraries gutted. In the Buddhist Institute in Phnom Penh, 40,000 documents were destroyed. When the Vietnamese defeated Pol Pot in 1979, the country was in ruins, and there was only a handful of Buddhist monks left.

Since 1979, Cambodia has painstakingly – and in the context of ongoing violence and war – attempted to rebuild its Buddhist heritage, gaining help from countries such as Sri Lanka, Japan, and Germany. The first priority was to rebuild the temples, after which came teachers and books. In 1992, the Buddhist Institute was re-opened. A deeper challenge than any of these has been to spark an interest in spiritual values in those Cambodians who had only known violence.

BUDDHISM ENTERS THE WEST

One consequence of China's invasion of Tibet was that thousands of Tibetans fled the country. Most went to India, Nepal, and Bhutan, but some travelled to Europe and America, internationalizing the Tibetan story, and spreading Tibetan forms of Buddhism. For instance in 1967 two Tibetans – Chogyam Trungpa Tulku Rinpoche (1939–87) and Dr Akong Tulku Rinpoche (b. 1939) – founded Kagyu Samye Ling monastery, near Eskdalemuir, southern Scotland, which has now become the largest Tibetan Buddhist centre in Europe, attracting numerous Westerners, a good number of whom have become monks and nuns.

Tibetan Buddhism, however, was not the first form of Buddhism to enter the West. In the nineteenth century, Buddhists came to British universities from countries such as Sri Lanka and Myanmar. Then, in 1893, the Anagarika Dharmapala (1864–1933), a key figure in the Buddhist Revival in Sri Lanka, visited Britain – although his principal goal was to attend the World's Parliament of Religions in Chicago – returning in 1896 and 1907. The first formal Buddhist mission to Britain, however, came from Myanmar in 1908, led by the second British person to become a Buddhist monk, Venerable Ananda Metteyya (Allan Bennett, 1872–1923), who was then living in Myanmar. The Buddhist Society of Great Britain and Northern Ireland was formed to welcome him. Allan Bennett had come to Buddhism through theosophy, and through Edwin Arnold's poem on the Buddha, *The Light of Asia*, published in 1879. This poem's presentation of the Buddha as compassionate hero drew on both Theravada and Mahayana textual sources and attracted countless readers.

The history of Buddhism in Britain and the West between 1908 and 1959 is a complex one. In 1924, the work of the Buddhist Society of Great Britain and Northern Ireland was taken over by a lawyer, Christmas Humphreys (1901–83), who combined it with a Buddhist centre he had started within the Theosophical Society, to form the Buddhist Lodge. In 1943 this was renamed The Buddhist Society, London, which continues today as the Buddhist Society. One of the inspirations for Christmas Humphreys was Daisetz Teitaro Suzuki (1870–1966), the Japanese Zen master who did more than any other person to bring Zen Buddhism to laypeople in the West. As a young man, he lived in La Salle, Illinois, but in 1921 became Professor of Buddhist Philosophy at Otani University, Tokyo. Following World War II, he resumed contact with the West, influencing a generation of Westerners, and producing more than thirty volumes on Buddhism and Zen in English.

Almost all schools of Buddhism are now present in the West, and new Buddhist organizations are emerging to meet the needs of Westerners. In Britain, for instance, Theravada Buddhism has a strong presence, with monasteries and educational centres catering for Buddhists from Sri Lanka, Thailand, Myanmar, and for Western converts. The Japanese Mahayana schools are represented – Zen, Pure Land, Tendai – and also newer lay movements such as Soka Gakkai, with its many Western followers, and Rissho Kosei-kai. The different Tibetan schools have also taken root, and there are movements such

Young Buddhist monks in Cambodia.

as the one founded in 1967 by the British Buddhist, Sangharakshita (Dennis Lingwood, b. 1925), the Triratna Buddhist Order, which aims to offer a Buddhism to Westerners that combines the best of all schools. Never in the history of Buddhism has one area of the world received so many forms of Buddhism within the same short time span.

Asian countries such as Thailand and Japan have been particularly affected by the internationalization of capital, and the individualism and consumerism that has followed in its wake. Since the mid-twentieth century, both countries have experienced phenomenal economic growth, which has led to an undermining of Buddhism's emphases on non-greed and community. On the other hand, new counter-cultural Buddhist voices have emerged, challenging forms of Buddhism that place individual well-being above the health of the whole community.

BUDDHISM, WAR, AND PEACE

Conditioned by forces such as those mentioned above, Buddhists are entering many contemporary debates. Their contribution falls into two broad categories: the dynamics of social engagement, and the benefits – and indeed necessity – of meditation as a way of preventing hatred, anger, and violence.

In Cambodia, after the fall of Pol Pot, in a situation of ongoing violence, a remarkable Buddhist movement, The Coalition for Peace and Reconciliation, grew up under the leadership of Maha Ghosananda (1929–2007), a monk who escaped the Pol Pot regime because he was in Thailand in 1975. During the 1990s, annual peace walks, or Pilgrimages for Truth (*Dhammayietras*), were held, passing through areas still torn by conflict. Monks and nuns, laywomen and men, took part, sometimes risking their lives as they walked through crossfire. Such costly witnesses for peace have characterized Buddhism in the modern world. However, Buddhists have not stood for non-violence in all situations.

The monk's vow

I shall eat whatever is given to me with appreciation.

From *The Monastic Code of Discipline, Vinaya IV 189*

Buddhism's nonviolent stance sets it against war in general. However, like followers of other faiths, Buddhists have struggled when this principle comes up against pressing and complex issues, and some strands of Buddhism developed a philosophy of the 'just war'. At times, this justification of war has seemed to predominate over nonviolence. For example, Japanese Buddhists aligned with – or at least did not resist – the militarization of Japan in the middle years of the twentieth century, an attitude criticized by Buddhists born later in the century, after the horror of Nagasaki and Hiroshima. In Sri Lanka, some Buddhist monks and laypeople have supported a military solution to the ethnic war that ravaged the country after 1983, arguing that defence of Buddhism is justified if it is seen to be threatened, though other Sri Lankan Buddhists have rejected this stance.

BUDDHISM AND WOMEN

In the Buddha's time, women received higher ordination and became nuns (Pali, *bhikkhunis*; Sanskrit, *bhiksunis*). This higher ordination was lost in Sri Lanka and Myanmar, and never transmitted to countries such as Tibet and Thailand. Even without higher ordination, however, women have left their families to become nuns, but have not officially been able to follow the complete *bhikkhuni* rule of discipline. This began to change after the founding in 1987 of Sakyadhita ('Daughters of the Buddha'), an international organization of Buddhist women. At Sakyadhita conferences, fully-ordained nuns from Mahayana countries such as Taiwan and Korea met 'contemporary nuns' from countries such as Sri Lanka. This eventually led to ordination ceremonies, at which nuns from countries such as Taiwan, together with sympathetic Theravada monks, ordained nuns from countries that had no higher ordination. This is a story still in process.

Restoring to all Buddhist women the opportunity to gain higher ordination is not simply about regaining lost 'rights'; it is about affirming what women can contribute to Buddhism. Whether all Buddhist women gain the option to renounce as fully-ordained nuns or not, Buddhist women are now coming together with urgency to meditate, to co-operate in joint projects, and to share their vision of a world transformed by the Buddha's teaching.

ENGAGED BUDDHISM

In 1989, the International Network of Engaged Buddhists was formed. Its founders included Sulak Sivaraksa (b. 1933), a lay Buddhist from Siam – he will not call himself Thai – and Thich Nhat Hanh (b. 1929), an exiled monk from Vietnam, who founded the Order of Interbeing in 1965. The Network asserted that Buddhism was not only about individual peace and liberation, but also about creating a better world now. Drawing on Buddhist concern for the elimination of suffering and the concept of interconnectedness, it sought to draw attention to the fact that the causes of much oppression, poverty, and suffering lay in unjust structures and the corporate greed of the rich. Engaged Buddhist movements are now found throughout the world. The members of the Amida Trust in Britain, for instance, draw inspiration from the Pure Land Tradition of Japan – which emphasizes that rebirth in the 'Pure Land', from where it will be easy to attain *nirvana*, is possible through relying on the compassion of the Buddha Amitabha – but direct this towards working for a 'Pure Land' here and now, a task they link with the original message of the Buddha.

Engaged Buddhists insist that meditation and social engagement go hand in hand, in line with the Buddha's message that we need to know how our minds and hearts work, if we are to act with wisdom rather than with greed and hatred. A growth of meditation centres catering for laypeople in Asia and the West is putting this message across strongly. In traditional Asian Buddhism, meditation practices – except for the most elementary – were linked with monastic life. Now, whether in Sri Lanka, Thailand, the USA, or Europe, meditation is becoming an important part of life for laypeople as well.

INTERFAITH RELATIONS

Although mistrust of Christianity is found in countries such as Sri Lanka, where Buddhists have experienced aggressive Christian missionary activity, many Buddhists across the world are involved in building bridges of understanding between faiths. Rissho Kosei-kai, for instance, a Japanese Buddhist lay movement started in 1938, was one of the founders of the World Conference on Religion and Peace in 1970, a pioneering international interfaith organization. In 1987 the US-based Society for Buddhist-Christian Studies was formed, and in October 1997 the European Network of Buddhist-Christian Studies.

Buddhism is changing, partly due to the interpenetration of Western and Eastern forms of Buddhism. The result is that Buddhism has become a positive, dynamic force in the world; one of the insights it can offer the world is that social engagement and compassionate action must go hand in hand with work on self, the work of meditation, the work of wisdom.

ELIZABETH J. HARRIS

QUESTIONS

1. Why is human experience so important for a follower of Buddhism?

2. Explain how the Four Noble Truths help Buddhists attain *nirvana*.

3. What is Mahayana Buddhism?

4. What is the difference between Theravada and Mahayana Buddhism, and why are they not directly comparable?

5. Why did Sanskrit become so important in Buddhism?

6. What is Tantric Buddhism and why is it regarded as controversial?

7. Why is abstention so important in Buddhist morality?

8. Explain the role of meditation in Buddhism.

9. Explain some of the different ways that Buddhism has been affected by encounters with the West.

FURTHER READING

Blomfield, Vishvapani, *Gautama Buddha: The Life and Times of the Awakened One*. London: Quercus, 2011.

Bui, Hum Dac, and Beck, Ngasha, *Cao Dai: Faith of Unity*. Fayetteville, AR: Emerald Wave, 2000.

Dalai Lama, *How to Practice: The Way to a Meaningful Life*. Trans. and ed. Jeffrey Hopkins. New York: Pocket Books, 2002.

Fisher, Robert E., *Buddhist Art and Architecture*. London: Thames & Hudson, 2002.

Gunaratana, Bhante H., *Mindfulness in Plain English*. Boston: Wisdom Publications, 2002.

Harvey, P., *An Introduction to Buddhism: Teachings, History and Practices*. Cambridge: Cambridge University Press, 1990.

Lopez, Donald S. Jr., *The Story of Buddhism: A Concise Guide to its History and Teachings*. New York: HarperCollins, 2002.

Queen, Christopher S., and King, Sallie B, eds., *Engaged Buddhism: Liberation Movements in Asia*. Albany: State University of New York Press, 1996.

Thich Nhat Hanh, *The Heart of the Buddha's Teaching*. New York: Broadway, 1999.

Williams, Paul, *Buddhist Thought: A Complete Introduction to the Indian Tradition*. New York, Routledge, 2000.

PART 5
CHINESE, KOREAN, AND JAPANESE RELIGIONS

SUMMARY

For as long as humans have lived in China, the country has had its own, highly distinctive, religious traditions, partly because the belief systems of China grew up in almost complete isolation from those elsewhere. From the very earliest traditions comes the conception of the balance of nature, well known today as yin and yang; while all Chinese traditions emphasize a supernatural concern with the wellbeing of humankind. As a result, Chinese traditions have tended to focus more on their conception of ethics than on speculation about the existence of a deity.

The ethical teachings of Confucius were augmented by later prophets, especially Mencius and Hsün-tzu, but the Taoist religion emerged almost as a foil to Confucianism's emphasis on service to society, concerned with seeking a mystical unity with the Tao – a metaphysical absolute – by the contemplation of nature. Both traditions – Taoism especially – changed through the influence of Buddhism. The extent of crossover between these three traditions in China is such that many see no problem in being a member of all three.

Korea's traditional religion, Sinkyo, has been central to Korean society throughout its history, and is grounded in the national mythology. Central to Sinkyo are the yin and the yang, whose harmonious coexistence is essential. Korean tradition has borrowed much from its neighbours – Confucianism, Taoism, and Buddhism – and in recent years has been challenged by the growth of Christianity in South Korea, and by repression in the Communist North.

Japan's rich and diverse religious culture is the product of two thousand years of history, and of its geography. Its religion has been strongly influenced by the Asian mainland. Shinto, formerly the state religion, has a history stretching back to around 300–600 CE, and is concerned with national mythology. The emperors had a special place in this narrative, as they were believed to descend from Amaterasu, the sun goddess. Buddhism has been present almost as long as Shinto, and exists in a number of forms. It is typical for most people to adhere to both Shinto and Buddhism.

CHAPTER 22

Chinese Religions

SAGES AND IMMORTALS

Chinese religion is unique. This is partly due to the fact that – alone among the great religions of humankind – Chinese religion first developed in isolation, without the influence of the other great world religions. Confucianism and Taoism (or Daoism), two of the three faiths of China, developed their distinctive forms before there was any significant contact with the rest of the world. For this reason, Chinese religion has taken a form that often seems quite unlike any other. For example, neither Confucianism nor Taoism is like Judaism, Christianity, or Islam – monotheistic religions with God at the centre. Confucianism, especially, became a religion without any great speculation on the nature and function of God. For this reason, it was often not even considered to be a religion. However, it is clear Confucianism is a religion, and that it was the dominant tradition of pre-modern China.

THE SHANG

The earliest forms of Chinese religion are not clear. We know hardly anything definite about the religion of the great Shang dynasty (1766–1122 BCE), the first historical dynasty. But although we know little of the detail, we are certain religion played a very important part in the life of the Shang. In fact, the Shang lived in a world of spirits and powers, who directly influenced the lives of the living – their success or failure – and who required sacrifice and appeasement.

The Shang sought to fathom the wishes of these spirits through a complicated system of divination. We have the records of these divinations, the famous 'oracle bones'. The diviner, at the request of the king, would put a question to the spirit, and record the question and its answer on the carapace of a turtle or the shoulder-blade of an ox. The Shang were concerned to know the will of the spirits almost everything they did.

Although the nature of Shang religion is clouded in mystery, a certain continuity remains between the Shang and later Chinese religion. There is a persistent belief in the balance of nature, an idea that was later explicitly defined as the famous concepts of *Yin* and *Yang*: the forces of dark and light, of soft and hard, of female and male. Another important idea which continues throughout the history of Chinese religion is a constant concern for the wellbeing of the people, an idea that later became the concept of *t'ien-ming* or the Will of Heaven.

Prior to the rise of Confucianism, certain elements of the Shang and Chou dynasties took more definite shape. If there is one idea that informs the entire history of the development of Chinese religion, it is a 'consciousness of concern'. Even in the western Chou and eastern Chou, we find the persistent claim that high Heaven itself has concern for the well-being of the people. In fact, Heaven is said to hear and see, as the people hear and see, and hence to have a most active concern for them.

This sense that concern is the basis of the cosmos makes Chinese religion different from such religions as Judaism, Christianity, or Islam, where a sense of awe, or dread, of a supreme power informs religious consciousness. Chinese religion has always had a close connection with the ethical thought of the people; a sense of concern and participation pervades the Chinese understanding of humanity's relationship to the transcendent and with other people.

PHILOSOPHY OR RELIGION?

What then are Confucianism and Taoism? Are they philosophies or religions? Do they have any kind of mystical traditions that seek to aid the faithful to achieve the perfected aims of a religious life?

There is a common Chinese distinction that is helpful in answering this question: the distinction between the terms *chia* (schools of thought, philosophy) and *chiao* (teaching, religion). The former refers more to the great thinkers and their teachings, and the 'great traditions'; the latter to the religious and, by extension, to the unique ways in which the great traditions have been appropriated by the people at grass-roots level. A distinction between the great intellectual traditions and the cultic and devotional side of religious life has been made in all the Chinese traditions: Confucianism, Taoism, and also Buddhism, after its introduction into China in the second century CE.

The Chinese traditions have never felt the need to contrast *chia* and *chiao* in a hostile fashion; in a characteristic way, they are said to represent two different parts of one continuum. They are different yet related. In traditional China, each of the great religions operated on both levels: there were great Confucian, Taoist, and Buddhist philosophers, as well as masters of the various religious arts of meditation, liturgy, and ritual.

CONFUCIANISM

The Latinized name, 'Confucianism', is a Western invention which has come down from seventeenth-century Jesuit missionaries. Interestingly, these early Western missionaries clearly saw the religious nature of Confucianism, even if they did not agree with its traditions and rituals.

The Chinese term for Confucianism, *Ju* (scholars, literati, with the special meaning of Confucian from the T'ang dynasty), points to its broader character as intellectual culture. It is usually regarded as philosophy (*chia*), although such terms as *Ju-chiao*, *K'ung-chiao* (K'ung being Confucius's family name), or *Li-chiao* (Li referring to Confucian rituals) are also used. All these terms refer to those elements of worship, ritual, and sacrifice that are religious teachings, which is, of course, what *chiao* itself refers to.

CONFUCIUS

Confucianism is best known for its moral philosophy, represented by Confucius (551–479 BCE), Mencius (371–c. 289 BCE), and Hsün-tzu (fl. 298–238 BCE), and is clearly grounded in religion – the inherited religion of the Lord-on-high, or Heaven. Even the great rationalist Hsün-tzu saw society founded on the penetrating insight of the sagely mind. Although Confucianism is less known for its mysticism, the *Book of Mencius* cannot be fully understood except in the light of mysticism. The *Chung-yung*, one of the 'Four Books' which became the basis for Confucian self-cultivation in the southern Sung (1126–1279 CE), explicitly states that the sage, having realized true integrity (*ch'eng*), becomes one with Heaven and Earth. Confucian moral metaphysics reaches over into the religious quest for unity with the ground of being.

Nonetheless, Confucianism gives primary emphasis to the ethical meaning of human relationships, finding and grounding the moral in the divine transcendence. The perfect example of this is Confucius himself, who is best remembered as a great teacher, and the basis of whose teaching was the concept of humanity (*jen*). Just as compassion is the greatest Buddhist virtue, and love the Christian, *jen* is the ultimate goal of conduct and self-transformation for the Confucian. Whereas most of Confucius' teachings stress the ethical dimension of humanity, he made it clear it was Heaven itself which protected him and gave him his message: 'Heaven is the author of the virtue that is in me.'

MENCIUS

Confucius stands as a prophet, giving an ethical teaching grounded in religious consciousness, whereas Mencius projects the image of a teacher of mysticism. He proclaims an inner doctrine, alluding to the presence within the heart of something greater than itself: 'All things are present in me. When I reflect upon myself in all sincerity, my joy is boundless.' What was an implicitly religious message in Confucius becomes explicit in Mencius. For example, Confucius is said not to have discussed the relationship between human nature and the Way of Heaven, whereas Mencius made his whole system of thought revolve around these two concepts, attempting to show how the very essence of the Way of Heaven, the divine power of the cosmos, became human nature. He felt that, if this human nature could be correctly cultivated and nurtured, even the common person could become a sage.

The Confucian classics (there are thirteen) prefer to discuss the work of spiritual cultivation in terms of emotional harmony and psychic equilibrium – a harmony of due proportions, rather than the absence of passions. The 'Doctrine of the Mean' (*Chung-yung*), one of the 'Four Books', distinguishes between two states of fundamental mind, the 'pre-stirred' state (before the rise of emotions), and the 'post-stirred' state (after contact with the things and events of the world). The meaning best expressed by the concept of true integrity (*ch'eng*) lies in the harmony of emotions that have arisen, but resembles the equilibrium of the 'pre-stirred' state. The *Chung-yung*, as we have seen, claims this harmony puts a person in touch with the cosmic processes of life and creativity: 'If they can assist in the transformation and nourishing process of Heaven and Earth, they can thus form a trinity with Heaven and Earth.'

HSÜN-TZU

The third founding father of Confucianism, Hsün-tzu, is best remembered for his doctrine of ritual action (*li*). If Confucius begins Confucianism with the dramatic – almost prophetic – demand that we live a life of *jen*, or perfect humanity, and Mencius expands upon the concept of *jen*, to show this is a life of heightened inter-subjectivity and intuition into the boundless joy of the enlightened sage, Hsün-tzu provides the practical side of Confucian religion. It is his genius to demonstrate the power of correct ritual action needed to transform the human heart, which is prone to err, into the mind of a sage. In doing so, Hsün-tzu provides a model for daily life that supports the religious and ethical intuitions of Confucius and Mencius. Without a life of ritual – a liturgy of daily life ennobled by humility and graced by beautiful conduct – the supreme insights of religious geniuses such as Confucius and Mencius would be impossible to maintain.

In the course of time, the meaning of the word 'Heaven' becomes ambiguous, shifting from the early reference to a supreme deity (the *Analects* of Confucius), to a vacillation between that and moral force (Mencius), to the universe itself (Hsün-tzu).

NEO-CONFUCIANISM

Confucian mysticism, especially in its second great phase, Neo-Confucianism, leans more and more in the direction of pantheism, as is borne out by the later philosopher, Chang Tsai (1020–77). Here Confucian religion and mysticism show the imprint of Taoist – and Buddhist – influences; yet Chang Tsai still shows a profoundly Confucian bent to his mystical vision of the unity of the world, by expressing this as one of a perfected family. In this vision, the whole world becomes related to him as his own family. The note of inter-subjective concern sounded by Confucius and Mencius is reaffirmed.

The first great flowering of Confucianism produced such diverse thinkers as Mencius and Hsün-tzu, while Neo-Confucianism gave us Chu Hsi (1130–1200) and Wang Yang-ming (1472–1529). Both the latter started from a desire to reform the Confucianism of

CHINA TIMELINE

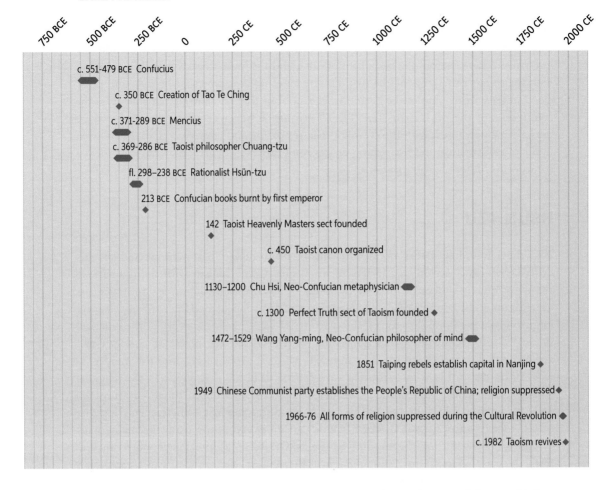

c. 551-479 BCE Confucius

c. 350 BCE Creation of Tao Te Ching

c. 371-289 BCE Mencius

c. 369-286 BCE Taoist philosopher Chuang-tzu

fl. 298–238 BCE Rationalist Hsün-tzu

213 BCE Confucian books burnt by first emperor

142 Taoist Heavenly Masters sect founded

c. 450 Taoist canon organized

1130–1200 Chu Hsi, Neo-Confucian metaphysician

c. 1300 Perfect Truth sect of Taoism founded

1472–1529 Wang Yang-ming, Neo-Confucian philosopher of mind

1851 Taiping rebels establish capital in Nanjing

1949 Chinese Communist party establishes the People's Republic of China; religion suppressed

1966-76 All forms of religion suppressed during the Cultural Revolution

c. 1982 Taoism revives

their day, and then sought to give practical guidance for the perfection of the mind. Their schools, respectively, were called 'the teaching of principle' (*li-hsüeh*) and 'the teaching of mind' (*hsin-hsüeh*). In fact, both were primarily concerned with the task of achieving sagehood: the great debate between them centred on how to achieve this.

Chu Hsi believed we must go through a long and arduous process of self-cultivation and ethical activity in order to reach jen. He stressed the method of 'the examination of things' (*ko-wu*) as the best means to achieve this end. But this was more than a scientific interest in the material matters of the cosmos; it was to be an examination of all the various ethical and spiritual states of the mind, an attempt to know the self, in order to perfect the original nature, which he held to be good.

Chu Hsi expressed his spiritual goal in this way:

> The mind of Heaven and Earth, which gives birth to all things, is humanity
> (jen). Man, in being endowed with matter-energy, receives this mind of Heaven

A SHORT INTRODUCTION TO WORLD RELIGIONS

and Earth, and thereby his life. Hence tender-heartedness and humanity are
part of the very essence of his life.

Wang Yang-ming agreed on the goal of sagehood, but rejected Chu Hsi's gradualist method. For Wang, only the 'enlightenment experience' of the absolute unity of our minds with the mind of the Tao (or Dao) would suffice to achieve sagehood. All other methods, including Chu Hsi's attempt at gradual self-cultivation, were a waste of time, if they did not provoke this realization of the enlightenment experience. After Wang himself had had such an experience he wrote:

My own nature is, of course, sufficient for me to attain sagehood. And I have
been mistaken in searching for principle in external things and affairs.

The great Neo-Confucians gave Confucianism a new lease of life, providing a new explanation of the Confucian vision that could compete philosophically with Taoism and Buddhism. But, even more, they provided a practical set of life-models for the earnest seeker of sagehood. Although Chu Hsi consulted gradualism, and Wang Yang-ming immediate experience, both sought that moment when the human mind – precarious in its tendencies to good and evil – would be transformed into the Mind of Heaven, the state of perfected excellence.

TAOISM

The great Taoist religion is, in many ways, the opposite of Confucianism. Confucianism seeks to perfect men and women within the world; whereas Taoism prefers to turn away from society to the contemplation of nature, seeking fulfilment in the spontaneous and 'trans-ethical'. The Tao, a metaphysical absolute, appears to have been a philosophical transformation of an earlier personal God. The way it teaches leads to a union with itself – a way of passive acceptance and mystical contemplation. Such is the teaching of the great Taoist thinkers, Lao-tzu and *Chuang-tzu*, about whose lives little is known, if indeed they ever existed. This is perhaps fitting for men who allegedly chose a life of obscurity, and taught a way of silence.

Taoism is not just passive contemplation. The texts of Lao-tzu and Chuang-tzu (also the name of the book, Chuang-tzu) served a later generation of religious-minded thinkers, anxious to transcend the limited conditions of human existence, whose ambition was to 'steal the secret of Heaven and Earth', to wrench from it the mystery of life itself, in order to fulfil their desire for immortality.

The goal of the Confucian was to become a sage, a servant of society, while the goal of the Taoist was to become an immortal (*hsien*). They revived belief in personal deities, practising a ritual of prayer and appeasement, and fostered the art of alchemy – an external alchemy, which 'internalized' the golden pill of immortality – and sought it through yoga and meditation. They saw sexual hygiene as another means of prolonging human life.

This new Taoism has been called 'Taoist religion', to distinguish it from the classical philosophy of Lao-tzu and Chuang-tzu with its acceptance of both life and death. This Taoist religion developed its own mystical tradition, embellished with stories of marvellous drugs and wonder-working immortals, of levitations and bodily ascensions to heaven. Basing itself on the early texts — the *Lao-tzu, Chuang-tzu, Huai-nan-tzu, and Lieh-tzu* — the Taoist religionists created long-lasting religious institutions.

Some of these groups still exist today, and trace their roots back to the Taoist movements at the end of the second century ce. With their esoteric and exoteric teachings, their lines of orthodox teachers, their social organizations, they more closely resemble the other great religious traditions of humankind. But their persistent Chinese style comes through: they seek unity with the Tao which cannot be named.

THE TAO

How can Taoism be distinguished from its great sister religion, Confucianism? One major goal of all the various schools and sects of Taoism was the quest for freedom. For some, it was freedom from the political and social constraints of the emerging Confucian state; for others, the more profound search for immortality; and for yet others, the search for oneness with the Tao itself. This Tao was the sum total of all things which are and which change, for change itself was a very important part of the Taoist view of reality. As the *Chuang-tzu* tells us, the Tao is 'complete, all-embracing, the whole: these are different names for the same reality denoting the One'. This One, this totality of the Tao, worked as a liberating concept for the Taoists; within the ceaseless flux of the Tao, they found the power to live life in a spontaneous fashion. Probably the most famous statement of the freedom of the Taoist immortal is that of Lao-tzu, where he says, 'The ways of men are conditioned by those of Heaven, the ways of Heaven by those of the Tao, and the Tao came into being by itself.' The Tao is therefore the principle of the universe, and also a pattern for human behaviour, often called 'uncontrived action' (*wu-wei*).

The Taoist imagination was totally unfettered by the confines of Confucian etiquette or sensibility, and provided the magic garden of the Chinese people. Some took this magic very seriously, while some found that this, too, was just another illusion of the changing Tao. For example, at the end of a report of a magical spirit journey attributed to King My of the Chou dynasty, the magician who has been his guide for the trip explains:

> *Your majesty feels at home with the permanent, is suspicious of the sudden*
> *and temporary. But can one always measure how far and how fast a scene may*
> *later turn into something else?*

Or, as the next story in the *Lieh-tzu* puts it:

> *The breath of all that lives, the appearance of all that has shape, is illusion.*

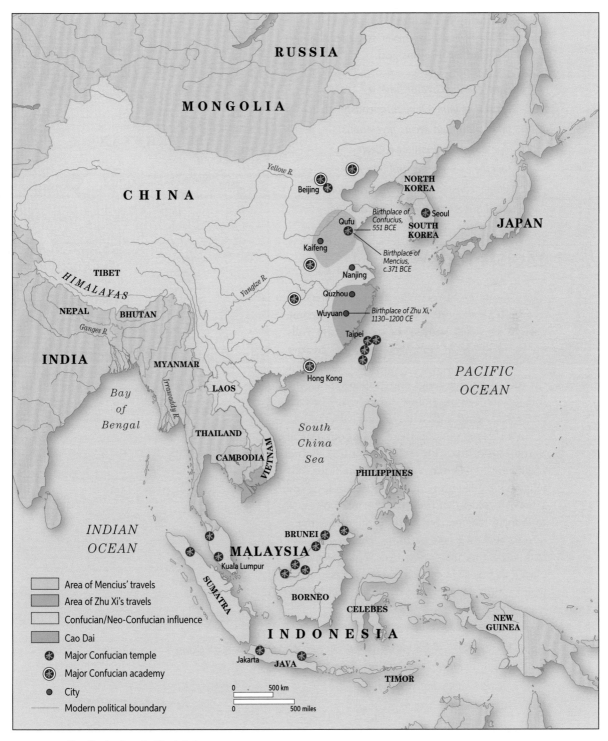

Confucianism in East Asia

Area of Mencius' travels
Area of Zhu Xi's travels
Confucian/Neo-Confucian influence
Cao Dai
Major Confucian temple
Major Confucian academy
City
Modern political boundary

0   500 km
0   500 miles

Birthplace of Confucius, 551 BCE
Birthplace of Mencius, c.371 BCE
Birthplace of Zhu Xi, 1130–1200 CE

RUSSIA
MONGOLIA
CHINA
Yellow R.
Beijing
NORTH KOREA
Seoul
SOUTH KOREA
JAPAN
Qufu
Kaifeng
Nanjing
Quzhou
Wuyuan
Yangtze R.
Taipei
Hong Kong
PACIFIC OCEAN
TIBET
HIMALAYAS
NEPAL
BHUTAN
INDIA
Ganges R.
MYANMAR
Irrawaddy R.
Bay of Bengal
LAOS
THAILAND
CAMBODIA
VIETNAM
South China Sea
PHILIPPINES
INDIAN OCEAN
SUMATRA
MALAYSIA
Kuala Lumpur
BRUNEI
BORNEO
CELEBES
NEW GUINEA
INDONESIA
Jakarta
JAVA
TIMOR

But unlike many of the great religions of India and the East, the Taoists never felt that the Tao could be called a conscious god.

> How can the Creator have a conscious mind? It spontaneously takes place, but seems mysterious. The breath and matter collect together, coagulate, and become shape: constant with transformation it continues on without ever ceasing.

TAOISM TODAY

Throughout its history, the diverse masters of Taoism have sought, in various ways, to become part of this 'self-so-ness' of reality. Life rolls on by itself in an unbroken wave of creative spontaneity; neither the Confucian Heaven, nor the rule of earthly kings and emperors, nor the folly of demons or goblins can defy it. The true immortal lives to learn a life in tune with the Tao.

In all Taoist religion there is a poetic touch, a realization that life is a beautiful – and frightening – panorama of transformations. No religion has been more successful at invoking the sense of wonder that these transformations cause to human beings. Set within their mountain retreats and their lake pavilions, the Taoists have truly been the poets of nature. The great T'ao Ch'ien (365–427 ce) expresses this sense of wonder, tinged with serene resignation and hope:

> Just surrender to the cycle of things,
> Give yourself to the waves of the
> Great Change,
> Neither happy nor yet afraid,
> And when it is time to go, then
> simply go,
> Without any unnecessary fuss.

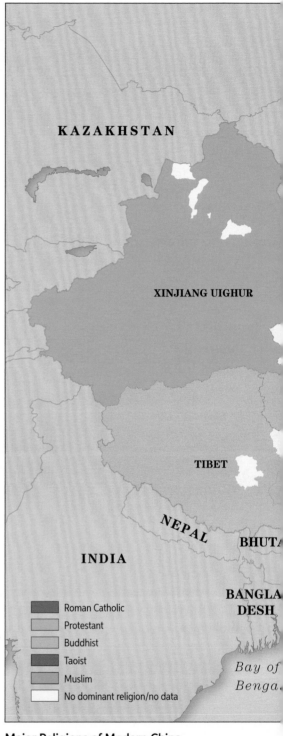

Roman Catholic
Protestant
Buddhist
Taoist
Muslim
No dominant religion/no data

Major Religions of Modern China

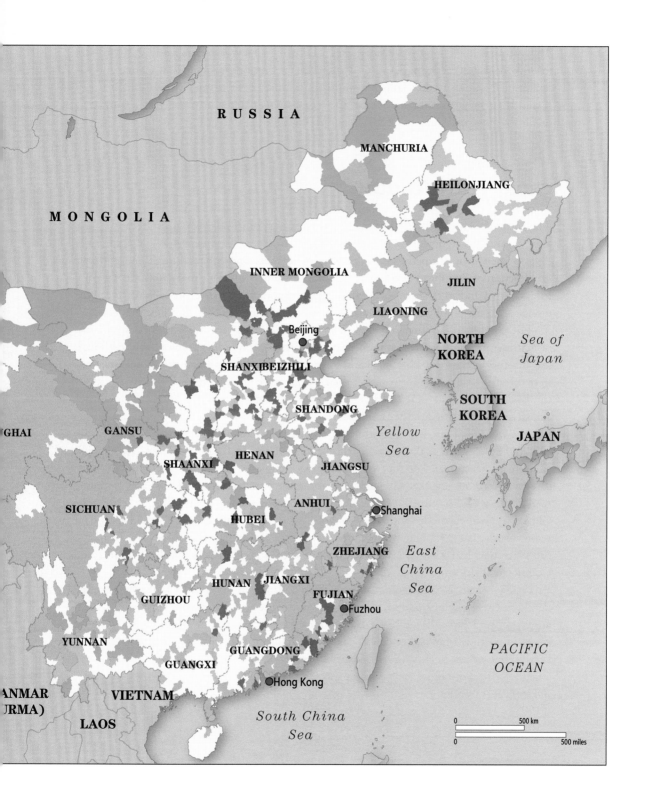

Today this sense of poetic beauty, and desire to achieve oneness with the Tao, still inform the Taoist religion. Because of the great revolutionary changes in China, and the determined animosity of Maoism towards traditional 'superstition', it was difficult to tell if and how Taoism could survive on the Chinese mainland. In recent years, however, a distinct *détente* concerning religious affairs has been noticeable.

CROSS-FERTILIZATION

The great Chinese religions have always influenced each other's development. In early China, great debates and arguments went on between the Taoists and Confucians, helping both sides develop their own distinctive attitudes. The picture becomes more complicated with the introduction of Buddhism into China. Both Taoism and Confucianism borrowed a great deal from the new Indian religion, with the Taoists reforming their religious structures, founding monasteries, and writing a huge canon of sacred texts in imitation of Buddhist models.

The great Neo-Confucian revival in the twelfth and eleventh centuries ce would also be unthinkable without the stimulus and challenge of Buddhist philosophy. Although the Confucians did not borrow nearly as much as the Taoists from the Buddhists, they were certainly stimulated to work out their own mature philosophic response to Buddhist thought – and on the practical level learned a great deal about meditation, which they called 'quiet-sitting', from the Buddhists.

The heyday of cross-fertilization of religions in China came in the Ming dynasty (1369–1644), when many religious thinkers, such as Lin Chao-en (1517–98), sought to effect a harmonization of the three great religions of China, declaring that the three religions are one. Lin sought to combine the best features of Taoist and Buddhist meditation with a Confucian sense of shared concern for fellow creatures, in a uniquely Chinese type of religious synthesis that is still present in China today. It would not be far wrong to say that most religious Chinese are, in fact, a mixture of all three great religions; the syncretists had such an effect that no one thinks it odd to be Buddhist, Taoist, and Confucian at the same time.

Finally, there is an element of Western culture in modern China's intellectual development. Religious and secular Western influence will, no doubt, have just as great an impact on China – witness the tremendous transformative power of Maoist thought, based in part on Marxist concepts – as did Buddhism. It is impossible to say what will survive; but we can be certain that what will emerge will be distinctively Chinese.

JOHN BERTHRONG

CHAPTER 23

Sinkyo: Korea's Traditional Religion

Korea's traditional religion, Sinkyo, has been called 'the religion without a name'. It is not so much a structured set of uniform beliefs, as a religious way of seeing the world and a person's sacred link with it – what used to be called 'animism'. Like other religions, it has five 'magnetic points':

1. **I and the cosmos**

   Humanity is in rhythm with the world. The forces of nature controlling life and death, fertility and sterility, become personified and god-like. This world is a religious arena, inhabited by spirits of heaven and the soil, water and the trees.

2. **I and the norm**

   The myth of Tangun, legendary founder of Korea, underlines that sense of cosmic norm to which the Korean must conform. Ung, the son of heaven, changed a bear into a woman. The bear-woman could find no one to marry, so Ung changed his form, married her, and fathered her child, Tangun. This myth is remembered on 'opening of heaven day' (*Kaechonjol*), an annual national holiday. Similar tales surround the archetypal tribal leaders, and mythical ancestors of present-day clan families.

3. **I and destiny**

   How do we reconcile the fact that we are active beings and also victims of fate or destiny? Borrowing from pre-Confucian roots, Sinkyo finds its answer in a cosmic pattern, where heaven, humankind, and nature make a harmony of opposites that complement each other. They are the great forces of the *yin* and the *yang*, non-being and being. The *yin* is negative, passive, weak, and destructive; the *yang* is positive, active, strong, and constructive. As they act and interact, harmony is achieved and recreated, again and again. Our individuality comes from these opposites: the *yin* is the female, mother, soft, dark, wet; the *yang* male, father, strong, hard, bright.

   Out of these opposites comes the system called 'geomancy'. 'Where shall we live?' becomes a religious question of choosing a good house-site or grave-site, in harmony with these opposites. The house or burial place, for instance, must be arranged in conformity to the cosmic workings of *yin-yang* and the harmony of the

KOREA AND JAPAN TIMELINE

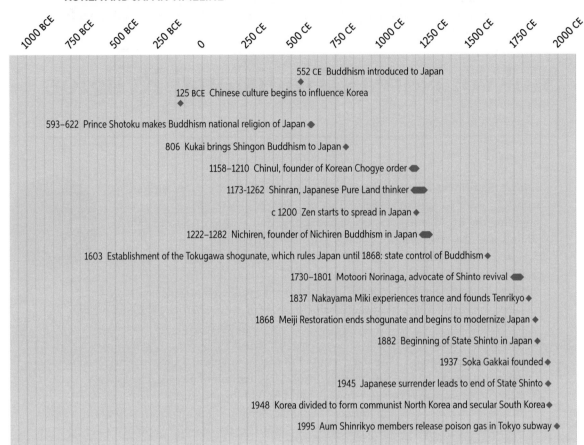

552 CE	Buddhism introduced to Japan
125 BCE	Chinese culture begins to influence Korea
593–622	Prince Shotoku makes Buddhism national religion of Japan
806	Kukai brings Shingon Buddhism to Japan
1158–1210	Chinul, founder of Korean Chogye order
1173-1262	Shinran, Japanese Pure Land thinker
c 1200	Zen starts to spread in Japan
1222–1282	Nichiren, founder of Nichiren Buddhism in Japan
1603	Establishment of the Tokugawa shogunate, which rules Japan until 1868: state control of Buddhism
1730–1801	Motoori Norinaga, advocate of Shinto revival
1837	Nakayama Miki experiences trance and founds Tenrikyo
1868	Meiji Restoration ends shogunate and begins to modernize Japan
1882	Beginning of State Shinto in Japan
1937	Soka Gakkai founded
1945	Japanese surrender leads to end of State Shinto
1948	Korea divided to form communist North Korea and secular South Korea
1995	Aum Shinrikyo members release poison gas in Tokyo subway

five elements: wood, metal, fire, water, earth. The interacting flow of these forces must not be disturbed.

4. **I and salvation**

Since this harmony is often broken, Sinkyo must also meet people's craving for salvation. When the rice paddies are ploughed in the spring, a farmers' band pacifies the spirits of the earth with music and ritual. When the ridge-pole of a new house is raised, wine and food are thrown at it, while a member of the household chants, 'Please, grandfather and grandmother of the ridge pole, bless us with good luck and long life, and many sons!'

Life is under a curse, a shadow darkening the cosmic harmony. The way back to 'paradise' is by ritual sacrifice. Throwing a stone on a simple altar keeps you from getting sore feet on a journey; spitting on the altar is a sign of purification, and wards off evil spirits. Earth spirits must be satisfied before a corpse can be laid to rest. The 'sin' is not that of personally violating the will of a personal 'god', but the corporate breaking of cosmic unity.

A SHORT INTRODUCTION TO WORLD RELIGIONS

The chief role in restoring unity is often played by the Mudang. Always a woman, her most important task is curing mental and physical disease. Like the shamans of Siberia, she also conducts communal sacrifice, assures the farmers of good crops, and fishermen of safe journeys and a good catch. She will produce sons for a barren woman, recall the spirits of the dead after a funeral and lead them to the kingdom of the blessed, and pacify the spirits of those who die violent or tragic deaths. Her role is regarded as beneficial.

Sinkyo feels deep horror at the threat of death, which destroys cosmic harmony. Two thousand years ago, it was common for Koreans to bury the dead with their personal belongings, including gold and silver. With the growing influence of Confucianism in Korea from the third century ce, Sinkyo saw the spirit world in a new way. The Confucian concept of filial piety as the summit of all virtues strengthened – if it did not create – Korea's early ancestor-cult. In the following years, food was offered to kinsmen at death and at memorial times, in the hope that the ancestor would favour the descendants.

5. **I and the Supreme Being**

Koreans read about the gods in the great picture-book we call the cosmos. Among the spirits of nature, the spirit of heaven (Hananim, or Hanunim) has a special place. Not a 'high god', remote and supreme, he is said to bring sunlight and rain – while lightning, drought, and other disasters are his judgment on the wicked. By his favour we live and breathe. When national disaster came, the king used to appeal to Hananim, by confessing his own sins and those of his people. In some sense a 'heavenly father', Hananim was the grandfather of Tangun, the aboriginal hero of Korea.

SINKYO AND THE NEW RELIGIOUS MOVEMENTS

As Korea was invaded by Confucianism, Buddhism, and Christianity, Sinkyo did not shrink, but was altered and strengthened. From Confucianism came the ethical codes surrounding the ancestor-cult. Taoism and Neo-Confucianism strengthened the magical side of Sinkyo and its geomancy. From Buddhism came a stress on suffering and pain, now linked with healing and divining.

Sinkyo has also provided the background for Korea's new religions. Chondogyo was founded in the mid-eighteenth century in reaction to the coming of Christianity, and reinforced humanity's sacred links with the universe. Sun Myung Moon, the Korean founder of the Unification Church, can be seen as the great link-man between the people and the spirit world.

HARVIE CONN

CHAPTER 24

Japanese Religions

A TAPESTRY OF TRADITIONS

Religion in Japan is a rich tapestry of diverse traditions, with a history of nearly 2000 years. Many Japanese people display some kind of allegiance to more than one religion: a person will usually be expected to have a Shinto wedding and a Buddhist funeral, though Buddhist and secular weddings are also possible.

Along with this may go a personal or family interest in a particular Buddhist denomination or practice, or membership of one of the various new religions, which attract almost a third of the population.

These different forms of religion have separate organizations, buildings, festivals, sacred writings, ministers or priests and so on. However, it should be remembered that the paths of these religions have touched at many points in Japanese history, and that they still meet in the lives of many Japanese people. For this reason, it is possible to speak both of 'Japanese religions' and of 'Japanese religion' – especially as the Japanese language itself does not usually distinguish between the singular and the plural.

LAND AND RELIGION

The general pattern of Japanese religion is, in some ways, a reflection of the country's geographical position and character. Japan has received a great deal from the Asian continent, almost entirely from or via Korea and China. The major imported religions are therefore Buddhism, mainly in its Mahayana form, and Confucianism. The influence of Taoism has been largely indirect, bearing partly on divination practices, and partly on the style of Zen Buddhism. It was in reaction to the powerful Buddhist and Confucian systems, with their scholarly prestige and political influence, that Japan's native Shinto faith first became clearly organized and defined. Indeed, the impact of Chinese, and then of Western, culture, and Japan's responses to these, provide the overall cultural perspective within which Japanese religion can be understood.

FOUR ISLANDS

The fact that the country consists mainly of four great islands, spread over a vast distance from north to south, has also had its effect:

1. **Honshu**

   The most famous historic Shinto shrines and Buddhist temples are found in the southern part of the main island, Honshu. Ancient Shinto shrines which are still of national importance are located at Ise, where the sun-goddess Amaterasu is revered, and where a new prime minister usually 'reports' on the formation of the cabinet, and at Izumo, where all the gods, or *kami*, of Japan are said to return once a year. Between these two sites are the former capitals, Nara and Kyoto, which themselves boast not only well-known Shinto shrines, such as the Kasuga Shrine at Nara, but also many fine Buddhist temples and images. The thirteenth-century sectarian development of Buddhism is reflected in the temple buildings and images at Kamakura, also on the main island of Honshu, but further east, near modern Tokyo.

2. **Shikoku**

   The smaller island of Shikoku has never been of political importance, and so lacks major religious monuments. But it does have a famous pilgrimage route, which takes in eighty-eight Buddhist temples. Today these are frequently visited by tourists, an example of the intimate link between holiday travel and religion in Japan today. Other pilgrimage routes are found in other parts of the country, the most famous being the thirty-three places in western Honshu, where the Bodhisattva Kannon-sama is revered.

3. **Hokkaido**

   The island of Hokkaido in the north was largely undeveloped until the nineteenth century. Today its people today practise the usual forms of Japanese religion.

4. **Kyushu**

   Kyushu, the southernmost major island, claims some of the oldest known historical sites in Japan, because of its proximity to Korea. Its importance as a maritime trading approach from the West meant it became the main base for Roman Catholic missions in the sixteenth century, and the scene of martyrdoms, especially at Nagasaki. Roman Catholic Christianity was suppressed partly because it was espoused by feudal lords in Kyushu who showed separatist tendencies. Kyushu was the geographical base for the Shinto-inspired reassertion of imperial power in the mid-nineteenth century, when the central military government in Edo (now Tokyo) came to the end of its two and a half centuries of undisturbed rule.

MOUNTAIN SHRINES

The mountainous terrain of the country has also had a major effect on the forms of Japanese religious life. Many mountains have shrines at their summit, and attract pilgrim groups seeking purification and heightened spiritual powers. The most famous is Mount Fuji itself, which is a quasi-religious symbol for the whole nation.

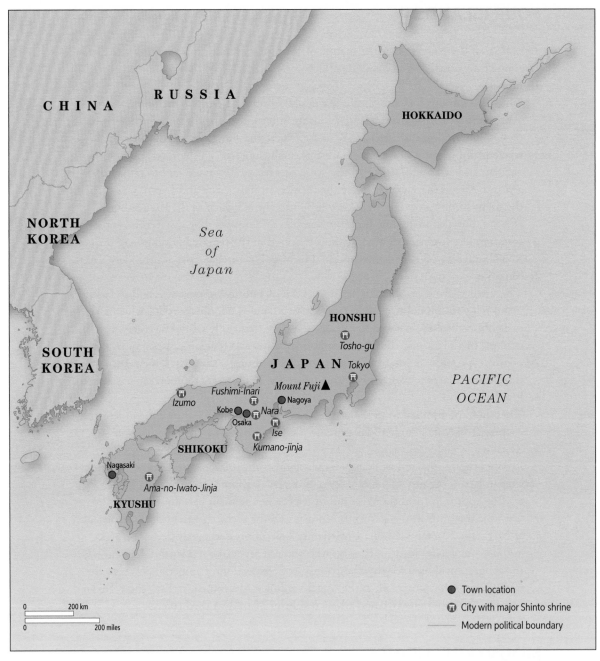

Major Japanese Shinto Shrines

A SHORT INTRODUCTION TO WORLD RELIGIONS

Buddhists had already used mountains in China as isolated retreats from the world, and this practice was carried over to Japan. The most famous example was Mount Koya, one of the leading headquarters of Shingon Buddhism (see below).

The mountain cult encouraged one of the most fascinating syncretistic movements in the history of religion, the Shugendo movement, which linked Buddhism and Shinto. This movement used ascetic exercises aiming at enlightenment in a quest for shamanic magical powers, performing spiritualist healing and fire-walking rites. It flourished in historical times, has by no means died out, and has had considerable influence on the formation of new religions.

SHINTO

Shinto is the name given to a wide conglomeration of religious practices with roots in prehistoric Japan. Little is known about Japanese religion before the emergence of a unified state in the Yamato period (fourth to seventh centuries ce), but in its simplest forms it was broadly animist, believing that a supernatural living force resided in natural objects such as mountains, trees, and animals.

The oldest literary works in Japan were composed on the basis of the combined myths and legends of the various clans that had been forged into political unity. The oldest of these official works is the *Kojiki* (712 CE), but this was soon replaced by the *Nihongi* (720 CE), or *Nihonshoki*. These two works retain to this day an honoured position in the minds of most Japanese people, and are considered especially important by the advocates of Shinto. However they are not recited – or even studied – by ordinary believers.

From the Yamato period onwards, the imperial household took a central position within Shinto. Its ancestry was traced back through legendary emperors and empresses as far as Ninigi, believed to have been the grandson of the sun-goddess Amaterasu. For this reason, the Ise Shrine has always had a close connection with the imperial household. From 1868 onwards, when the monarchy was restored to a central position in Japanese politics under Emperor Meiji (1852–1912), until the end of the Pacific War in 1945, the Shinto religion was focused sharply on the Ise Shrine and the emperor cult. After the war, the emperor's semi-divine status was officially denied and Shinto disestablished. Since then, religious teaching has no longer been given in state-run schools, and the observance of Shinto practices has become voluntary. Nevertheless, the imperial family still enjoys high esteem among the people, and leading Shinto shrines remain important symbols of Japanese nationhood.

SHINTO SHRINES

Shinto today is based fundamentally on each individual shrine. Although most shrines large enough to have an organizing staff are affiliated to the Association of Shinto Shrines, the majority of people who visit a shrine, or take part in a festival, are hardly aware of this.

Each shrine has some individual reason for its existence, whether a natural phenomenon, such as a mountain, a historical event of importance to the local community, or an act of personal devotion or political patronage. For example, the ancient shrine at Kashima, near the Pacific coast of Honshu, is patronized particularly by those devoted to the martial arts, such as swordsmanship and *kendo*. At the same time it has various sub-shrines within its grounds. One of these celebrates a spring of fresh water tumbling out of the side of a hill, and has its symbolic gate planted in the pool at the foot. Another is a fenced enclosure surrounding a mighty stone, of which only the rounded top is visible, sticking up through the sand. This stone is supposed to hold beneath the earth the giant catfish that is believed to be responsible for earthquakes.

The god, or *kami*, of a shrine may be the natural object itself, one of the divinities mentioned in the *Kojiki* or the *Nihongi*, or a legendary or historical person. In shrines where a specific object is kept in the inner sanctuary, it is usually not known what the object is, for nobody ever sees it.

Shinto shrines have certain common features that are almost always to be seen. The first of these is a large, symbolic gate, consisting of two uprights and two crossbars, marking the entrance to the shrine, called *torii*. Inside the precinct there is a large trough of clean water, usually sheltered with a roof, and provided with clean wooden ladles. Here the worshipper rinses face and hands, in a simple act of purification. The main shrine buildings consist of a worship hall (*haiden*), with a main hall (*honden*) standing behind. The main hall is usually smaller and is not entered, being the physical location of the *kami* itself.

The worship hall is entered from time to time by small groups for petitionary prayer. Individual visitors to the shrine stand outside, toss a coin into the offerings box, pull on a dangling rope with a bell or clanger at the top, clap their hands twice, bow briefly in prayer, clap their hands again, and leave. The sound of the clanger and the handclap are intended to alert the kami to the believer's presence. The front of the worship hall is often decorated with a thick rope (*shimenawa*) and folded white paper strips, which are used to designate a sacred area or sacred object. Sometimes these are strung around a rock or a tree, indicating that these too are considered as shrines for the *kami* of the rock or tree.

There are three main types of shrine:
1. Shrines of local significance, housing the *kami* of the locality (*ujigami*);
2. Shrines of a particular recurrent type, such as the Inari Shrines, which are visited with a view to winning business success, and can be found in any part of the country;
3. Shrines of national and semi-political importance, such as the Ise and Izumo Shrines mentioned earlier, the Meiji Shrine in Tokyo, honouring the former emperor Meiji, and the Yasukuni Shrine, also in Tokyo, commemorating the souls of Japan's war dead. Since the end of the Pacific War, the status of Ise Shrine, and of Yasukuni Shrine, has been a matter of some controversy, because critics fear a revival of Shinto-led nationalism.

Other types of shrine that recur throughout the country include the Hachimangu Shrines, dedicated to the *kami* of war and martial prowess; the Toshogu Shrines, sacred to the memory of the dictator-general Ieyasu (d. 1616), reflecting the colourful pomp of his mausoleum at Nikko; and the Tenmangu Shrines, where a loyal but wrongfully banished aristocrat is revered, and believers pray for success in literature and study.

SHINTO PRACTICE

Much of Shinto practice is an individual matter, as when a person simply visits a shrine to make his or her own request – before a journey, before an exam, before some new enterprise, or perhaps because they just happen to be passing. In such cases the form of worship is as described earlier. Family occasions also involve visits to the shrine. It is common, though not universal, to take a newborn baby there, so prayers can be said for its health. Shinto priests officiate at the majority of Japanese weddings, though these usually take place in a purpose-built hall, run on business lines, with reception rooms and other facilities.

Shrines are visited by large numbers at New Year, especially on 1 January, but also on 2 and 3 January. Some people go just after midnight on 31 December, while others go at dawn. Some visitors to mountain shrines make a point of observing the rising sun and bathing their faces in its first rays. At the New Year, there is a brisk sale of feathered wooden arrows (to drive off evil), protective charms, and stiff paper strips bearing the name and seal of the shrine (*fuda*). These are taken home and kept on the kami shelf or in a high place for the coming year. The previous year's accessories are taken back to the shrine at New Year to be burned.

Another personal charm sold in great numbers at this time of year is the papier-mâché *daruma* doll, originally a representation of the Zen Buddhist master Daruma (or *Bodhidharma*). Though Buddhist in origin, these dolls are on sale at the entrance to many shrines. Some Buddhist temples share in the New Year practices, encouraging a first visit on a specified day in January, selling various kinds of talisman, and offering prayers for safety in the home and in traffic, prosperity in business, and avoidance of bad luck.

SHINTO FESTIVALS

Perhaps the most important feature of Shinto practice is the festival (*matsuri*), the main occasion when a particular shrine takes on meaning for all its worshippers at once. A Shinto festival usually includes a procession, or a fair with stalls and side-shows, and so draws large numbers of people.

Festivals famous throughout Japan for their huge floats include the Gion Festival in Kyoto, the Takayama Festival in the Hida region, and the Chichibu Festival in the mountains north-west of Tokyo.

In many cases, the floats, or the standards and banners, are taken through the town by groups of young men wearing clothes representative of their part of the town. They are usually fortified with plenty of rice wine (*sake*), which is particularly associated with Shinto.

Sometimes the processions recall a historical event, such as a battle, in which case period costumes are worn. Often the focal point of a procession is a portable shrine (*mikoshi*), taken from the main shrine to various points in the locality, symbolizing a journey made by the *kami*. Not all of those taking part in a procession enter the worship hall of the main shrine; usually only representatives go inside with the priests to present offerings.

JAPANESE BUDDHISM

The history of Japanese Buddhism can be traced back to the early sixth century CE, when images and *sutras* (Buddhist scriptures) were sent from Korea. The first major act of patronage took place when Prince Shotoku, regent from 593–622 CE, established Buddhism as a national religion, linking it with Confucian ideals of morality and statecraft.

A stream of eminent monks brought more knowledge of the new religion from Korea and China, and the early traditions at the capital of Nara were superseded in 805 CE by a much bigger Buddhist establishment on Mount Hiei, overlooking the new capital of Kyoto. This new Buddhist centre drew its inspiration from the Chinese T'ien T'ai school, which came to be known in Japan as Tendai Buddhism.

This in turn was rapidly affected by the doctrines and practices of an esoteric form of Buddhism, not unlike that of Tibet. Almost immediately, a rival headquarters for this type of Buddhism was set up on the then almost inaccessible Mount Koya, some distance south of Kyoto. This school – Shingon Buddhism – was established by the famous monk Kukai (744–835), posthumously known as Kobo Daishi, and revered as a great saint.

The Tendai and Shingon sects were rapidly supplemented by others, partly drawing on trends in Chinese Buddhism, and partly resulting from Japanese innovation. The *Lotus Sutra* had already been of great importance in Tendai Buddhism, but Nichiren (1222–82) gave it a new centrality, and his interpretative writings provided the basis for a number of sects. Among these are some of the most influential lay Buddhist movements of modern times. Nichirenite sects share the recitation of the simple formula '*Nam(u) Myoho Renge Kyo*' ('Hail Wonderful Dharma Lotus Sutra'). In their various ways these sects all express significant themes in the tradition of Mahayana Buddhism, which spread from India across East Asia. While some people have a clear allegiance to one or other sect, especially in the case of the *nembutsu* sects and the Nichirenite sects, many features of popular devotion cut across sectarian distinctions.

Two of the most widely revered saviour figures are the Bodhisattvas Jizo-sama and Kannon-sama. Jizo-sama is believed to care especially for children, and for infants who die during childbirth or pregnancy. Kannon-sama (*Avalokiresvara* in Sanskrit) offers many kinds of protection and solace, and is found in many places, not least in the precincts of Soto Zen temples.

BUDDHISM IN THE HOME

Many families are reminded of Buddhism by the presence of a domestic Buddhist altar (*butsu-dan*). This usually contains a central Buddhist image or other symbol, tablets commemorating ancestors, a booklet with portions of Buddhist scriptures, a place for lighting incense, and various other accessories. As a morning devotion, a small offering of food may be placed on the altar, a passage recited from a *sutra*, and a stick of incense lit. Individual sects introduce many variations.

Buddhism is also particularly influential as the religion of funerals and cemeteries. Again, the different sects make slightly different provisions, though cremation and a stone memorial are universal. Thin wooden posts placed by visitors at the tombstone bear texts written in heavy black ink and reflecting the distinctive faith of the temple in question. Cemeteries are visited particularly at *higan*, at the spring and autumn equinoxes. The other main commemoration of the dead is in midsummer at *o-bon*, marked by outdoor fires and dancing.

BUDDHIST FESTIVALS

To some extent, Japanese Buddhism borrows the Shinto concept of festival (*matsuri*). In early April, for example, some Buddhist temples celebrate a flower festival centred on the commemoration of the Buddha's birthday on 8 April. A small standing statue of the infant Buddha is placed in a framework decorated with flowers, and worshippers anoint it with liquid from a bowl beneath.

Another well-known festival, climaxing at a Buddhist temple in Tokyo, is that of the forty-seven masterless Samurai (*ronin*). These forty-seven have been applauded for centuries, because they avenged the unjustly forced suicide of their master, and then committed suicide themselves, in one of the classic cases of premeditated ritual suicide (*hara-kiri*), carried out in connection with a feat inspired by loyalty. This theme is worked out in the well-known traditional drama *Chushingura*, regularly shown at the time of the festival in December. The festival itself consists of a procession re-enacting the arrival of the forty-seven Samurai at the temple to report the completion of their deed of vengeance. Following this, crowds of people light incense at their tombs.

Buddhism is linked to Japanese culture at many points: through the traditional way of the Samurai, generally known as *bushido*; through the austere *no* drama, with its many Buddhist themes; through the tea ceremony, which is intended to communicate simplicity and naturalness; through calligraphy and painting, and so on. The liveliest aspect of Japanese Buddhism, however, remains the popular faith directed towards the various Buddhas, Bodhisattvas, and saints of the Mahayana Buddhist tradition.

NEW RELIGIONS

Innovation is an accepted feature of Japanese religious life. Many Shinto shrines are the result of some fresh religious experience, or message from a medium, long since incorporated into the general pattern of Shinto. In some more recent cases such initiatives have led to the growth of separate religious bodies.

One of the best known of these is the Religion of the Heavenly Wisdom (*Tenrikyo*), founded in the early nineteenth century by Nakayama Miki (1798–1887). This religion began with her revelations and healings, but instead of merging into the wider pattern of Shinto, it formulated its own independent sacred writings, constructed its own sacred city named Tenri, and shaped its own forms of worship, including a special dance.

Another well-known example is the popularly named Dancing Religion (*Odoru Shukyo*), which also has the longer formal name of *Tensho Kotai Jingu Kyo*, incorporating alternative names for the goddess Amaterasu and the Ise Shrine. Its founder, Kitamura Sayo (1900–67), believed a *kami* was speaking through her abdomen, and these revelations are the basis of the religion's teaching. She also initiated a form of ecstatic dance that encourages believers to experience a state of not-self (*muga*), one of the 'three marks' of Buddhist teaching. The 'Teaching of the Great Source' (*Omotokyo*) is another major independent religious group, combining a Shinto background with belief in a new revelation of its own.

Other new religions have moved further from the traditional faiths of Japan. The Syncretic House of Growth (*Seicho no Ie*) claims to overcome disease and suffering through its new teachings propounded by Taniguchi Masaharu (1893–1985), a former *Omotokyo* member. The Church of World Messianity (*Sekai Kyuseikyo*) is also loosely derived from *Omotokyo*. Its leader, Okada Mokichi (1882–1955), preached freedom from disease and poverty, and his following grew rapidly after the Pacific War. PL Kyodan, which claims a membership of around two million, sees the whole of life as art, and religion as a means of realizing this vision in the member's experience. The 'PL' in its name stands for 'Perfect Liberty'.

NEW BUDDHIST MOVEMENTS

Japanese Buddhism also gives scope for innovation, since the proliferation of sects and independent temple organizations is accepted as a normal feature of religious life. It is hardly surprising that several of Japan's new religions are recently developed forms of Buddhism.

The most influential are those based on the *Lotus Sutra*, which together claim about one fifth of the population as adherents. Of these, the Reiyukai began as a movement caring for untended tombs, stressing the virtues of gratitude and loyalty towards ancestors.

Several groups split off from the Reiyukai, in a series of organizational and doctrinal disputes. Of these the largest is the Rissho Kosei-kai, claiming more than six million members, strongly influenced initially by the religious messages of Naganuma Myoko

(1899–1957). The dominant figure, however, was the founding president, Niwano Nikkyo (1906–99), who emphasized the exposition of the *Lotus Sutra* as the doctrinal basis of the movement. After taking over the leadership, his son Nichiko (b.1938) also emphasized political activities, such as anti-nuclear campaigns and the promotion of world peace. This is a lay movement, entirely independent of any previously existing monastic sect. The main emphasis is on a form of group counselling, in which the individual's problems are analyzed in Buddhist terms, though, of course, the *Lotus Sutra* is recited and studied too.

Also based on the Lotus Sutra, but with different doctrinal tendencies, is the lay movement commonly known as Soka Gakkai. This is linked with a monastic sect named Nichiren Shoshu, claiming a direct tradition back to Nichiren himself; the full name is Nichiren Shoshu Soka Gakkai. Members support one of Japan's larger political parties, the Komeito (Clean Government Party), founded under the stimulation of Soka Gakkai leaders, although legally distinct.

PRESENT AND FUTURE

The new religions draw in many ways on the wider religious culture of Japan, which is formed mainly by traditional Shinto and Buddhism, but is also influenced by Confucian ideas and values, and to a lesser extent by a Western-looking Christianity. Historically, Confucianism has provided the main moral backing for Shinto, emphasizing family duty and loyalty, and extending these concepts to school, industry, and state. Though Confucianism has no organization of any note, many religious bodies in Japan stress such values as loyalty or sincerity (*makoto*), gratitude, correctness of behaviour, and brightness of attitude.

Modern Christian missions have had little impact numerically or ideologically, but have had some unintentional influence on other Japanese religious bodies. A number of Buddhist sects now run Sunday schools, for example, and some of the new religions use books that look remarkably like Christian Bibles and prayer-books. Christianity has a total membership of less than 1 per cent of the population, probably because it is strongly identified with the West. Christian churches in Japan have only very tenuous links with the general religious culture of the country.

In spite of the startling success of several of the newer religious movements, it would be wrong to think Buddhism and Shinto have lost support. In some ways, particularly in politics and education, Japan has become remarkably secularized, and there is much ignorance about the deeper teachings of the religions. At the same time, most Japanese people are involved in various kinds of religious behaviour at certain times of the year and at the appropriate points in their lives.

MICHAEL PYE

QUESTIONS

1. How have the concepts of *yin* and *yang* influenced religion in China?

2. Is Confucianism a religion? Explain your answer.

3. Mencius or Hsün-tzu: who was more important in the development of Confucianism – and why?

4. How do Confucianism and the Taoist religion differ?

5. How have Confucianism, Buddhism, and Taoism influenced each other in China?

6. Why is ritual sacrifice important in Sinyo?

7. How has Confucianism influenced Sinkyo?

8. How has geography influenced the development of religion in Japan?

9. How has Buddhism shaped wider Japanese culture?

10. Why have elements of Shinto been controversial in recent decades?

FURTHER READING

Berthrong, John H., and Evelyn Nagai Berthrong, *Confucianism: An Introduction*. Oxford: Oneworld Publications, 2000.

Ching, Julia, *Chinese Religions*. London: Macmillan; Maryknoll, NY: Orbis, 1993.

Kohn, Livia, *Daoism and Chinese Culture*. Cambridge, MA: Three Pines Press, 2001.

Lopez, Donald S., Jr, ed., *Religions of China in Practice*. Princeton: Princeton University Press, 1996.

Miller, James, *Daoism: A Short Introduction*. Oxford: Oneworld Publications, 2003.

Oldstone-Moore, Jennifer, *Confucianism: Origins, Beliefs, Practices, Holy Texts, Sacred Places*. New York: Oxford University Press, 2002.

Yao, Xinzhong, *An Introduction to Confucianism*. Cambridge: Cambridge University Press, 2000.

Buswell, Robert, *Korean Religions in Practice*. Princeton: Princeton University Press, 2003.

Lee, Peter H., and Bary, William Theodore de, eds., *Sources of Korean Tradition*. New York: Columbia University Press, 1997.

Nelson, John, *Enduring Identities: The Guise of Shinto in Modern Japan*. Honolulu: University of Hawai'i Press, 2000.

Reader, Ian T., *Religion in Contemporary Japan*. Honolulu: University of Hawai'i Press, 1991.

Tanabe, George, Jr, ed., *Religions of Japan in Practice*. Princeton: Princeton University Press, 1999.

PART 6
JAINISM

SUMMARY

Jainism, like Hinduism and Buddhism, emerged from the Vedic culture of northern India, about the fifth century BCE, and is based around the teachings of Mahavira, whom Jains venerate as the twenty-fourth *jina* ('conquerer') of the last cosmic cycle. Jains hold that all living beings have a soul, and that these souls, undergoing a continuous cycle of death and rebirth, can only be liberated if the individual adopts the lifestyle of an extreme ascetic, in order to become omniscient, following the example of Mahavira himself. In the years after Mahavira's death, Jains broke into two main sects, Digambara and Shvetambara, which are divided by their views on scripture – Shvetambara Jains believe their canon descends directly from *The Twelve-limbed Basket*, the collection of Mahavira's teachings, while Digambara Jains believe this has been lost – and by the question whether there have been female *jinas*. Monasticism has an important role in Jainism, because of the value placed on asceticism, and the co-dependence of ascetics and the laity is central to the structure of traditional Jain society. Because of their belief that all living beings have souls, Jains are bound by a strict code of ethics, centred on the principle of non-violence, which forbids causing harm to any creature.

In the centuries after Mahavira's death, Jainism spread out through India, which remains its primary home to this day. Diaspora communities do exist, though these are small, and somewhat restricted by the absence of ascetics, who may travel only on foot. Alongside this, Jains – whether living in India or elsewhere – often have to compromise on some of the stricter ethical rules in order to live everyday lives in the modern world.

CHAPTER 25

A Historical Overview

Jainism originated in India, its name deriving from the term *jina* (conqueror). *Jinas* are also called *tirthankaras* — the terms are synonymous — meaning 'ford-makers'. The *jinas*, or *tirthankaras*, are religious teachers who, Jains believe, have attained enlightenment and omniscience by conquering *samsara*. Their state of omniscience means their teachings have indisputable authority, and can provide Jains with a crossing or ford — hence 'ford-maker' — from *samsara* to liberation.

Early in its history, Jainism split into two main sects: Digambara Jainism predominates in South India, Shvetambara in North-West India. Some scholars suggest the difference in beliefs and practices emerged gradually, the sects bifurcating after the Council of Valabhi, at Saurashtra, in the fifth century CE, during which the Shvetambara canon was fixed, in the absence of any Digambara representation. Today, Jainism has many different branches, most of them associated with either Digambara or Shvetambara Jainism.

THE *JINAS*

Twenty-four *jinas* are born and preach during the third and fourth phases of each half of the cosmic cycle. Jains of the Digambara sect believe all twenty-four *jinas* of the last cosmic cycle were men; Shvetambara Jains believe the nineteenth *jina*, Mallinath, was a woman. The twenty-fourth, and most recent, *jina* was called Mahavira. Jain tradition states that, just a few years after Mahavira's death, the cosmos entered the fifth phase of its regressive half-cycle, which will last for approximately 21,000 years. The first *jina* of the next group of twenty-four will not be born until the third phase of the next progressive cycle. Historians of religion sometimes associate Jainism's point of origin with the birth of Mahavira. Jains themselves subscribe to a timeless history, in which Mahavira is one of a perpetual cycle of spiritual masters. Textual evidence verifies Mahavira as a historical figure who was contemporary with the Buddha. Evidence also supports the historicity of the twenty-third *jina*, called Parshva, who lived in Varanasi about 250 years before Mahavira.

MAHAVIRA

Jain temple on Mount Shatrunjaya, near Palitana, 'City of Temples', Gujarat, India.

Mahavira lived towards the end of the Vedic period, when religious culture centred on rituals to preserve the health and prosperity of individuals, as well as cosmic equilibrium and political stability. Rituals, which sometimes involved animal sacrifice, were commissioned by high-caste householders, but performed by members of the priestly caste (Brahmans), who monopolized religious authority and had an important status in Indian society. From about the seventh century BCE, a number of 'renouncer' traditions (*shramana*) emerged. Breaking with Vedic culture, they shifted the emphasis of their religious practice from external ritual to renunciation and asceticism. Jainism and Buddhism are two examples.

Mahavira lived and preached near Patna, in the state of Bihar, and died aged seventy-two. Historians date his death at around 425 BCE; Digambara Jains believe he died in 510 BCE, Shvetambara Jains in 527 BCE. Jains celebrate five auspicious moments in Mahavira's life: his conception, birth, renunciation, enlightenment, and final spiritual liberation (*moksha*). These five auspicious events, which occur in the lives of each of the *jinas*, are thought to authenticate the *jina's* identity as a *jina*.

Mahavira's life story and teachings are recorded in Jain scriptures. The *Kalpasutra* describes how, after Mahavira's previous incarnation as a celestial being, Indra, the king of the gods, arranged for Mahavira to be transported to his mother's womb. Shvetambara Jainism tells how Mahavira was mistakenly delivered to a Brahman woman before reaching his

> On reaching the most excellent asoka tree, he [Mahavira] ordered his palanquin to be placed beneath it. Then he came out of the palanquin. Thereafter, with his own hand, he took off his wreaths, fineries, and ornaments. Having taken them off, he himself tonsured his head in five handfuls.
>
> *Kalpa Sutra*, trans. K. C. Lalwani
> (Motilal Banarsidass, 1999) verse 116

intended mother, Trisala, who was the wife of King Siddhartha. *Jinas* are always born into the caste of warriors and noblemen, in contrast to Vedic culture, in which holy men were always Brahmans. The impact of Mahavira's renunciation is enhanced by the luxurious lifestyle that he left. Trisala had a series of auspicious dreams during her pregnancy, which were interpreted as predictions that Mahavira would be a great political or spiritual leader.

Humans and gods rejoiced when Mahavira was born. Indra took the infant to Mount Meru, at the centre of the universe, where he was anointed and consecrated. Mahavira was originally named Vardhamana ('increasing'), because his family had prospered during his mother's pregnancy. Much later he was given the name Mahavira ('great hero') in recognition of the strict asceticism he practised as an adult. Shvetambara tradition recalls that, when Mahavira was a young man, he married Princess Yasoda, who bore him a daughter. Digambara tradition denies this: when Mahavira was thirty, the gods beseeched him to pursue his destiny as a *jina*. Heeding them, Mahavira was initiated as an ascetic, the gods officiating at the ceremony. As part of his initiation, Mahavira renounced all his possessions, and even pulled the hair from his head. Novice Jain ascetics still pull the hair from their heads during their initiation ceremonies.

For the rest of his life, Mahavira wandered homeless and without possessions. Digambara tradition states he was naked from the outset. Shvetambara tradition tells how his white robe caught on a bush, and Mahavira was too deep in contemplation to notice its disappearance. He depended on alms from villagers for sustenance, although the people he encountered often abused him. He practised non-violence, undertook extreme fasting, and meditated continually on the nature of the soul. After twelve and a half years, Mahavira attained enlightenment and omniscience.

Mahavira's enlightenment is a vital moment in Jain history, because it was from this point that his career as the twenty-fourth *jina* began. The assemblies (*samavasarana*) at which he preached are depicted frequently in Jain art. Mahavira took the central position, surrounded in concentric rings by his congregation, who consisted of gods, humans, and animals. Mahavira faced east, but so that the whole congregation could hear and see him, the gods replicated his image to face each cardinal point. According to Digambara Jainism, Mahavira's body emitted a divine sound (*divyadhvani*) during his sermons, which his disciples translated for the congregation.

During his life, Mahavira is believed to have established a Jain community of 36,000 nuns, 14,000 monks, 318,000 laywomen, and 159,000 laymen. His first disciples were three Brahman priests: Indrabhuti Gautama and his two brothers, Agnibhuti and Vayubhuti, who converted after Mahavira defeated them in debate. They were soon joined by a further eight Brahman converts, bringing the total of Mahavira's closest disciples to eleven. These eleven disciples had hundreds of disciples of their own, who also converted to Jainism. Mahavira's eleven closest disciples all attained enlightenment under his guidance.

ASCETIC AND LAY COMMUNITIES

Soon after Mahavira's death, the community of Jain ascetics began to branch into groups. Having taken a vow of non-possession, they depended for survival upon alms from a laity who shared their values of non-violence and vegetarianism, and lay communities probably developed in tandem quite early. Inscriptions describing donations by tradesmen and artisans date from the beginning of the Common Era. By the fifth century CE, alms-giving had escalated from food offerings into the construction of ascetics' dwelling-halls. By the eleventh century CE, numerous ascetic communities existed, each led by a religious teacher (*acharya*), and supported by a lay following. In Shvetambara Jainism, an *acharya's* religious authority was — and continues to be — authenticated by a lineage traced back to Mahavira's disciple, Sudharman.

> *Still in meditation, [Mahavira] attained the supreme knowledge and faith, kevala by name, unsurpassed unobstructed, unlimited, complete, and full.*
>
> *Then Sramana Bhagavan Mahavira became the venerable, victor, omniscient, all-knowing, all observing.*
>
> Kalpa Sutra verses 120 and 121.

THE SPREAD OF JAINISM IN INDIA

Jains soon began to migrate from the north-east to other regions in India, ascetics to uphold their vows as wandering mendicants, the laity to pursue mercantile opportunities. Some followed a western caravan route towards Delhi, Mathura, and finally Gujarat; others followed the southern caravan route towards Orissa, Chennai, and Mysore. Mathura was an important Jain centre for trade and culture from about 100 BCE to 100 CE, perhaps even earlier; an inscription dated 157 CE at a Jain shrine here implies the shrine was already of considerable antiquity by that date. By about the fourth century CE, pressure from the ruling Gupta Empire and international trading opportunities led some Jains to travel further west to Valabhi, which became an important centre of Shvetambara Jainism.

Jain presence in South India is confirmed from about the second century BCE by inscriptional evidence at Kalinga. Digambara Jainism continued to be a major religious and cultural influence in South India for almost a millennium. By the sixth century CE, Jains were largely divided by geography and sect: Shvetambara Jains in the west, Gujarat, Rajasthan, and Punjab; Digambara Jains in the south, Maharashtra, and Karnataka. Very few Jains remained near Mahavira's homeland in the north-east.

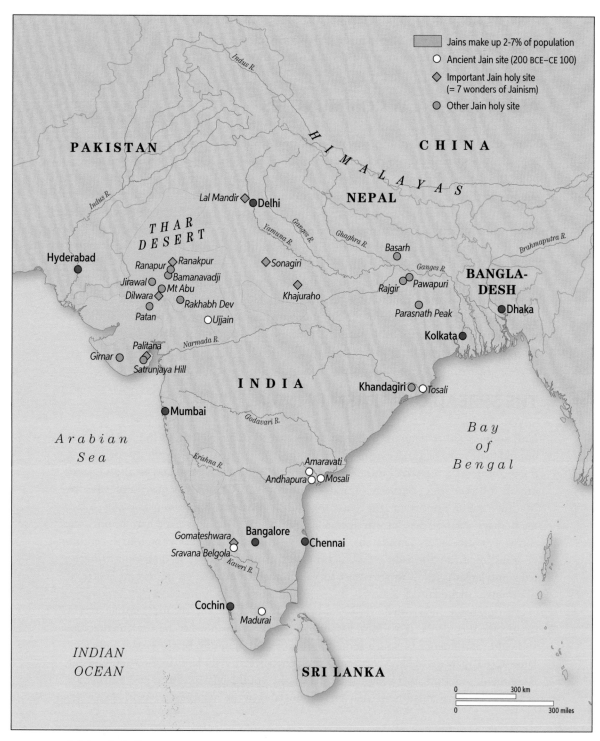

Jainism in India

Jains make up 2-7% of population

○ Ancient Jain site (200 BCE–CE 100)

◇ Important Jain holy site
(= 7 wonders of Jainism)

● Other Jain holy site

JAINISM TIMELINE

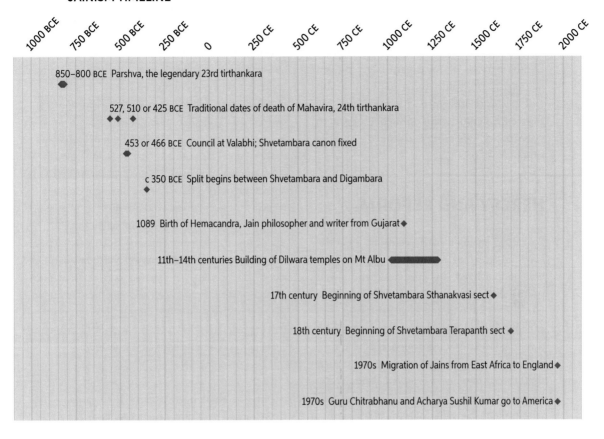

1000 BCE — 750 BCE — 500 BCE — 250 BCE — 0 — 250 CE — 500 CE — 750 CE — 1000 CE — 1250 CE — 1500 CE — 1750 CE — 2000 CE

850–800 BCE Parshva, the legendary 23rd tirthankara

527, 510 or 425 BCE Traditional dates of death of Mahavira, 24th tirthankara

453 or 466 BCE Council at Valabhi; Shvetambara canon fixed

c 350 BCE Split begins between Shvetambara and Digambara

1089 Birth of Hemacandra, Jain philosopher and writer from Gujarat

11th–14th centuries Building of Dilwara temples on Mt Albu

17th century Beginning of Shvetambara Sthanakvasi sect

18th century Beginning of Shvetambara Terapanth sect

1970s Migration of Jains from East Africa to England

1970s Guru Chitrabhanu and Acharya Sushil Kumar go to America

ROYAL PATRONAGE

The development of Jainism benefited from periods of royal support. King Srenika, who ruled in Bihar during the period that Mahavira preached, was sympathetic to Mahavira's message. The pro-Jain Nanda dynasty, followed by the Chandragupta Maurya dynasty, ruled in Bihar until the third century BCE. In Gujarat, King Vanaraja, who had been raised by a Shvetambara ascetic, established Jainism as the state religion from 746 CE to 806. Jain ascetics sometimes forged links with royal patrons, such allegiances affording protection to Jain communities, and helping to promote Jainism. Acharya Hemachandra (1087–1172) was court scholar to Jayasimha Siddharaja, King of Gujarat (1092–1141), and to Siddharaja's heir, Kumarpala, who ruled until 1165. With Hemachandra at his side, Kumarpala employed Jain values in the running of his kingdom. He took Jain lay vows, practised vegetarianism, outlawed animal slaughter, and erected Jain temples – for example, at Taranga Hill, in Gujarat.

Digambara Jains in South India enjoyed almost seven centuries of political stability, under the rule of the Ganga dynasty in Karnataka, which came to power in 265 CE, with the assistance of a powerful ascetic called Simhanandi. Two other southern dynasties that supported Jainism were the Rashtrakutas in the Deccan, between the eighth and twelfth centuries CE, and the Hoysalas in Karnataka, between the twelfth and fourteenth centuries. During periods of royal patronage, Jainism in North and South India grew in wealth and political influence. However, by the thirteenth century, this influence began to wane, under increasing Muslim rule and the Hindu *bhakti* movement.

HERESY AND REFORM

By about the fourth century CE, the spiritual ideal of wandering Jain ascetics was jeopardized by ascetics who lived permanently in monasteries. In Shvetambara Jainism these sedentary mendicants were called *caityavasi* (temple-dwellers). Temple-dwelling ascetics questioned the religious validity of perpetual wandering, and argued that their presence preserved Jainism, by keeping Jain temples active. However, their behaviour was challenged by reformed Jains, who upheld the value of non-possession, and who regarded sedentary mendicants as lax and irreligious. In 1024 a reformed ascetic called Jinesvara Suri defeated in debate a temple-dwelling ascetic at the royal court in Patan, Gujarat. During the mid-fifteenth century, a famous layman from Gujarat called Lonka Shah established the Lonka Gaccha. These Jains sought to return to Mahavira's teachings, which, according to Lonka Shah's interpretation, meant no *caityavasi,* and no use of temples and images during worship.

During the twelfth century, an institution of clerics developed within Digambara Jainism. *Bhattarakas* ('venerable ones') underwent minimal ascetic initiation. They managed temple ritual and temple-dwelling ascetics, supervised vow-taking by the laity, maintained libraries, and oversaw lay religious education. *Bhattarakas* also acted as emissaries between Jain communities and other religious and political authorities, and, in this role, often wielded significant political influence. *Bhattarakas* are credited with negotiating political protection for Jains, and for promoting Jainism through the spread of education and publications. However, as an institution, *bhattarakas* are regarded retrospectively as an emblem of spiritual decline in Jainism, because their claim to religious authority was not verified by the moral authority of ascetic renunciation. By the early twentieth century, most of the thirty-six *bhattaraka* seats in India had become obsolete.

EMMA SALTER

LEADERS AND ENLIGHTENMENT

Indrabhuti Gautama and Sudharman were the only two of Mahavira's eleven closest disciples to survive him. Tradition tells how Indrabhuti Gautama's enlightenment was obstructed by his supreme attachment to Mahavira. He was initially distraught by Mahavira's death, but his passion ceased within a few hours, when he realized the truth of Mahavira's *moksha,* and he became enlightened too. Jains celebrate the combined events of Mahavira's *moksha* and Indrabhuti Gautama's enlightenment during a festival in November called Dipavali.

Sudharman led the ascetic community, until he too achieved enlightenment and was succeeded by his disciple Jambu, who also attained enlightenment. Early in the Common Era, Jains started to believe that, since Jambu, enlightenment was no longer possible during the current cosmic era. This protects Jainism's claim that its spiritual leaders were omniscient, because no living person's omniscience can be tested.

CHAPTER 26

Sacred Writings

Jain sacred writings are not a tidy affair. Jainism has no single textual equivalent to, for example, the Christian Bible. Throughout Jainism's history, a variety of religious texts has become regarded as sacred: some are ancient texts, but many reflect the teachings of relatively recent saints. In Jainism, the sacredness of a text is not judged necessarily by its antiquity, but by the religious value of its content, and by its use during worship. Jains may regard as sacred writings both an ancient scripture written by an illustrious ascetic, and a nineteenth-century hymn written by a pious layman.

ANCIENT SCRIPTURES

It is not known when ancient Jain scriptures (*agamas*) were first written down. Jainism's ancient scriptural tradition began orally. Each of Mahavira's disciples is said to have compiled an oral recension of Mahavira's teachings, known collectively as the *Twelve-limbed Basket*. Early texts were written in Ardhamagadhi, a form of Prakrit, and later in Sanskrit. The current extant Jain canon was not written by a single person at a single point in history, although it is accepted by Jains as a reflection of Mahavira's teachings.

Digambara and Shvetambara Jainism do not refer to the same canon. Shvetambara Jains believe their scriptures descend directly from the *Twelve-limbed Basket*, whereas Digambara Jains believe this early literature to have been lost by the second century CE, and therefore question the authority of the Shvetambara canon. Nevertheless, some Digambara ascetics accept the authority of some Shvetambara scriptures. Possibly the migration to South India dislocated Digambara Jains from their early scriptural tradition, though some scholars suspect their rejection of Shvetambara scripture was a strategy to establish a clear division between the two sects. Evidence suggests that both scriptural traditions have the same roots.

THE DIGAMBARA CANON

The oldest text accepted by Digambara Jainism is the *Scripture of Six Parts*, which originated with the recollections of the ascetic Dharasena, who lived during the second century CE. Soon after, another ascetic, Gunabhadra, composed the *Treatise on the Passions*. These are the only two texts Digambara Jains accept as belonging to the ancient scriptural tradition; both discuss the nature of the soul and its liberation from *samsara*.

Over the centuries texts written by revered Digambara ascetics have been collated into a corpus of literature that has acquired canonical status. This is organized into four groups, known as the *Expositions*:

1. One of the most famous texts in the first group is the *Universal History*, which describes among other things the origins of Jainism and society, and the lives of Mahavira and the other *jinas*. The *Universal History* was written during the eighth century by an ascetic called Jinasena and his pupil Gunabhadra. Shvetambara Jainism has its own version of the *Universal History*.
2. The second exposition includes texts about cosmology.
3. The third exposition includes texts about codes of behaviour for ascetic and lay Jains. Some of the most important texts in this group were composed by a famous Digambara *acharya* called Kundakunda, whom some historians place in the eighth century CE, although Digambara tradition places him several centuries earlier.
4. The fourth exposition includes a broad range of metaphysical works and devotional hymns.

THE SHVETAMBARA CANON

The Shvetambara canon was formed during three councils at which senior Shvetambara ascetics — but no Digambara ascetics — recited what they could remember of the oral tradition, and their recollections were recorded and collated into textual scripture. The first council was held in Patna, 160 years after Mahavira's death; the second, 827 years after his death, was held simultaneously at Mathura, in the north, and at Valabhi, in the west. This led to some discrepancies, but Shvetambara Jains generally accepted the Mathura version as the first official canon. The third council, at which the Shvetambara canon was finally closed, was held at Valabhi, during the first half of the fifth century. The problem for scholars attempting to reconstruct the early Shvetambara canon is that no lists of the texts accepted at any of these councils remain.

The Shvetambara canon is organized into three groups:

1. The *Purva*, the tradition of lost scripture that Digambara and Shvetambara Jains accept as authoritative.
2. The *Twelve Limbs*, of which the twelfth text is lost.
3. A group divided into five categories of subsidiary texts that originate not with Mahavira's disciples, but with later ascetic teachers.

This is a broad and inclusive outline of the Shvetambara canon; not all Shvetambara Jains accept all these texts as authoritative. For example, two branches of Shvetambara Jainism, Sthanakvasi Jains and Terapanthi Jains, reject texts that advocate image worship.

TATTVARTHASUTRA

One important text accepted by both Digambara and Shvetambara Jainism is the *Tattvarthasutra*, written during the

Mahavira Temple, Osian, near Jodhpur, India.

fourth or fifth century CE by the ascetic Umasvati, about whom little is known, although Digambara and Shvetambara Jains both claim he belonged to their sect. The *Tattvarthasutra* was the first significant Jain text to be written in Sanskrit, and the first to organize the main aspects of Jain doctrine into a single volume. The opening verse of the *Tattvarthasutra* identifies the essence of Jain doctrine as correct faith, correct knowledge, and correct conduct – a triad that became known as 'the three jewels of Jainism'.

ATTITUDES TO SCRIPTURE

Historically, only ascetics were allowed to study scripture. Laypeople were precluded, because they couldn't read the non-vernacular language of the texts, and because scriptural study without the qualification of ascetic rigour was considered dangerous. The laity

> *The enlightened world-view, enlightened knowledge, and enlightened conduct are the path to liberation.*
>
> Umasvati, *That Which Is (Tattvartha)*, trans. Nathmal Tatia (HarperCollins, 1994) verse 1.1.

encountered sacred literature at religious lectures delivered by ascetics, and through their devotional practices. Partly as a result of this, Jainism lays claim to a substantial quantity of devotional texts written by laypeople in their vernacular languages. More recently, attitudes have changed, and edited editions of some sacred Jain texts have been published, which has widened access for lay Jains and non-Jains. However, a vast corpus of sacred literature remains the exclusive domain of ascetic communities.

EMMA SALTER

CHAPTER 27

Beliefs

Much of Jain doctrine is concerned with the nature of the soul, and its liberation from bondage. Every living being has a soul that is trapped in *samsara*, the continuous cycle of birth, death, and rebirth that binds a soul to its worldly existence. A soul bound in *samsara* is believed to be suffering, even if the body in which it is incarnated enjoys a happy life, because bound souls are unaware of their true nature, which is omniscience and absolute bliss. Omniscience is pure and simultaneous knowledge of all things. Once a soul becomes fully aware of its true nature, it is released from *samsara* and becomes a liberated soul – *arhat* or *kevalin* – that endures no more incarnations, and suffers no further worldly entrapment. The *jinas* were *arhats* who were distinguished by their vital roles as religious teachers.

When the physical body in which a liberated soul is incarnated dies, the liberated soul attains *moksha*, a state of absolute purity and perfection, and is called *siddha*. *Siddhas* do not have physical bodies; they reside at the topmost part of the universe, where they exist in a constant state of omniscience and bliss, and have no further dealings with mundane, worldly affairs. The soteriological goal of Jainism is to attain *moksha* and become *siddha*.

BONDAGE

Souls are trapped in *samsara* because of the effects of *karma*. In Jainism, *karma* is believed to be physical matter that permeates the entire universe, but which is so fine that it is imperceptible. Under certain conditions, *karma* 'sticks' to the soul, and obscures the

> *The five causes of bondage are: deluded world-view, non-abstinence, laxity, passions, and the actions of the body, speech, and mind. Because of its passions, the soul attracts and assimilates the material particles of karmic bondage. The result is bondage.*
>
> Tattvarthasutra verses 8.1 to 8.3

soul's knowledge of its true, pure nature, as dust on a mirror prevents the mirror from giving a clear reflection. A soul generates energy by motivating the body to perform mental, verbal, or physical actions, and this energy attracts free-floating *karma* towards the soul.

Karma is unable to stick to the soul of its own accord. For this to happen, *kashaya* – which translates loosely as 'passion', and includes feelings of anger, pride, deception, and greed – needs to be present. The soul produces *kashaya* in response to attachment, of which there are two types: attraction to an event or thing, and aversion to an event or thing. Eventually *karma* 'stuck' to the soul matures and produces an effect – a mental, verbal, or physical action, usually reflecting the activity by which it was attracted – before falling naturally away. This is why Jains sometimes refer to the circumstances of peoples' lives as resulting from their *karma*.

Karma sometimes produces unpleasant results, sometimes pleasing results, but – as all *karma* traps the soul in *samsara* – it is anomalous to describe any *karma* as 'good'. The action *karma* induces the soul to take generates energy that attracts more *karma* towards the soul. The soul's response of attraction, or aversion, to the action causes more *karma* to stick to the soul, and so the cycle continues. Thus, *karma* traps the soul in *samsara* because it deludes it of its own pure nature, and entangles it in a perpetual cycle of action and reaction. A soul has to be reincarnated over and over again, to expel the *karma* it has accrued, whilst at the same time continuing to accrue more *karma*. The type of *karma* accrued determines the soul's next incarnation.

LIBERATION

Jains state that the binding effect of *karma* is not the same as predestination – in which a person has no free will to affect the events of her or his life – because the soul is an intellectual force that exerts free will by the way it chooses to respond to life's events. Jains aim to control the type and quantity of *karma* attracted to their soul through their religious practices. Strategies for overcoming the mechanism of bondage therefore provide a moral framework for Jains to live by.

Jains do not depend upon an external figure of salvation, but have to take personal responsibility for their own liberation. Mahavira's teachings describe *how* Jains can cleanse their souls of *karma*, but Mahavira cannot undertake the process *for* them. The path of religious practice leading to liberation, *moksha marg*, is charted by the *gunasthanas*, fourteen stages of purity through which a soul has to pass on its way to *moksha*:

- The fourth stage is a vital turning point in a Jain's spiritual journey, because at this stage a Jain experiences *samyak darshana*, true insight. Jains interpret the experience of *samyak darshana* differently: for some, it is a deep personal commitment to their religion, for others, religious commitment coupled with a spiritual experience of communion with their soul.
- The *anuvratas* (lay vows) are taken at the fifth *gunasthana*, and the *mahavratas* (ascetic vows) at the sixth *gunasthana*. Jains believe only ascetics can attain liberation. Shvetambara Jains believe women ascetics can attain liberation, whereas Digambara Jains believe liberation can be achieved only by men.
- At the thirteenth *gunasthana*, all deluding *karma* is finally dispelled, and the soul attains omniscience.
- At the moment of death, all *karma* associated with embodiment is exhausted, and the liberated soul attains *moksha*. This is the fourteenth *gunasthana*.

Jains believe that, in this part of the universe, and during the current cosmic era, it is not possible to progress beyond the seventh *gunasthana*.

GOD AND DIVINITY

Jains do not believe in a creator-God, so Jainism is sometimes described as atheistic. This is a misrepresentation. In Jainism, liberated souls are venerated as divine being, and it is these — and most specifically the *jinas* — whom Jains worship. The hierarchy of beings worthy of veneration is expressed in the *Panch Namaskara Mantra*:

> *I bow before the* arhats
> *I bow before the* siddhas
> *I bow before* acharyas
> *I bow before ascetic teachers*
> *I bow before all ascetics*
> *This fivefold salutation*
> *Which destroys all sin*
> *Is pre-eminent as the most auspicious of all auspicious things.*

adapted from P. S. Jaini, *The Jaina Path of Purification*

The recital of this, the most popular and widely used mantra in Jainism, is incorporated into most patterns of worship, and is accepted, with small variations, by all Jain sects. The *arhats* — embodied, liberated beings — are the first to receive veneration, because they perpetuate Jain teachings. *Siddhas* have attained *moksha*, and so no longer engage in worldly affairs.

THE SOUL

Physical bodies consist of matter: they cannot act, think, or respond to the world, unless 'inhabited' by a soul, which is their sentient force. The soul is the only type of substance in the universe that has the capacity for consciousness — which is its fundamental quality. Two other qualities of the soul are energy and bliss. Only liberated souls can fully experience bliss.

Jains believe all living beings have a soul. They also believe the entire universe is permeated by infinite, minute, life monads that exist alongside more substantial life forms, such as plants, animals, humans, celestial beings, and hell beings. When a living being dies, its soul is immediately reincarnated into another body, although not necessarily of the same type. For example, a human being may not necessarily be reincarnated as another

> *Morality is perfect forgiveness, humility, straightforwardness, purity (freedom from greed), truthfulness, self-restraint, austerity, renunciation, detachment, and continence.*
>
> *Tattvarthasutra* verse 9.6

human being. Although souls are not material, they expand or shrink, to fit precisely the size and shape of their current corporeal form. Just as the light from a lamp will fill different size rooms, so a soul will fill different size bodies.

Souls are eternal, which means they can be neither created nor destroyed, and every soul is likely to have experienced every conceivable embodiment, millions of times over. Jains therefore generally adopt an attitude of respect to all living beings, in the belief that one may have been similarly incarnated in a previous life, and that most beings have the potential of becoming *siddha* in a future incarnation. Jains believe all living beings – no matter how small – have the capacity for suffering, because all living beings have a soul, and are therefore conscious. Causing harm to another soul is believed to generate an influx of *karma* to one's own soul. For this reason, Jains take great lengths to avoid harmful behaviour. Non-violence is Jainism's principal ethical value, and the emphasis Jains give to it has earned them a reputation for compassion and tolerance. Their commitment to non-violence, combined with their belief in the ubiquity of life, has resulted in many of Jainism's characteristic religious practices, such as vegetarianism. Jainism's doctrine of non-violence is said to have inspired Mahatma Gandhi in his peaceful protest for India's freedom from British rule.

COSMOLOGY

Jains believe the cosmos is uncreated and eternal. It is dualistic, consisting of consciousness, determined by the presence of souls, and that which is not conscious, which includes both matter and aspects that are neither material nor conscious, for example, space, time, motion, and non-motion.

Matter has shape, colour, taste, smell, and density. From a philosophical perspective, Jainism regards matter as both permanent and temporary. It is permanent, because the physical atoms that make up material substances are constant so can be neither created nor destroyed; at the same time it is temporary, because substances with particular qualities and modes are formed when atoms combine, but when the combined atoms dissipate, the substance they have formed is destroyed. Atoms then rejoin in different combinations, to form new substances, with different qualities and modes.

The Jain cosmos is finite in size, but vast beyond human imaginings. Its shape is sometimes described as two drums balanced on top of each other, or as a human figure, standing legs apart and hands on hips. At the base of the cosmos are seven realms of hell, inhabited by hell beings who suffer hideous tortures, as a result of the bad *karma* they have accrued during previous incarnations. Above the seven realms of hell is a middle realm, *madhya loka*, the smallest cosmic realm, and the domain of human habitation. Above *madhya loka* are seven celestial realms, inhabited by celestial beings who live in great luxury and splendour, as a result of the meritorious *karma* they have accrued during previous incarnations. At the very top of the cosmos is *siddha loka*, also known as *isatpragbhara* – 'the slightly curving place' – where liberated souls, free from *karma*, reside in a state of *moksha*.

From a soteriological perspective, *madhya loka* is the most significant cosmic realm, because it is where humans live. Liberation is only possible from a human incarnation, and then only as an ascetic. *Madhya loka* undergoes perpetual cyclical phases, like a wheel constantly rotating. There are six phases of ascent, during which *madhya loka* becomes increasingly more spiritual and human suffering decreases, followed by six phases of descent, during which spiritual purity declines and suffering increases. Twenty-four *jinas* are born and preach in *madhya loka* during the third and fourth phases of each half cycle. It is only possible to attain *moksha* during these phases, because during the other phases society is either in such a state of suffering that it cannot accept the possibility of liberation, or in such a state of contentment that it cannot accept the necessity for liberation. Jains believe our world entered the fifth phase of the descending cycle soon after Mahavira's death. Only one region in *madhya loka* – called *mahavideha*– is immune to the cycle of ascent and descent. Here a *jina* – currently

Pilgrim entering an ancient marble Jain temple, Ranakpur, Rajasthan, India.

Simadhar Svami – is always preaching, so *moksha* can be attained at any time. The structure and mechanism of the cosmos explains why liberation is not currently possible in our world, but encourages religious effort, by the opportunity of rebirth in *mahavideha*.

EMMA SALTER

CHAPTER 28

Worship and Festivals

In Jainism, worship is directed towards ascetics, because their commitment to renunciation and non-violence is thought to represent the religious ideal taught by Mahavira and the other *jinas*. Lay Jains venerate ascetics, and ascetics venerate their superiors. The *Panch Namaskara Mantra*, which is recited by ascetic and lay Jains, venerates all ascetics, from the novice to the liberated soul. Ascetics are believed to have progressed further along the path of liberation — *moksha marg* — than lay Jains, and therefore to have attained a higher level of spiritual purity.

Whenever a lay Jain meets an ascetic, whether at a public sermon or private interview, she or he performs a rite of veneration, *guru-vandan*, bowing twice to the ground before the ascetic, and reciting a short prayer of veneration. Often the ascetic will then offer a blessing. Devout Jains visit ascetics' lodgings daily to perform *guru-vandan*. Theoretically, lay Jains do not personalize their veneration towards one particular ascetic, because all Jain ascetics are equal representatives of Jainism's religious ideal; in practice, they sometimes revere a particular ascetic as their special guru.

VENERATION OF THE *JINAS*

The twenty-four *jinas* were perfect, liberated ascetics, who taught the path of liberation, and attained *moksha*, and are thus the principal focus of worship. Jains worship the *jinas* during rituals called *puja*, and also express their veneration of them in a rich tradition of devotional songs.

Shvetambara Jains of the Terapanthi and Sthanakvasi sects, and Digambara Jains of the Taranapanthi sect, do not use images of the *jinas* during worship, as they do not believe the practice to have been sanctioned by the *jinas*. Ascetic and lay Jains who belong to these sects perform their worship in plain halls, usually attached to the ascetics' lodgings, venerating the *jinas* through *mantra* chanting, meditation, and scriptural study. If available, a senior ascetic teacher may provide a focal point; otherwise a scriptural text may be used as a substitute. In either case, it is the *jinas'* teachings that are the focus of veneration.

Other Shvetambara and Digambara sects use images of the *jinas* during their worship. Usually crafted in marble or metal, they depict the twenty-four *jinas* as identical to each

other; with robust male physiques, broad shoulders, and narrow waists — always meditating, either sitting or standing. A symbol carved at the base

Stone statue of an elephant outside the ancient Jain temple of Indra Sabha, carved out of solid rock, at Ellora Caves, near Auranabad, India, between the fifth and tenth century CE.

of each image identifies which *jina* it represents: for example, images of Mahavira are identified by a lion, whilst images of Parshvana — the twenty-third *jina* — have a canopy of cobra hoods. Digambara images are plain and naked, depicting the *jinas* in their ascetic role; Shvetambara images depict the *jinas* as nobility, before they became ascetics, and so are bejewelled, dressed in royal regalia, and adorned with gold or silver crowns. A Digambara or Shvetambara temple is often very ornate and beautiful, and usually dedicated to a single *jina*, an image of whom is the focal point. Large temples may also house images of other *jinas* and associated deities.

Most ritual worship in the temple is non-congregational. One simple ritual — *darshan* — involves gazing upon the image of a *jina* with a feeling of devotion and humility. Another ritual — *aarti* — is usually performed in the evening, and involves placing five small candles — representing five different types of knowledge — on a special tray. Worshippers then wave the tray in clockwise, circular motions before the image, while singing devotional hymns. Another ritual many Jains perform daily is the '*puja* of eight substances'.

As liberated beings, who have transcended worldly affairs, the *jinas* take no reciprocal role during worship. Worship does not appease them, nor do they respond to it by granting favours. Despite this, Jains feel immense love and devotion towards the *jinas*. The most important aspect of Jain worship is the devotional sentiment of the worshipper, regardless of ritual patterns, and whether or not an image is present. For this reason, Jains have to perform their own worship; no one else can do it on their behalf. Substances used during rituals are not offerings from the worshipper to the *jinas*, who have no use for them, but gestures of renunciation on the part of the worshipper. This is one reason why ascetics cannot perform temple rituals; they own nothing, and therefore have nothing to renounce.

FESTIVALS

Festivals are a time when lay Jains worship collectively, and often lay and ascetic communities come together. Most Jain festivals celebrate an aspect of the lives of the *jinas*: for example, *Mahavira Jayanti* in March/April celebrates Mahavira's birthday. Jains share some festivals with Hindus, and in mid-October celebrate *Diwali*. For Jains, however, *Diwali* signals the start of a new ritual and commercial year ,and celebrates Mahavira's transcendence to *moksha* and the enlightenment of his disciple Gautama.

PARYUSHAN

Paryushan ('abiding') is an important Shvetambara festival, closing the old year. It occurs in August/September, and lasts for eight days. Jains may attend the temple more often than usual, and some observe fasts, ending in a celebratory feast on the last

THE PUJA OF EIGHT SUBSTANCES

This ritual varies slightly between Jain communities, and is usually performed in the morning after bathing.

- Upon entering the temple, the worshipper bows before the *jina* image, while saying *nisihi* ('abandonment'), signifying that she or he has left the mundane world and entered the sanctity of the temple.
- The worshipper then circumambulates the image three times clockwise.
- Shvetambara Jains anoint the image with milk mixed with water, and, while reciting special prayers, use the third finger of their right hand to apply camphor and sandalwood paste to nine parts of the image in the following order: left and right big toes, right and left knees, right and left wrists, right and left shoulders, crown, forehead, throat, chest, and navel. Digambara Jains do not touch their *jina* images, so for this part of the ritual they sit before the image, pouring water – or a mixture of milk and water – from one vessel into another, and reciting prayers.
- Shvetambaras and Digambaras place a fresh flower by the image, and, in a circular motion, waft incense, followed by a camphor lamp.
- The worshipper then performs a joyous dance before the image, while waving a yak-tail fan.
- Next, the reflection of the *jina's* image is observed in a hand-held mirror.
- The worshipper then places a handful of dry rice on a special plate, forming it into the shape of a swastika, representing four possible incarnations: human, animal, celestial being, or hell being. Some food – usually sweets, fruit, or nuts – and sometimes a small amount of money, is placed on top of the rice swastika.
- At the end of the ritual, the worshipper says *nisihi* again, perhaps spends some time in spiritual contemplation, and usually sounds a bell upon departure.

> *The observer of vows should cultivate friendliness towards all living beings, delight in the distinction and honour of others, compassion for miserable, lowly creatures and equanimity towards the vainglorious.*
>
> *Tattvarthasutra* by Umasvati chapter 7 verse 6.

day of the festival. Fasting is an important and frequently performed religious practice amongst Jain laity. It is usually women who fast, men often claim to be restricted by their professional obligations. In addition to spiritual benefits, the completion of an arduous fast may improve the social prestige of the family of the person fasting. Pious lay Jains may stay at the mendicants' lodgings, having taken temporary vows of asceticism, and others make a pilgrimage to a holy site, such as Mount Shatrunjaya, in Gujarat, or Shravana Belagola, in Karnataka.

Ascetics deliver sermons daily for the first three days of *Paryushan,* and twice daily for the remaining five days. On the fourth to seventh days, this involves a public reading of the *Kalpasutra,* the Shvetambara scripture containing histories of the twenty-four *jinas.* The description of Mahavira's birth, on the second day of the reading, is accompanied by an elaborate ritual and great celebration.

On the final day, Jains perform *pratikraman,* a congregational ritual that is a communal statement of atonement and repentance for any harmful actions that may have been committed during the year. For more pious Jains, *pratikraman* is also a daily practice. At the end of *Paryushan,* many Jains send cards or emails to relatives and friends, seeking forgiveness for any wrong-doing. A devout Jain carries no grudge or quarrel over into the new year.

The equivalent Digambara festival is called *Dashalakshanaparvan* ('Festival of Ten Religious Qualities') and lasts ten days. The ten chapters of the *Tattvarthasutra* are recited publicly, with laypeople taking an active role, as there are relatively few Digambara ascetics. Towards the end of the festival, a special *puja* with flowers is performed to Ananta, the fourteenth *jina.* On the last day, rites of atonement are performed, similar to those of *Paryushan.*

ASCETIC PRACTICES

By taking ascetic initiation, a Jain dedicates her or his life to spiritual progression. The vows of renunciation ascetics take mean they no longer have a secular role in society; their worldly possessions are replaced with those things necessary for their ascetic lifestyle. For Digambara ascetics, this is a broom made from naturally shed peacock feathers and a water pot. They do not wear robes; *Digambara* literally meaning 'sky-clad', that is, naked. It is socially unacceptable for women to be 'sky-clad', which is one reason Digambaras – unlike Shvetambaras – do not accept that women can attain liberation. Shvetambara ascetics receive a set of simple white robes, a bowl for collecting alms, and a broom made from naturally shed cow-tail hair. As well as relinquishing worldly possessions, renunciation also means giving up anything that may be pleasing to the senses, such as tasty food, or comfortable living quarters.

Of the five ascetic vows, the most famous is commitment to non-violence: not harming any creature — however small or seemingly insignificant — by action, speech, or thought, and not condoning such actions by others. Ascetics use their broom to sweep gently the ground before them free from insects, so they do not tread on them. During the rainy season, they do not travel, because the risk of harming creatures is too great. Terapanthi and Sthanakvasi Shvetambaras wear cloth mouthshields, to protect tiny airborne creatures from being harmed by their breath. During alms collection, donations are accepted only if they meet the ascetics' strict ethical requirements, food being inspected for insects and other impurities prior to consumption. Collecting or eating alms after dark is prohibited, because cooking-fires may lure insects to their deaths. Jain commitment to non-violence also includes honesty, respect, and compassion towards others.

Ascetic practices, which can be internal or external, are believed to 'burn off'

Ceiling of the marble Jain temple at Ranakpur, Rajasthan, India, dedicated to Adinatha.

karma already attached to the soul. Internal practices develop spirituality, and are met by the six obligatory actions. External practices involve enduring physical hardships. The most frequently performed is fasting, which includes total abstinence from food for a designated period, reduction — for example, eating every other day — or denial of certain types of food. The most dramatic form is *sallekhana* (elective fasting until death). The ascetic meditates throughout, to maintain a state of equanimity, which is believed to result in a meritorious rebirth. Ascetics are permitted to perform *sallekhana* only if they are already facing death by terminal illness or old age, and the process must be overseen by a senior ascetic. Few perform *sallekhana*, but those who do are highly celebrated.

EMMA SALTER

I AM A JAIN

I am a Jain nun, and have been practising Jainism for nineteen years. I joined my monastery when I was eighteen. Jain ascetic life is very simple: I have two sets of clothes; I eat pure vegetarian food in handmade wooden bowls; I have no monetary assets – no property, no bank balance; I have given up family attachments; and I am happy, having no desires for material possessions.

I did not become a nun because I was unhappy. I had incredibly happy moments with my parents, my two sisters and brother. I was born in Chennai, in southern India. My father is a physician and radiologist, my mother a housewife. We always said prayers and meditated for an hour on Sunday. The inspiration of my family, and the religious environment in which I was brought up, made a deep impression on me and developed within me. My parents are not only followers of the Jain religion, but have applied Jain principles throughout their lives. Their deep spirituality and religious commitment influenced me a lot.

Eventually I started to learn more about Jainism, by discussing and spending time with many Jain monks and nuns who visited Chennai. Their simple way of life appealed to me. After finishing my education at high school, I sought the permission of my parents to join the training institution for nuns. I had to wait a couple of years, to convince my parents of my commitment to the religious life: they needed to be sure this was what I really wanted. I wanted a life that was peaceful, purposeful, productive, and progressive. I wanted something special, that gave me a feeling of contentment and fulfilment. Finally, I chose this path. In the Jain training centre, I read not only the holy scriptures, but also comparative studies of different religions, philosophies, and ideas. I studied for a Master's degree in comparative religion and philosophy at the Jain Vishwa Bharati Institute at Ladnun, in Rajasthan. This period of study helped me to understand my beliefs and values with more clarity.

After six years of training, my spiritual gurus, Acharya Tulsi and Acharya Mahaprajna, initiated me, at a gathering of thousands of people. It was a deeply spiritual celebration. I took vows of non-violence, truth, non-stealing, celibacy, and non-possession. It is a lifelong commitment, with self-discipline and self-control. That day I was so happy – my dream was coming true. I was at the feet of my guru, receiving blessings for this new journey of spiritual enlightenment. I was dressed in a white robe and my head was shaved. I was named 'Samani Charitra Prajna'.

Acharya Tulsi and Acharya Mahaprajna established the Saman Order in 1980. Their vision was to propagate and reinforce the message of non-violence, peace, and harmony throughout the world. In Jainism, we believe that water, air, fire, earth, and plants are living beings. Although it is not possible to be completely non-violent, we try to prevent unnecessary violence by our actions, words, and thoughts. Acharya Tulsi established a new form of monastic life. The lifestyle of a *saman* or *samni* is very similar to that of a monk or nun in other Jain monastic communities, but there are differences. For example, we use transport to educate and enhance human life and values at the global level.

As a *samni,* my lifestyle is totally different from that of a secular person. I spend four to five hours a day in meditation, prayer, chanting, and reading the holy scriptures. Twice a day, before sunrise and after sunset, I recite a special prayer known as *pratikraman*, in which I ask for forgiveness from, and give forgiveness to, all living beings; if I have committed sins, or violated any kind of vows, I repent and resolve not to repeat them. I freely admit my flaws and mistakes, and seek to improve myself.

I observe *preksha* meditation every day. A scientific technique, it is aimed at transforming my inner personality; it is known to have an impact on the endocrine system, by changing the biochemicals and balancing the hormones. It helps me a lot, enabling me to eliminate negative emotions and regenerate positive qualities, and benefits me by relaxing me and giving me peace of mind. As a *samni,* I do not eat and drink before sunrise or after sunset. This has a basis in science, as it has been shown sunlight is needed for good digestion.

Along with the daily practice of meditation and prayer, once a year I celebrate eight special days of spiritual enhancement and uplifting of my soul. This is called *paryushan* – 'being closer to your soul' – and is practised not only by monks and nuns, but by the whole Jain community. We listen to sermons, fast day and night, and practise living simply, with detachment from the material world and self-control. The last day of *paryushan* is very important, because this is the day when we recall all our past mistakes and sins, ask forgiveness from those against whom we have sinned, and give forgiveness to those who have sinned against us.

Jainism emphasizes a process of self-purification. All my efforts are focused on freeing the soul from the bondage of *karma*.

As a *samni,* ten months a year I travel extensively in India and overseas, lecturing at universities, colleges, national and international conferences, and to various associations. I have often participated in interfaith dialogues and discussions, and have conducted many camps, workshops, and seminars on stress management, anger management, the science of living, and ailments such as diabetes, high blood pressure, anxiety, obesity, allergies, and heart attacks. The rest of my time I spend in the presence of my guru, whose holy presence clarifies many doubts and queries.

I am very happy I have dedicated my whole life to a good cause, and to be following the message of non-violence, and a soul-oriented religion that emphasizes human values.

Samani Charitra Prajna

CHAPTER 29

Jainism in the Modern World

Jainism is a dynamic religion, remaining relevant in the modern world, by responding to social change, and to scientific and technological innovations. Some Jains embrace modernization, while others prefer to uphold established traditions; the different points of view have sometimes led to tension within the Jain community. The estimated 100,000 Jains living outside India face additional challenges, in that Jain ascetics play a vital role in the religious practices of Jain laypeople, yet are allowed to travel only on foot, and not permitted to travel outside India.

SOCIAL CHANGE AND MODERNIZATION

Changing social values have influenced traditional Jain practices. For example, most Jain sects no longer allow children to take ascetic initiation. Jains sometimes attempt to demonstrate the validity of Jain doctrine by reference to current social issues, such as associating vegetarianism with healthy living, or associating non-violence with cultural tolerance.

Jainism has also responded to scientific discoveries. Some Jains have suggested science proves the truth of Jain doctrine and, therefore, the authority of the *jinas*, because Jain teachings about the formation of matter from particles correspond with scientific discoveries about atoms. Where science and doctrine are not reconciled, as with the structure of the cosmos, Jains have to decide whether to accept scientific discovery and reclassify their doctrinal beliefs as mythical, or reject scientific discovery and hold fast to their doctrinal beliefs.

Technological advances have presented Jains with new ethical dilemmas. Some progressive mendicants use microphones during their sermons, to ensure the entire congregation can hear them; while other mendicants refuse to use electrical equipment, out of concern that electricity may harm tiny airborne creatures. Advances in printing, publishing and information technology have made Jain literature increasingly accessible to a broad readership that includes lay Jains and non-Jains. Some Jains hope this will further the understanding of Jainism, while others are concerned that sacred texts may be misinterpreted, or treated irreverently. Modernization also obliges Jains to rethink the motivation behind certain religious practices. For example, today most lay Jains live in houses or apartments where it is no longer appropriate to suggest eating after dark increases the risk of harming insects. If they do not eat after sunset, they have to justify this as exercising discipline and respect for tradition, rather than as an act of non-violence.

Today many Jains are well educated; religious rituals that appear to hold little meaning beyond tradition may not satisfy them. However, numerous independent educational programmes are being established in India and abroad, to teach lay Jains about Jainism, and revitalize their commitment, by explaining the doctrinal reasons for their religious practices. The first Jain university was established in 1970 at Ladnun, Rajasthan, under the direction of Acharya Tulsi (1914–97).

THE JAIN DIASPORA

> It doesn't matter if you become a Jain, aspire to become a good man, a moral person.
>
> Acharya Tulsi

Towards the end of the nineteenth century, many Indian people emigrated to East Africa, where they established homes and businesses. By 1926, a Jain temple had been built in Nairobi, Kenya, and another was constructed in Mombasa in 1963, indicating the religious community's growth. However, during the late 1960s and 1970s, Indian people were persecuted by East African political regimes, and many fled to Britain and North America, where they took up citizenship, while endeavouring to establish a communal identity.

To Jains who do not live in India, the absence of ascetics presents a difficulty, since ascetics have religious authority, and play a vital role in the religious practices of Jain laypeople, offering instruction, administering vows, performing initiation and consecration ceremonies, and giving laypeople the opportunity to gain spiritual merit through alms-giving. Some diaspora Jains travel to India, either regularly or occasionally, to be in the presence of ascetics, though family, work, and financial restraints make such trips difficult for many. This difficulty is compounded by ascetics being peripatetic for eight months of the year. Some modern movements have – consciously or not – addressed the problem of ascetic absence. Terapanthi Jainism, the followers of Chitrabhanu, Shrimad Rajachandra, and Kanji Swami all have different organizational structures, but each is an example of progressive and modernized Jainism.

EMMA SALTER

QUESTIONS

1. What is the role of a *jina*?

2. Explain the main points of disagreement between Digambara and Shvetambara Jains.

3. Why is asceticism so important in Jainism?

4. Explain why Jains do not believe enlightenment is possible during the current cosmic era.

5. Why is the Digambara scriptural canon so much smaller than the Shvetamara canon?

6. Explain the Jain conception of *karma* and its role in trapping a soul in *samsara*.

7. Why do Digambara and Shvetambara Jains have different views about the role of women?

8. Why do Jains have such a strong position on non-violence?

9. What attracts Jains to an ascetic lifestyle?

10. Why does modern life pose so many problems for strict Jains?

FURTHER READING

Carrithers, Michael, and C. Humphrey, *The Assembly of Listeners: Jains in Society*. Cambridge: Cambridge University Press, 1991.

Cort, John E., *Jains in the World: Religious Values and Ideology in India*. New York: Oxford University Press, 2004.

Dundas, Paul, *The Jains*. New York: Routledge, 2002.

Jaini, Padmanabh, *The Jaina Path of Purification*, 2nd ed. Columbia, MI: South Asia Books, 2001.

Laidlaw, James, *Riches and Renunciation: Religion, Economy, and Society among the Jains*. New York: Oxford University Press, 1996.

Vallely, Anne, *Guardians of the Transcendent: An Ethnography of a Jain Ascetic Community*. Toronto: University of Toronto Press, 2002.

PART 7
JUDAISM

SUMMARY

More than any other world religion, Judaism can be thought of as the religion of a particular people – or indeed as *being* that people, rather than their religion. In part, this goes back to the shared, though disputed, story of national origin transmitted to us by scripture. According to this tradition, the people of Israel are bound by a covenant as God's elect to fulfil his obligations, in return for their special status. This tradition is central to the religion today: Judaism's most popular festivals, such as Passover and *Hanukkah*, commemorate key events from this version of the community's past. The religion of the ancient Judeans, based around the maintenance of the covenant through sacrificial rites, in time gave way to the rabbinic tradition, centred upon the synagogue, serving as a place of prayer, praise, and study.

The diaspora that followed the destruction of the Temple at Jerusalem in 70 CE carried Judaism across much of the Middle East, North Africa, and Europe. During the medieval period, many Jews – especially those in Muslim lands – made significant contributions to the arts and sciences, while those living in Christendom were frequently subjected to persecution and changing royal whim. By the twentieth century, though, Jewish communities formed part of the fabric of many European states. Reform of Judaism's tradition formed one distinct strand of the European Enlightenment, and the increasing separation of church and state at this time provided a framework into which Judaism could comfortably fit. More recently of a variety of schools of thought has emerged within Judaism, maintaining different approaches to doctrine and worship, and sometimes differing over how to respond to the changes and challenges of the secular world.

Much of recent Jewish history is overshadowed by the Nazi Holocaust, and for many the memory of this event highlights the importance Jewish traditions and of the community itself. Since 1948, the state of Israel has been a centre for this community and home – along with many other countries – to the diverse schools of thought that together make it up.

CHAPTER 30

A Historical Overview

Rabbinic Judaism today sees itself as a direct development from the time of Moses, the giver of the Torah, more than 3000 years ago. To understand the developing beliefs and practices of Judaism, we need to know something of the social and political events that affected Jewish communities. We also need to observe the ideas of their neighbours in order to understand the influence of the cultures with which they came into contact. Greek thought, Christianity, Islam, medieval philosophy, and charismatic movements have all affected the intellectual activity and popular customs of Judaism.

EXILE AND AFTER

The story of the early development of Judaism is much debated. The commonly accepted narrative, largely based on the polemical biblical texts of Ezra and Nehemiah — which actually refer to 'people of Israel' rather than 'Jews' — has been important for the later development of Jewish self-understanding, but is not necessarily founded in historical reality.

This popular story of Judaism begins in the late sixth century BCE, when the Persian Empire was dominant in the Middle East. In 586 BCE, Nebuchadnezzar II, King of the

I was glad when they said to me,

'Let us go to the house of the Lord!'

Our feet have been standing within your gates, O Jerusalem!

Jerusalem, built as a city which is bound firmly together,

to which the tribes go up,

the tribes of the Lord,

as was decreed for Israel,

to give thanks to the name of the Lord.

There thrones for judgment were set,

the thrones of the house of David.
Pray for the peace of Jerusalem!

'May they prosper who love you!

Peace be within your walls,

and security within your towers!"

For my brethren and companions' sake

I will say, 'Peace be within you!'

For the sake of the house of the Lord our God,

I will seek your good.

Psalm 122, Old Testament, Revised Standard Version

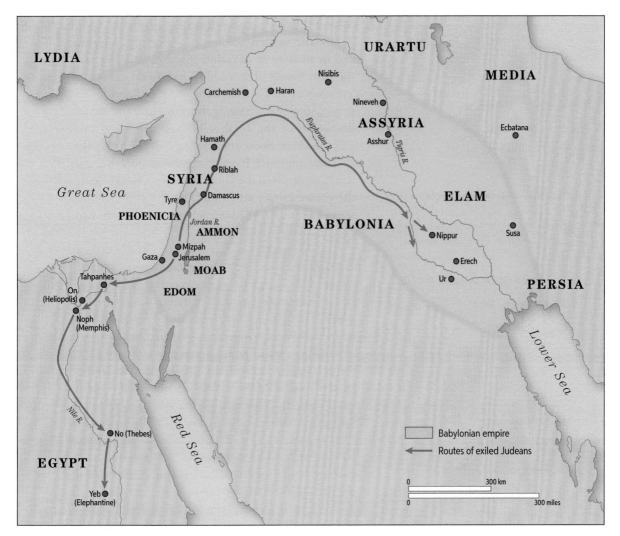

The Judean Exiles, c. 560 BCE

neo-Babylonian Empire, destroyed Jerusalem, and many its people were taken captive to Babylon, along with much of the population of Judea. In both Babylon and Egypt there were now communities of people who still considered themselves Judeans — consisting largely of mercenary soldiers and of prisoners of war and their families — some of whom were agents of the ruling power, and for that reason privileged. In Egypt, where this caused much resentment, the Judeans remained separate, following the religion and customs they brought with them.

The Judeans believed there should be just a single Temple, the only place where religious sacrifice could be carried out. While they lived in Judah, it was possible for all to make the pilgrimage to this Temple in Jerusalem; but in exile this became difficult, if not impossible — though the Jews of the Dispersion apparently made great efforts

*By the rivers of Babylon we sat
and wept*

when we remembered Zion.

There on the poplars

we hung our harps,

*for there our captors asked us
for songs,*

*our tormentors demanded songs
of joy;*

*they said, 'Sing us one of the songs
of Zion!'*

How can we sing the songs of the Lord

while in a foreign land?

If I forget you, O Jerusalem,

may my right hand forget its skill.

*May my tongue cling to the roof of
my mouth*

if I do not remember you,

if I do not consider Jerusalem

my highest joy.

Psalm 137:1–6, Old Testament,
New International Version

to visit Jerusalem and worship in obedience to the Torah, the written teaching. To meet this obstacle, and in an attempt to maintain some continuity with the past, houses of assembly — *beitei knesset* in Hebrew, 'synagogues' in Greek — were set up in Babylon, and prayer, singing or chanting, teaching, and reading and discussion of the Torah — but not sacrifice — took place in them. Some time during this period, scribes also first appeared. Based in the synagogue, their role was to understand the Torah and interpret its rules for the contemporary situation. This 'guild of scholars' seems eventually to have evolved into the rabbis of rabbinic Judaism.

In 539 the army of Cyrus II, 'the Great', of Persia captured Babylon, and Cyrus gained nominal control of the Babylonian Empire. According to Ezra I:3, he permitted the Hebrews to return from exile and rebuild their Temple in Jerusalem. When Hebrew religious leaders returned to Jerusalem, the city was apparently established as a Temple community, led by the priests, as Cyrus would not allow the restoration of the monarchy. According to Ezra/Nehemiah, a strict separation between Judean — 'Jews' — and non-Judean in Judah was enforced by the Hebrews' leaders, Ezra and Nehemiah, a separation apparently marked by circumcision, observance of *Shabbat* — the Jewish Sabbath — and of the Sabbatical year, recognition of the Torah (the first five books of Jewish scripture), and obligations to the Temple in Jerusalem. Rigorists also required that marriage arrangements should be made only between Judeans.

THE HELLENISTIC KINGDOMS

After Alexander the Great won the Battle of Issus in 333 BCE, an era of prosperity commenced in the region. Cities founded on the Greek pattern grew rapidly, with Alexandria becoming the leading city in Egypt within a few years of its foundation. The Judean community there was substantial, and Greek — rather than Aramaic — became their language. People even tried to look Greek! The Greek language was the medium by which Greek ideas, attitudes, and ways of reasoning were passed on. People who could read Greek — especially those living in Alexandria — might have had an opportunity to read the great Greek philosophers in the original. But it seems Greek-speaking Jews were not drawn away from their customs as much as some feared, and still visited Jerusalem to celebrate the festivals in the Temple.

After the death of Alexander, his empire broke up into smaller units, principally the kingdoms of Macedonia, Egypt, and the Seleucids. When the Parthian Empire rose to power in the third century BCE, the Seleucid Kingdom, which had included Babylon, was gradually reduced to only the Syrian region, and Babylon came under Parthian control. The Jews remaining in Babylon were now cut off from other Jewish communities, and Aramaic remained their language, adding a linguistic barrier to that of politics. The Jewish communities of Babylon and of the Greek-influenced, or 'Hellenized', kingdoms inevitably developed differently, though they were united by a common scripture and emphasis on Jerusalem and its Temple, where priests were leaders, and the high priest politically and economically powerful.

TENSION AND REVOLT

In 191–190 BCE the Romans, turning their eyes towards the East, defeated King Antiochus III of Syria; it was probably prisoners of war from this conflict who founded the Jewish community in Rome. Jews also settled in Antioch, Syria, and in Asia Minor, modern Turkey. The Romans exacted tribute from Antiochus, which meant increased taxes. Consequently tension grew between rich and poor in Jerusalem and Judah, which – along with the political and cultural divisions between those for and against Hellenism – made for a volatile situation.

The explosion came during the reign of Antiochus IV Epiphanes (175–164). When the Jews resisted his nominee for the high priesthood, he sent troops to sack Jerusalem, established pagan practices in the Temple, and attacked the Jewish religion. Some Jews submitted, but those who adhered to the Torah, especially the *Hasidim* – 'The Pious' – suffered greatly. Eventually there was full-scale revolt, led by the Maccabee family, and – against the odds – Judas Maccabeus came to terms with the Syrians in 165 BCE, marched on Jerusalem, and ritually cleansed the desecrated Temple. This victory, and the reconsecration of the Temple, is celebrated today in the Festival of Lights, or *Hanukkah*.

The Maccabee family now began a line of rulers – the Hasmonean dynasty – many of whom, ironically, became typical Hellenistic despots. However they won a measure of freedom for the Jewish realm before the Romans, under Pompey, annexed Judea in 63 BCE.

UNDER THE ROMAN EMPIRE

Judea now became a vassal of Rome. The current Hasmonean king was confirmed as the nation's leader and high priest, but the Romans refused to recognize him as king.

In 40 BCE, following a Parthian invasion of Syria and Judea, the Rome gave Herod (c. 73–4 BCE), son of Antipater the Idumean, the title 'king of the Jews'. Although his personal life was disastrous, the country prospered under his rule, and Herod 'the Great' is remembered as a builder of cities such as Sebaste and Caesarea, of fortresses such as

Masada and Herodium, of palaces, theatres, and amphitheatres, and of the Jewish Temple in Jerusalem. Those who opposed Rome and Hellenism hated and opposed him.

During the Roman period Jewish hopes rose for a messiah – a king of David's line, for some, a priest-king – who would rescue his people from the Romans and restore the Judean state. There were several revolts in Judea during the time of Herod and his successors, and 'prophets' attracted large followings. The most serious threat to the Jews came during the reign of the Emperor Caligula (37–41 CE), who demanded that all his subjects worship him, and ordered a statue of himself as Zeus to be placed in the Jerusalem Temple.

THE TEMPLE DESTROYED

Judea became increasingly unsettled. In the coastal cities, conflict between Greeks and Jews was constant, and tension mounted between the Roman governors and the people. Finally in 66 CE the Jews rose in revolt against Rome, but initial success was followed by crushing defeat, Jerusalem was taken, and its Temple destroyed in 70 CE.

The destruction of the Temple was decisive for the future of Judaism. The Temple, the priesthood, and the council – the Sanhedrin – were finished. No longer could Jerusalem act as a unifying force within Judaism, the focus of pilgrimage. Jewish communities now became just one group within larger communities; although distinct, they were inevitably affected by the culture of the city or nation in which they found themselves.

HELLENISTIC JUDAISM

The life of the ordinary Jew in Greek-speaking areas centred on the synagogue, where worship and practical matters of community life were conducted. Strangers were lodged, the poor helped, discipline enforced, public gatherings held, and children taught in the synagogue. Visiting preachers might give a sermon, but the resident scholars probably did not. Authority was in the hands of the 'ruler of the synagogue'. Associated with the synagogue was the 'house of study' (*bet midrash*), where the Bible was studied and scholars could consult a library.

Some Hellenistic rabbis drew up rules of biblical interpretation. Philo of Alexandria (20 BCE–50 CE) attempted to explain the Bible from the point of view of Greek philosophy, presenting the great events of Israel's history as allegories of eternal truths and adopting

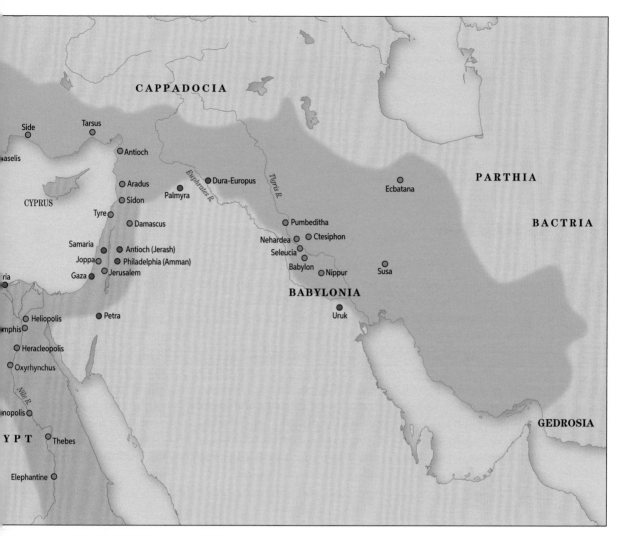

The Jewish Diaspora c. 240 BCE

the Stoic idea of Reason (*Logos*), which he called a 'second God', an intermediary between God and the world.

RABBINIC JUDAISM

A seemingly insignificant event provided a new direction for Judaism when Johanan ben Zakai (30–90 CE) founded a school at Jamnia, or Yavneh, Galilee, where *rabbi* (master) became the formal title for teachers. Though Johanan may not have been a Pharisee, his successor, Gamaliel the Elder, was, and the school's ethos was essentially Pharisaic, the stance of emerging rabbinic Judaism. The school at Jamnia came to exercise the function of a council, and even adopted the name 'Sanhedrin'. Johanan fixed the calendar for Jews abroad – once the prerogative of the high priest – and Jews began to look to this council for advice and judgments. The rabbis of this early period are known as *Tanna* – plural *Tannaim*, 'teachers'. Their earliest surviving works are 'sayings' in the *Pirkei Avot*, sometimes known as the 'Ethics of the Fathers', and second-century written Hebrew versions of Jewish oral traditions known as the Mishnah.

Most other varieties of Judaism gradually died out. Jewish Christianity survived into the second century CE, although the rabbis tried hard to exclude Jewish Christians from the synagogues after about 90 CE. In the Greek world, Christians broke entirely with Judaism, often becoming anti-Jewish.

PERSECUTION

Jewish revolts against Roman rule continued widely and were brutally put down. The Judean revolt of 132 CE may have been ignited by the establishment of the new Roman city of Aelia Capitolina upon the ruins of Jerusalem; the Old City of present-day Jerusalem is the linear descendant of this Roman town. This revolt was led by Simon ben Kosiba, also known as Simon bar Kokhba – 'Son of a Star', who claimed to be the messiah, and who was supported by the greatest rabbinic scholar of the day, Rabbi Akiva ben Joseph (c. 40– c. 137 CE). But the uprising was hopeless, and the casualties inflicted on the Romans only made the final defeat more harsh.

The governors of Palestine – the name the Romans now gave the country – were now higher-ranking Romans than previously. Construction of Aelia Capitolina was completed, and Jews forbidden to enter the city. Galilee now became a centre of Jewish life, and several different towns in succession became the seat of the Jewish council. Judaism was not banned, but the circumcision of converts was forbidden, making conversion difficult, if not impossible.

PALESTINIAN PATRIARCHATE

Simeon ben Gamaliel II became president of the 'Great Sanhedrin' and first Palestinian Patriarch with – at least in theory – authority over all Jews of the Roman world. His son, Judah I, the Prince (b. 135) – also known as Rabbi HaQadosh – appears to have exercised considerable power. A noted scholar, during his time the Mishnah was codified and published. The Palestinian Patriarchate came to an end with the execution by the Romans of Gamaliel VI in 425, and the Sanhedrin was also dissolved as a result of Roman oppression.

The conversion of Constantine to Christianity in 313 was not auspicious for Jews. Although Judaism was never made illegal, life became difficult for Jews, as Jewish-Christian tensions grew. In Egypt, the Jewish community began to recover, though numbers were never as high as in earlier centuries. Greek culture was on the wane, and with it Hellenistic Judaism.

BABYLONIAN EXILARCHS

In Babylon, the ruler of the Jews of the Diaspora were known as an 'exilarch', or head of the exiles. This hereditary position was recognized by the state and, later, under Arab rule by the Muslims. But from the fifth century onward, relations between the Jews and the Persian authorities became difficult, and the Jews there welcomed the Arab conquerors. Similarly, in Palestine, the harshness of the Byzantine rule caused the Jews to look for help abroad, aiding the invading Persian forces in 614. However uprisings among the Jerusalem Jews in 617 were subdued by military force when the Byzantine army re-entered the city, and the Jews were once more expelled.

JUDAISM AND ISLAM

Islam arose and spread with extraordinary rapidity in the seventh and eight centuries CE. Muslim Arabs defeated the Byzantine army in 634, conquered Syria and Palestine, defeated Persia in 637, and Egypt soon after. Muslims invaded Spain in 711, and set up a Muslim state. Within a century, many Jews had come under Muslim rule. For most, living conditions improved considerably, and the Jews shared in the intellectual ferment of the Arab world. Arabs translated and studied the learning of Greece, Persia, China, and India, and drawing on these resources, Muslim and Jewish scholars made great advances in mathematics, astronomy, philosophy, chemistry, medicine, and philology. One of the greatest Jewish philosophers, Saadiah Gaon (882–942), grappled with the problem of 'faith and knowledge', discussing proofs of God's existence.

BABYLON: THE AGE OF THE GAONS

In Babylon, the authority and importance of the Gaons – the heads of the Babylonian academies – grew immensely after 600. The Gaons ensured that the Babylonian Talmud – documents compiled in the Babylonian academies between the third and fifth centuries – became accepted more widely. In the ninth century a gaonate was established in Palestine, and was recognized as authoritative by Jews in Spain, Egypt, and Italy. Under the Gaons collections of Talmudic laws were made, synagogue poetry written, prayer-books drawn up, and the text of the Bible was fixed and annotated. Most influential were the *Responsa* (Hebrew, *She'elot ve-Teshuvot* – questions and answers) – questions on matters of practice sent to the Gaons, debated in the academies, and answered in their name.

Variants from rabbinic Judaism arose. In eighth century Babylon, Anan ben David (c. 715–c. 795), and Karaite movement he possibly founded, rejected the Talmud and all forms of oral law, such as the Mishnah, taking a stand on the Bible only. It seemed the Karaites might divide the Jewish world, but the movement soon became merely a sect, which still survives today in small numbers.

SCHOLARSHIP IN SPAIN

Jews rose to influential positions at court in Spain, where 'Sephardic' Judaism developed, with its own synagogue rituals and a Spanish-Jewish dialect, Ladino. Solomon ibn Gabirol (c. 1021– c. 1058) attempted to reconcile Jewish thought with Neo-Platonism – which posits that God is separated from the world by a descending series of 'emanations' – which contributed to the development of the Jewish mystical tradition known as the Kabbalah (see below). Judah Halevi of Toledo (1085–1140) wrote a fictional dialogue between a Jewish scholar and the king of the Khazars – a Turkish tribe converted to Judaism – showing that philosophy could prove God's existence, but that revelation was then necessary to know more of him.

JEWS IN WESTERN EUROPE

From the mid-eleventh century Jewish scholars in the West became more important than the Gaons. The French scholar Rabbi Solomon ben Isaac (Shlomo Yitzhaki, 1040–1105), known, from his initials, as Rashi, produced standard commentaries on the Bible and Talmud. With additions by his successors, his commentaries are still printed in the Talmud.

> *This God is one. He is not two nor more than two, but one. None of the things existing in the universe to which the term one is applied is like unto his unity.*
>
> Moses Maimonides,
> *Mishnah Torah*

In the eleventh century there was a shift in philosophical thought, as Aristotle supplanted Plato. Aristotle's science seemed to leave no room for religion, and Jewish scholars debated whether his philosophy could be reconciled with biblical religion. In Córdoba, Spain, the Rabbi Moshe ben Maimon (Moses Maimonides, 1135–1204) presented a code containing all the *halakhah* in his Mishneh Torah. Exiled from Spain to Egypt, he wrote in Arabic the great philosophical work *The Guide for the Perplexed*, discussing the difficulties Aristotle's philosophy presented for the believer. Although Judaism had been – and is – far more based on right behaviour – orthopraxis – than orthodoxy, Maimonides saw 'right belief' as of great importance, for which he was much criticized. Maimonides also drew up thirteen 'roots' of Judaism, the 'Thirteen Principles of the Faith'.

THE RISE OF ANTI-SEMITISM

From the tenth century onwards, anti-Jewish sentiment and riots became common in France, and life in Christian Europe generally became difficult for Jews. The Crusading armies marching to the 'Holy Land' looted and slaughtered Jews as they went, and the capture of Jerusalem – hailed by Christendom as a great triumph – meant death for the Jews there. Many Jews regarded such death as martyrdom, the ultimate form of witness, or 'sanctification of the Name' (*kiddush haShem*), and some committed suicide rather than renouncing their faith. Jewish rules of conduct (*halakhah*) stated that in some situations death was preferable to the

JUDAISM TIMELINE

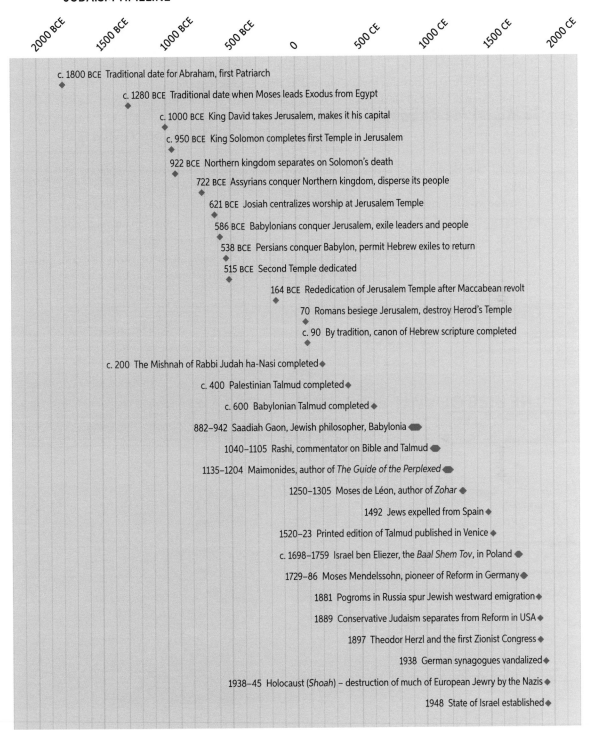

2000 BCE   1500 BCE   1000 BCE   500 BCE   0   500 CE   1000 CE   1500 CE   2000 CE

c. 1800 BCE Traditional date for Abraham, first Patriarch

c. 1280 BCE Traditional date when Moses leads Exodus from Egypt

c. 1000 BCE King David takes Jerusalem, makes it his capital

c. 950 BCE King Solomon completes first Temple in Jerusalem

922 BCE Northern kingdom separates on Solomon's death

722 BCE Assyrians conquer Northern kingdom, disperse its people

621 BCE Josiah centralizes worship at Jerusalem Temple

586 BCE Babylonians conquer Jerusalem, exile leaders and people

538 BCE Persians conquer Babylon, permit Hebrew exiles to return

515 BCE Second Temple dedicated

164 BCE Rededication of Jerusalem Temple after Maccabean revolt

70 Romans besiege Jerusalem, destroy Herod's Temple

c. 90 By tradition, canon of Hebrew scripture completed

c. 200 The Mishnah of Rabbi Judah ha-Nasi completed

c. 400 Palestinian Talmud completed

c. 600 Babylonian Talmud completed

882–942 Saadiah Gaon, Jewish philosopher, Babylonia

1040–1105 Rashi, commentator on Bible and Talmud

1135–1204 Maimonides, author of *The Guide of the Perplexed*

1250–1305 Moses de Léon, author of *Zohar*

1492 Jews expelled from Spain

1520–23 Printed edition of Talmud published in Venice

c. 1698–1759 Israel ben Eliezer, the *Baal Shem Tov*, in Poland

1729–86 Moses Mendelssohn, pioneer of Reform in Germany

1881 Pogroms in Russia spur Jewish westward emigration

1889 Conservative Judaism separates from Reform in USA

1897 Theodor Herzl and the first Zionist Congress

1938 German synagogues vandalized

1938–45 Holocaust (*Shoah*) – destruction of much of European Jewry by the Nazis

1948 State of Israel established

A HISTORICAL OVERVIEW

alternative – for instance to avoid idolatry, incest, or murder, or to 'sanctify the Name'.

In Europe, two vicious lies circulated: the 'blood libel' and the 'libel of desecration of the host'. The blood libel claimed Jews were guilty of ritual murder, using the blood of Christian children during Passover. The 'libel of desecration of the host' spuriously claimed that Jews stole the host – the consecrated bread of the eucharist, believed to be the body of Christ – and stabbed or burned it, thus re-enacting the crucifixion of Jesus.

Jews entered England during the eleventh century, but were expelled in 1290, not to return until after 1650. Between 1290 and 1293, Jewish communities in southern Italy were almost wiped out and many forced conversions were made. The Jews were expelled from France in 1306, and massacres occurred in 1348. Jews were falsely accused of poisoning wells and causing the Black Death, a plague that killed off one third of the population of Europe in 1348. From Spain to Poland, Jews were persecuted and massacred.

In the twelfth century Christians attempted to recapture Spain from the Muslims. In response, the Muslim Almohades from North Africa pushed into Spain and, not showing their usual tolerance towards Jews, drove them northwards. Christian leaders at first welcomed these Jews. With other means of livelihood closed to them, many became moneylenders, since usury was forbidden for Christians. But tolerance did not last, and in

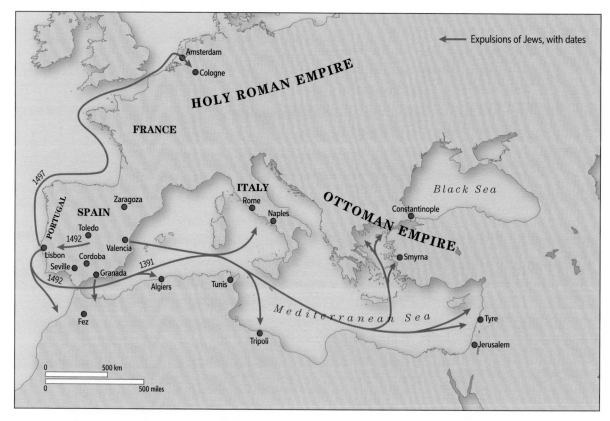

The Jews are expelled from Spain

Christian Spain attacks on Jews reached a peak in 1391. Many Jews professed conversion to Christianity, and were known by the insulting name of *Marranos* (swine). In 1492 Jews were offered the choice of converting or leaving; thousands fled to other parts of Europe and beyond, such as Safed in Galilee.

JEWISH MYSTICISM

Another important strand of Judaism is mysticism: belief in some kind of direct 'vision' of divine things, a way of experiencing things other than through our ordinary senses. The Kabbalah, a Jewish mystical tradition, developed in Spain, bringing together earlier traditions, such as ideas from the Talmud and the Book of Creation (*Sefer Yetsirot*), which emphasized the mystical meaning of the letters in the Hebrew alphabet and from Neo-Platonism a concept of how God related to the world.

UNDER THE OTTOMANS

During the sixteenth and seventeenth centuries, the Muslim Ottoman Empire was in the ascendant, capturing Palestine in 1515, Egypt in 1517, and expanding into Europe, until halted in Vienna in 1683. Most Jews now lived either in Christian Poland–Lithuania, or under the Muslim Ottoman Empire, where conditions were generally less difficult, but where they were still subject to arbitrary or capricious acts of the rulers. In Christian Italy, severe penalties were inflicted on the Jews in this period.

The Protestant Reformers on the whole favoured Jews, but Martin Luther changed from tolerance and defence to rabid anti-Jewish abuse. The rite of non-Sephardic Jews in Europe – especially in Germany – known as 'Ashkenazi' dates to the sixteenth century, and has its own German-Jewish dialect, Yiddish.

Anti-Jewish riots continued, but the authorities now more often protected the Jews, who were seen as useful for their money-lending and trading. In Ukraine and Poland many Jews were killed in massacres in 1648 and 1649, when Jewish leaders were seen by the peasantry to be economically and politically at one with the Polish overlords.

HOPE OF A MESSIAH

In the late seventeenth century a number of Jewish messianic movements arose, partly a product of the insecurity of Jewish life. The most important was centred on Shabbetai Zevi (1628–1716) and his prophet, Nathan of Gaza (1643–80), who called for repentance, strict ascetic practices, and mortification of the body – including fasting, bathing in freezing water, and constant prayer. Shabbetai was imprisoned in Gallipoli in 1665, and in 1666, under coercion, converted to Islam. His remaining followers were viewed with deep suspicion by the Jewish community, and the episode resulted in general disillusion with Messianism.

HASIDISM

Eighteenth century Poland saw the rise of Hasidism, a popular movement that gave hope and excitement to people who were frightened and deprived, with its emphasis on emotion and devotion. The movement focused on the individual and direct experience of the divine, and was thus accessible to ordinary labourers, who could not afford the long hours of study required by rabbinical Judaism. The key figure in the growth of Hasidism was Israel ben Eliezer (1700–60), known as the Baal Shem Tov, 'Master of the Good Name'; a dynamic, charismatic figure, widely known as a miracle worker, whose teaching contained much from the Kabbalah, especially the *Zohar*.

Many legends are told about Baal Shem Tov, and much popular belief – indeed superstition – was caught up into the movement. But at the core was a passionate devotion to God, expressed in ecstatic prayer, singing, and dancing. From outside, Hasidic life may seem a narrow existence, but it is sustained by Hasidic 'joy' – a genuine religious 'high'.

The leaders of Hasidic groups were more gurus than rabbi-like scholars. The leader, *rebbe*, or *zaddiq*, is a man who lives the life of devotion, and acts as intermediary between his followers and God. His word is absolute: his followers leave their families to be with him, and even contest for a share of the food he has touched. There are a number of different branches of Hasidism today. Women played a much more prominent role in the beginnings of the movement than they do today. Generally, Hasidism is a man's world; Hasidic women lead separate lives.

The Hasidic movement met strong opposition from the Jewish establishment, with something of a class struggle, as *rebbes* replaced the rich and learned. One of the most hostile opponents was the Gaon of Vilna, Elijah ben Solomon (1720–97), an ascetic intellectual who excoriated Hasidism. The Hasidic Jews were sometimes excluded from the community – and even betrayed to hostile authorities. Influenced by Shneur Zalman of Liadi (1745–1812), his Chabad branch of Hasidic Judaism was reconciled to Talmudic study and thus accepted by the wider Jewish community.

GO WEST

From the early seventeenth century, Jews gradually began to move from Poland and the Ottoman Empire into the cities of the West. There was a growing recognition of the value of Jewish commercial activity, and Jews began to be associated with the more developed social and economic systems. During the nineteenth century, large numbers of Jews migrated to America. Judaism remained the target for abuse and oppression, but there was a growing tolerance. During the nineteenth century equal rights were eventually obtained in many countries, though often with great difficulty.

JEWISH ENLIGHTENMENT

The 'Jewish enlightenment', *Haskalah*, pointed to another new direction within Judaism. Its founder, Moses Mendelssohn (1729–86), advocated the separation of church and state, so that religious bodies should not be able to compel, only persuade. He emphasized the universal principles of religion within Judaism, and translated the Torah into German. After his death, this movement, now led by Leopold Zunz (1794–1886), became more radical, rejecting the Talmud and traditional ideas – even the idea of revelation.

At the beginning of the nineteenth century, emancipation in France, Italy, and Germany allowed Jews to leave the ghetto and – as a result of *Haskalah* – develop reformed Judaism. Emancipation also aided the assimilation of Jews – sometimes even their cultural disappearance, when Jews merged through marriage into the surrounding society. After emancipation, the lifestyle of many Jews began more closely to resemble that of their non-Jewish fellow citizens.

> *All things that are, are in God, and must be conceived through God, and therefore God is the cause of the things which are in himself. This is the first point. Further, no substance can be granted outside God, that is, nothing which is outside God exists in itself; which was the second point. Therefore God is the immanent, but not the transcendent, cause of all things.*
>
> Baruch Spinoza, *The Ethics* (1677).

The dark counterpoint to increased tolerance was anti-Semitism, based on a belief in the 'soul' of a people; a contrast was drawn between the 'Semitic' nature of Jews and that of the 'Aryan' or 'Slavonic'. Strongly anti-Semitic movements were promoted in Germany and France from the 1880s, the direct consequence of which was the destruction between 1939 and 1945 of six million people in the Holocaust, simply because they were Jewish. European Jewry almost ceased to exist, and one-third of world Jewry was killed.

GEOFFREY COWLING
REVISED BY TIM DOWLEY

CHAPTER 31

Sacred Writings

The texts of Judaism have long been central to its life and culture, as can be seen in many expressions. In the Torah, Deuteronomy 30:14, we read: '. . . the word is very near to you; it is in your mouth and in your heart for you to observe' (literally: for you to do). Psalms and wisdom also hint at the centrality of texts. For example, the psalmist proclaims: 'I treasure your word in my heart, so that I may not sin against you ... Your word is a lamp to my feet and a light to my path' (Psalm 119:11, 105).

In the reign of King Josiah (c. 639–609 BCE; see 2 Kings 22–23), it is the discovery of the 'book of the Law' (an early form of Torah) that inspires Josiah's reforms. From the late biblical period until classical rabbinic Judaism, the scribe, from the copyist to the 'maker' of scrolls or books, has been regarded as something of a hero, often on a par with a sage and, eventually, a *reb* or rabbi.

A Jewish legend reflects the sacredness of texts. It tells of a Roman soldier who defaced a Torah scroll in the first century CE, and whom the authorities put to death to avoid insurrection. Since the destruction of the Temple in 70 CE, and the final revolt against Roman authorities (132–35 CE), sacrifice and pilgrimage to the Temple was replaced with the study of Scripture and other sacred texts, prayer, and works of piety.

The study of texts made Judaism a portable tradition. Jews of the diaspora, or exile, were able to worship God anywhere, and the study of sacred texts could also be done anywhere. Today, the sacredness of texts is expressed in other ways too. Since the advent of printing, Jewish writers and publishers have been at the forefront of the book industry. Modern *halakhot* (observances) include stipulations about the proper treatment of books. Judaism has always exhibited a remarkable love of the word, of manuscripts, and of books.

There are three major textual traditions:
- Tanakh (Hebrew scriptures)
- Mishnah (tractates and regulations on the Law)
- Talmud (exposition of the Mishnah and Torah)

TANAKH

In Jewish practice and theology the term 'torah' is used in three senses:

- the first five books of the Scriptures, traditionally ascribed to Moses
- the whole of the Jewish Scriptures (written torah)
- ethical teaching of the rabbis (oral torah)

This article only uses the term in the first sense, referring to the first five books. In referring to the whole of Hebrew scripture, we use the term 'Tanakh', which derives from the tradition since late antiquity of dividing the Hebrew scriptures into three distinct sections.

Much debate surrounds how and why particular books came to be included in the Jewish canon, and in what order. The order is significant. For example, in the Jewish canon the Book of Ruth is in the Writings and belongs to a group of five books (the *megillot*) that are read cyclically at festival times, Ruth being read at harvest.

In Judaism the notion of canon itself has evolved over the centuries. From the earliest records, what mattered was the pragmatic nature of texts: which texts manage to speak with immediacy – beyond the context of their composition –to the ongoing life and identity of the faith community? Once identified, those texts are 'biblical'. These are texts that, for whatever reason, accrued existential value for the community who used them.

> *There is one way to salvation: to go back to the sources of Judaism, to Bible, Talmud, and Midrash; to read, study, and comprehend them in order to live them … the seekers after knowledge will go back to the ancient fountains of Judaism, Bible, and Talmud and the one effort will be to obtain the concept of life out of Judaism.*
>
> Samson Raphael Hirsch, *The Nineteen Letters on Judaism* (1836), transl. B. Drachman (New York: Feldheim, 1960).

MISHNAH

The Mishnah is a collection of tractates consisting of *halakhot*, observances which cover every conceivable area of Jewish daily life and ritual purity. Its first tractate, the sayings of the fathers, *Pirqe Avot*, begins by laying down some principles for interpretation and for practice. The first verse sets the tone:

> *Moses received Torah from Sinai and passed it on to Joshua, and Joshua to the Elders, and the Elders to the Prophets; and the Prophets passed it on to the men of the Great Assembly. They said three things: 'Be careful in giving judgment, raise up many disciples, and make a fence around the Torah.'*

In other words, like Jewish writers after them, the authors of the Mishnah saw themselves as part of an unbroken chain of tradition. Jews who fulfilled the ordinances of the Mishnah would in turn be fulfilling the Torah, building a hedge around it in a mutually beneficial exchange: guard the Torah and it will guard you. From its inception (c. 200 CE), the Mishnah became the key reference for decision making among the diaspora Jews. However, within fifty to a hundred years large portions of it were thought to be terse and obscure, and an explanatory companion soon evolved.

TALMUD

The Talmud ('teaching'), a vast collection of writings containing the teaching of the rabbis, appeared in the rabbinic academies of diaspora Judaism out of the continuing debate about the significance and implementation of the Tanakh – especially the Torah – and the Mishnah, with tractates and groups of tractates gradually becoming authoritative through use.

There are two Talmuds: the Palestinian – also known as the Jerusalem Talmud – a record of discussion in the rabbinic schools of Galilee, especially Tiberias, during the fourth century CE; and the longer Babylonian Talmud, completed in the seventh or eighth century CE, recording the opinions of more than a thousand rabbis between 200 and 650 CE. The Babylonian Talmud was used by Jews living in the Muslim Empire, whilst the Palestinian Talmud was influential in Italy and Egypt.

These lengthy collections – the Babylonian Talmud amounts around 4 million words – contain many kinds of literature. The scholar Solomon Schechter (1847–1915) described the Talmud as 'a work too varied, too disconnected, too divergent in its elements, to be concisely defined at all, or even approximately to be described within the limits of an English sentence'. For this reason, we have to be careful about taking any particular opinion in the Talmud as 'the teaching of Judaism'. The Talmud records many views, so it is necessary to discover who said what, how authoritative it was, whether it was accepted by the later authorities, and what later commentaries said about it.

The range of topics the Talmud covers is astounding. Hyam Maccoby's anthology of the Talmud, *The Day God Laughed*, organizes its material into such categories as: Enjoying Nature, Against Asceticism, Physical Beauty, Eating and Drinking, Rejoicing, Studying; Tall Stories, The Value of Argument, Arguing for Pleasure, Arguing with God, and Privy Etiquette. The Talmud is at pains to blur any distinction between holy and profane, and is not concerned with answers. It is far more concerned with questions – and the process of answering them. One of its most celebrated passages captures this:

> *On that day, Rabbi Eliezer put forward all the arguments in the world, but the sages did not accept them.*
>
> *Finally, he said to them, 'If the* halakhah *is according to me, let that carob-tree prove it.'*
>
> *He pointed to a nearby carob-tree, which then moved from its place a hundred cubits, some say, four hundred cubits. They said to him, 'One cannot bring a proof from the moving of a carob-tree.' …*
> [Two more miracles were performed by Rabbi Eliezer in a bid to have his argument accepted.]
>
> *Then said Rabbi Eliezer to the Sages, 'If the* halakhah *is according to me, may a proof come from heaven.'*

Then a heavenly voice went forth, and said, 'What have you to do with Rabbi Eliezer? The halakhah *is according to him in every place.'*

Then Rabbi Joshua rose up on his feet, and said, 'It is not in the heavens.' [Deuteronomy 30:12 – he goes on to explain that since the Torah has already been given on Sinai, we do not need to pay attention to a heavenly voice.]

Rabbi Nathan met the prophet Elijah. He asked him, 'What was the Holy One, blessed be He, doing in that hour?'

Said Elijah, 'He was laughing, and saying, "My children have defeated me, my children have defeated me."'

Bava Metsia 59b

In other words, God's children are grown up enough to argue with him; for the rabbi, it is even a responsibility. In this sense, the Talmud captures something essential, not just of the historical period and contexts it emerges from, but also of the ongoing life of Judaism: God is in the argument, and he may well be found in the delight of vigorous human discourse.

In some ways, for modern Judaism the Tanakh is not the most important text. In matters of practice, the texts of classical rabbinic Judaism, of its subsequent commentators— such as the biblical *Targums* (paraphrases) and medieval texts such as the *Mishneh Torah* ('Copy of the Torah') of Maimonides, and commentaries by Rashi and Abraham ibn Ezra — and of a whole range of popular prayer books and guides to Jewish life, including the *Zohar* and *Shulhan Arukh* (c. 1565) – are often the first port of call. Yet for the composers of the Mishnah, Tanakh was the foundation not just of the laws being composed, but of life itself; and for the Talmud, Mishnah and Tanakh were foundational.

Judaism's sacred texts, then, can be envisaged as concentric circles: The innermost three circles are the Tanakh, at the very centre, Torah, followed by *Nevi'im* (the prophets), and *Ketuvim* (the writings). After that come Mishnah, Talmud, and *Midrash* ('commentary') – the ongoing tradition of commentary and critique, a potentially never-ending circle that includes all texts that manage to become, in some way, of existential value to the Jewish community.

ERIC S. CHRISTIANSON

DIVISIONS OF THE HEBREW SCRIPTURES

Torah
Genesis, Exodus, Leviticus, Numbers, Deuteronomy

Nevi'im (Prophets)
Former: Joshua, Judges, Samuel, Kings
Latter: major: Isaiah, Jeremiah, Ezekiel
Minor: the book of the twelve: Hosea, Joel, Amos, Obadiah, Jonah, Micah, Nahum, Habakkuk, Zephaniah, Haggai, Zechariah, Malachi

Ketuvim (Writings)
Psalms, Proverbs, Job, Song of Songs, Ruth, Lamentations, Ecclesiastes, Esther, Daniel, Ezra, Nehemiah, Chronicles

CHAPTER 32

Beliefs

In the Hebrew Bible, the Israelites experienced God as the Lord of history. The most uncompromising expression of his unity is the *Shema* prayer: 'Hear, O Israel, the Lord our God is one Lord' (Deuteronomy 6:4–9). According to Scripture, the universe owes its existence to the one God, the creator of heaven and earth, and since all human beings are created in his image, all men and women are brothers and sisters. Thus, the belief in one God implies, for the Jewish faith, that there is one humanity and one world.

GOD AND CREATION

For the Jewish people, God is conceived as the transcendent creator of the universe; that is to say, God is distinct from that which he has created, above and beyond the world. He is 'wholly other' than anything that is not God. Unlike creation, God is uncreated and does not depend upon anything for his existence. Thus he is described as forming heaven and earth:

> *In the beginning God created the heavens and the earth. The earth was without*
> *form and void, and darkness was upon the face of the deep; and the Spirit of*
> *God was moving over the face of the waters.*

> Genesis 1:1–2

Throughout the Bible this theme of divine transcendence is repeatedly affirmed. The prophet Isaiah proclaims:

> *Have you not known? Have you not heard? Has it not been told you from the*
> *beginning? Have you not understood from the foundations of the earth? It is he*
> *who sits above the circle of the earth, and its inhabitants are like grasshoppers;*
> *who stretches out the heavens like a curtain and spreads them like a tent to*
> *dwell in.*

> Isaiah 40: 21–2

Despite this view of God as remote from his creation, he is also viewed as actively involved in the cosmos. In the Bible, the belief that he is always omnipresent is repeatedly stressed. In the rabbinic period, Jewish scholars formulated the doctrine of the *Shekhinah* to denote the divine presence. As the indwelling presence of God, the *Shekhinah* is compared to light. Thus the Midrash paraphrases Numbers 6:25, 'The Lord make his face to shine upon you, and be gracious to you': 'May he give thee of the light of the *Shekhinah*'. In the Middle Ages the doctrine of the *Shekhinah* was further elaborated: according to Saadiah Gaon, the *Shekhinah* is identical with the glory of God, and serves as an intermediary between God and human beings during the prophetic encounter. Judah Halevi of Toledo argued in his *Kuzari* that it is the *Shekhinah* rather than God himself who appears to prophets.

Some feminists today see the *Shekhinah* as a way for women to connect spiritually to the divine, distinct from the normalized male attribute of God that occurs in many Jewish contexts.

TIME AND ETERNITY

The Hebrew Bible also depicts God as having neither beginning nor end, a teaching that was elaborated by the rabbis. According to the Talmud, there is an unbridgeable gap between God and humans:

> Come and see! The measure of the Holy One, blessed be he, is unlike the measure of flesh and blood. The things fashioned by a creature of flesh and blood outlast him; the Holy One, blessed be he, outlasts the things he has fashioned.

God's eternal reign is similarly affirmed in midrashic literature. Yet the rabbis discouraged speculation about the nature of eternity. The Mishnah states:

> Whoever reflects on four things, it were better for him that he had not come into the world: What is above? What is beneath? What is before? and What is after?

> Whither shall I go from thy Spirit?
>
> Or whither shall I flee from thy presence?
>
> If I ascend to heaven, thou art there!
>
> If I make my bed in Sheol, thou art there!
>
> If I take the wings of the morning
>
> and dwell in the uttermost parts of the sea,
>
> even there thy hand shall lead me,
>
> and thy right hand shall hold me.
>
> Psalms 139:7–12, Old Testament, Revised Standard Version

Despite such teaching, in the Middle Ages Jewish theologians debated this issue. In his *Guide for the Perplexed* Maimonides argued that time itself was part of creation; when God is described as existing before the creation of the universe, the 'time' should not be understood in its normal sense. This concept was developed by Joseph Albo in his *Ikkarim* (fifteenth century), where he argues that the concepts of priority and perpetuity can only be applied to God in a negative sense. That is, when God is described as being 'before' or 'after' some period, this only means that he was not non-existent before or after that time. However, terms indicating a time-span cannot be applied to God himself.

According to other Jewish thinkers, God is outside time altogether: he does not live in the present, have a past, or look forward to the future, but lives in the 'Eternal Now'. Hence, God is experiencing every moment in the past and future history of the created world simultaneously and eternally. What for us are fleeting moments rushing by are, for God, a huge tapestry, of which he sees every part continually.

OMNIPOTENCE AND OMNISCIENCE

Allied to this is the Jewish conviction that God is all-powerful and all-knowing. From biblical times the belief in God's omnipotence has been a central feature of the faith. Thus in Genesis, when Abraham's wife Sarah expressed astonishment at the suggestion that she should have a child at the age of ninety, she was criticized. Similarly, when Jerusalem was threatened by the Chaldeans, God declared: 'Behold, I am the Lord, the God of all flesh; is anything too hard for me?' (Jeremiah 32:27).

In the Middle Ages, however, Jewish thinkers wrestled with the concept of divine omnipotence. Maimonides, for example, argues in his *Guide for the Perplexed* that, although God is all-powerful, there are certain actions that he cannot perform because they are logically impossible:

Modern statue of Moses Maimonides, Rabbi Moshe ben Maimon (1135–1204), in Córdoba, Spain.

That which is impossible has a permanent and constant property, which is not the result of some agent, and cannot in any way change, and consequently we do not ascribe to God the power of doing what is impossible.

Regarding God's omniscience, the Bible proclaims:

The Lord looks down from heaven, he sees all the sons of men ... he who fashions the hearts of them all, and observes all their deeds.

Psalms 33:13, 15

Following the biblical view, rabbinic Judaism asserted that God's knowledge is not limited by space and time. Rather, nothing is hidden from him. Further, the rabbis declared that God's foreknowledge of events does not deprive human beings of free will. Thus, in the Mishnah, the second-century sage Akiva declares: 'All is foreseen, but freedom of choice is given.' In his *Guide for the Perplexed*, Maimonides claims that God knows all things before they occur. Nonetheless, human beings are unable to comprehend the nature of God's knowledge because it is of a different order from theirs. Similarly, it is impossible to understand how divine foreknowledge is compatible with free will.

THE ELECTION AND MISSION OF ISRAEL

The Bible asserts that God controls and guides the universe. The Hebrew term for such divine action is *hashgahah*, derived from Psalm 33:14: 'From where he sits enthroned he looks forth on all the inhabitants of the earth.' Such a view implies that the dispensation of a wise and benevolent providence is found everywhere: all events are ultimately foreordained by God. Such a notion was developed in rabbinic literature, where God is depicted as the judge of the world, who provides for the destiny of individuals as well as nations on the basis of their actions.

Jews further affirm that God chose the Jews as his special people:

> For you are a people holy to the Lord your God: the Lord your God has chosen
> you to be a people for his own possession out of all the peoples that are on the
> face of the earth.
>
> Deuteronomy 7:6

Through its election, Israel has been given a historic mission to bear divine truth to humanity. God's choice of Israel thus carries with it numerous responsibilities:

> For I have chosen him, that he may charge his children and his household after
> him to keep the way of the Lord by doing righteousness and justice.
>
> Genesis 18:19

THE TORAH

To accomplish this task, God revealed both the oral Torah and the written Torah to Moses on Mount Sinai. As Maimonides explains:

> The Torah was revealed from Heaven. This implies our belief that the whole of
> the Torah found in our hands this day is the Torah that was handed down by
> Moses, and that it is all of divine origin. By this I mean that the whole of the
> Torah came unto him from before God in a manner which is metaphorically

called 'speaking'; but the real nature of that communication is unknown to everybody except to Moses.

In rabbinic literature, a distinction is drawn between the revelation of the Pentateuch – the first five books of the Bible, and Torah in the narrow sense – and the prophetic writings. Such a distinction is frequently expressed within Judaism: the Torah was given directly by God, whereas the prophetic books were given by means of prophecy. The remaining books of the Bible were conveyed by means of the Holy Spirit rather than through prophecy. According to the rabbis, the expositions and elaborations of the written Law were also revealed by God to Moses on Mount Sinai, subsequently passed from generation to generation, and through this process additional legislation was incorporated, a process referred to as 'the oral Torah'. Thus traditional Judaism affirms that God's revelation is twofold and binding for all time.

> Before the mountains were brought forth,
>
> or ever thou hadst formed the earth and the world,
>
> from everlasting to everlasting thou art God.
>
> Psalm 90:2, Old Testament, Revised Standard Version

According to tradition, God revealed 613 commandments to Moses. These *mitzvot* are recorded in the Five Books of Moses and classified in two major categories:
- statutes concerned with ritual performances, char acterized as obligations between human beings and God;
- judgments consisting of ritual laws that would have been adopted by society even if they had not been decreed by God.

All these laws, together with their expansion in rabbinic sources such as the Mishnah and Talmud, are binding on Jewry for all time.

Rabbinic Judaism teaches that there are two tendencies in every person: the good inclination (*yetzer ha-tov*) and the evil inclination (*yetzer ha-ra*). The former urges individuals to do what is right, whereas the latter encourages sinful acts. At all times a person is to be on guard against the assaults of the *yetzer ha-ra*.

ESCHATOLOGY

Eschatology is teaching about the 'last things', such as the end of time, the afterlife, heaven, and hell. Traditional Judaism asserts that, at the end of time, God will send the Messiah to redeem his people and usher in the messianic age. In Scripture, such a figure is depicted in various ways, and as time passed the rabbis elaborated the themes found in the Bible and Jewish literature of the Second Temple period. In the midrashim and the Talmud they formulated an elaborate eschatological scheme, divided into various stages.

First there will be the time of the messianic redemption. According to the Babylonian Talmud, the messianic age will take place on earth after a period of decline and calamity, and will result in the complete fulfilment of every human wish. Peace will reign on earth; Jerusalem will be rebuilt; and at the close of this era the dead will be resurrected and joined with their souls, and a final judgment will come upon all humankind. Those who are judged righteous will enter heaven (*Gan Eden*), whereas those deemed wicked will be condemned to everlasting punishment in hell (*Gehinnom*).

However, 'when the Messiah comes' is also a colloquial way of saying 'never', and modern Judaism has become increasingly eschatology-neutral, particularly as a result of disillusion following such messianic disappointments of Bar-Kochba and Sabbati Zevi.

CHANGING BELIEFS IN MODERN TIMES

From biblical times Jews have subscribed to a wide range of beliefs about the nature of God and his activity in the world. In modern times, these have been increasingly called into question. In the nineteenth century, reformers sought to reinterpret this belief system for modern Jews. In their view, it no longer made sense to believe in the coming of the messiah and the eschatological scheme as outlined in rabbinic sources. Subsequent movements, such as Reconstructionist and Humanistic Judaism, rejected the supernaturalism of the past, and called for a radical revision of Jewish theology for the contemporary age. In more recent times, the Holocaust has raised fundamental questions about belief in a supernatural God who watches over his chosen people. Today there is widespread uncertainty in the Jewish world about the central tenets of the faith.

DAN COHN-SHERBOK

CHAPTER 33

Worship and Festivals

An annual cycle of worship and festivals gives Judaism its distinctive form. There is a major or minor festival almost every month of the year. Beginning with *Rosh Hashanah*, New Year's Day, on the first day of *Tishrei*, and proceeding to the period of penitence that begins in the twelfth month, *Elul*, Jews are able to express and celebrate their identity through the regular re-enactment of stories that explore life's meaning and purpose. High and low points of the Jewish story are remembered year by year.

THE HEART OF JUDAISM

Maimonides' 'Thirteen Principles of the Faith' help define Judaism. They were not intended to become a creed — indeed, Judaism is based much more upon practice than belief — and can be summarized in the three great themes that underpin the Jewish religion: creation, revelation, and redemption.

At the heart of Judaism is the profound idea that human beings can bring God into the world through their everyday actions and interactions. Although Judaism acknowledges a huge distance between the infinity of God and the limitations of human beings, it believes we are called to be partners with God in the task of creation. This understanding of the divine–human relationship can be traced back to the Babylonian Talmud (*Shabbat* 10a, 119b, *Sanhedrin* 38a). The supreme moment of revelation was when the people received the commandments at Mount Sinai; hence, Jewish religious expression or worship occurs when *mitzvoth*, the commandments, are followed, as one practises *halakhah*, or 'walking in God's way'.

> *Judaism is a very practical and also a very joyful religion. 'Happy are we! How good is our lot! How pleasant is our destiny! How beautiful our heritage! Happy are we who, early and late, evening and morning, twice each day declare: Hear O Israel, the Lord is our God, the Lord is One!'*
>
> *The Jewish Prayer Book*, extract from the Morning Service.

HOME AND SYNAGOGUE

The object of greatest religious importance in Judaism is a scroll of the Law, a *Sefer* Torah. It is a moving moment when the Torah scroll is taken out of its protective ark in the synagogue during the course of a service of worship and held up before the people. The synagogue is important as a meeting place, a focus for prayer, and house of study. But it is not the only significant place of worship, in the sense in which a mosque or a church may be; Jews often refer to the synagogue simply as *shul*, school.

The home is the focus of many of the most central aspects of Jewish religious life, such as *Shabbat*, the festivals, and the dietary laws, as well as education across the generations. Every effort is made to involve children in the celebration of the major festivals. It is a child who asks the questions concerning the special night at the *Seder* celebration during *Pesach*, Passover. It is children who enjoy drowning out the sound of Haman's name whenever it is mentioned during the reading of the book of Esther at Purim. It is children who are given the best places in front of the lights of the *menorah*, candelabrum, at the festival of *Hanukkah*.

THREE PILGRIMAGE FESTIVALS

Three of the most popular biblical festivals are known as 'pilgrimage' festivals, since they recall the three annual occasions when Jews made the journey to worship in Jerusalem when the Temple played a central role in Jewish life. These are the eight-day festival of *Pesach* (Passover), *Shavuot* (Pentecost), and *Sukkot* (Tabernacles), also an eight-day festival. Together, they form an annual re-enactment of the special events that forged the relationship between the Jews and their God.

- *Pesach* (15–21/22 *Nisan*) remembers the Exodus from Egypt under the leadership of Moses, and celebrates the passage from slavery to freedom. The highlight is the first evening, with the observance of the *Seder*. Around the table in the home, Jews relive the story, often reading from the *Haggadah*, 'telling', the order of the Seder, and reflect how it must have felt to be a slave in Egypt (Exodus 13:8).
- *Shavuot* (6 *Sivan*) marked the bringing of the first fruits in the days of the Temple, and celebrates the giving of the Torah by God to Moses on Mount Sinai.
- *Sukkot* (15–20 *Tishrei*) commemorates the time when God protected the people in the desert.

In many ways, the story of the Exodus from Egypt did not end with Moses gaining freedom for a small group of people centuries ago. The theme of Passover gives a context

> The three Pilgrim festivals have in common the theme of joy in God's presence: 'And you shall rejoice on your festivals' (Deuteronomy 16:14–16) … The festive joy is traditionally expressed in feasting with meat and drink, and with the purchase of new garments for the women. It is a joy which is only complete when allied with concern for the needy; as the verse continues, 'with … the strangers, orphans and widows among you.'
>
> Rabbi Norman Solomon

SEDER MEAL

Through the ritual and symbolism of the *Seder* meal, Jews tell the story of how their ancestors left Egypt. The foods placed upon the often beautifully decorated *Seder* plate are symbolic and comprise: three wafers of unleavened bread, *matzot*, to symbolize the bread eaten by the Israelites when they left Egypt in a hurry (Exodus 12:39); bitter herbs, *maror*, to recall the experiences of slavery in Egypt (Exodus 1:14); a sweet paste, *haroset*, made from almonds, apples, and wine, to represent the mortar used for building in Egypt as slaves, and symbolize both the toils of slavery and the sweetness of redemption and freedom; a bowl of salt water to represent the bitter tears of slavery, with parsley used for dipping; a roasted bone, as a reminder of the Paschal lamb; and a roasted egg, as a reminder of the offering brought to the Temple for the festival with the Paschal lamb – these last two items being left on the *Seder* plate during the meal, and not eaten. It has also been the custom, since Rabbinic times, to drink four cups of wine during the *Seder* to represent the four stages of redemption, from the Exodus to the future coming of the messiah.

for exploration of the issues of freedom and slavery, and the accompanying themes of risk, choice, hope, disappointment, leadership, hardship, and sacrifice. Moses has inspired many people who have struggled to gain freedom from prejudice and oppression; issues of marginalization and possibilities for liberation in the contemporary world are often discussed during the *Seder* meal.

ROSH HASHANAH

The new year festival of *Rosh Hashanah* (1–2 *Tishrei*), as in many traditions, is a time for making resolutions about the future. However, for the Jews it is a serious occasion. A month earlier a forty-day period of penitence begins – the Ten Days of Awe, '*yamim noraim*' – and *Rosh Hashanah* marks the beginning of the last ten of these days. The foods eaten at the meal on New Year's Eve symbolize sweetness, blessings, and plenty. Bread is dipped into honey – rather than the usual salt – and the following prayer is said: 'May it be your will to renew for us a good and sweet year.' Prayers at the morning service the following day, which lasts up to six hours, focus on the characteristics of God as creator, king, and judge: the God who will show mercy and compassion to those who sincerely turn towards him, '*teshuva*'. The sounding of the ram's horn, '*shofar*', regularly through the service is literally a wake-up call to the people (see Amos 3:6).

> *From the* Seder *liturgy*
>
> *This is the bread of affliction which our fathers ate in the land of Egypt.*
>
> *Let all who are hungry come and eat.*
>
> *Let all who are in want come and celebrate the Passover with us.*
>
> *May it be God's will to redeem us from all trouble and from all servitude.*
>
> *Next year at this season, may the whole house of Israel be free!*
>
> From the *Seder Haggadah, The Union Haggadah,* ed. The Central Council of American Rabbis, 1923.

YOM KIPPUR

The Day of Atonement, '*Yom Kippur*' (10 *Tishrei*), is a fast day marking the end of the Ten Days of Awe, and is the holiest day in the Jewish liturgical year, when Jews solemnly review their record of behaviour and literally turn to face a new year. The whole day is spent in prayer for forgiveness and for a good year ahead, and for at least part of it synagogues are full to overflowing. *Yom Kippur* marks one of the most emotionally charged times of the Jewish year. The theme is return to God, '*teshuva*' – a major religious theme within Judaism, involving a renewed commitment to walk in the right path. *Kol Nidrei* – a declaration in Aramaic – forms the beginning of the synagogue service, often sung to a moving melody, and sets the tone as the congregation gathers in awe.

Work is forbidden, as on *Shabbat*. There are five further prohibitions, '*innuyim*', or forms of self-discipline, that apply during the *Yom Kippur* fast, and also the fast of *Tisha b'Av*, discussed below. Jews must abstain from eating and drinking, anointing with oils, sexual relations, washing for pleasure, and wearing leather shoes.

The Closing of the Gates, '*Ne'ilah*', is the final service, as the fast ends, and emphasizes the importance of the last hour in which the gates of heaven remain open for a returning to God. *Avina Malkenu*, 'our father, our king', is chanted to express the congregation's commitment to the unity of God, followed by a final blow on the *shofar*.

A Jewish family in Israel celebrate Passover together with the *Seder* meal.

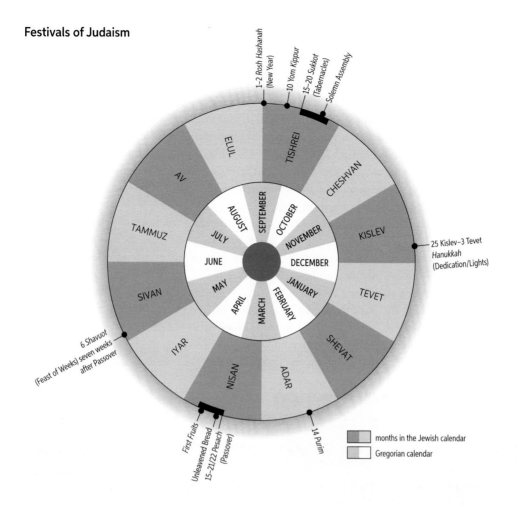

The diagram shows the Jewish calendar months and Gregorian calendar with festival markings:

- 1–2 Rosh Hashanah (New Year)
- 10 Yom Kippur
- 15–20 Sukkot (Tabernacles)
- Solemn Assembly
- 25 Kislev–3 Tevet Hanukkah (Dedication/Lights)
- 6 Shavuot (Feast of Weeks) seven weeks after Passover
- First Fruits
- Unleavened Bread
- 15–21/22 Pesach (Passover)
- 14 Purim

Jewish calendar months: ELUL, TISHREI, CHESHVAN, KISLEV, TEVET, SHEVAT, ADAR, NISAN, IYAR, SIVAN, TAMMUZ, AV

Gregorian calendar months: SEPTEMBER, OCTOBER, NOVEMBER, DECEMBER, JANUARY, FEBRUARY, MARCH, APRIL, MAY, JUNE, JULY, AUGUST

Legend:
- months in the Jewish calendar
- Gregorian calendar

MINOR FESTIVALS

The most popular of the minor festivals are *Hanukkah* (25 *Kislev* – 2 *Tevet*), Purim (14 *Adar*), and the New Year for Trees, *Tu biShevat* (15 *Shevat*).

Hanukkah celebrates the rededication of the Temple in about 165 BCE, after its defilement by the Greeks. On each of the eight nights of the festival, a light is lit to commemorate the 'miracle of the oil'. The Hasmoneans, seeking to rededicate the Temple, could only find one cruse of oil, enough to keep the Temple *menorah* burning for a day – yet it lasted for eight. This is interpreted as symbolic of God's creative action in the world.

Between the destruction of the first Temple and the building of the second, many Jews were threatened with massacre by Haman's scheming with Ahasuerus, King of Persia, but Queen Esther and her uncle Mordechai were used by God to avert catastrophe. Purim celebrates this deliverance with parties and sending gifts of food to people in need, and the scroll of the book of Esther, *Megillah*, is read in the synagogue.

Judaism celebrates a new year for trees, *Tu biShevat*, a popular festival with the return to the land of Israel in modern times. In Israel it is marked by a school holiday and tree-planting ceremonies.

OTHER FAST DAYS

Of the other fast days the most important is 9 *Av* (*Tishah b'Av*), when the destruction of the two Temples, in 586 BCE and in 70 CE, is commemorated, as well as other tragedies of Jewish history. Reform Jews often use the day to commemorate the Holocaust.

On *Yom Kippur* and on *Tishah b'Av* people fast for twenty-five hours, instead of the twenty-four hours required for other fast days. Nothing is eaten or drunk during this time, unless there is a practical reason for not undertaking this discipline.

SECULAR JUDAISM

Many Jews who describe themselves as 'secular' nevertheless experience a sense of belonging to the wider Jewish community at times such as *Pesach* or *Yom Kippur*. Official Israeli holidays can also strengthen the links between communal identity and liturgy:

* Holocaust Day, *Yom HaShoah* (27 *Nisan*) remembers the Holocaust and the six million Jews who were murdered.
* Memorial Day, *Yom HaZikaron* (4 *Iyar*) remembers the soldiers killed defending the state of Israel.
* Independence Day, *Yom Ha-Atzma'ut* (5 *Iyar*) marks the anniversary of the founding of the State of Israel in 5708 (1948 CE).
* Jerusalem Day, *Yom Yerushalayim* (28 *Iyar*) commemorates the reunification of the city of Jerusalem in 5727, 1967 CE.
* The Israeli Declaration of Independence, proclaimed on 14 May 1948, is celebrated with social activities, in Israel and throughout the world, and special psalms and prayers are said in the synagogue, but is somewhat controversial, for both religious and political reasons.

LIZ RAMSEY

I AM A JEW

 My paternal grandparents immigrated to Western Europe from Lithuania at the turn of the twentieth century to escape the effects of anti-Semitism and grinding poverty. My mother was born and brought up in Frankfurt-am-Main, Germany. She fled Germany at the end of June 1939, a refugee from Nazi persecution. She and her father were the only members of my maternal line to survive, the rest of the family are numbered among the millions of Jews murdered in the Holocaust. We live in a predominantly secular world, where religion and spiritual values are often assigned a very low priority. But, for me, my Jewish faith and family history have shaped and defined my identity. I attach great value to the traditions of democracy, freedom of speech, and equality before the law. I also feel a personal responsibility to contribute to building a better understanding and harmonious relations between the Jewish community and the non-Jewish majority among whom we live.

I also think I am incredibly lucky to be Jewish. I draw inspiration from the courage and fortitude with which my mother confronted both the difficulties of her childhood and the humiliation and poverty of being a refugee. No less inspiring is the example of friends who are Holocaust survivors. They are often the sole surviving members of their families, whose homes and communities were completely destroyed. Their suffering and loss is unimaginable. They were brutalized and terrorized solely because they were born Jewish. Yet despite all this, so many of the survivors have chosen to renew and rebuild their lives firmly rooted in the Jewish faith and tradition into which they were born. This, for me, is proof of the eternal and enduring nature of their Jewish faith. The triumph of their humanity is truly inspiring.

Many of those murdered in the Holocaust were condemned in part because of the failure of so many countries, including the Western democracies, to take in Jewish refugees. So for me, and most Jews living in the diaspora (that is, Jews who live outside the borders of Israel), Israel represents a life insurance policy, a place of safety to which we can go if we feel we are once again endangered by anti-Semitism. Israel is, therefore, very important for the worldwide Jewish community. I have visited Jerusalem twice. It is at the heart and geographical centre of the Jewish world. Synagogues around the world are all built facing Jerusalem. The festival of *Hanukkah* and the fast days of *Tevet*, *Tammuz,* and *Av* have their origin in the sieges of Jerusalem and the desecration of the Temple. Each time I prayed at the *Kotel* – formerly known as the 'Western Wall' or 'Wailing Wall' – I sobbed uncontrollably.

For me Judaism is not just a religion, but a complete and distinctive way of life. It defines my relationship with God, my relationship with other people, Jewish and non-Jewish, and my obligations as a human being. The central and defining principal of Judaism is belief in a single God who is responsible for the creation of the universe and everything in it. The foundation of Judaism is the Torah, also known as the Five Books of Moses. I remember as a five-year-old schoolboy going after school to *cheder*, where I was taught to read Hebrew. At school I had to attend assembly each morning for Christian prayers, while at home, at the synagogue, and at *cheder* I was expected to follow Jewish religious practice and traditions. For a few years I found this mixture of Jewish and Christian teaching all very confusing, especially when one day at school I was beaten up because, according to my accuser, I had 'murdered little Lord Jesus'!

Every Jew is obliged to obey the law of the land, to do all they can to preserve human life, *pikuach nefesh*, and give to charity. This includes not only donations of money or goods, but acts of kindness, the promotion of education, and caring for the sick, needy, and elderly. On *Shabbat,* Jews are obliged to refrain from all forms of work: using machines, operating mechanical or electrical equipment, cooking, handling money, and travelling in a vehicle. For me, *Shabbat* is the one day of the week to which I always look forward: it is truly a day of physical and spiritual renewal.

David Arnold

CHAPTER 34

Branches of Judaism

The majority of Jews throughout the world today are descendants either of the Sephardim or the Ashkenazim. Before being driven from Spain by the Inquisition in 1492, the Sephardim had been closely involved with the Muslim world, enabling them to develop a unique intellectual culture. Sephardic Jews – 'Sepharad' means Spain – created the Ladino language, a mix of Spanish and Hebrew.

The Ashkenazim came from central Europe, mainly Germany and France, and later moved to Poland and Russia. 'Ashkenaz' means the area inhabited by the Ashkenazim, who adhere to *minhag Ashkenaz* – a region that coincides with modern-day Germany, but also extends from France to the Pale of Settlement, the region within which Jews were allowed to reside by Imperial Russia. Ashkenazi Jews developed Yiddish – a mixture of Hebrew and medieval German – as their language and around it produced a culture rich in art, music, and literature. The difference in cultural background between the Ashkenazim and Sephardim is evident in Israel today, where each supports its own chief rabbi.

But the Jews are not a race, and Judaism is not an unchanging institution. Due to intermarriage, conversion, and dispersion among the nations, there has been a branching out over the centuries, and wide cultural differences between Jews have resulted. The difference between the black Falasha Jews of Ethiopia and the Indian Jews of Mexico, for instance, is immense.

In addition to these cultural groupings, several religious branches can be distinguished within Judaism today. Modern Judaism is rooted in rabbinic, or Talmudic, Judaism, and both evolved from biblical Judaism.

ORTHODOX JUDAISM

Orthodox Judaism regards itself as the only true Judaism. During the first half of the nineteenth century it developed into a well-defined movement, seeking to preserve traditional (classical) Judaism against the emerging Reform movement in East Europe.

Orthodox Jews are characterized by a 'Torah-true' approach to life, teaching that God personally and decisively revealed himself, in giving the Torah at Sinai, and that the words of the Torah are therefore divine and hence fully authoritative – the changeless revelation of God's eternal will. Every aspect of the Orthodox Jew's life is to be governed by the commandments (*mitzvot*). Jews are to study the Torah daily, and conform their lives to its propositions and rituals, including the strict rules of *Shabbat* observance, dietary laws, and prayer three times a day. In short, Orthodox Judaism is 'mitzvahcentric'.

At the start of the nineteenth century many East European Jews in rural areas lived in a close-knit community known as a *shtetl*, a stockaded, traditional culture shut off from the secular world. However, as large numbers started to emigrate to the United States, Orthodox leaders such as Rabbi Samson Hirsch (1808–88) encouraged Jews to involve themselves in the contemporary culture of the Western world, pursue secular university education, and develop philosophical thinking. Today, most Orthodox Jews believe adjustment to the modern world is legitimate, so long as it does not conflict with the teachings of the Torah.

Orthodox Jews maintain a high regard for the rabbi as teacher and interpreter of the Torah, and place a strong emphasis upon education, particularly day-schools where traditional learning can be acquired. Most Orthodox Jews are Zionist, supporting the state of Israel, and many hope for a personal messiah: an ideal man who will one day fully redeem Israel, although exactly what is meant by 'ideal' and 'redeem' is the subject of some debate. However few today would accept the divine authority of the Torah, the old test of 'Orthodoxy', and it is not uncommon for Jews to belong to both an Orthodox and a Progressive or Liberal synagogue. The term 'Orthodox' was originally used as a label for traditionalists opposed to radical change; now there are many shades of Orthodoxy, as the energy inspired by the Reform movement influences most Jewish groupings.

REFORM JUDAISM

Reform Judaism had its origins in Germany, where the Enlightenment of the eighteenth century stressed reason and progress. Emancipation in the following century opened the Jewish people to new freedoms, to equal rights as citizens, and to new opportunities to explore secular society. Jews quickly began to adapt to this new age, geared to change, growth, scientific inquiry, and critical evaluation. To meet this move away from Jewishness, Abraham Geiger (1810–74) and others declared that modern people could no longer accept the revelation of the Torah as factual and binding, and encouraged changes in ritual law and worship. Dietary laws were abandoned, prayers were translated from Hebrew into the vernacular, and synagogue worship was changed – the organ was introduced, services shortened, and the 'family pew' replaced segregation of the sexes. Some Jews even began to worship on Sunday rather than *Shabbat*.

In the USA, the Reform movement was led by Isaac Wise (1819–1900), who founded an organization of Reform congregations, and in 1875 set up the Hebrew Union College, the main seminary for training Reform rabbis. While Reform Judaism is one of the most progressive major branches of modern Judaism, active in the area of dialogue between faiths, the smaller Reconstructionist and Renewal movements are more radical in such areas as gender and political activism. Since the 1970s, Hebrew Union College has ordained women rabbis.

Liberal (Reform) Judaism[1] is still evolving – as revelation is seen to be a continuing process – and seeks to keep current with each new generation, using reason and experience to establish the relevance or truth of a proposition. Thus the ethical teachings of the prophets are emphasized rather than the ritual Law. Reform Judaism provides an individualized, non-authoritarian approach to religion; a law is observed, not because God said so, but because it is meaningful to modern religious experience.

Many Jews claim the Reform movement is now the most creative component within Judaism. With younger Jews no longer feeling that Judaism is defined by suffering and persecution, they are exploring the boundaries of cultural experience and convey a sense of expectancy for a new age of Judaism.

CONSERVATIVE JUDAISM

Many European Jews were uncomfortable with the radical changes introduced by Reform Judaism, and as a result Conservative Judaism arose at the end of the nineteenth century, emphasizing the historical elements of the Jewish tradition. As president of the newly-founded Jewish Theological Seminary, Solomon Schechter (1850–1915) led the movement in the USA, stressing commitment to tradition – with adjustments if necessary. Conservative Judaism thus has roots in Orthodoxy and Reform, and combines the ideals of both, preserving traditional Jewish practices, but holding that Jewish law can be reinterpreted in the light of modern views and trends – such as the findings of modern historical criticism.

Conservativism has maintained a strong emphasis on the people of Israel and modern Zionism. Laypeople have considerable influence: some congregations, for instance, permit the use of the organ, while others do not; some emphasize dietary laws, others do not. Conservative Judaism is possibly the largest single Jewish grouping in North America. In Israel and Britain, where it has been a more recent development, it is known by its Hebrew name, *Masorti*.

RECONSTRUCTIONIST JUDAISM

Reconstructionist Judaism is an outgrowth of Conservative Judaism, based on the work of the scholar Mordecai Kaplan (1881–1983), who stressed Judaism as an evolving culture, giving equal importance to religion, ethics, and culture. Reconstructionist Judaism doesn't fit neatly into the traditional/liberal, observant/non observant continuum. Although

---

1   In the UK, there is a difference between Liberal/Progressive Judaism, which is closer to American Reform Judaism, and Reform Judaism, which is somewhat closer to the American Conservative movement.

there are few Reconstructionist groups outside the United States and Israel, the movement has influenced Judaism, contributing to a reappraisal of basic concepts such as God, Israel, and Torah. Since its inception in the late 1960s, Reconstructionism has developed the use of inclusive language, encouraged women to be fully involved in liturgical practice, and accepted people with one Jewish parent as Jewish. Reconstructionists are actively involved in developing liberal Judaism in Israel.

THE HASIDIM

The Hasidim, founded by Baal Shem Tov, have many sects around the world, each led by its own *rebbe*. However, there is — and has been historically — much controversy over whether the Hasidim inappropriately substitute the judgment of the *rebbe* for the laws of Torah.

In some Hasidic groups the men have a distinctive style of dress, including black coats and hats, and wear ear-locks. They have a joyful form of worship, involving song and dance. In the United States, the Lubavitch and Satmar sects are especially influential. Some Hasidim are ultra-Orthodox, living in isolation from the Gentile world. The Renewal Movement, with roots in the 1960s counter-culture, attempts to reinvigorate Judaism, drawing on elements from Jewish mystic, Hasidic, musical, and meditative traditions, and has been criticised by some as 'New Age'.

HUMANISTIC JUDAISM

Humanistic Judaism began in 1965 with the rejection or reinterpretation of the beliefs of traditional Judaism. For example, supernatural beliefs are denied, and the Exodus from Egypt is seen as a myth. Humanistic Jewish worship is very different from traditional worship, and rarely uses the word 'God'. Unlike traditional Judaism, Humanistic Jews 'welcome into the Jewish people all men and women who sincerely desire to share Jewish experience regardless of their ancestry.' The principal institution of Humanistic Judaism is the International Federation of Secular Humanistic Jews.

ULTRA-ORTHODOX JUDAISM

The Haredim, or Ultra-Orthodox Jews, view the total separation of Judaism from the modern world as a religious obligation. Whereas Sephardic Haredim generally support Zionism and the State of Israel, many Ashkenazi Haredim oppose both.

> *The Reconstructionist philosophy emphasizes our obligation as Jews to work for social justice and* tikkun olam, *the 'repair of the world'. Reconstructionists reject any distinction between 'religious life' and 'real life'.*
>
> A member of the Jewish Reconstructionist Congregation, Evanston, Illinois

> *We believe in the value of human reason and in the reality of the world which reason discloses. The natural universe stands on its own, requiring no supernatural intervention. We believe in the value of human existence and in the power of human beings to solve their problems both individually and collectively. Life should be directed to the satisfaction of human needs. Every person is entitled to life, dignity and freedom. We believe in the value of Jewish identity and in the survival of the Jewish people. Jewish history is a human story.*
>
> Proclamation stating the ideology and aims of Humanistic Judaism

RECENT DEVELOPMENTS

The collapse of the Soviet Union led to a rapid acceleration of Jewish immigration to Israel. Due to the earlier Soviet restriction of religious freedom, however, many of these immigrants came to Israel severely limited in their understanding and practice of Judaism. Unemployment, housing needs, and political unrest among Israelis and Palestinians created additional hardships associated with return to the Land.

The increased secularization of society has continued to threaten Jewish religious and community life through assimilation and intermarriage. To help counter these and other challenges, Chabad Lubavitch launched a successful programme of outreach towards unaffiliated Jews.

MARVIN WILSON
REVISED BY TIM DOWLEY

CHAPTER 35

Judaism in the Modern World

Jewish communities can be found in most parts of the modern world, which means there are great cultural and social variations as well as religious diversity within Judaism. Out of a worldwide total of around 13 million Jews the largest groupings live in Israel – 5,000,000 or 78.7 per cent of local population – and the USA – 5,700,000 or 2.1 per cent of local population. Although Jews account for no more than 0.25 per cent of the world's population, it would be hard to find another group of people who have had so much influence on the world in so many ways over such a long time. There is little sign of this influence lessening, in spite of the challenges facing Jewish survival. In the technological and scientific developments of the modern age, Jewish knowledge and expertise have a high profile, from medicine and genetic engineering to art and architecture. Jews are also prominent in the worlds of entertainment, law and politics. It is amazing how influence on this scale has been maintained despite the appalling loss of people and centres of learning that took place between 1933 and 1945.

WHO IS A JEW?

This question is hotly debated within contemporary Judaism. The Orthodox insistence that a Jew must be born of a Jewish mother – or convert according to Orthodox criteria – is largely disregarded by Reform Jews, but can lead to painful situations concerning identity and status for partners and children. The Reform view is that a person is a Jew if one parent is Jewish and that person is raised in a Jewish community. Moreover, conversion to Reform Judaism is a much simpler process. However, the term 'Judaism' does not only refer to a religion; more than fifty per cent of all Jews in Israel today call themselves 'secular', and half of the Jews in the USA do not belong to a synagogue or temple. Jews can be described as a 'nation' or 'people' – but the question of whether Judaism is a religion or ethnicity or peoplehood is complex and hotly debated.

> 'Lo alecha ha-mamlacha ligmor,' *says the Mishnah.*
>
> *'It is not incumbent on you to complete the work (of repairing the world), but neither are you free to evade it.'*
>
> Pirkei Avot 2:16

ISRAEL

Since its establishment in 1948, the state of Israel has been the focus of the Jewish world. In this tiny strip of land, only twelve miles wide in places, Jews from more than one hundred cultures mingle. All Jews, inside or outside Israel, feel an obligation to assess their relationship with Israel. Within Israel there are serious tensions between secular, Orthodox, and Ultra-Orthodox Jews concerning their attitudes to it. Some groups of Orthodox Jews do not support the existence of a Jewish state at all, and consider the militarism involved in preserving the state to be a contradiction of fundamental Jewish values.

The Zionist movement, dating back to Theodor Herzl (1860–1904), includes many supporters who prioritize the preservation of the Jewish people over the preservation of the Jewish religion. Herzl's dream was simply to establish a Jewish homeland after centuries of exile.

A common Israeli view, shared by many Jews in the diaspora, is that Israel needs to be strong in order to provide a safe haven for Jews all over the world, to provide a feeling of security and, perhaps even more importantly, hope for the future.

A minority fundamentalist group, *Gush Emunim*, 'Bloc of the Faithful', founded in 1974 in the wake of the

Interior of Eldridge Street Synagogue, Lower East Side, Manhattan, the oldest Eastern European synagogue in the USA.

Yom Kippur War, claims a divine right to the settlement of the West Bank, the Gaza Strip, and the Golan Heights — and sometimes as far as the Euphrates — as part of Israel.

JEWISH RELIGIOUS LIFE

Religious Jews pray and study Torah. They observe the dietary laws, keep the Sabbath and the festivals, and try to apply Jewish ethics in a global context of commerce and business. Jews are keen to observe religious regulations that emphasize the importance of the family and marriage. They are also aware of the responsibilities involved in being members of a community that is international as well as local, including praying together, providing welfare support, sharing in times of sadness and joy, and becoming involved in the cycle of rituals and festivals. In so doing, the religious Jew receives a glimpse of what heaven on earth might be like.

From the first century CE onwards, the rabbinic tradition bonded the Jewish people. Today there are more Jews studying in rabbinical seminaries than at any time since the great Babylonian academies. But following the rabbinic tradition is only one way of being Jewish.

Committed Jews remain faithful because the continuing story of Judaism depends on such commitment. Traditionally, Jews have shared a strong sense that there is a divine purpose for humanity, and that they have a special role in achieving it. The covenantal relationship between the Creator and creation, described in the Torah, means that together God and human beings may embark on the task of repairing or mending the world, *tikkun olam*.

Jews and Judaism have shown an amazing capacity to adapt to changing times and circumstances, while preserving the vital traditions central to the faith — a capacity closely linked to a strong emphasis on interpretation as well as revelation. For many Jews do not view revelation as something that happened solely once and for all in the distant past, but that there are different layers of meaning of Torah that can be rediscovered and interpreted in the light of contemporary contexts and needs.

> *To be a Jew means first belonging to the group ... Judaism is an evolving religious civilization.*
>
> Mordecai Kaplan

At the core of Jewish life is an immense store of moral energy. 'Social justice' is much the highest scoring factor that Jews in the United States give as relevant to what being Jewish involves. The restless drive to 'perfect the world under the sovereignty of God' remains after other practices have been abandoned. Judaism puts a high value on the dignity and responsibility of human beings, an emphasis that can provide the stimulus for creative dialogue and shared action between Jews, Muslims, and Christians with regard to the responsible stewardship and management of the world's resources, though there may never be more than an agreement to differ as far as theological issues are concerned.

DIVERSITY

The Jewish world reflects the pluralistic nature of the wider society in which Jews live. All Jews today contend with conflicting influences. One option is to cut off modern influences as far as possible, and seek refuge in tradition. Another is to abandon Judaism. The path that young Jews are increasingly choosing goes beyond the fractiousness between and within different groups with regard to authority, Torah, the role of women, modernity and cultural change and the state of Israel, and seeks to transform Judaism. But it is a mistake to define movements within modern Judaism as if they were sects or denominations. It is more accurate to use the term 'schools of thought'. There is a saying among Jews, 'Where you have two Jews you will have three opinions.'

THE FUTURE

The continuity of Judaism cannot be taken for granted. People are freer to be Jews than at any other time in history. They are also freer not to be. There is real concern about the continuation of the Jewish faith when in the United States one in two Jews either does not marry or marries a non-Jew. The long and painful history of anti-Semitism has understandably made some people uncertain about wanting their children to be overtly Jewish. There are many examples of people changing their name in order to hide their Jewishness.

A new generation of Jews sometimes express a desire to be free of the burden of memory that has traditionally been the hallmark of being Jewish. In complex, pluralist, and multicultural societies, some argue that Jewish identity has become superfluous. However, Jews and Judaism have an incredible capacity to survive.

There is also today a greater confidence in the continuation of the story that is Judaism than there has been since the Holocaust. Jewish people have managed to outlive a succession of oppressors. At the same time, they have increased the depth and richness of Jewish spirituality. More non-Jews than ever before find inspiration from the study of Judaism, as it has entered the curriculum of institutions of higher learning.

With rising levels of anti-Semitism across the world, the need for education and dialogue is acute. Contrary to many people's perceptions, Judaism combines universalism with the exclusivity of an ethnic religion. Jewish ideas of salvation extend to the non-Jewish world. Neither Christianity nor Islam would be conceivable without Judaism. Since the Holocaust, many Christians have commenced a more positive exploration of their Jewish roots. The monotheistic religions share a distinctive ethical focus that can inspire greater efforts on the part of human beings to work together to perfect the world.

LIZ RAMSEY

QUESTIONS

1. Explain the differences between the religion of the ancient Judeans and rabbinic Judaism.

2. What were the implications for Judaism of the destruction of the Temple in 70 CE?

3. Why was medieval Europe often such an inhospitable place for Jews?

4. Explain the importance of the covenant to Judaism.

5. How important are Maimonides' Thirteen Principles of the Faith for Judaism?

6. Explain the different roles of *Tanakh*, Mishnah, and Talmud in rabbinic Judaism.

7. Why are there such different views within Judaism about the coming of the Messiah?

8. Explain the main differences between Orthodox and Reform Judaism.

9. Why is the state of Israel so important in Judaism today?

10. How is modern Judaism able to contain such diverse views on questions of belief and practice?

FURTHER READING

Barnavi, Elie, ed., *A Historical Atlas of the Jewish People: From the Time of the Patriarchs to the Present*. New York: Knopf, 1992.

Biale, David, ed., *Cultures of the Jews: A New History*. New York: Schocken Books, 2002.

Cesarani, David, *Final Solution: The Fate of the Jews 1933–1949*. Macmillan, 2016.

Friedman, Richard E., *The Bible with Sources Revealed*. San Francisco: Harper, 2003.

Gaster, Theodor H., *The Festivals of the Jewish Year*. New York: William Sloane Associates, 1952.

Newman, Louis I., ed., *The Hasidic Anthology: Tales and Teachings of the Hasidim*. New York: Scribner, 1934.

Schama, Simon, *The Story of the Jews and the Fate of the World*. London: Bodley Head, 2013.

Seltzer, Tobert, *Jewish People, Jewish Thought*. New York: Macmillan 1980.

Steinsaltz, Adin, *The Talmud, the Steinsaltz Edition: A Reference Guide*. New York: Random House, 1989.

Steinsaltz, Adin, *A Guide to Jewish Prayer*. New York: Schocken, 2002.

PART 8
CHRISTIANITY

SUMMARY

With around one third of the world's population as adherents, Christianity is easily its largest religion. This fact, though, belies Christianity's humble origins, as what was essentially a small Jewish sect. For his early followers, Jesus was a Jewish teacher commanding strong loyalty, who provided direction through his preaching and a code for life, but was also more than a mere prophet. Christianity's divorce from Judaism was the result of its acceptance of Jesus himself as the Messiah of Jewish teaching, as the Son of God, and as a sacrifice made by God to redeem his followers from sin. Jesus' message not only supersedes that of the Old Testament in Christianity, but his life also furnishes it with its distinct rituals and festivals: baptism, communion, and, above all, Easter, are all taken from the Gospels, rather than from Jewish tradition.

While the earliest history of Christianity is one of anti-establishment insurgency, a threat to both Jewish and Roman authority, much of its subsequent history is closely bound up with European high politics. Christianity rapidly advanced into Asia and North Africa, and after 324 was officially recognized in the Roman Empire, a development that eventually saw much of the church's life centred on Rome itself. This ancient church subsequently broke up during three schisms that resulted from conflicts over doctrine and authority.

If Christianity today is the world's largest religion, it is also its most diverse. This is in part due to the division of the ancient church, producing distinct Orthodox, Catholic, and Protestant branches, but also due to more recent developments, such as the adaptation of churches in the global South to the needs and cultures of their local communities. In the West, too, older churches have been shaped by their different reactions to social and scientific developments, as well as by the emergence of new trends, such as the Pentecostal and Charismatic movements. The strength of Christianity increasingly lies outside the West, however, and in much of the world it faces competition from other faiths, especially Islam.

CHAPTER 36

A Historical Overview

Christianity rapidly spread beyond its original geographical region of Roman-occupied Palestine into the entire Mediterranean area. Something of this process of expansion is described in the Acts of the Apostles, in the New Testament. For example, it is clear that a Christian presence was already established in Rome itself within fifteen years of the resurrection of Christ. The imperial trade routes made possible the rapid traffic of ideas, as much as merchandise.

THE EARLY CHURCH

Three centres of the Christian church rapidly emerged in the eastern Mediterranean region. The church became a significant presence in its own original heartlands, with Jerusalem emerging as a leading centre of thought and activity. Asia Minor, modern-day Turkey, was already an important area of Christian expansion, as can be seen from the destinations of some of Paul's letters, and the references to the 'seven churches of Asia' in the book of Revelation. This process of expansion in this region continued, with the great imperial city of Constantinople, modern-day Istanbul, becoming a particularly influential centre of mission and political consolidation.

Yet further growth took place to the south, with the important Egyptian city of Alexandria emerging as a stronghold of Christian faith. With this expansion, new debates opened up. While the New Testament deals with the issue of the relationship of Christianity and Judaism, the expansion of Christianity into Greek-speaking regions led to the exploration of the way in which Christianity related to Greek philosophy. Many Christian writers sought to demonstrate, for example, that Christianity brought to fulfilment the great themes of the philosophy of Plato.

Yet this expansion was far from unproblematic. The 'imperial cult', which regarded worship of the Roman emperor as determinative of loyalty to the empire, was prominent in the eastern Mediterranean. Many Christians found themselves penalized for their insistence on worshipping only Christ. The expansion of Christianity regularly triggered off persecutions. These were often local – for example, the Decian persecution of 249–51, which was particularly vicious in North Africa. Christianity was not given official recognition as a 'legitimate religion' by the Roman state until 313, when Constantine, a recent convert, was joint emperor. From that point onwards, Christianity became not merely a recognized faith, but in time the official religion of the Roman state.

This period of Christian history was marked by a series of controversies over the identity of Jesus Christ and the Christian doctrine of God. A series of councils was convened to resolve these differences, and to ensure the unity of the Christian church throughout the empire. The most important of these was the Council of Chalcedon (451), which set out the definitive Christian interpretation of the identity of Jesus Christ as 'true God and true man'.

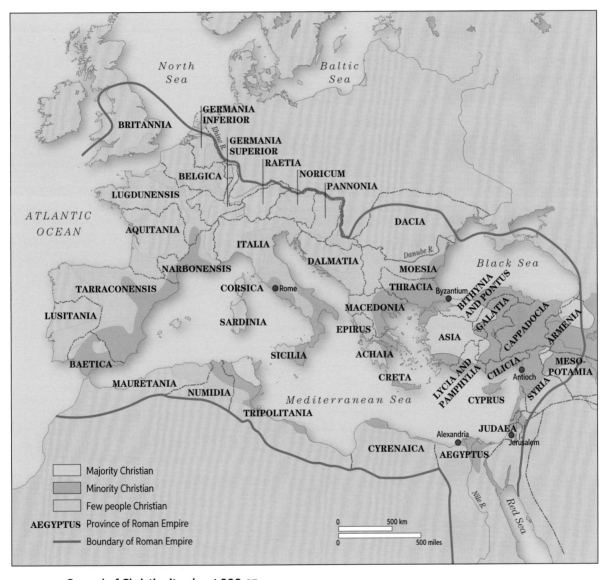

Spread of Christianity about 300 CE

CHRISTIANITY TIMELINE

0 • 200 CE • 400 CE • 600 CE • 800 CE • 1000 CE • 1200 CE • 1400 CE • 1600 CE • 1800 CE • 2000 CE

c. 30 Death of Jesus

c. 49 Council in Jerusalem debates the status of Jews and Gentiles

c. 65 Death of the apostle Paul

c. 301 Armenian King Tiridates III baptized

312 Constantine's reported vision of the cross

325 First Council of Nicaea

354–430 Augustine of Hippo, pre-eminent theologian

451 Council of Chalcedon

476 Roman Empire falls in the West

529 Benedict establishes first monastery

638 Muslims conquer Jerusalem

842 Orthodox iconoclastic controversy ends

862 Cyril and Methodius' mission to Moravia

1054 Break between Eastern and Western Christianity

1095 Pope Urban II calls for crusade

1099 Crusaders take Jerusalem

1187 End of Latin Kingdom of Jerusalem

c. 1225–74 Thomas Aquinas, author of *Summa Theologiae*

1517 Martin Luther posts his 95 Theses

1534 King Henry VIII becomes head of Church of England

1536 Calvin's *Institutes* published

1563 Council of Trent ends

1738 John Wesley's conversion experience, London

1781 Immanuel Kant's *Critique of Pure Reason*

1830 *Book of Mormon*

1859 Charles Darwin, *On the Origin of Species*

1870 First Vatican Council ends

1910 *The Fundamentals* published in USA

1948 First assembly of the World Council of Churches

1965 Second Vatican Council ends

The fall of the Roman Empire – traditionally dated to 476 – led to widespread insecurity within the Western church. In the East, the church continued to flourish, as the Eastern Empire, based at Constantinople, was largely unaffected by the attacks from northern European invaders which eventually ended Roman power in the West. The removal of Rome as a stabilizing influence, however, gave a new role to the church in the West, and particularly to its monasteries. The founding of the first Benedictine monastery at Monte Cassino around 525 is seen as a landmark in this process. The increasingly important role of the pope as a political force also began to emerge during this period.

The major disruptions within the Roman Empire in the fifth century led to a growing rift between the Western and Eastern churches. Increasing tension over political as much as theological issues led to the 'Great Schism' of 1054. By this stage, the influence of the Eastern Church had extended as far north as Moscow. While the story of Christianity in Eastern Europe at this time is important, most attention focuses on developments in the Western church.

THE MIDDLE AGES AND RENAISSANCE

Christianity underwent a major renaissance in Western Europe during the period 1000–1500. This era – often referred to as the 'Middle Ages' – saw the renewal of church life at every level. It was a period of consolidation of the political and social influence of the church, with the personal authority of the pope to intervene in political disputes of the region reaching unprecedented levels. The form of theology known as 'scholasticism' began to develop around this time, with thirteenth-century writers such as Thomas Aquinas and Duns Scotus achieving new levels of theological sophistication.

Yet scholasticism was not universally acclaimed. The European Renaissance, which began to become a major cultural force in Western Europe during the fourteenth century, emphasized the importance of returning to the roots of Christendom through the simple language and imagery of the New Testament. The humanist movement, linked with the Renaissance, believed it was essential to study the Bible in its original languages, rather than in unreliable Latin translations, such as the Vulgate, thus creating irresistible pressure for new Bible translations. Yet it became clear that some medieval

'Prayer of St Francis'

Lord, make me an instrument of your peace.

Where there is hatred, let me sow love.

Where there is injury, pardon.

Where there is doubt, faith.

Where there is despair, hope.

Where there is darkness, light.

Where there is sadness, joy.

O Divine Master,

grant that I may not so much seek to be consoled, as to console;

to be understood, as to understand;

to be loved, as to love.

For it is in giving that we receive.

It is in pardoning that we are pardoned,

and it is in dying that we are born to Eternal Life.

Attributed to Francis of Assisi (1181–1226)

theological ideas were ultimately based on translation mistakes in the Vulgate. Some form of review of teachings was seen to be necessary, in the light of the new biblical scholarship.

The rise of Islam in the seventh century had a significant impact on Christianity in North Africa and Palestine. However, its influence seemed poised to reach new levels in 1453, when Islamic armies finally managed to take Constantinople, the city widely seen as the gate to Europe. By the early sixteenth century, Islam had become a significant presence in the Balkans, and was poised to enter Austria. Martin Luther (1483–1546) believed it was only a matter of time before Europe became an Islamic sphere of influence. In the event, a series of decisive military defeats limited this influence to the Balkans. By this stage, however, Western Europe was convulsed by new controversies, as the movement we know as the Reformation gained momentum.

REFORMATIONS

The sixteenth century gave rise to a major upheaval within Western Christianity, usually referred to as the Reformation. This movement had its origins in the Renaissance, especially its demand for a return to the original sources of Christianity in the New Testament. Alarmed at what they perceived to be a growing disparity between apostolic and medieval visions of Christianity, individuals such as Martin Luther and Huldrych Zwingli (1484–1531) pressed for reform. For Zwingli, it was the morals and institutions of the church that required reform. Luther, however, judged that a deeper level of reform was required. The teachings of the church had been either distorted or inflated during the Middle Ages, and needed to be brought back into line with Scripture. For Luther, the whole question of how we enter into a right relationship with God – technically referred to as the 'doctrine of justification' – needed radical revision in the light of the biblical witness.

Although the need for reform was widely conceded within the church, such reforming agendas proved intensely controversial. In the end, both Luther and Zwingli found themselves creating reforming communities outside the mainline church, instead of reforming that church from within, as they had hoped. By the time of John Calvin (1509–64) and his reformation of the city of Geneva, Protestantism had emerged as a distinct type of Christianity in its own right, posing a very significant threat to the Catholic Church.

In the late 1540s, the Catholic Church itself began a major process of reformation and renewal, referred to as the Catholic Reformation – previously as the Counter-Reformation. The religious orders were reformed, and many of the beliefs and practices which reformers such as Luther found objectionable were eliminated. Nevertheless, significant differences remained between Protestantism and Catholicism. In many ways, the Reformation debates defined the contours of modern Christianity, and many remain live to this day.

Christianity in Europe about 1650 CE

THE MODERN PERIOD

A period of political uncertainty developed during the eighteenth century, with major implications for the future of Christianity in the West. Growing hostility towards the church in France was one of the contributing causes to the French Revolution of 1789, which saw Christianity publicly displaced from French society. Although the French Revolution did not achieve the permanent removal of Christianity from the nation, it created an atmosphere of instability. Revolutionary movements throughout Europe sought to repeat the successes of their French counterparts, creating serious difficulties for the Catholic Church in many parts of Europe, especially Italy.

Christianity also faced new challenges in the West. During the 1840s, the German philosopher Ludwig Feuerbach (1804–72) argued that the idea of God was simply a projection of the human mind. Karl Marx (1818–83) declared that God was invented by people to console themselves in the face of social and economic hardship: all that was necessary for the elimination of religious belief was the radical alteration of the social conditions which brought it into being in the first place. Sigmund Freud (1856–1939) argued that religion was simply an illusion, a 'wish-fulfilment'. By about 1920, many had concluded that Christianity was intellectually untenable.

By then, other difficulties had arisen. Perhaps the most important of these was the Russian Revolution of 1917, which led to the establishment of the world's first explicitly atheist state. The Soviet Union actively sought to eliminate religion from public and private life, especially during the 1930s. The Allied defeat of Nazi Germany in World War II led to large areas of Eastern Europe coming under Soviet influence, and the state adoption of explicitly anti-religious policies. With the fall of the Berlin wall in 1989, a new openness towards religion developed throughout the former Soviet sphere of influence, with Christianity – especially in its Orthodox forms – and Islam experiencing a major renaissance. Yet by this stage the epicentre of Christianity had moved away from this region altogether.

WORLDWIDE EXPANSION

The sixteenth century saw the beginnings of a process which would have a decisive impact on the shaping of Christianity. During the Middle Ages, Christianity was primarily a European religion. Although it was present in parts of India and the Middle East, its numerical strength was heavily concentrated in Europe. The discovery of the Americas opened up new mission fields, and led to a new interest in spreading the gospel abroad. The Society of Jesus, the 'Jesuits', founded by Ignatius Loyola in 1540, took the lead within the Catholic Church, and sent missionaries to the Americas, India, China, and Japan.

Protestant missionary activity was later in developing. There was a surge of missionary activity from Britain during the closing years of the eighteenth century. The Baptist Missionary Society, founded in 1792 and initially known as 'The Particular Baptist

Society for the Propagation of the Gospel';
the London Missionary Society, founded
in 1795, and initially known as 'The
Missionary Society'; and the Church Missionary Society, founded in 1799, and originally
known as 'The Church Missionary Society for Africa and the East', all played a major
role in planting Christianity in Africa, India, and Oceania. American missionary societies
also played important roles in establishing Christianity in various regions of the world,
especially Korea.

Statue of *Cristo Redentor* – Christ the Redeemer, at the peak of Corcovado mountain, Rio de Janeiro, Brazil.

Yet Christianity expanded by other means too. One of the most important was large-scale emigration from Europe to North America, beginning in the late sixteenth century. Initially, the immigrants were primarily Protestant refugees from England; however, these were later joined by Lutherans from Scandinavia, Anabaptists from Germany, Calvinists from Holland, and Catholics from Ireland and Italy.

Today, Christianity is primarily a faith of the developing, rather than developed, world. Although European and American missionaries played a significant role in planting Christianity in regions such as Asia and Africa, these are now largely self-sufficient. The implications of this massive shift from the West to the developing world have yet to be fully explored. It is nevertheless clear that a new phase in the history of the Christian church has begun, with momentous implications for the future.

ALISTER MCGRATH

CHAPTER 37

Jesus

Christianity is founded on the worship of Jesus Christ – 'Jesus the messiah' – as Son of God, the unique self-revelation of God to the human race. At the same time, it remembers Jesus as a real historical figure, a man of insignificant social standing, during his life unknown outside the obscure corner of the Roman Empire where he lived and died.

Almost all we know about Jesus comes from the four accounts of his life, the Gospels of Matthew, Mark, Luke, and John, in the New Testament. This account is based on those Gospels. Although scholars disagree at some points about the historical value of the Gospel records, the following general picture is widely agreed.

MESSIAH

Born just before the death of Herod the Great, King of Judea, around 4 bce, Jesus lived for a little more than thirty years, scarcely travelling outside Palestine throughout his life. At this time, the Jews were a subject people, who lived either under local princes appointed by the Roman Emperor, or under the direct rule of Rome itself. They had long hoped for 'the day of the Lord', when God would act to save his people. There were several different hopes of a 'messiah', a saviour, whom God would send, and these hopes ran high at the time of Jesus.

Jesus was born at Bethlehem, in Judea, but was brought up in Galilee, and most of his public activity was in that region. Luke's account of the baby, cradled in a manger in a stable, visited by shepherds, has become one of the best-known stories in the world. But the Gospels record it was far from ordinary. Angels proclaimed him the promised saviour, and it was maintained he was not conceived by human intercourse, but by the power of God. This bringing together of earthly poverty and obscurity with a miraculous birth is typical of the Gospels' portrait of Jesus, as truly human but also uniquely the Son of God.

Virtually nothing is known of Jesus' life from his infancy until about the age of thirty. The event that launched Jesus' public ministry was the mission of his relative, John 'the Baptist', in Judea. John called the Jews to return to God, and baptized those who responded in the River Jordan. He attracted a large following, and Jesus joined him, was baptized, and himself began preaching. When John was put in prison, Jesus moved back to Galilee, and continued to preach in public.

HEALING AND PREACHING

The Gospels summarize Jesus' activity as preaching, teaching, and healing. He and his closest followers deliberately adopted a wandering and dependent style of life.

As a preacher, Jesus drew large crowds, who followed him constantly. He taught with a vivid simplicity, and with an authority that contrasted sharply with other Jewish religious teachers.

From the beginning of his public activity, Jesus was well known as a healer. The Gospels record his curing many different types of illness and deformity, usually by a simple word and a touch, sometimes by a word alone. He is also recorded as an exorcist, driving out demons by a word of command. It was apparently as much for his healing power as for his teaching that Jesus was sought out by the Galilean crowds.

Most of Jesus' recorded miracles are healings, but there were also a number of incidents where he displayed a supernatural control over nature. The Gospels present him as one whose personal authority extended beyond his words to a control over nature, which inevitably made a deep impression on those around him.

Like many other Jewish teachers, Jesus quickly gathered a group of committed followers, known as his 'disciples'. An inner group of twelve were his constant companions. Much time was spent in teaching his disciples privately, preparing them to continue his mission. Jesus told them he would soon be killed, and expected them to be the focus of the new community created by his work.

OPPOSITION

Jesus quickly aroused the opposition of the Jewish leaders. His attitude was in many ways unconventional, and he posed a threat to the Jewish religious establishment. He refused to recognize the barriers that divided people in society. His habit of mixing with ostracized classes earned him the name 'friend of tax-collectors and sinners'. Women held an unconventionally high place in his following, and not all of them were 'respectable'.

Jesus did not share the general Jewish disdain for Samaritans — a despised minority of mixed blood. Although he seldom travelled outside Jewish territory, Jesus welcomed the faith of a non-Jewish soldier and a Syrian woman. As for economic barriers, Jesus deliberately gave up a secure livelihood, and made no secret of his contempt for affluence.

On religious questions he was equally radical. Jesus clashed with the religious authorities because of his liberal attitude to the observance of the Sabbath, the day of rest, and his declaration that ritual purification mattered less than purity of heart. His bold reinterpretation of the Jewish law moved away from an external observance of rules to a deeper, more demanding, ethic.

Nor did he please the Sadducees, the priestly rulers. Jesus taught that the Jewish nation was ripe for God's judgment, and even predicted the destruction of the Temple, upon which their national religion was centred. In a symbolic gesture, he 'purified' the Temple, by violently expelling the traders whose presence the priests encouraged. His popular following threatened to upset the delicate balance of the Sadducees' cooperation with Rome.

Jesus made it clear his idea of salvation was not a political one, so gradually his popular following dwindled, as those who wanted a military messiah became disillusioned. Even one of his twelve closest disciples betrayed him in the end, and none of them understood his true purpose till after his death.

DEATH AND RESURRECTION

The opposition to Jesus came to its climax at the annual Passover festival in Jerusalem. Jesus rode into the city in a deliberately messianic gesture on a peaceable donkey, and was enthusiastically welcomed by the crowds.

Eventually Jesus was arrested by the Jewish leaders, with the help of Judas – his disillusioned disciple – and tried under Jewish law on a charge of blasphemy, because he claimed to be the messiah and Son of God. A death sentence was passed, but a Roman conviction was required to make it effective. This was secured by a charge of sedition, pressed upon the Roman governor, Pontius Pilate, by the religious leaders.

Jesus was executed by crucifixion, the barbaric method reserved by Rome for slaves and rebels, and buried in a nearby tomb. The cross has become the symbol of Christianity: in Jesus' death, with all its cruelty and injustice, is the focus of salvation.

The Beatitudes

Happy are those who know they are spiritually poor;

the Kingdom of heaven belongs to them!

Happy are those who mourn;

God will comfort them!

Happy are those who are humble;

they will receive what God has promised!

Happy are those whose greatest desire is to do what God requires;

God will satisfy them fully!

Happy are those who are merciful to others;

God will be merciful to them!

Happy are the pure in heart;

they will see God!

Happy are those who work for peace;

God will call them his children!

Happy are those who are persecuted because they do what God requires;

the Kingdom of heaven belongs to them!

Happy are you when people insult you and persecute you and tell all kinds of evil lies against you because you are my followers.

Be happy and glad, for a great reward is kept for you in heaven. This is how the prophets who lived before you were persecuted.

From Jesus' Sermon on the Mount, Matthew 5:3–12, *Good News Bible*, 1976.

A SHORT INTRODUCTION TO WORLD RELIGIONS

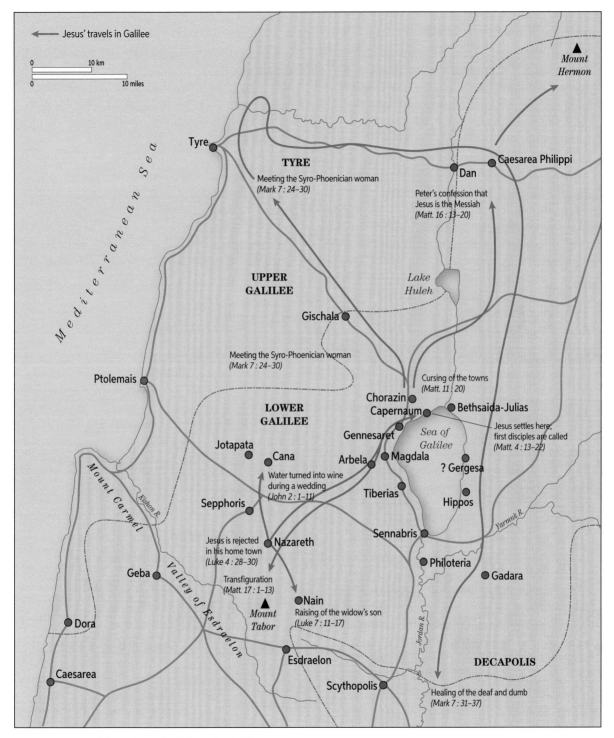

Mediterranean Sea

Mount
Hermon

Tyre

TYRE

Meeting the Syro-Phoenician woman
(Mark 7 : 24–30)

Dan

Caesarea Philippi

Peter's confession that
Jesus is the Messiah
(Matt. 16 : 13–20)

**UPPER
GALILEE**

*Lake
Huleh*

Gischala

Ptolemais

Meeting the Syro-Phoenician woman
(Mark 7 : 24–30)

Cursing of the towns
(Matt. 11 : 20)

Chorazin

**LOWER
GALILEE**

Capernaum

Bethsaida-Julias

Gennesaret

*Sea of
Galilee*

Jesus settles here;
first disciples are called
(Matt. 4 : 13–22)

Jotapata

Cana

Arbela

Magdala

? Gergesa

Mount Carmel

Kishon R.

Water turned into wine
during a wedding
(John 2 : 1–11)

Tiberias

Hippos

Sepphoris

Yarmuk R.

Jesus is rejected
in his home town
(Luke 4 : 28–30)

Nazareth

Sennabris

Geba

Valley of Esdraelon

Transfiguration
(Matt. 17 : 1–13)

Philoteria

Gadara

Dora

▲
*Mount
Tabor*

Nain

Raising of the widow's son
(Luke 7 : 11–17)

Jordan R.

Caesarea

Esdraelon

DECAPOLIS

Scythopolis

Healing of the deaf and dumb
(Mark 7 : 31–37)

Jesus' Travels and Ministry in Galilee

BRANCHES OF THE CHURCH

The New Testament is witness to the vision that the church should be one – and to the reality that it is not. The history of Christianity since then is, for the most part, a history of fragmentation. Only in the twentieth century were serious attempts made to seek reconciliation between churches separated by centuries of misunderstanding and mistrust. The various branches of the Christian church owe their existence to three historic crises. The first was the splintering of Eastern Catholic Christendom in the fifth century. The second was the so-called 'Great Schism' between East and West, usually dated at 1054, that resulted in the division between 'Catholic' and 'Orthodox' Christianity. The third was the Reformation in the sixteenth century, which, together with its seventeenth- and eighteenth-century aftermath, left as its legacy Protestantism in its various forms. This article deals only with the principal branches of the church as they have emerged in the history of Christianity.

The Eastern Churches

These include the Orthodox Churches, together with those that share with them in a spiritual and cultural ethos that derives from the Byzantine Empire. The church in the East suffered its most serious divisions following the Councils of Ephesus (431) and Chalcedon (451), called to determine the orthodox Christian teaching on the relationship between the deity and the humanity of Christ. The Nestorian Church, centred historically on Persia, and the Monophysite Churches, such as those of Syria, Egypt, and Ethiopia, date from this period.

The final separation of the Eastern Churches from Western Christendom lay in their conflict with Rome over the papal claim to supreme authority, and in their rejection of the Filioque clause, added by the Western church to the original text of the Nicene Creed, in which the Holy Spirit is said to proceed 'from the Son' as well as the Father. The Orthodox Churches extend across Eastern Europe, the Slav nations, and eastern Mediterranean. The patriarchates of Constantinople,

Alexandria, Antioch, and Jerusalem are given special honour, but authority belongs to the whole church, whose rich liturgical life and icon-based spirituality is seen as the living embodiment of divine love on earth. It is estimated that there are over 322 million Orthodox Christians today.

The Roman Catholic Church

Numbering around 1,200 million members, the Roman Catholic Church is the largest single Christian grouping. Roman Catholics, or simply 'Catholics', trace their lineal descent from the Western Catholic Church of the Middle Ages. They acknowledge the primacy

Ave Maria

Ave Maria, gratia plena,

Dominus tecum.

Benedicta tu in mulieribus,

et benedictus fructus ventris tui, Iesus.

Sancta Maria, Mater Dei,

ora pro nobis peccatoribus,

nunc, et in hora mortis nostrae.

Hail Mary

Hail Mary, full of grace,

the Lord is with thee.

Blessed art thou amongst women

and blessed is the fruit of thy womb, Jesus.

Holy Mary, Mother of God,

pray for us sinners,

now, and in the hour of our death.

One of the most popular Roman Catholic prayers. Of unknown origin, it was incorporated into the liturgy in the 15th century.

and authority of the Supreme Pontiff, the bishop of Rome, who is traditionally regarded as Christ's representative, or 'Vicar', on earth, and the successor of St Peter. When speaking with full authority – *ex cathedra* – and defining matters of faith or morals, the pope's utterances are regarded as infallible and binding on Catholics.

The Second Vatican Council (1962–65) resulted in far-reaching reforms, including greater emphasis on the role of bishops acting as an episcopal college, more open relationships with non-Catholic churches, and the simplifying of the liturgy. Along with the Orthodox Churches, Roman Catholicism recognizes seven sacraments: baptism, confirmation, marriage, ordination, penance – the sacrament of reconciliation, extreme unction – anointing of the sick, and, at the centre of the sacramental system, the Mass. Especially in developing countries, Roman Catholics are often prominent in supporting the struggles of the oppressed, and in the pursuit of justice and peace generally. In the early twenty-first century the church was shaken by revelations of sexual abuses committed by a number of priests.

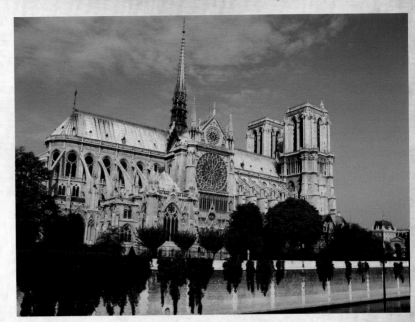

The Cathedral of Notre Dame de Paris, France, built at the peak of medieval European Christendom.

Churches of the Protestant Reformation

The Anglican Church

The Anglican communion is a worldwide family of autonomous churches in communion with the Archbishop of Canterbury, who has presidential status amongst the heads of other Anglican Churches. Largely anglophone, its members number around 85 million. The parent Church of England has its roots both in the Celtic Christianity of the earliest Britons, and in the Roman form of the faith brought to England by Augustine of Canterbury (r. 597–604).

The Anglican Church claims to be both Catholic and Reformed, and has adhered to the Catholic threefold ministry of bishops, priests, and deacons, but with a conservatively reformed liturgy. *The Book of Common Prayer* of Archbishop Thomas Cranmer (1489–1556) retained many of the texts of the medieval church, while recasting them in a clearly Protestant direction. Nowadays, Anglicanism is an inclusive church embracing members of at least three persuasions: Anglo-Catholic, Liberal, and Evangelical, and for this reason is often seen as a 'bridge' church between Protestantism, Roman Catholicism, and Orthodoxy.

The Lutheran Churches

These represent the chief Protestant presence in Germany and Scandinavia, as well as being a significant worldwide Christian denomination, which speaks through the Lutheran World Federation. Following the teaching of the German reformer Martin Luther (1483–1546), the doctrine of justification by faith is its central tenet, embodied in the Augsburg Confession (1530). Some Lutheran Churches have retained the Catholic threefold ministry, while others are more presbyterian or congregational in government. Like Anglicanism, Lutheranism adopted a conservative attitude to liturgy, although the preaching of the sermon has always been central, and music has always played an important part. Lutherans worldwide number around 75 million.

The Reformed Churches

Protestantism in France, Switzerland, the Low Countries, and Scotland at the time of the Reformation shared many of the central tenets of Lutheranism, but following the principles of John Calvin (1509–64), applied them in a more thoroughgoing way. The authority of the Bible is paramount, and the preaching of the Word is central to its liturgy. There are two principal forms of church organization: presbyterian – local churches grouped together under the government of a regional synod of ordained presbyters and lay elders – and congregational – local churches as independent congregations, responsible for their own life and order. Reformed churches have around 75 million members worldwide.

The Free Churches

These all derive from the various churches of the Reformation as a result of movements in subsequent centuries.

Interior of a traditional American Episcopalian church. It shares many characteristic features with other Protestant churches, with a prominent pulpit and simple altar.

The Baptist Churches are a worldwide family of independent congregations that reject the baptism of infants, claiming baptism is a sign of an adult profession of faith. Worship tends not to follow set liturgical forms. The Southern Baptists of the USA are a particularly influential conservative evangelical grouping. There are around 100 million Baptists across the world.

The Methodist Churches originate in the Evangelical Revival of the eighteenth century, and in the preaching of John Wesley (1703–91). Historically indebted to Anglicanism, which Wesley never renounced, congregational hymn-singing is one of its distinctive contributions to the church at large. Social action is emphasized. Their worldwide number is around 75 million.

The Society of Friends, or Quakers, was founded by George Fox (1624–91). It rejects all liturgical forms – including sacraments – ecclesiastical structures, and definitions of faith. Members meet for silent worship to attend to the 'inner light'. Quakers have a strong commitment to radical involvement in justice and peace issues. They number 400,000 in all.

The Salvation Army was founded by William Booth (1829–1912) as a mission to the poor of London. Now a worldwide movement, it gives equal place to the preaching of the gospel and to social action amongst the needy. Worship is informal and Bible-centred: the sacraments are not observed. Organization is along the lines of the armed forces. There are around 1.1 million Salvationists.

The Pentecostal Churches, numbering around 130 million, amongst them the Assemblies of God, date from the early twentieth century. Charismatic renewal is particularly strong in Latin America and Africa. The gifts of the Spirit, ecstatic experience, healing, and speaking in tongues, are central to church life and worship.

The Charismatic movement

This has profoundly influenced churches in most denominations, including the Roman Catholic Church.

The African Independent, or Initiated, Churches are vigorous and fast growing communities of black Christians for whom the black experience is crucial to their self-understanding. In various degrees, they are influenced by liberation theology, as a people who have known oppression, charismatic renewal, and the indigenous religion of their ancestors. They number around 40 million.

House Churches, or New Churches, are a growing phenomenon within the conservative evangelical movement. 'Restorationists' reject the institutional church with its ordained ministry, returning to what is seen as a New Testament pattern of worship in members' homes. Worship is informal, and often charismatic in style.

The Ecumenical Movement

The Ecumenical Movement, from the Greek *oikoumene*, meaning 'the inhabited world', is the product of the twentieth century. It was increasingly realized that Christian witness in the world is severely compromised by the deep historic divisions between the churches. While organic unity, or even inter-communion, between the churches remains a long way off, the churches now recognize the validity of one another's baptism. The mutual recognition of ministries, especially by Roman Catholics of non-Catholic ministries, remains problematic. All the mainline denominations are publicly committed to the task of reconciliation between Christians.

Statue of the Protestant reformer Martin Luther (1483–1546), Dresden, Germany.

The World Council of Churches was constituted in 1948 as a fellowship of churches united in their loyalty to Jesus Christ 'as God and Saviour'. The Council exists to enable the churches to debate matters of common concern, and where possible, to speak and act as one. It has been particularly vigorous – sometimes controversially so – in development work, in education, and in taking up the cause of oppressed minorities. Assemblies of the Council meet every seven years. Councils of churches exist in many places, enabling local congregations to worship, work, and study alongside one another. More formal ecumenical agreements enable sharing of buildings and ministries to take place on a regular basis.

Michael Sadgrove

> '*I am the bread of life. He who comes to me will never be hungry.*'
>
> '*I am the light of the world. Whoever follows me will have the light of life and will never walk in darkness.*'
>
> '*I am the gate for the sheep … whoever comes in by me will be saved.*'
>
> '*I am the good shepherd, who is willing to die for the sheep.*'
>
> '*I am the resurrection and the life. Whoever believes in me will live, even though he dies; and whoever lives and believes in me will never die.*'
>
> '*I am the way, the truth and the life; no one goes to the Father except by me.*'
>
> '*I am the vine, and you are the branches. Whoever remains in me, and I in him, will bear much fruit; for you can do nothing without me.*'
>
> Jesus' great statements about himself, from John's Gospel, *Good News Bible.*

Two days later, Jesus' disciples found the tomb empty. The meaning of this was brought home to them by a series of encounters with Jesus himself, alive and real. He explained to them again the meaning of his life and death, and the mission that he had entrusted to them. Then he left them, and they began to preach to the world that Jesus — triumphant even over death — was Lord and Saviour. The resurrection of Jesus formed the focus of the earliest Christian preaching; it was the risen Lord whom they worshipped.

WHO WAS JESUS?

Jesus was hailed as a prophet, a man sent by God. In his preaching, teaching, and healing he matched up to that role. But Christians believe, and his own life and teaching suggest, he was much more than that.

Jesus called for faith in, and loyalty to, himself, and presented himself as the final arbiter of people's destiny. He not only proclaimed forgiveness and salvation: by his own life, suffering, and death he achieved it. He is the messenger — but he is also the heart of the message. He calls people to God, but he is also himself the way to God.

During Jesus' earthly life, his disciples only dimly understood this. But after his resurrection, they quickly came to speak of him as more than just a man, and to worship him as they worshipped his Father. During his earthly teaching, Jesus had prepared the way for this, by speaking of himself as the Son of God in a unique sense, and of God as his Father in an exclusive relationship quite different from the sense in which his disciples could use the term.

The worship of Jesus the man as the Son of God did not have its origin in some fanciful piety, long after his death, but in the impression he made on his disciples

> *The Father and I are one.*
>
> John 10:30, *Good News Bible.*

during the three years of his ministry. His resurrection deepened that impression and confirmed it. Without in the least doubting his real humanity, they believed they had been walking with God.

RICHARD FRANCE

CHAPTER 38

Sacred Writings

The word 'Bible' comes from the Greek *Biblia*, meaning simply 'the Books'. The plural is significant: the Bible is a collection of books written over a period of more than 1000 years, in widely differing cultural and historical situations, and in a rich variety of styles and language. This collection has come to be regarded by Christians as a single unit, 'The Bible', as its books have been recognized as standing apart from other books.

THE OLD TESTAMENT

There are two unequal parts to the Bible. The first, and by far the larger, called by Christians 'the Old Testament', is simply the Hebrew and Aramaic scriptures of Judaism, which present the history and religious thought of the people of God up to the time when Jesus came. Christians have always regarded themselves as the legitimate heirs to the religion of ancient Israel, and so accept the books of the Hebrew Bible as fully 'canonical', or part of scripture. Without them, the specifically Christian scriptures could hardly be understood.

A number of later Jewish works in Greek are also included in Roman Catholic editions of the Old Testament, sometimes distinguished as 'deutero-canonical', of lesser importance than the Hebrew scriptures. Protestant Bibles do not include these works in the Old Testament; but they are sometimes printed after the Old Testament, as a separate section, known as 'the Apocrypha'. Protestant Christians do not accept them as Scripture.

THE NEW TESTAMENT

The specifically Christian books of the Bible, known as 'the New Testament', comprise twenty-seven writings by Christians of the first century CE, mostly quite short. While most of the writers were of Jewish origin, the books are in Greek, which was the common language of the Roman Empire.

They consist firstly of four 'Gospels', setting out from different points of view the life and teaching of Jesus, together with the 'Acts of the Apostles', which is a continuation of the Gospel of Luke telling the story of the first thirty years of Christianity. There are then thirteen letters by Paul, the great missionary leader, to churches and individuals; eight other letters by early Christian leaders; and the 'Revelation of John', a visionary work cast in the mould of Jewish apocalyptic literature.

The New Testament writings, although produced within a relatively short period compared with the many centuries of the writing of the Old Testament, are mixed in style and content; even the literary quality of the Greek varies widely. The different interests and personalities of the writers are clear on even a superficial reading.

THE INSPIRATION OF THE BIBLE

Christians have regarded these varied writings of both the Old and New Testaments as a unity, often called the 'Word of God'. They have spoken of the Bible as 'inspired', meaning not merely that it is great literature, or that it brings spiritual enlightenment, but that it comes from God. But the classic Christian belief is that what they wrote in their own language, and in their own historical setting, was directed by God, so that the result was no less his word than theirs.

> *All scripture is God-breathed and is useful for teaching, rebuking, correcting and training in righteousness, so that the man of God may be thoroughly equipped for every good work.*
>
> 2 Timothy 3:16, New International Version.

So, while the biblical books must be interpreted with proper attention to their background and literary form, what they declare is, Christians believe, God's word to his people. This is why the Bible, for all its variety, is treated by Christians as a unity, progressively revealing not only God's acts, but his mind and will.

THE AUTHORITY OF THE BIBLE

In theory, therefore, all Christians accept the Bible as authoritative, both in guiding their actions and in forming their beliefs. In practice, Christians have differed on this. The Protestant Reformation aimed to restore the Bible to a place of authority above the pronouncements of the leaders of the church and the traditions that had grown up. Within Protestant Christianity, the Enlightenment of the eighteenth century led to a new confidence in human reason as the ultimate guide to truth, and the Bible began to be treated only as a record of human religious development, not as a divine revelation.

> *The Holy Scripture is the only sufficient, certain, and infallible rule of all saving knowledge, faith, and obedience.*
>
> Second Westminster Confession (1677)

Today, while evangelical Christianity accepts the Bible as its supreme authority, more liberal Protestantism questions its importance. In Roman Catholicism, since the Second Vatican Council, there has been a resurgence of interest in the Bible.

RICHARD FRANCE

CHAPTER 39

Beliefs

The Christian faith is directly descended from the religion of the Jews. At the time of Jesus this had the following characteristics, as taught in the sacred book of the Jews, the Old Testament:

- Belief in the existence of one God (monotheism), the Creator and Lord of the universe, who is sovereign over all.
- Belief in the fact that human beings are made in the image of God, but have rebelled against their Creator, and stand in danger of judgment.
- Belief that God, who is the righteous judge, is also gracious and merciful. He has provided a way for people to be set free from judgment, by the penitent offering of sacrifices.
- Belief that God revealed himself to the nation of Israel and called them to be his people.
- Belief that God would some day establish his rule in a sinful world, setting his people free from their enemies, and appointing his chosen agent, the messiah, to rule over them for ever.
- The practice of a moral life, under the guidance of the Law given in the Old Testament; the maintenance of a religious ritual based on the Temple and involving the offering of sacrifice.

THE SIGNIFICANCE OF JESUS

These beliefs were decisively affected by the coming of Jesus, his followers' confident reports of his resurrection from the dead, and their receiving of the gift of the Spirit of God at Pentecost. There remained a basic similarity with the Jewish religion, but there were some fundamental changes.

> I believe Christ's teaching; and this is what I believe. I believe that my welfare in the world will only be possible when all men fulfil Christ's teaching.
>
> Leo Tolstoy, *What I Believe* (1884).

The most important of these changes was due to the Christian understanding of Jesus. From a very early date, the Christians began to realize that the Jewish hope of God's chosen agent coming to set up his rule had been fulfilled in Jesus. He was the messiah whom the Jews awaited. It is the rejection of this identification by Jews that constitutes the decisive difference between them and Christians. For Christians, the coming of Jesus means that God's future plan, announced in the Old Testament, has already begun to happen. God's rule is being established in a new way.

But the way in which it has happened is different from what the Jews had come to expect. They thought that God's rule would be achieved by the military overthrow of their enemies, and would lead to their own establishment as the dominant nation. But Jesus did not speak out against the external enemies of the Jews; rather, he proclaimed the need of everybody for a change of heart. The rule of God advances by the conversion of individuals to a new way of life, and the way of violent revolution is firmly rejected.

THE DEATH OF JESUS

God's action in Jesus was also seen as including sacrifice. The death of Jesus was understood as a means of cancelling sin, provided by God himself, and displaying his love for sinners. Sinfulness must inevitably bring separation from God, or death. But Jesus died this death himself. A variety of pictures — drawn from the slave market, the law court, the Temple, and personal relationships — are used to express the fundamental belief that the death of Jesus is the means of reconciling God and human beings, and freeing them from the fear of judgment.

The effect of this understanding was to bring to an end the system of animal sacrifices, which were understood as pictures pointing forward to the spiritual sacrifice of Jesus, and now made obsolete by the offering of the perfect sacrifice. Christian worship was no longer a matter of offerings in a temple; rather it was the expression of gratitude to God for his provision of a sacrifice.

At the same time, the coming of Jesus was seen as bringing to an end the ritual Law of the Jews which regulated the Temple worship and a host of other matters. The ethical principles which lay behind the Law, seen especially in the Ten Commandments, were not abolished, but the detailed ritual and other observances were no longer needed.

In practice, the Jews had come to regard the observance of the Law in minute detail as the means of gaining and maintaining a good relationship with God and obtaining his favour. It was Paul who insisted that God's favour could not be gained by keeping the Law: all have sinned and come short of God's glory. So the proper relationship of human beings with God can only be that of faith, the grateful and obedient trust which comes to God on the basis of what he has done, in contrast to the approach of works, which insists that the individual must do something to merit God's favour.

Though Christian worship abandoned the Temple, it was deeply influenced by the synagogue, the Jewish meeting-house in which the teaching of the Law was central. But the rejection of the Law as the means of salvation led to a shift in the understanding of the Old Testament. Interest turned more to its prophetic character, as a book which looked forward to the coming of Jesus, and it was increasingly studied for what it taught about him. At the same time, other writings were increasingly placed alongside it as equally inspired and authoritative scriptures. The writings of the infant church, the letters written by its leaders, and the accounts of the actions and preaching of Jesus in the Gospels, were seen as a corpus of scriptures alongside the Old Testament. The whole collection became the Bible of the Christian church.

The recognition that observance of the Jewish Law was no longer binding on Christians, together with the simple fact that almost from the beginning non-Jews – the Gentiles – were attracted by the message, led quickly to the development of a community composed of both Jews and non-Jews. Despite initial uncertainties, it was recognized that non-Jews did not need to adopt the practices of the Jewish Law, especially circumcision and the observance of Jewish holy days, in order to become Christians. Christianity, which might have remained a Jewish sect, was thus poised to become a world faith, open to everyone on the basis of belief in Jesus.

The characteristic rites of the new faith, which roughly parallel the Jewish rite of circumcision and the festival of the Passover – which celebrated the deliverance of the people of Israel from slavery in Egypt – were baptism and the Lord's Supper. Baptism was a ritual washing with water which signified cleansing from sin, the reception of God's Spirit, the dedication of the baptized persons to God, and their entry into the new people of God. The Lord's Supper, or Eucharist – 'thanksgiving' – was a token meal of bread and wine: elements used by Jesus at his Last Supper before his death to point to his self-sacrifice and the shedding of his blood to open up a new covenant or agreement between God and his people.

THE RESURRECTION OF JESUS

Alongside the death of Jesus, belief in his resurrection was the crucial thing for the development of Christianity. Christians saw it as God's vindication of Jesus, after he had been rejected by the Jewish leaders and put to death. It was the confirmation of his claims to be God's agent, and above all it demonstrated that he was triumphant over the power of sin and death. The resurrection was seen as the decisive stage in the ascent of Jesus to share the throne of God in heaven – to use the picture-language of the New Testament. This belief had several important consequences.

> *All things are possible to him that believes, more to him that hopes, even more to him that loves, and more still to him that practises and perseveres in these three virtues.*
>
> Brother Lawrence, *The Practice of the Presence of God* (1691)

- First, it confirmed the Christian belief that God would act again in history through the return of Jesus at the end of the world. The exaltation of Jesus meant that he was the agent appointed by God to carry out final judgment and to bring in God's eternal reign in peace and justice.
- Second, it led to the conviction that Jesus was to be seen as divine. Already in his lifetime, he had displayed a unique consciousness that he was God's Son, and that God was his Father. After the resurrection, Christians recognized increasingly that all the functions of God were exercised through Jesus, and that he shared in the rule of God. He was to be regarded as the Son of God, who had 'come down' into the world in human form and then 'ascended' to be with God. The consequences of this belief were shattering: Jews and others who believed that there was one God could not accept the

Christian claim. Christians, for their part, had to revise their ideas about God, and recognize that, though God is one, alongside the Father there was also the Son; they were each divine in nature, yet in such a way that the Son could be regarded as dependent on the Father. The earthly Jesus was the Son of God made flesh – 'incarnate' – become a human being.

- Third, now that Jesus has been exalted to heaven, he remains active and living, in the same way as the Father is the living God. Sharing the status of the Father, Jesus is now the Lord, so that the relation of the Christian to him is not simply one of belief and trust, but also of obedience and commitment. To be a Christian is to make the confession 'Jesus Christ is Lord', a confession that he is both the Lord whom the believer obeys, and also the one to whom the whole universe will one day bow the knee.

The ancient Christian monastery of Mar Saba is located in the Judean Hills, near Bethlehem, Israel.

Such faith and obedience is part of a spiritual relationship between Christians and Jesus. Christians can be said to be united with Jesus, a whole variety of metaphors from the language of personal relationships being used to express the reality of this link. The new life which they begin when they believe in Jesus is the reproduction of the life of Jesus in them. They die to their old way of life, and rise again to a new God-centred and divinely inspired life, in the same way as Jesus died and rose again by the power of God. The Christian community is a vast organism, or body, through which the spiritual life of Christ flows.

THE HOLY SPIRIT AND THE BIRTH OF THE CHURCH

After the resurrection came the third decisive event that determined the character of Christianity. The Jews already believed in the communication of God's power and guidance to particular individuals – especially the prophets – by the activity of the divine Spirit. The birthday of the church is reckoned from the day of Pentecost, when all the believers in Jesus became conscious of the gift of the Spirit given to each one personally. So universal is the gift, that a Christian can be defined as a person who has received the gift of the Spirit. The initial experience can be spoken of as a second, spiritual birth, bringing the new life of Jesus to the believer. The Spirit works in the Christian community by giving different abilities to different individuals, to enable them to lead and help the church as a whole. He also acts in the life of each Christian, to foster the qualities of love and freedom from sin which were seen in Jesus himself.

Thus the Spirit can be seen as the personal agent of God in the lives of individuals and the Christian community. This meant a further development in the understanding of God. The Spirit was recognized as being divine in the same way as the Father and the Son, so that the Christian concept of God had to recognize a fundamental 'three-ness' or 'Trinity' in the nature of God as one being who exists in three persons. Thus the understanding of God as Trinity, which in this form is peculiar to Christianity and sharply differentiates it from other religions in the same Judaic tradition — Judaism and Islam — sums up the distinctive and vital elements in Christian faith.

Christian belief takes the holiness and judgment of a righteous God seriously. This is seen in the character of the Christian message, which includes the warning that all people are sinners who have rebelled against God and therefore face judgment. It is only against this background that the Christian message makes sense as 'gospel', good news that the same God is merciful and longs for the salvation of all, and has provided the way of forgiveness and life in Jesus. Thus the gospel presents everyone with the alternatives of judgment or life.

VARIETY AND DIFFICULTY

The Christian message has naturally been subject to fresh thinking and reformulation down the ages, as theologians have tried to express the biblical teaching in ways that are philosophically acceptable and logically coherent. It is not surprising that there have been differences in understanding in different times and places, and that some expressions of Christianity have veered away from the biblical witness.

The doctrines of the Trinity and the incarnation have caused particular difficulty. Since the nature of God, who is infinite, lies beyond the scope of our finite understanding, attempts to explain his nature can lead to misunderstandings and one-sided statements. This has led to a variety of attempts to simplify the doctrine of God, by restricting full divinity to the Father, or by regarding the three persons simply as three different aspects of one God. Some theologians have found it hard to believe that Jesus is the eternal Son of God, and sometimes he has been regarded as a separate, subordinate being. The tendency in modern times has been to deny that God could truly be united with a human being in one person, and to say that Jesus was a good man who possessed the divine Spirit to an unusual degree, or that true humanity is the same thing as divinity. Another tendency has been to regard the Spirit as less than a full person.

The Christian understanding of the work of Jesus has also been the cause of difficulty. Some Christians have denied that any sort of action is necessary to enable God to forgive sins, and have seen in the death of Jesus nothing more than a demonstration of supreme love. Others have carried the idea of sacrifice over into Christian worship, and seen the Lord's Supper as some kind of repetition of Christ's sacrifice on the cross.

At times there have been tendencies to legalism: the need to do good works in order to merit salvation has been taught. The church has on occasions claimed an authority almost equal to that of God, and developed a hierarchy, or set of graded authorities, surrounded by pomp and prestige. At other times, the doctrine of God as judge has been watered down, and replaced by a belief that God will ultimately save everyone, no matter how they have behaved in this life.

Over against such views, mainline Christianity affirms that Christian teaching must be based on the Bible, and any developments in understanding must be consistent with its supremely authoritative position as the written form of God's revelation of himself and his will for his people. It therefore insists that people must recognize that the nature of God is a complex unity in which there are three persons, Father, Son, and Spirit, and that the Son became a human being in the person of Jesus. In the life and death of Jesus is seen the activity of the one God entering into the sinful plight of the world and bearing its painful consequences, so that believers might be delivered from its guilt and its power, and share in the life of God himself.

Within this basic framework of belief, as summed up in the historic creeds and confessions of the church, there is room for confession of people's inability to understand God fully, and there can be variety of understanding over matters that are of lesser significance, as the existence of the various denominations of the church shows. At all times Christians need to go back to the Bible and to test their beliefs and their practice by its teaching. Jesus himself — the Christ of the Bible and of experience — is believed to be far greater than any human formulation of dogma or teaching about him.

I. HOWARD MARSHALL

The Nicene Creed

We believe in one God, the Father, the Almighty, maker of heaven and earth, of all that is, seen and unseen.

We believe in one Lord, Jesus Christ, the only Son of God, eternally begotten of the Father, God from God, Light from Light, true God from true God, begotten, not made, of one Being with the Father; through him all things were made.

For us and for our salvation he came down from heaven, was incarnate from the Holy Spirit and the Virgin Mary, and was made man.
For our sake he was crucified under Pontius Pilate; he suffered death and was buried.

On the third day he rose again in accordance with the Scriptures;

he ascended into heaven and is seated at the right hand of the Father.

He will come again in glory to judge the living and the dead,
and his kingdom will have no end.

We believe in the Holy Spirit, the Lord, the giver of life,
who proceeds from the Father and the Son,

who with the Father and the Son is worshipped and glorified,
who has spoken through the prophets.

We believe in one holy catholic and apostolic Church.

We acknowledge one baptism for the forgiveness of sins.

We look for the resurrection of the dead, and the life of the world to come. Amen.

CHAPTER 40

Worship and Festivals

All institutions live by their rituals, and religious institutions are no exception. The New Testament is, from one standpoint, the history of the religious life – including the 'cultic', or worshipping, life – of the people of God: its pages record the beginnings of Christian worship.

It is recorded in the book of Acts that the infant church began a rhythm of church life which, in outline, is what would be called 'worship' today – indeed, a modern pattern for a communion service might well have the same elements. The believers gathered for the apostles' teaching, for prayer, fellowship, and 'the breaking of bread'.

EUCHARIST

The Lord's Supper, Communion, or Eucharist was the distinctive event of Christian worship. Jesus himself commanded it, and there is reason to think that the church observed it as a weekly – sometimes a daily – event from the outset. Originally, the commemoration of Jesus, especially his death and resurrection, which the 'sacramental' bread and wine signified, was held within the context of a larger meal, called an *agape*, or love-feast. But for various reasons, this context fell away in the first hundred and fifty years after the resurrection, and a ritual meal of solely bread and wine remained.

BAPTISM

The New Testament also describes what has been called the Christian initiation rite, baptism. This was certainly a means for the new convert to enter the life of the church; but in sharp distinction to contemporary mystery religions, it was open and simple. Baptism was a public 'washing', identifying the believer and his household with the death and rising again of Jesus.

Today, churches which are Baptist in conviction hold that this should only take place on confession of personal faith, at an age appropriate for the confession to be credible as the candidate's own. Others baptize not only adults and others able to confess the faith personally, but also young children and newborn infants in believing households. The intention is that such infants and children should be brought up as Christians, but they are usually expected to make a personal profession of faith at 'confirmation', or a similar rite, at a mature age.

There is other evidence in the New Testament of early church practice. Psalms and hymns were sung. To express corporate solidarity with missionaries, elders, or deacons serving the church, there was 'laying on of hands' at their commissioning. The sick were anointed and prayer made for their recovery. Money was collected for other, poorer churches. The 'ministry' of the church was divided amongst those who had the 'gifts of God's Spirit' for both practical and spiritual leadership.

There seems to have been no such concept as 'having a service'. The 'business' part of church life, such as organizing for the care of widows or the relief of famine, was all bound up with the 'worship' part, of praying, singing, and teaching.

LITURGY AND LEADERSHIP

In the post-apostolic years, patterns gradually settled down, and a clear structure of leadership emerged, in which the bishop would normally preside over the worship of the local church. Bishops wrote down for themselves the great thanksgiving prayer which they uttered over the bread and wine of communion, and these 'eucharistic prayers' began to be used regularly, and over wide areas, as others copied them.

As congregations grew, they sometimes overflowed from the homes in which they originally met. Groups started – occasionally even in times of persecution – to put up special buildings for worship. They produced an ever more detailed pattern of the church's year – not only keeping the 'week' of creation, though making the first day of the week holy in place of the seventh, but also keeping annual commemorations: first of all the Passover – when Jesus had died and risen – then – when the Spirit had come – and finally Christmas – celebrating Christ's birth – and the 'death day' of the various martyrs.

The Peace of Constantine, or Peace of the Church (313 CE), gave a new tolerance to Christians to worship freely, and also boosted church building. The assimilation of church and state that followed not only encouraged the use of pagan festivals for Christian commemorations – as happened with Christmas – but also started to shape church organization on the lines of the official civic structures. Whole communities were baptized, and the Western concept of 'Christendom' was born. Later, the natural conservatism of the followers of any institution which observes rituals ensured that Latin remained in use rather than the language of everyday speech, that fourth-century garments remained in use by those who led the worship – even though fashions changed for other uses – and that church building attracted the energies of architects and builders whilst other civic buildings were neglected.

In many ways the Eastern Orthodox Churches have remained closer than any other to the spirit of the fourth and fifth centuries. Generations of a minority position have built

Festivals of Christianity

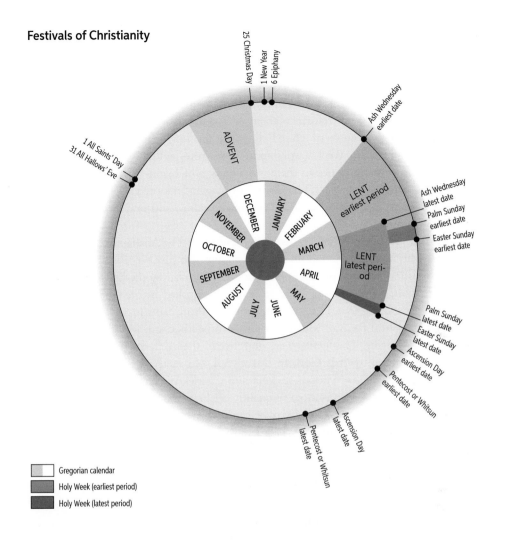

Gregorian calendar

Holy Week (earliest period)

Holy Week (latest period)

up a great regard for tradition and its conservation. The East has never had a Reformation or any equivalent of the Roman Catholic Second Vatican Council.

In the Middle Ages in the Western church, the role of the clergy became much more dominant. Celibacy added to the mystique of the clergy, who alone took an active part in worship. The concept of their special – indeed miraculous – power to transform the bread and wine into the body and blood of Christ gave them the functions of a priesthood. The part of ordinary believers was to attend Mass and to adore the presence of Christ. The people could not understand the Latin used for the Bible readings and prayers, nor did they receive communion, except at Easter, and then – from the late thirteenth century onwards – only the bread.

REFORM

The sixteenth-century Reformation, which took a stand against these perceived abuses, involved the return to God's Word written in the Bible, and a swing in ritual away from drama, colour, and movement to a word-centredness, emphasizing intelligibility and an understanding of doctrine. The reformers themselves often strove to bring the celebration of communion into the centre of church life, but the long-standing habits of their congregations defeated them. Weekly worship in most Protestant churches focused on the sermon, and in the Lutheran churches there was a growth of hymn-singing to accompany services of the Word and of prayers. The Church of England adopted a sober Prayer Book routine, in which the daily round of Bible readings, psalms, and prayers took on more importance than preaching.

The Reformation also gave birth to distinctive traditions. The Anabaptists, for example, included those who not only rejected infant baptism, but also gave voice to their emotions in worship, expressing personal piety in prayer in gatherings 'led by the Spirit'. And in the seventeenth century the Quakers, originally quite literally, 'quaked' before God in worship.

A big change started to affect English-speaking Protestantism in the eighteenth century. The Evangelical Revival, which gave birth to Methodism, was characterized by enthusiastic hymn-singing. The hymns were objective in their rich doctrinal content, but also expressed emotions towards God. In this revival, old metrical psalters were swept aside, and the hymns of Isaac Watts and John and Charles Wesley started to take their place. Also, the Lord's Supper was more frequently celebrated.

Hymns apart, Protestantism has tended to be like Roman Catholicism, in that its worship is usually dominated by the minister or leader, and in its solemnity: for the congregation, religion is not only passive, but also serious. But in the second half of the twentieth century, a 'liturgical movement' among both Catholics and Protestants began to strive for just those ends which seem so often to have been missed – active participation by the whole congregation, understandable services, and a genuine building up of the fellowship of the body of Christ.

In the Church of Rome, this led in 1962–65 to the Second Vatican Council's reforms of the liturgy, including the admission of local languages into worship, after 1600 years of Latin. The

The elaborate interior of St Paul's Anglican Cathedral, London, England.

A SHORT INTRODUCTION TO WORLD RELIGIONS

spill over from this movement into Protestantism, along with other shifts of conviction, led to a new emphasis on the corporateness of the sacrament, and on lay participation. Many denominations gained a new sense that worship might be more than a sermon with some formal preliminaries.

As a direct result of this new openness in the Church of Rome there were many doctrinal conversations designed to clear away misunderstandings. In the area of worship, the Anglican/Roman Catholic International Commission led in 1971 to an agreed statement on the Eucharist, or holy communion. The great multilateral convergence about worship has been precipitated through the World Council of Churches' Faith and Order report, *Baptism, Eucharist and Ministry* (1982), to which churches all over the world responded in the decade following.

PENTECOSTALISM

There have always been more radical movements. The twentieth century, for instance, saw the rise of the Pentecostal denominations. These are 'Spirit-directed' rather than 'Word-directed', and the characteristic expression in worship involves a full release of feelings, a free use of body movements, and an openness to contributions — not always, but quite often, 'tongues', 'interpretation of tongues', and 'prophecies' — from all the worshippers. 'Ministries of healing' are also widely practised within public worship. In South America, for instance, Pentecostalism is the main alternative to Roman Catholicism.

A parallel, indeed related, movement has been the 'charismatic' movement, often initially called 'Neo-Pentecostalist'; here Pentecostalism, instead of separating from the historic churches, has found a strong home within the 'mainline' Protestant denominations, and even in the Church of Rome.

TODAY

The religious face of the earth is changing. Eastern Orthodoxy has resurfaced in Russia and other Eastern European nations since the collapse of Communism — whilst Islam and Eastern religions have come, largely by migration, into Western nations.

Christianity is once again in a missionary situation in the West, as Christendom fades into secularism. But the various Western forms of Christianity are not now confined to the West. Young churches flourish in Asia, Africa, and elsewhere, varying in their worship from being as traditional as the Western churches from which they sprang, to the use of their genuine freedom to be culturally relevant to their contexts, frequently showing a freshness and liveliness hard to find in Western historic churches.

COLIN BUCHANAN

I AM A CHRISTIAN

I am twenty-seven years old and live in Memphis, Tennessee, USA. My wife Emily and I have a six-month-old boy named Noah. We are members of an Evangelical Presbyterian congregation.

I was raised as a Christian in a family that took the faith seriously. I went to a Christian private school until I was fourteen. At home I was taught to read the Bible daily. I enjoyed reading it – especially the Old Testament books of Proverbs and Psalms – and read it in its entirety before the age of thirteen. My sister and I were raised on Bible stories, right behaviour, and respect for our parents and others. More than that, we were encouraged to seek God on our own. My parents held, as I do now, that beliefs must be heartfelt. A relationship with God is personal and must be freely entered into. Although instruction and example guided me in my formative years, my own public profession of faith and a personal prayer of surrender, forgiveness, and acceptance seemed to demarcate the beginning of my individual life of faith. It was then, and remains today, a life I base on the fact that God is perfect, I'm not, and Jesus makes up that infinite difference.

I feel confident in my personal relationship with Jesus, who I believe to be Lord and God, and I am continually trying to bring every element of my life under God's authority. This means, with the help of God's Spirit, continually working to understand the Bible and live by its principles, bringing my desires in line with God's guidelines, which I believe are revealed in the Bible. My aim is to live a life of gratitude for the gracious love God has shown me, living in the peace and joy that comes from knowing I am loved and accepted by my maker. I've sometimes tried to live by ideas that run contrary to what I believe the Bible teaches and, frankly, have wound up hurting myself and others.

My practice of faith is not very ceremonial or ritualistic. For me, faith is more about believing and practising what the Bible teaches. I believe Christianity is about a relationship with Jesus as a personal saviour, lord, and friend. One of my guiding principles is Jesus' commandment to love others in the same way that he has loved us. For example, after college I spent four years teaching and mentoring inner city youths. My wife and I currently live with her parents so that she can help care for her mother, who is paralysed. These experiences have taught how difficult such love and commitment can be. Following Jesus has also helped me to respect others, learn from them, and seek ways to increase their health and well-being.

Jesus' example of love has led my wife and me to tithe our earnings, sharing ten per cent of our income every month with our church and others. That said, we understand ten per cent to be a benchmark, and seek to give more. For example, having won some money on a game show, we felt strongly that at least half of it should be donated to a relief fund. Loving others means making sure that whatever I do in life – including my occupation and all other activities – I do for God's glory and the benefit of others, not primarily for my own gain, reputation, or personal satisfaction.

Because God loves the whole world, and because a person's greatest good is found in a relationship with Jesus, I feel obliged and privileged to share Jesus with believers and unbelievers, always being sensitive to the needs and rights of others.

The fact that my wife and I were both Christians was of paramount importance to us in our decision to marry, and also very important to our families. Having said that, the marriage was not arranged. Our parents were not involved in the decision-making process. However, I did formally ask my wife's father for her hand in marriage. Following this, we received the blessing and encouragement of both our families. My wife and I take our relationship of love to each other and to God seriously. We pray together frequently, discuss the Bible, and talk honestly as partners on a shared journey, never making big decisions without first seeking God's will.

Study of the Bible is central for many Christians.

One of the most important parts of being a follower of Jesus is living in community with other Christians. I feel enormously privileged and grateful to be part of the large, global Christian family – imperfect, to be sure, but a real family nonetheless. The main gathering of our local branch is the church service on Sunday morning, which always includes thanksgiving for what God has done, prayers of petition and confession, hymns of worship, statements of belief about God and salvation, and a talk/sermon on a passage from the Bible.

Sunday is a special day to us, when we celebrate a day of rest and worship. It is the Lord's Day, a day of the week that reminds us of Jesus' resurrection. Other important celebrations are Christmas, when we celebrate the event of God becoming human in the person of Jesus, and Easter, when we remember Jesus' death on a cross for sinners and his subsequent victory over death and evil in his resurrection from the dead.

Since our church is quite large, we break down into groups for social and educational purposes, meeting on Sundays and during the week. Our group consists of newly-married couples, and within this group there are smaller 'mentor groups' which meet for intimate conversation, prayer, and Bible study. Whereas the larger groups are led by pastors, the smaller group is led by an older couple with more wisdom and experience in life than we possess. These groups and leaders are important to us. I always pray before making important decisions, and seek counsel from my group leaders, pastors, and peers.

Finally, the heart of my religion and religious experience can be summed up in the word 'love'. I celebrate the love God has for me and others, and I love God in return. My deep desire is that my love for Jesus and his love for me and others will be evident in my life in all places and at all times.

Jason Hood

CHAPTER 41

Contemporary Christianity

The history of the Christian movement across the centuries is full of surprises. From the beginning this faith has displayed an ability to take root and flourish in new areas and different cultural settings. One way of explaining this is to say that Christianity is a faith capable of being translated into new languages and cultural forms.

Today, while the churches of Europe and North America face the challenges of secularization – the process by which a society becomes increasingly secular or non-religious – the faith is growing at a rapid rate in diverse cultural settings in the non-Western world. At the very point in the mid-twentieth century when the colonial empires were receding, indigenous forms of Christianity displayed considerable growth, demonstrating that the faith had put down roots in the soil of local cultures and languages. The outcome has been the emergence of 'World Christianity', which is increasingly recognized as a central feature of our globalized world.

MODERN EXPANSION

The growth of the religion across the southern continents in modern times is unprecedented. While Western missions played a crucial role in the initial act of communicating the Christian gospel across cultural and linguistic barriers, the key players in the spread of the faith have invariably been local believers, able to express their new religion in surprising and dynamic ways, in contexts frequently marked by social and cultural crisis. This is the case whether in the evangelization of West Africa by repatriated slaves, or the contribution of thousands of ordinary Christians who – faced with the challenge of urban living in the burgeoning cities of the south – have proved adept at sharing their faith and planting new churches. In addition, a powerful impetus has come from the ministries of prophetic preachers and evangelists, who applied the faith to local situations, presenting Christ in ways that resonated with the felt needs of their own people, achieving mass movements of converts on a scale that equals, and probably surpasses, previous revival movements in Christian history.

This growth of Christianity across the southern continents has resulted in a shift in the centre of gravity of the religion, which now has its roots firmly planted in the soils of non-Western cultures. For example, in South America the extraordinary growth of indigenous forms of Pentecostal Christianity, involving the conversion of upwards of 160 million people, has taken both theologians and social scientists by surprise. The secular experience of Europe, far from being the vanguard of a global trend, may actually be unusual and exceptional.

AFRICA

The continent of Africa provided evidence of rapid Christian growth during the twentieth century. Despite the existence of ancient Christian traditions, the faith arrived in most sub-Saharan countries in the course of the nineteenth century. Yet so great has been the Christian growth witnessed across this continent, that Africa is rapidly displacing Europe and North America as the chief Christian heartland. Both the Roman Catholic Church and major Protestant groupings are being transformed by these changes, as the number of their adherents in Africa dwarfs the parent churches in Europe and North America. For example, the Archbishop of Canterbury presides over a worldwide communion of around 85 million Anglicans, of whom the vast majority are in the southern continents, including more than 18 million in Nigeria alone. One estimate suggests that the total Christian population of that country may reach 120 million by the middle of this century, and figures like this can be replicated elsewhere in Africa. Africa also saw a plethora of Independent churches, especially in the Zionist tradition, blossom in the 1980s and 1990s, as well as many other charismatic and Pentecostal churches.

Young African Christians worshipping.

ASIA

In Asia, the picture appears to be rather different. In many countries across this vast region, Christians remain small minorities, in contexts shaped by ancient non-Christian religious traditions. There are exceptions – notably in South Korea – where growing churches display remarkable missionary passion, as well as Singapore and the Philippines. However, a narrow focus on percentages of Christians can easily conceal the reality of significant Christian movements in the context of Asian religious pluralism. For instance the relatively small Christian community in Japan has given birth to some gifted theologians and writers. Similarly, the church in India has incarnated the Christian gospel in the context of the Hindu culture of the subcontinent, and there are indications it is experiencing growth.

The story of Christianity in modern China is of great significance. Seventy years ago, Western scholars were inclined to dismiss the church in China. Its apparently ineradicable foreignness limited its influence, and seemed to condemn it to being an ephemeral feature of colonial history. However, following the removal of Western missions after the Communist revolution, the unexpected occurred, so that scholars now speak of a flood of manifestations of the revival of religion, and acknowledge that Christianity has shed its image as a foreign import, and is now clearly identified as a Chinese religion. Estimates as to the number of Christian believers vary between 30 and 105 million. While claims at the top end of this range should be treated with scepticism, there is solid evidence of a tenfold increase in the Chinese churches since 1949. This in part reflects the continuing impact of the Home Church Movement in China, where the number of congregations increased from some 50,000 in 1970 to 400,000 twenty-five years later.

WORLD CHRISTIANITY

What are the implications of these changes? Until recently it was possible to assume the churches of Europe and North America could simply be transplanted to other continents, together with their inherited patterns of theology and practice. This assumption rested on the conviction that Western Christianity was a culture-free expression of the faith revealed through Christ and his apostles, and possessed absolute status and importance. In the new context created by the emergence of the non-Western churches, such assumptions have to be abandoned. The church looks very different in societies that stress the importance of the community over the rights of the individual, while theology takes surprising directions in cultures relatively unaffected by Western modernity.

As to Christian mission, the older approaches in which this was a one-way affair – from the West to the rest – have now been replaced by a far more complex pattern, in which mission is 'from everywhere to everywhere'. The massive migrations from the southern continents into Europe and North America is resulting in the appearance of 'Southern' forms of Christianity in the great urban centres of the Western world, where they often become by far the largest and most dynamic of Christian communities.

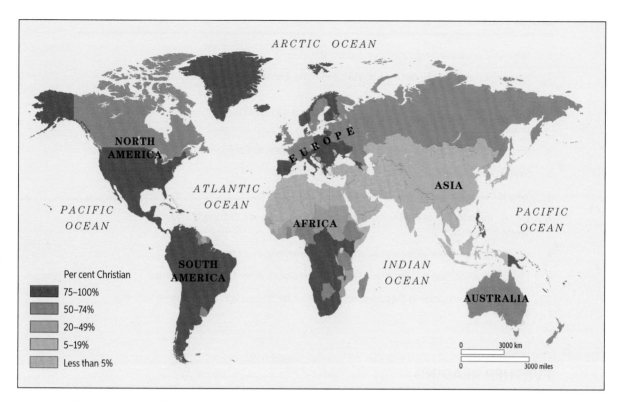

Per cent Christian
75–100%
50–74%
20–49%
5–19%
Less than 5%

Christianity Worldwide Today

For the vast majority of Christians in the southern hemisphere, religious pluralism is not a new experience. Faith in Christ is confessed, and the life of discipleship lived out, in continual interaction with one's Muslim, Hindu, Buddhist, or Confucian neighbours. Non-Western churches are overwhelmingly churches of the poor, existing in social and economic conditions largely dictated by forces beyond their control, in a world shaped by the phenomenon of economic globalization. The growth of non-Western churches in contexts inevitably characterized by ongoing dialogue with people of other faiths holds the possibility that fresh insights into the meaning of Christ and salvation will emerge from these new heartlands in the course of the twenty-first century.

DAVID SMITH

QUESTIONS

1. Why did Christianity separate from Judaism?

2. How important was the decision in 313 CE to make Christianity the Roman state religion for the future of the religion?

3. Why is it so important in Christianity that Jesus is the Son of God, rather than merely a prophet?

4. Why is the death and resurrection of Jesus so important to Christians?

5. Explain why Jesus' teaching was so radical at the time.

6. Why is baptism important in Christianity?

7. Explain the doctrine of the Trinity, and how it differs between Orthodox and Western Churches.

8. What was the Reformation, and what did its leaders hope to achieve?

9. How do the Catholic, Anglican, and Reformed traditions differ from one another?

10. 'Christianity is no longer a European religion.' How far do you agree or disagree with this statement?

FURTHER READING

Barrett, C. K., *The New Testament Background: Selected Documents*. Rev. ed. San Francisco: Harper & Row, 1989.

Barrett, David B., ed., *World Christian Encyclopedia*. Nairobi: Oxford University Press, 1982.

Bettenson, Henry S., ed., *Documents of the Christian Church*. 3rd ed. London: Oxford University Press, 1999.

Dowley, Tim, *Christian Music: A Global History*. Minneapolis: Fortress, 2011.

Hastings, Adrian, *The Church in Africa, 1450–1950*. Oxford: Oxford University Press, 1994.

Hastings, Adrian, ed., *A World History of Christianity*. London: Cassell, 1999.

MacCulloch, Diarmaid, *A History of Christianity: The First Three Thousand Years*. London: Penguin, 2009.

McManners, John, ed., *The Oxford History of Christianity*. Oxford and New York: Oxford University Press, 1993.

Noll, Mark, *A History of Christianity in the United States and Canada*. Grand Rapids MI: Eerdmans, 1992.

Pelikan, Jaroslav, *Jesus through the Centuries: His Place in the History of Culture*. New Haven: Yale University Press, 1985.

PART 9
ISLAM

SUMMARY

The history of Islam, one of the most significant cultural forces in the world today, began around 610 CE in the city of Mecca, when, Muslims believe, Muhammad began to receive revelations from God, which were recorded as the *Qur'an*. Muhammad's message – that there was only one God, who was omnipotent and merciful, and who will judge all humanity at the end of time – was initially not well received in Mecca, and he was forced out. In time, though, the new religion grew, both through conversions and – as a rising imperial power as well as a religion – military expansion. Within a hundred years of Muhammad's death, Islam dominated much of the Mediterranean world, including part of Europe. A schism had emerged, however, between the *Sunni* majority and the *Shi'a* over the succession to Muhammad.

Acceptance of the Muslim creed, which recognizes one God alone, with Muhammad as his prophet, is the first of five pillars which together shape believers' lives. The routine of daily prayers, *salah*, is the most obvious ritual element, but importantly, these are not just individual: by praying in the direction of Mecca, Muslims around the world demonstrate their unity. This sense of a community of believers is perhaps most obvious during Ramadan, the month of fasting, and in the fulfilment of *Hajj*, the duty to make a pilgrimage to Mecca at least once. Early on, Muslim scholars developed a complex legal system, *Shari'a*, to govern their community, while others made major contributions to the development of the arts and sciences.

Today Islam is thriving, not just in its traditional heartlands, but also in much of the West, as a result of significant migration since World War II. There has also been tension with the West, in part because of foreign policy questions, in part for more fundamental reasons. Some, such as the leaders of Iran's revolution of 1979, go further, seeing Western secularism as irreconcilable with Islam; while others are more comfortable with their faith's place in a pluralistic world.

CHAPTER 42

A Historical Overview

Islam began in Mecca about 610 CE. The dominant religion of Arabia at this time was a form of the old Semitic religion, with shrines of various gods and goddesses in many places. There also appears to have been a widespread belief in a high god, or supreme god, Allah. The other gods were sometimes regarded as angels, and could be asked to intercede with the supreme god on behalf of the worshippers.

Most of the Arabs were members of nomadic tribes, and believed more in human excellence than in any divine power. They believed that what happened to them was determined by Fate or Time, which they thought of, not as a being to be worshipped, but simply as 'the course of events'. Some tribes, or parts of tribes, had become Christian, and there were Jewish communities in Medina and elsewhere in western Arabia. Thus, certain Jewish and Christian ideas were familiar to many Arabs.

BEGINNINGS

Islam began, not among nomads, but among city-dwellers engaged in far-flung commercial enterprises. Towards the end of the sixth century, the merchants of Mecca gained a monopoly of trade between the Indian Ocean and the Mediterranean, which passed up the west coast of Arabia by camel caravan. Mecca had a sanctuary, the Ka'ba, which was an ancient pilgrimage centre, and the surrounding district was sacred. All this facilitated the growth of trade, but the wealth that poured into Mecca led to social tensions, especially among the younger men.

Muhammad was born in Mecca, around the year 570 CE. In about 610, he came to believe he was receiving messages from God, which he was to convey to his fellow Meccans. These messages, or revelations, revealed over 23 years, were later collected and form the *Qur'an*. They asserted that God was One (Allah), and that he was both merciful and all-powerful, controlling the course of events. On the Last Day, he would judge people according to their acts, and assign them to heaven or hell. Part of the conduct he expected of people was a generous use of wealth. In the revelations, Muhammad himself was spoken of, sometimes as simply a warner, telling of God's punishment for sinners, sometimes as a prophet, or messenger, of God. Muhammad sincerely believed these revelations were not his own composition, but the actual speech of God, conveyed to him by an angel. This is still the belief of Muslims.

Muhammad gained a number of followers, who met frequently with him, and joined him in the worship of God. But his messages were not all well received. The Meccan merchants were roused to vigorous opposition by the criticisms of their practices implied in the *Qur'an*. The merchants spoke of the old pagan gods, but the *Qur'an* came to emphasize that there is only one God – that 'there is no deity but God'. As opposition grew, the Quranic messages began to speak of former prophets who had met with opposition, and of the way in which God had preserved them and their followers, and brought disaster on their opponents. Among the stories were those of Noah and the Flood, Lot and the destruction of Sodom, and Moses escaping from Pharaoh.

> *He is Allah, besides whom there is no other god. He is the Sovereign Lord, the Holy One, the Giver of Peace, the Keeper of Faith; the Guardian, the Mighty One, the All-powerful, the Most High! Exalted be He above their idols! He is Allah, the Creator, the Originator, the Modeller. His are the gracious names. All that is in heaven and earth gives glory to Him. He is the Mighty, the Wise One.*
>
> The Qur'an, Surah 59:23–24.

EMIGRATION TO MEDINA

Muhammad's followers were now persecuted in various ways by his opponents, who were often their own relatives. Eventually it became impossible for him to carry on his religious activity in Mecca. An initial emigration of a handful of Muslims took place to the neighbouring Christian kingdom of Abyssinia, whose Christian ruler regarded kindly the message of Islam, and refused to hand over the Muslims to their adversaries from Mecca. Later, these emigrants joined the others in the main emigration of Muslims from Mecca in 622, when Muhammad, preceded by about seventy men and their families, emigrated to Medina. This emigration, the *Hijrah*, became the event that marked the beginning of the Islamic era. Medina was a fertile oasis, and the inhabitants were divided into two hostile groups. Most of them accepted Muhammad as prophet, and agreed that they and the emigrants from Mecca would form a single community or federation. Possibly they were more ready to accept Muhammad because they had heard from local Jewish clans that a messiah was expected. They were also hopeful that he would help them to overcome their divisions.

> *If you ask them who it is that has created the heavens and the earth and subjugated the sun and the moon, they will say 'Allah', How then are they turned away?*
>
> The Qur'an, Surah 29:61.

At Medina the religion of Islam took shape. The main ritual forms, modelled on Muhammad's example, were: worship (or prayer), almsgiving, fasting for the whole month of Ramadan, and the pilgrimage to Mecca, including ceremonies at neighbouring sites. The messages revealed to Muhammad at Medina included legal regulations for matters where Arab custom was unsatisfactory, such as the inheritance of wealth and the avoidance of incest.

The Jewish clans in Medina were associated with Muhammad's federation, as allies of Arab member clans, but nearly all the Jews refused to accept him as prophet. They mocked parts of the *Qur'an*, and sometimes actively opposed the Muslims. Muhammad expelled two Jewish clans from Medina, and had the men of a third executed. Until after the conquest of Mecca, he had few contacts with Christians.

At first, Muhammad had no special political powers at Medina, beyond being head of the emigrants from Mecca. After a year or two, however, all his followers there — now called Muslims — became involved in hostilities with the pagan Meccans. By 630, Muhammad was strong enough to take Mecca. He treated his enemies generously, and won most of them over to become Muslims. Many tribes all over Arabia also joined his federation and became Muslims. Because of his successes, Muhammad's authority as head of state was unquestioned.

THE FIRST CALIPHS

'He who honours Muhammad must know that he is dead. But he who honours the God of Muhammad must know that He is living and immortal.' Muhammad died in 632, and with these words his first successor, Abu Bakr (c. 573–634), encouraged the Muslim community and pointed them to the task ahead.

On his death, Muhammad left both a religion and a state. At first, the state had the form of a federation of tribes or clans, but as it expanded it became more organized. The head of state was known as the 'caliph' (*khalifa*) — the 'successor' or 'deputy' of Muhammad. Raiding their neighbours had been a normal occupation of the nomadic Arab tribes, and Muhammad and the first caliphs realized they could not keep peace within the federation unless they found some outlet for the energies of the tribesmen. They therefore organized raiding expeditions (*ghazawat*) in the direction of Syria and Iraq. The aim of these was to obtain booty, including domestic animals, and the first raids from Medina were very successful. There was a power vacuum in the region, because the two great powers of the day — the Byzantine and Persian Empires — had been almost constantly at war for half a century, and were now exhausted. In a few decisive battles, the Muslims overcame such opposition as the empires presented. Instead of returning to Medina after each campaign, they established forward base camps, so that they could go further afield in the next expedition. Following this strategy, within twelve years of Muhammad's death they had occupied Egypt, Syria, and Iraq, and were advancing westwards into Libya and eastwards into what is now Iran.

The Byzantine and Persian governors of the provinces fled, and the Muslims made treaties with the local inhabitants, giving them the status of 'protected minorities'. These groups ordered their own internal affairs, but paid tribute, or tax, to the Muslim governor. The status of protected minority was open only to 'people of the book' — communities who believed in one God and possessed a written scripture, such as Jews and Christians. The *jizya* – tax – that these protected minorities paid was in lieu of the *zakat* – poor-due – paid by Muslims, this not being required of minorities. However, the *jizya* did act as an incentive for minorities to accept Islam.

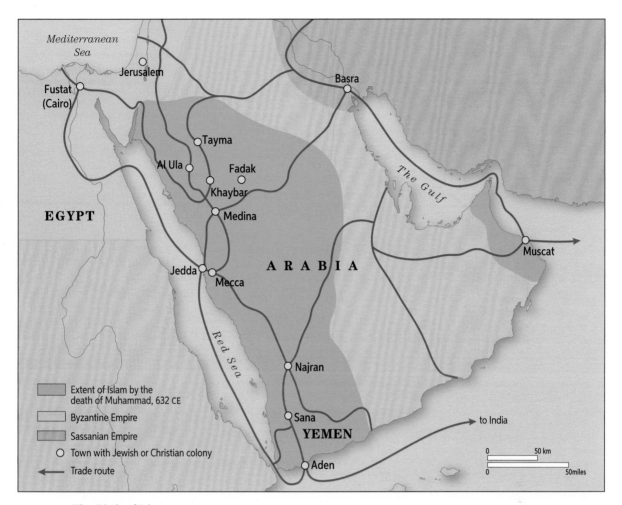

Labels on map:

Mediterranean Sea

Jerusalem

Fustat (Cairo)

Basra

Tayma

Al Ula

Fadak

Khaybar

The Gulf

Medina

EGYPT

ARABIA

Muscat

Jedda

Mecca

Red Sea

Najran

Extent of Islam by the death of Muhammad, 632 CE

Byzantine Empire

Sassanian Empire

O Town with Jewish or Christian colony

← Trade route

Sana

YEMEN

to India

Aden

0   50 km
0   50 miles

The Birth of Islam

THE EXPLOSION OF ISLAM

Apart from some periods of civil strife among Muslims, this expansion continued for a century. Westwards the Muslims occupied North Africa to the Atlantic, crossed into Spain, and for a few years held the region round Narbonne, in southern France. At the Battle of Tours, France, in 732 a Muslim raiding expedition was defeated by a French army, but this did not loosen the Muslim hold on Spain. Northwards, they raided as far as Constantinople (modern Istanbul), but failed to occupy any of Asia Minor (Turkey). Eastwards, after occupying the whole of Persia and Afghanistan, they penetrated into central Asia, and crossed the line of the River Indus in modern Pakistan. Until 750, this vast area remained a single state, ruled by the caliphs of the Ummayad dynasty.

Most of the inhabitants of these regions were not immediately converted to Islam, but became protected minorities. The military expeditions, though dignified with the title of

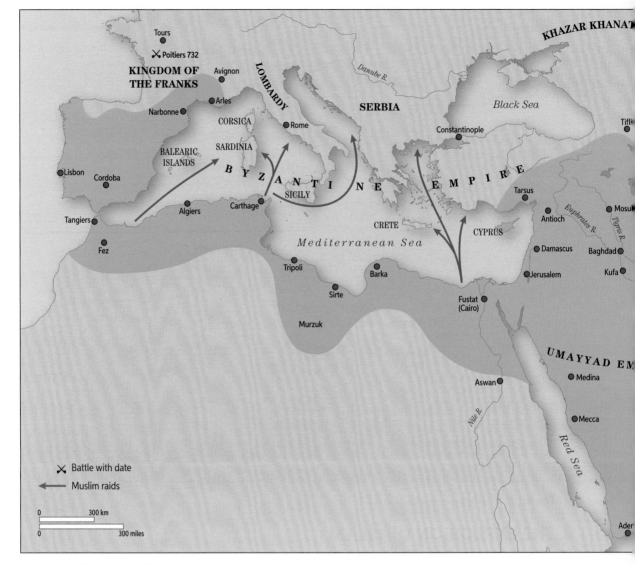

The Extent of Islam in 750 CE

'holy war' (*jihad*), were raids for booty — and not to make converts. The idea that opponents were given the choice of 'Islam or the sword' is false, except in the case of pagan Arab tribes. The protected minorities were on the whole well treated, since Muslim rulers felt it to be a point of honour that their 'protection' should be effective. Members of these minorities, however, saw themselves as second-class citizens, and over the centuries there was a steady trickle of converts to Islam. In this way Islam became the dominant religion in lands which were the original home of Christianity. In the seventh century though, Zoroastrianism — the official religion of the Persian Empire — was in decline, and conversion from it to Islam was quite rapid and extensive.

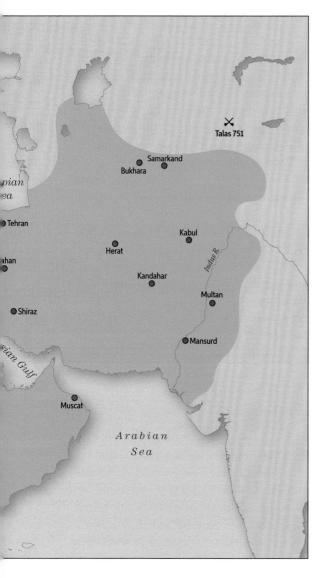

Talas 751

Samarkand
Bukhara

Tehran

Kabul

Herat

Kandahar

Multan

Shiraz

Mansurd

Muscat

*Arabian
Sea*

CONSOLIDATION

In 750 the Ummayad dynasty of caliphs, based in Damascus, ended, and for the next 500 years, the 'Abbasid dynasty ruled from Baghdad. They never took over control of Islamic Spain, and gradually lost authority over other outlying provinces. A local governor with a powerful army would insist on being succeeded by a person of his choice, maintaining only weak links with the caliph. In 945 the 'Abbasid caliph was even forced to delegate supreme political and military authority over Baghdad and the central provinces. However, there continued to be 'Abbasid caliphs in Baghdad, though without political power, until the destructive Mongol invasion in 1258.

Whereas the Ummayad period was one of growth and adaptation for Islam and the Arabs, the first century or two of 'Abbasid rule was marked by consolidation. All the cultural forms needed for the life of a great empire flourished. A central place was given to the development and elaboration of Islamic law, the *Shari'a*, which formed the basis of social structure. The *Shari'a* was derived in part from rules in the *Qur'an*, but to a greater extent from the example of Muhammad, known from the collections of *Hadith* — sometimes translated 'traditions' — stories about his deeds and sayings. This study of law, or jurisprudence, became the core of Islamic higher education.

Subordinate scholarly disciplines were concerned with the text of the *Qur'an*, the interpretation of the *Qur'an*, grammar, lexicology, and theological doctrine. There were also the 'foreign sciences' — Greek philosophy, medicine, mathematics, and natural science. Many Greek books were translated into Arabic, and considerable advances were made in the sciences, literature, the arts, and the skills of government and administration. Almost at the same time, scientific and mathematical advancement were further enhanced, as advances made in the Muslim East seeped back to the West, with increasing interaction between the worlds of Islam and Europe.

TO THE EAST

After 750, military expansion slowed, and almost the only advance was further into India, where the climax of Islamic power was under the Mughal emperors from 1556 until 1707, when most of the subcontinent was subject to them. Hindus were treated as 'people of the book' because their philosophers – though not most ordinary Hindus – were monotheists. Though there were group conversions to Islam, most of the population remained Hindu.

Islamic rule also spread by peaceful methods. Muslim traders with camel caravans took it into the West African steppe, and sea traders carried it to the East African coast. From India it spread – mainly through trade – to Malaysia, Indonesia, and the Philippines; and from central Asia it moved into eastern China.

Local people were impressed by the confidence and high culture of the Muslim traders, allowed them to marry local women, and often after a time decided themselves to become Muslims. Converts often kept many of their old customs, and did not immediately observe the *Shari'a* fully. But over the centuries they moved closer to standard Islam, and at the same time the number of Muslims kept increasing.

Prior to 1500 the main area where Islam contracted was Spain. Christian military pressure gradually whittled away the area under Muslim control, and in 1492 the last Sultan of Granada had to surrender. Muslims continued in Spain for a time, but were executed or driven out by the Inquisition.

THE IMPACT OF EUROPE

A new era in the history of Islam began about 1500. The Portuguese sailor Vasco da Gama (c. 1460–1524), having rounded the Cape of Good Hope and disrupted the Muslim trade on the East African coast, reached India in 1498. This was the beginning of the impact of Europe on the eastern part of the Islamic world. In the west, the Ottomans took over the caliphate, and conquered much of south-east Europe and the southern coast of the Mediterranean during the fifteenth and sixteenth centuries, and were then in military and diplomatic contact with European states, as well as having commercial dealings. The full force of the European impact, however, was not felt until after the Industrial Revolution.

The impact of Europe on the Islamic world – as on Asia and Africa generally – was many-sided: economic, political, intellectual, and religious. It began with ocean-borne trade, but went on to political interference and finally colonization. As European technology developed, in the nineteenth and twentieth centuries, richer Muslims wanted to share in its comforts and conveniences, and independent rulers wanted their countries to have railways and other forms of communication, plumbing, electricity for lighting, telephones, and so forth. Military hardware was also high on the list, and it then became necessary to train men to use it. Colonial powers also introduced Western-type education, to train men for minor administrative posts. After 1800, the Christian churches sent

The Masjid-i Jahan-Numa ('world-reflecting mosque'), usually known as the Jama Masjid, is the principal mosque of Old Delhi, India, and was built by the Mughal Emperor Shah Jahan between 1650 and 1656 CE.

missionaries to most parts of the world, but in Islamic lands they made relatively few converts; their chief contribution was to develop education and medical care.

By the early twentieth century, informed Muslims were aware of their situation. Movements for political independence grew and were eventually successful. Some industry was developed, based on Western technology. Most Muslim countries adopted an essentially Western educational system, because religious leaders were not prepared to adapt the traditional Islamic education they controlled. In many Muslim countries this has led to two parallel systems of education: a secular system inherited from Europe, and a traditional religious system of education, revolving around *madrassahs* (Islamic schools). The discovery of vast quantities of oil in the Middle East was at first exploited by Westerners, but later, when taken over by Muslim governments, became a weapon in world politics. Until the end of World War II, Muslim countries were united in their struggle to be free of colonialism. Since then, splits between 'progressive' and 'conservative' groups have become increasingly apparent; and the conservative and reactionary groups have been strengthened by the development of Islamic fundamentalism.

MONTGOMERY WATT

ISLAM TIMELINE

500 CE   1000 CE   1500 CE   2000 CE

570   Birth of Muhammad

622   Muhammad's hijrah from Mecca to Medina: Muslim Year 1

632   Muhammad dies; leadership passes to the caliph

661   Umayyad caliphate moves to Damascus

680   Death of Hussein at Karbala; commemorated as martyr by Shi'ites

711   Islamic Arab armies reach Spain

732   Battle of Poitiers stops Muslim expansion into France

762   Mansur establishes Baghdad as Abbasid capital

1071   Seljuk Turks defeat Byzantines

1058–1111   al-Ghazali, Sufi scholar, synthesizer of faith and reason

1099   Crusaders capture Jerusalem

1165–1240   Ibn al-'Arabi, philosopher of the mystical unity of being

1258   Mongol invaders destroy Baghdad

1207–73   Rumi, Persian mystical poet

1291   Muslims expel Crusaders from Palestine

1492   Christians take Granada, final Muslim outpost in Spain

1529   Ottoman Turks reach Vienna

1703–92   Ibn 'Abd al-Wahhab, leader of traditionalist revival in Arabia

1838–97   Jamal-ad-Din al-Afghani, promoter of modern Islamic cultural revival

1924   Kemal Ataturk, modernizer and secularizer, abolishes caliphate in Turkey

1947   Pakistan formed as Islamic state

1979   Ayatollah Khomeini (1902-89) sets up a revolutionary Islamic regime in Iran

2001   Taliban, Afghanistan hardliners, demolish 1500-year-old Buddha statues in Bamiyan as 'idols'

2001   Osama bin Laden launches terror attacks in USA

CHAPTER 43

The Unity and Variety of Islam

Islam has two basic groups – the Sunni and Shi'a. Their origins can be traced back to a question which faced the first generation of Muslims: how was Muhammad, 'the Seal of the Prophets', to be succeeded as leader of the Muslim community? For Muslims this question was always a religious as well as a political one.

SUNNIS: COMMUNITY CONSENSUS

The answer of the Sunnis, who constitute the Muslim majority of approximately 85 per cent, can be summarized as follows. No one could succeed Muhammad in his nature and quality as prophet, for the *Qur'an* finalized and perfected the revelation of divine guidance, and declared Muhammad to be 'the Seal of the Prophets'. Muhammad's successor could therefore be no more than the guardian of the prophetic legacy. He would be a caliph (*khalifa*) with subordinate authority as leader of the believers, having responsibility for the administration of community affairs, in obedience to the *Qur'an* and prophetic precedent. By the process of consensus (*ijma'*), the community would select its caliph from amongst the male membership of the Quraish tribe to which Muhammad belonged.

Following Muhammad's death in 632 CE, caliphal succession passed from Abu Bakr (632–634) to 'Umar (634–644), 'Uthman (644–656), and 'Ali (656–661). These, 'the four rightly guided caliphs' are deemed to have lived so close to the Prophet that their example, together with Muhammad's, is taken to comprise the authoritative *sunnah*, or custom, for all later generations of Muslims to follow.

The Sunnis gradually developed a comprehensive system of community law, the *Shari'a*, which provided cohesion within the community, while allowing for variance between four orthodox law schools, the Malikis, Hanafis, Shafi'is, and Hanbalis. The principle of *ijma'* remained central; notionally the consensus of the whole community, though in practice that of the legal scholars.

After the 'rightly guided caliphs', the caliphate became a dynastic institution, regarded as the guardian of the *Shari'a*. But in 1924, with the demise of the Ottoman Caliphate, it was abolished. The *ijma'* of contemporary Sunni Islam seems to be that, if the *Shari'a* is observed by the national governments of Muslim states, there is no need for the transnational office of caliph to be restored.

SHI'A: AUTHORITY AND LEADERSHIP

The Dome of the Rock, on the Temple Mount, Jerusalem, built by the fifth caliph, 'Abd-al-Malik, is the third holiest place in Islam.

For Shi'a Muslims, the principal figure of religious authority is the *imam*. Muhammad completed 'the cycle of prophethood', and with it the possibility of further divine revelation. But Shi'a Muslims believe he instituted 'the cycle of initiation' for the continuing guidance of the community, by appointing as his successor an *imam*, invested with the qualities of inspired and infallible interpretation of the *Qur'an*. Accordingly, the Shi'a speak of themselves as 'people of appointment and identification'.

The first *imam* was 'Ali. As cousin, adopted son, and later son-in-law of Muhammad, by marriage to Fatima, he was not just a member of Muhammad's tribe, but also of 'the people of his house'. This intimate family relationship is significant: the Shi'a believe 'Ali inherited Muhammad's 'spiritual abilities', his *wilayah*. He was infallible in his interpretation of the *Qur'an* and leadership of the community, and passed on these qualities to the sons of his marriage with Fatima, Hasan, and Husayn, and they to their descendants in the line of *imams*. The Shi'a believe that 'the cycle of *wilayah*' will continue until the end of human history when – on the Last Day – humankind will be resurrected and judged for the afterlife.

The majority of Shi'a, known as Imamis, most of whom live in Iran, believe the cycle will be completed with the messianic return of the twelfth *imam*, often referred to as the '*imam* of the period'. He is said to have been withdrawn into 'occulation' since the third century of Islam. His guidance is still accessible through 'doctors of the law' (*mujtahidun*), of whom the most senior in Iran are the *ayatollahs*, who have the right to interpret the *Shari'a* and to make religious rulings.

The history of the Imamis has seen two important offshoots. The Zaidis, mostly found in Yemen today, do not limit the number of *imams* to twelve, and interpret their function in a manner similar to the Sunni caliph. The Isma'ilis, meanwhile, have developed highly esoteric doctrines surrounding the *imam*. They have two major groups, the Nizaris, who look to the Aga Khan as their *imam*, and the Musta'lis – more commonly known as the Bohra Muslims– who believe in a hidden *imam* who is represented on earth by their leader, the Da'i.

SUFISM

Sunni and Shi'a Islam reflect the diversity of the Muslim response to divine revelation. Sunni Islam tends to be more concerned to create and preserve structures of society within which the community may fulfil its God-given responsibilities. Shi'a Islam began in the martyrdoms of 'Ali and his son, Husayn, and has always been conscious of suffering and alienation in the human condition. It searches for answers in a more esoteric interpretation of the *Qur'an* and *Shari'a*. But there is no hard and fast distinction: Sunni Islam is also concerned with the inner life, and Shi'a with the outer. Moreover, the important mystical tradition of Sufism has seen a confluence of Shi'a and Sunni consciousness.

Sunnism and Shi'ism represent the major doctrinal varieties of Islam: Sufism denotes the inner spiritual life of both. Sufis are not a distinct group or sect; they are simply Muslims – Sunnis or Shi'as – who seek intimacy with God through a discipline of spiritual purification. The heart of Sufism is the love of God, and is built on the Quranic assurance that 'God loves the God-fearing' (*surah* 3:76), and fulfils their devotions in love. God is heard to say in a Holy *Hadith:*

> *The complete mystic 'way' includes both intellectual belief and practical activity; the latter consists in getting rid of the obstacles in the self, and in stripping off its base characteristic and vicious morals, so that the heart may attain to freedom from what is not God and to constant recollection of Him.*
>
> Al-Ghazali, *Deliverance from Error* (12th century).

> Nothing is more beloved to Me than that my servant approaches Me with constant acts of devotion. And when I love him I am the eye by which he sees and the ear by which he hears. When he approaches a span, I approach a cubit; and when he comes walking, I come running.

Among early Muslims remembered for their devotional insight ranks a woman from Baghdad, Rabi'a al-'Adawiyya (eighth century CE), who prayed:

> O Beloved of my heart, I have none like unto Thee, therefore have pity this day on the sinner who comes to Thee. O my Hope and my Rest and my Delight, the heart can love none other than Thee.

Later treatises on Sufi devotion defined love as that which 'obliterates from the heart everything except the Beloved'.

It is misleading, therefore, to think of Sufism as an 'ism'. The English word comes from the Arabic *tasawwuf*, which could be translated 'self-purification', provided we understand that human endeavour is incomplete unless fulfilled by divine love. *Sufi* (feminine, *sufiyya*) denotes a person whose heart is purified from the pollution of this world.

The prophet Muhammad is venerated by Muslims as a Sufi. Religious tradition tells of the miraculous cleansing of his heart as a child, and of his ascension to heaven (*mi raj*) by night when, through prayer, he experienced the mystery of God's all-embracing unity. Amongst his early followers were the so-called 'people of the bench' (*'ahl al-suffa*), who rarely left the mosque in Medina, due to the constancy of their prayers. They wore a simple tunic made of wool (*suf*), symbolizing their obedience to the example of the many prophets – especially Jesus son of Mary (*Isa ibn Mariam*) – who practised asceticism in rejection of worldly comforts.

Strictly speaking, a Sufi should never describe himself, nor a Sufiyya herself, by this term. They use the related word *mutasawwif* (feminine, *mutasawwifa*), 'one who tries to be a sufi'. The difference is critical. A classical Persian Sufi authority (al-Hujwiri) explained it as follows:

> *The sufi is he that is dead to self and lives by the Truth; he has escaped from the grip of human faculties and has truly attained to God. The* mutasawwif *is he that seeks to reach this rank by means of self-mortification, and in his search rectifies his conduct in accordance with the Sufis' example.*

> *God dwells in the heart, according to the Tradition, 'Neither my earth nor my heavens contain me, but I am contained in the heart of my servant who believes.'*
>
> Ibn al-'Arabi, *Tarjumanu al-Ashwaq* (13th century).

The way of purification through self-mortification involves the spiritual path, *tariqah*, which is modelled on the prophet's heavenly ascent. The prophet Muhammad once said that the paths are equal in number to the true believers, meaning that each person should develop his or her own spiritual practice.

As Islam developed and spread, Sufis seeing the danger of undisciplined spiritual practices, insisted that a *mutasawwif* must follow the guidance of a spiritual master (*shaykh, pir*). To dispense with a spiritual master is to follow the devil. So the path was institutionalized in a variety of spiritual fraternities, or orders, which followed different masters. They stretched across the medieval Muslim world, and though they varied greatly from one another, each united its followers from different continents in common spiritual disciplines.

All these orders drew a fundamental distinction in the nature of spiritual practice. Acts of self-mortification are called *mujahadat* – a word connected to the Arabic term *jihad*, which means 'striving'. The Prophet Muhammad explained that the highest level of *jihad* is the inward striving of the soul for purification. In a clear reference to the word *jihad*, referring to the personal struggle for self-purification, the *Qur'an* says that Allah 'will surely guide those who strive hard [conduct *jihad*] for Our cause.' (The *Qur'an*, surah 29:69)

DAVID KERR

CHAPTER 44

Sacred Writings

For Muslims, the *Qur'an* represents the supreme revelation of God's word in written form. It is unique among revealed books, universal in its application, and eternal in its relevance. It is extracted from a tablet on which God's word is recorded and kept in heaven. Orthodox belief among the Sunni majority considers the *Qur'an* to be co-eternal with God. According to the great Muslim scholar and jurist Abu Hanifa (d. c. 767), 'its letters, vowel points, and writing are all created, for these are the works of man; but God's word is uncreated... he who says that the word of God is created is an infidel'.

Muslims show great reverence for the *Qur'an*, handling and storing it with great care. Reading the *Qur'an* is widely considered to bring rewards, increasing with each word read; the reader will be brought closer to God through frequent reading. Memorizing the Quranic text is considered an act of considerable piety: anyone who memorizes the entire text (a *hafiz*) is highly respected. Furthermore, the pages of the *Qur'an* are considered by many Muslims to have healing qualities.

There is a supplementary body of sacred writing in Islam: the *Hadith* collections, or Prophetic Traditions, much more voluminous than the *Qur'an*, which serve as a model for Muslims around the world in their daily lives.

THE QUR'AN

> *When the* Qur'an *is read, listen to it with attention, and hold your peace: that ye may receive Mercy.*
>
> The Qur'an, surah 7:204.

The *Qur'an* is divided into 114 chapters. With the exception of chapter one, The Opening, these are arranged in order of decreasing length. Each chapter (*surah*) has a number and a title, which is typically based on a key word or theme in the chapter: The Women (4), The Cave (18), The Moon (54). The basic unit of a chapter is the verse (*ayah*). In all, the *Qur'an* has more than 6200 verses. The Quranic chapters are identified with two periods: those revealed to Muhammad at Mecca, and those revealed at Medina. The former tend to reflect the voice of Muhammad as protester, criticizing the Meccan status quo centred on idolatry, social injustice, and other evils. The Medinan chapters reflect Muhammad's role as community leader, addressing legal issues, matters to do with building the structures of state, inter-ethnic, and inter-religious relations.

The Qur'an presents a holistic theology, claiming authority over all aspects of life, allowing no separation between sacred and secular. It includes diverse themes, containing morals indicating right from wrong, as well as injunctions to obey and fear God. There are parables, or allegorical stories teaching a lesson, which Muslim scholars stress are not designed as entertainment, but rather for instruction. Passages of sheer ecstasy, relating to Muhammad's revelatory experiences, were later to become models for Islamic mystics. There are legal passages, designed to assist with the organization of the

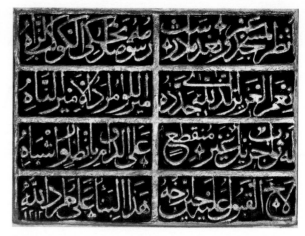

Bronze casting of a *surah* from the *Qur'an*.

Muslim community; chapters of encouragement, especially those revealed when the embryonic Muslim community was facing dangers and challenges; sections presenting oral traditions relating to Biblical characters and events; sections including sarcasm, argumentation, response, mercy, and even ruthlessness; and biographical material, from which a life of Muhammad can be constructed.

With such diverse themes, revealed over the final twenty-three years of Muhammad's lifetime, some verses appear to contradict others. This is addressed by the *Qur'an* itself in *surah* 2:106, which explains that, where the content is contradictory, later verses abrogate earlier verses. Muslims consider this does not point to error in the earlier verse; rather, the relevance of the verse being abrogated was specific to a time or context, with the later verse addressing a broader or later context. So prayer in the direction of Jerusalem, referred to in *surah* 2:143, was abrogated by *surah* 2:144, stipulating prayer towards Mecca. This reflected the changing relationship between the emerging Muslim community and the Jewish community of Arabia.

> *Whatever communications We abrogate or cause to be forgotten, We bring one better than it or like it. Do you not know that Allah has power over all things?*
>
> The Qur'an, surah 2:106

COMPILATION AND TRANSLATION

According to the Prophetic Traditions, the first official collection of the *Qur'an* took place under the first Caliph, Abu Bakr. However, regional variations occurred in copies of the *Qur'an* written or memorized, so the third Caliph, 'Uthman, made an official collection in 649/50. Oral traditions continued to circulate and diversify, and this variety was compounded by the inadequacies of contemporary Arabic script. Further reform and standardization were considered necessary, and this was undertaken by Abu Bakr bin Mujahid (d. 936). As a result of his efforts, seven readings of the Quranic text were accepted as canonical.

The *Qur'an* in its Arabic original has been prescribed in liturgical contexts by three of the four Sunni law schools since the earliest period of Islamic history. Only the Hanafite school has shown some flexibility, with founder Abu Hanifa allowing worshippers with no Arabic to recite the opening *surah* of the *Qur'an* in Persian, a right subsequently extended to speakers of other languages. In the twentieth century, there was further liberalization of attitudes towards translation – especially in Turkey and Egypt – amongst other schools of thought besides the Hanafite school. Nevertheless, translated texts are still considered as commentaries on the *Qur'an*, not the *Qur'an* itself.

Muslim prayer

In the name of God, Most Gracious, Most Merciful.

Praise be to God, The Cherisher and Sustainer of the Worlds;

Most Gracious, Most Merciful;

Master of the Day of Judgment.

Thee do we worship, and Thine aid we seek.

Show us the straight way,

The way of those on whom Thou hast bestowed Thy Grace,

Those whose (portion) Is not wrath,

And who go not astray.

The *Qu'ran*, Surah 1, transl. Yusuf Ali, 1934.
Used daily many times as a prayer.

THE *HADITH*

Hadith accounts are divided into two groups. The sacred *Hadith qudsi* are considered to include God's direct words, mediated through Muhammad, as in the case of the *Qur'an*; whereas the prophetic *Hadith sharif* record Muhammad's own wise words and deeds. The influential scholar al-Ghazali (1058–1111) shows the importance of the *Hadith* collections when he says:

> God has but one word, which differs only in the mode of its expression. On occasions God indicates His word by the Qur'an; on others, by words in another style, not publicly recited, and called the Prophetic tradition. Both are mediated by the Prophet.

The *Qur'an* recognizes earlier sacred writings: the Torah given to Moses, the Psalms to David, and the Gospel to Jesus. However, it charges both Jews and Christians with corrupting these earlier revelations, by changing the text, or wilfully misinterpreting it. Hence, the *Qur'an* sees itself as the final, perfect revelation, supplanting those which went before. Some Islamic thinkers recognize a measure of divine authority in the earlier scriptures, but challenge their interpretation by Jews and Christians.

PETER G. RIDDELL

CHAPTER 45

Beliefs

The Arabic term *iman* is used to designate the system of belief in Islam, drawing on Quranic verses.

ONENESS OF GOD

The Islamic belief system is centred on an uncompromising monotheism, called *tawhid*, the oneness of God. Many Quranic verses provide an insight into the attributes and characteristic features of God:

> *Allah is He besides Whom there is no god, the Everliving, the Self-subsisting by Whom all subsist; slumber does not overtake Him nor sleep; whatever is in the heavens and whatever is in the earth is His; who is he that can intercede with Him but by His permission? He knows what is before them and what is behind them, and they cannot comprehend anything out of His knowledge except what He pleases. His knowledge extends over the heavens and the earth, and the preservation of them both tires Him not, and He is the Most High, the Great*

> (surah 2:255).

God is supreme, eternal, and omnipotent. He sees all things and is present everywhere. He is the sole creator and sustainer of the universe, and controls life and death for all creatures. God has ninety-nine names, according to Muslim belief, representing his numerous attributes and aspects. The *Hadith* accounts provide the most important source for these names. Some relate to compassion and love, yet the depiction of God within Muslim theology is more of a God whom one reveres, of whom one is in awe, and to whom one is obedient.

The nature of God can be gleaned in part by a series of negative statements made within the Islamic sacred writings:

> *In the name of Allah, the Beneficent, the Merciful. Say: He is Allah, the One! Allah, the eternally Besought of all! Whom all creatures need. He neither eats*

nor drinks. He begetteth not nor was He begotten. And there
is none comparable unto Him

(The Qur'an, surah 112).

God is not a trinity, but is one. God has not been created, nor is he in a relationship of father, brother, or son with any other. He depends on no one, and has no needs. Nothing resembles him. He is without imperfections.

ANGELS

Belief in angels is another important article of faith. The *Qur'an* records that angels are created from light, and are so numerous that only God knows their exact number. Angels have no offspring, being neither male nor female, and serve God in various ways. The classical commentator Tabari defines angels as: 'God's messengers between Him and His prophets, and those of His servants to whom they are sent'.

The greatest of the angels is Jibril, or Gabriel, who was, according to Muslim belief, the angel who transmitted the *Qur'an* to Muhammad. Jibril also functions as the Holy Spirit within Islamic belief. An angel was the means used by God to tell Mary of the impending birth of her son Jesus:

> *When the angels said: O Mariam, surely Allah gives you good news with a Word*
> *from Him (of one) whose name is the Messiah, Isa son of Mariam, worthy of*
> *regard in this world and the hereafter, and of those who are made near (to Allah)'*

(The Qur'an, surah 3:45).

Angels are assigned other tasks by God, according to Islamic belief. They utter continuous praise of God, they bear his throne, and accompany believers in prayer. According to the *Hadith*, angels also record the deeds of every person. The angel Izra'il is responsible for drawing out the souls of the dying, while Israfil will sound the trumpet on the Last Day, the Day of Judgment. Other angels guard hell and direct its affairs. The *Qur'an* warns that opposing the angels is tantamount to opposing God, as they are his envoys:

> *Whoever is an enemy to Allah and His angels and apostles, to Gabriel and*
> *Michael – Lo! Allah is an enemy to those who reject Faith*

(surah 2:98).

REVEALED BOOKS

Sacred Scriptures revealed to humankind throughout history are of two types. The more substantial ones are called *Kutub* (books), while the smaller ones are known as *Suhuf* (scrolls). More than 100 works are believed to have been revealed throughout history, including scrolls revealed to Adam, Seth, Enoch, and Abraham, but now lost.

Only four revealed scriptures have survived, according to Islamic belief, and are mentioned by name in the *Qur'an*. The first is the *Tawrat*, the Jewish Torah, given by divine inspiration to Moses, according to the Quranic record: 'And before [the *Qur'an*] was the Book of Moses as a guide and a mercy…' (*surah* 46:12). This was followed by the *Zabur* (Psalms), revealed to David; the *Injil* (Gospel), revealed to Jesus; and the *Qur'an*, revealed to Muhammad. The various revealed books represented God's blueprint for people to live according to God's law.

For Muslims the *Qur'an* is the last and the definitive revelation, the repository of perfect truth, and it supplants all earlier revelations sent by God to humankind through the prophets. This is stated clearly in *Hadith* accounts anticipating events in the End Times:

> *Narrated Abu Huraira: Allah's Apostle said 'How will you be when the son of Mary [that is, Jesus] descends amongst you and he will judge people by the Law of the* Qur'an *and not by the law of Gospel?'*
>
> (Sahih Bukhari, Vol. 4, Book 55, No. 658).

God thus sends his angels with revealed books to the created world. A key link in this chain is provided by messengers and prophets, who must transmit the content of the revealed books to all people. Islamic belief considers a messenger (*Rasul*) to be a prophet (*Nabi*) of a specific type. A messenger is given a new set of divine laws and a new revealed book, whereas a prophet who is not a messenger is sent to transmit and implement previously revealed dispensations. The *Qur'an* mentions some twenty-five messengers by name, while the *Hadith* collections refer to a total of 124,000 prophets, of whom 313 were messengers. All prophets, whether messengers or not, are believed to perform miracles. The *Qur'an* also mentions that prophets — who have also been labelled 'guides' (13:7) and 'warners' (35:24) — have come to 'every nation', so Muslims accept that the founders of other great religions, such as Hinduism and Buddhism, may also have been prophets in their own time and place.

The words of the prophets are not their own, but those of God. The medieval scholar Ibn Khaldun (1332–1406) portrays this prophetic role as mediator in the following terms:

> *Allah has chosen individuals from among humankind whom He has honoured by Himself speaking to them to mould them according to His understanding, and to make them the mediators between Himself and His servants.*

It is in this context that Islamic prophets are believed to be free from sin.

Many of the prophets named in the *Qur'an* have counterparts in the Bible:

> *And We bestowed upon [Abraham] Isaac and Jacob; each of them We guided; and*
> *Noah did We guide aforetime; and of his seed (We guided) David and Solomon*
> *and Job and Joseph and Moses and Aaron. Thus do We reward the good'*

> (surah 6:84).

However, this is not the case with all: for example, Hud, Salih, and Luqman are all considered as Arabian prophets.

Muhammad represents the last messenger and prophet of God. Furthermore, according to the Islamic sacred writings, he is the greatest of all the prophets, having been given special functions:

> *Narrated Jabir bin 'Abdullah: Allah's Apostle said, 'I have been given five*
> *things which were not given to any amongst the Prophets before me'*

> (Sahih Bukhari, Volume 1, Book 8, No. 429).

These comprise divine assistance in achieving victory over his enemies, the right of prayer for his followers anywhere in the world, the right to take booty after battle, a mission to all humankind, and the right of intercession on the Day of Judgment.

RESURRECTION AND JUDGMENT

The message transmitted by the prophets, contained in revealed books, borne by angels, and originating from God, warns Muslims of an impending Day of Resurrection and Judgment. The exact time of the Day of Judgment is unknown to all except Allah. All that is known is that it will be on a Friday, the tenth day of the month of Muharram.

The *Hadith* collections point to signs of the approaching Day of Judgment. These include an increase in sin in the world, widespread disobedience of parental authority and disrespect for elders, an increase in debauchery, an increase in the numbers of women vis-à-vis men in the world, and incompetent people of lowly station assuming positions of leadership.

On the Day of Judgment, all people will be judged according to their sincere repentance and good deeds, measured by the degree to which they have followed God's law (the *Shari'a*). Everyone's deeds will be weighed on scales, and no last minute repentance will be accepted:

> *And repentance is not for those who go on doing evil deeds, until when death*
> *comes to one of them, he says: Surely now I repent; nor (for) those who die*
> *while they are unbelievers. These are they for whom We have prepared a*
> *painful chastisement*

> (The Qur'an, surah 4:18).

The Islamic sacred writings describe an afterlife, with the descriptions being especially graphic in the *Hadith* collections. If one earns favour from God on the Day of Judgment, according to good deeds, right belief, and sincere repentance of sins, heaven is the reward. This is a place of eternal bliss, resembling a garden with rivers, carpets, cushions, fruit, and pure maidens.

In contrast, an eternal hell awaits those who have not followed God's law, or held right belief. Hell is a place of great torment, with fire and boiling water, where skin is scalded, renewed, and scalded again. The Tree of Zaqqum provides bad fruit, and the damned are forced to eat from it:

> … *the tree of Zaqqum? Surely We have made it to be a trial to the unjust.*
> *Surely it is a tree that grows in the bottom of the hell; its produce is as it were*
> *the heads of the serpents. Then most surely they shall eat of it and fill (their)*
> *bellies with it. Then most surely they shall have after it to drink of a mixture*
> *prepared in boiling water. Then most surely their return shall be to hell*
>
> (surah 37:62–68).

Belief in God's decrees is the final article of faith. The *Qur'an* stresses that all is decreed by God:

> *And the sun runs on to a term appointed for it; that is the ordinance of the*
> *Mighty, the Knowing. And (as for) the moon, We have ordained for it stages till*
> *it becomes again as an old dry palm branch*
>
> (surah 36:38–39).

God controls the past, present, and future of each individual Muslim. Among the Muslim masses, this translates to a firm belief in God's preordination of all things, often verging on fatalism. This receives sustenance from Quranic verses such as the following:

> *Wherever you are, death will overtake you, though you are in lofty towers, and if*
> *a benefit comes to them, they say: This is from Allah; and if a misfortune befalls*
> *them, they say: This is from you. Say: All is from Allah, but what is the matter with*
> *these people that they do not make approach to understanding what is told (them)?*
>
> (surah 4:78).

At the level of Islamic scholarship, this article of faith has given rise throughout history to a dynamic debate about the degree of human ability to determine events, within an overall framework of God's predestination.

PETER G. RIDDELL

CHAPTER 46

Worship and Festivals

The *Qur'an* sees men and women as religious beings. 'I created … humankind only that they might worship me,' the Muslim hears God say in the *Qur'an*. Each individual is an *'abd* of God, a term which conveys the twin meanings of 'worshipper' and 'servant' in a single word. And this description applies to all aspects of human life, all of which is lived under the command of God. There is no distinction between worship and the wholeness of human life.

SUBMISSION TO GOD

Islam understands itself fundamentally as being 'natural religion', in that every created thing exists in dependence upon God, in obedience to his creative and sustaining power, and with the purpose of expressing adoration to God. For the human, this should lead to a conscious commitment to a life of thankful and praise-giving obedience to God. The word *muslim* means one who lives his life according to God's will; Islam means 'submission to God'.

> O believers, when you stand up to pray, wash your faces, and your hands up to the elbows, and wipe your heads, and your feet up to the ankles. If you are defiled, purify yourselves.
>
> The Qur'an, surah 5:8.

Worship (*'ibada*) and the activities of the workaday world (*mu'amalat*) are joint expressions of the character of *'abd*. The mosque cannot be separated from the marketplace. As far as worship is concerned, the *Qur'an* sees body and spirit as inseparably combined in the wholeness of human worship. Islam has no term for 'spirituality'; for its religious devotion seeks to preserve an equilibrium between the 'outward' and the 'inward' in worship. Believers' external acts of worship depend on their internal intention, and the *Qur'an* is concerned that both should be 'for the pleasure of God'. So while the holy law provides a code of practice as a framework for Muslim worship, the worship depends on the inner dynamic of thankful and praise-giving obedience, the discipline of the soul to 'remember God always'.

> Public worship is seventeen times better than private worship.
>
> Al-Ghazali

THE *SHAHADAH*

The Islamic code of conduct is founded upon the bedrock of the testimony of faith, the *shahadah*. This is the first pillar of Islam. When spoken in Arabic, and with sincere intention, it is a commitment to obey God and follow the prophet.

'I bear witness that there is no god but God; I bear witness that Muhammad is the Apostle of God.' These are the first words breathed into a child's ear at birth, and the last which Muslims would utter with their dying breath – the lantern for life and the hope for the mercy of God in the life hereafter. They point to the one God, who has spoken finally through the *Qur'an*; and they point to Muhammad, 'the Seal of the Prophets', sent to all humankind to transmit and interpret the *Qur'an*. The words of the *shahadah* summon Muslims to worship throughout the world, and their meaning is the heart of prayer and meditation.

PRAYING TOGETHER

The *Qur'an* identifies a human being as 'worshipper', and also places the individual worshipper, male or female, in the context of a worshipping community.

> *Hold fast, all of you, to the rope of God, and do not separate ... and may there spring from you a community who invite to goodness, enjoin right conduct and forbid indecency; such are they who are successful.*

The Qu'ran, surah 3:103

The *Shari'a* codifies and coordinates the practice of a worshipping community. Worship is a communal act, as well as one of individual commitment. To affirm the unity of God (*tawhid*) is

Muslim men, barefoot, pray together, facing Mecca.

A SHORT INTRODUCTION TO WORLD RELIGIONS

necessarily to affirm the unity of the created order and of humankind in right worship.

This community orientation of Islamic worship is symbolized and demonstrated in the ritual of *salah*, the liturgical form of prayer, which it is the duty of all Muslims to observe at fixed hours. Prayer is the second pillar of Islam. There are five prayer times, each preceded by obligatory ritual washing: dawn, midday, mid-afternoon, sunset, and night. They serve to remind Muslims, in a regular and disciplined manner, of their status before God as 'worshipful servants'. From the moment of the *muezzin's* call, and the preliminary washings, Muslims practise *salah*. On Fridays *salah* is a communal act.

> ... proclaim thy Lord's praise before the rising of the sun, and before its setting, and proclaim thy Lord's praise in the watches of the night, and at the ends of the day ...
>
> The Qur'an, surah 20:130.

> A mosque that was founded upon godfearing from the first day is worthier for thee to stand in; therein are men who love to cleanse themselves; and God loves those who cleanse themselves.
>
> The Qur'an, surah 9:109.

Festivals of Islam

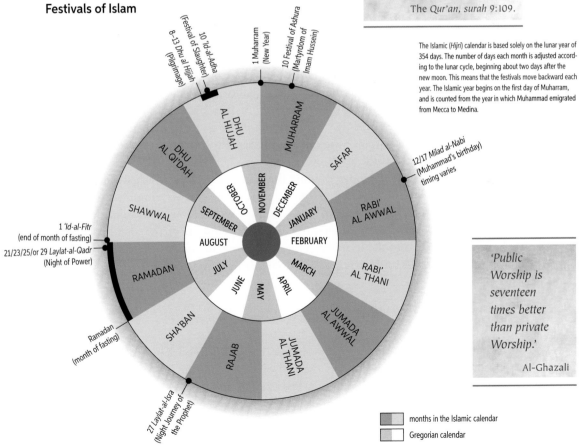

The Islamic (*Hijri*) calendar is based solely on the lunar year of 354 days. The number of days each month is adjusted according to the lunar cycle, beginning about two days after the new moon. This means that the festivals move backward each year. The Islamic year begins on the first day of Muharram, and is counted from the year in which Muhammad emigrated from Mecca to Medina.

> 'Public Worship is seventeen times better than private Worship.'
>
> Al-Ghazali

months in the Islamic calendar

Gregorian calendar

An expression of this is the common direction – towards the Ka'ba in Mecca – in which all Muslims turn in prayer. Around the globe, all are united in direction, and in intention, within a human circle of worshippers. At a signal from the prayer leader – the *imam* – men and women assemble separately in rows, at the mosque, or in the home or place of work, taking care that each person is close to the next. Carefully following the lead of the *imam*, they pray as a single body, quietly reciting words of prayer from the *Qur'an*. At the same time, they bow their bodies in a series of ritual movements until, from an initial standing position, all are upon their knees, with foreheads touching the floor – the whole congregation enacting, as a single body, its submission before the majesty of God, and asking for his guidance and mercy. Each of the five sets of prayers includes the repetition of *Allahu akbar* – 'God is greatest' – and of the first *surah* of the *Qur'an*, itself a prayer. At the end of the prayer, each person passes the Arabic words of peace to neighbours on right and left: *as-salamu alaikum*, 'peace be upon you'. Private prayers often follow the public service.

ALMSGIVING

'O you who believe, perform the *salah* and give the *zakah*.' Prayer is linked closely with almsgiving, the third pillar of Islam, often described by modern Muslims as the pillar of social action. Externally, *zakah* is the duty of sharing one's wealth with the poor, the needy, the debtor, the prisoner, the wayfarer – all who are less fortunate than oneself, but equally part of the worshipping community and equally precious to God. The *Qur'an* is less concerned with the quantity, and more with the quality, of giving. When it is offered 'in search of God's pleasure and for the strengthening of their own souls, it is as the likeness of a garden on a hill; the rainstorm smites it and it brings forth its fruit twofold'. The inward attitude is all-important; discretion is preferred to ostentation, and reproach on the part of the giver makes the action worthless.

The *Shari'a* is meticulous in determining the amounts of alms which should be given on different categories of possessions, but contemporary practice simplifies the matter to an annual rate of 2.5 per cent of one's cash balance. However Muslim devotional literature reflects equally the inwardness of *zakah* as 'purification' of the soul. It is a mercy to the giver as much as to the recipient; a means to atone for sins which are motivated by human self-centredness, or by irresponsible stewardship of possessions.

FASTING

Special alms are given on the two main religious festivals of the Islamic calendar, the first of which, *'Id al-Fitr* or *Bairam*, marks the end of Ramadan, the holy month of fasting. Fasting (*sawm*) is the fourth pillar of Muslim worship, and involves total abstinence from food and drink through the daylight hours of the entire month, from early dawn to sunset.

In some ways this is the most obviously communal of the duties of Islamic worship. The physical discipline means that social behaviour of the whole community has to change for the duration of the month; the pace of life slows down, and there is time for reflection. It is a period when social relationships are reaffirmed, reconciliations encouraged, and the solidarity of the community is expressed. Mosque attendance swells, particularly on the Night of Power (*laylat al-qadr*), towards the end of the month, when Muslims commemorate the descent of the *Qur'an* from heaven, and the beginning of Muhammad's ministry.

The fundamental intention of fasting is thanksgiving. Inwardly, the fast is thought of as a disciplining of the soul, to wait patiently upon God who guides and provides. This inward aspect is of great importance. Muhammad is reported to have said that, of all the duties of worship, *sawm* is the most loved by God, since it is seen only by him.

THE *HAJJ*

The fifth of the fundamental duties of Islamic worship — to be fulfilled once in a lifetime if at all possible — is the *Hajj*, the pilgrimage to Mecca and its vicinity. Here are the most holy places for Muslims, full of 'memorials' of God's guidance in times past. There are associations with Muhammad, who began his life and ministry in the city, and also with his prophetic precursor, Abraham, who, according

Throngs of Muslims, clothed in white, walk around the Ka'ba, Mecca, in the first rite of their pilgrimage.

to the *Qur'an*, built the Ka'ba, helped by his son, Ishmael, as a sign of their submission to God, with the prayer that God would show them 'our ways of worship'.

A visit to Mecca has religious significance for Muslims at any time of the year. But with the twelfth month of the calendar, *Dhu al Hijjah*, the season of the *Hajj*, or Great Pilgrimage, arrives. At any other time it is known as *Umra*, the Little Pilgrimage. Pilgrims flock to Mecca, each wearing the simple pilgrimage clothing of white cloth, denoting the state of ritual purification. They congregate in the Great Mosque, and the first rite of pilgrimage is performed – the circumambulation around the Ka'ba. This is followed by running seven times between two small hills, recalling the plight of Hagar and her son, Ishmael, who, in Islamic, Jewish, and Christian tradition, were saved from certain death by a spring of water which God caused to break through the desert sands. This well is named in the Islamic tradition as *zamzam*, and from it the pilgrims may draw holy water, before journeying a few miles out of Mecca to Mount Arafat, where the *Hajj* comes to its climax. Here the pilgrims observe the rite of 'standing' from midday to sunset in meditation before God. Then they begin the return journey to Mecca, stopping overnight at Mazdalifa, where each pilgrim gathers pebbles. The following day, these are thrown ritually against three stone pillars, in the neighbouring village of Mina, recalling the moments in Abraham's life when he resisted Satan's temptations to disobey God. God had commanded him to prepare his son Ishmael for sacrifice as a test of his obedience (*islam*). The *Qur'an* tells how the child was ransomed 'with a tremendous victim', and in joyful recollection of this act of divine mercy, the pilgrims offer the ritual sacrifice of sheep or camels, the meaning of which is clearly stated in the *Qur'an*: 'their flesh and blood reach not to God, but your devotion reaches him'.

With the intention of magnifying God, and remembering him 'with a more lively remembrance', Muslims throughout the world join with the pilgrims in Mina for the Feast of the Slaughter, which brings the *Hajj* to an end. Muslims remember their corporate identity and responsibility, as a worshipping community created by Muhammad. Muhammad believed this festival was the fulfilment of the Muslim community for which Abraham is said to have prayed before the Ka'ba:

> *Our Lord make us submissive to thee, and of our seed a community submissive to thee, and show us our ways of worship, and turn towards us. Lo! thou, only thou, art the Relenting, the Merciful*

> (The Qur'an, surah 2:128).

The Islamic (*Hijri*) calendar is based on the lunar year of 354 days. The number of days each month is adjusted according to the lunar cycle, beginning about two days after the new moon, which means the festivals move backward each year. The Islamic year begins on the first day of Muharram, and is counted from the year in which Muhammad emigrated from Mecca to Medina.

DAVID KERR

CHAPTER 47

The Law of Islam

Down the centuries, the traditional education of Muslims has rested on twin pillars: theology taught them what they should believe, and the sacred law prescribed how they should behave. In practice, the law has been the senior partner, for Islam has always been far more explicit about the quality of life God has ordained for his creatures than about the nature of the Creator himself. Although the role of Islamic law has changed considerably in recent years, it can still be described as 'the epitome of Islamic thought, the most typical manifestation of the Islamic way of life, the core and kernel of Islam itself'.

SHARI'A

The sacred law of Islam is called the *Shari'a* – a word which originally meant 'the way to a watering-place', but came to be used of the path of God's commandments. It is regarded by Muslims as firmly based on divine revelation, derived from four main sources:
1. The *Qur'an,* which, they believe, has existed eternally in Arabic in heaven, and was revealed piecemeal to Muhammad by the angel Jibril (Gabriel) as occasion demanded.
2. The *sunnah,* or practice of the Prophet, as enshrined in countless traditions of what he said, did, or permitted.
3. The *ijma',* or consensus of the Muslim community, or of its leading scholars.
4. *qiyas* – analogical deductions from the first three sources.

Orientalists have, however, shown that the raw material of the *Shari'a* was provided by pre-Islamic customary – and even codified – law and the administrative practices of early Islam, systematized and Islamicized by scholar-jurists in the light of those Islamic norms which had come to be accepted. They also insist that, for a number of decades, the law was wide open to foreign influences current in the conquered territories, or ingrained in the minds of converts to Islam.

The *Shari'a* has often been classified under five categories:
1. What God has commanded
2. What God has recommended, but not made strictly obligatory

3. What God has left legally indifferent
4. What God has deprecated, but not actually prohibited
5. What God has expressly forbidden.

As such, its scope is much wider than any Western concept of law, for it covers every aspect of life. Obviously a great deal of it could never be enforced by any human court, and must be left to the Day of Judgment. But, in theory, the *Shari'a* was a divinely revealed blueprint, to which every Muslim – from caliph to slave – must attempt to approximate.

In theory, human regulations were only appropriate in those matters which God had left 'legally indifferent'. In practice, from a very early date, even the official courts allowed a number of 'devices' which eased the inconvenience of some of the *Shari'a's* precepts.

Muslim rulers, moreover, found its standards of proof too exacting for the maintenance of public order. Muslim merchants found its prohibitions too restrictive for the life of the markets, while local communities of Muslims found its rigid prescripts too alien to their age-old customs. So less rigid courts soon appeared beside the official *qadis'* courts. But the fact remains that, until little more than a century ago, the *Shari'a* remained the basic and residual law – to which lip-service, at least, was almost always paid – throughout of the Muslim world.

INTERPRETING THE LAW

But the *Shari'a* was not a system of law that was either codified or uniform. Although it is regarded as firmly based on divine revelation, it has been developed and elaborated by generations of legal scholars, who interpreted the relevant verses in the *Qur'an* and those traditions which they accepted as authentic. They also drew from these sources a plethora of analogical deductions. At first, moreover, any adequately qualified jurist had the right of *ijtihad* – going back to the original sources to derive a rule of law to cover any problem that arose.

At a very early date, the Muslim community became divided between the Sunni, or 'orthodox', majority and the Shi'a and Khariji minorities, which split into further exclusive sub-sects, while the Sunni majority divided into a number of different schools or 'rites'. As these schools and sects crystallized, the right of independent deduction was progressively replaced by the duty to accept the authority of the great jurists of the past (*taqlid*). Today, even the most learned Sunni jurists are normally considered to be under this authority. The Ithna 'Ashari sub-sect of the Shi'a, which remains the dominant sect in Iran, still recognizes *mujtahidun* who may exercise *ijtihad* in certain circumstances. It is only among the Isma'ili Shi'as that the *imam* – or, in some cases his representative, the Da'i Mutlaq – can give a wholly authoritative ruling.

CIVIL LAW

Since about the middle of the nineteenth century, the position of Islamic law has changed radically throughout the greater part of the Muslim world. First in the Ottoman Empire, next in what was then 'British India', and subsequently elsewhere, the impact of modern life has loosened the sway of the *Shari'a* in two major ways. In many spheres of life, the *Shari'a* has been displaced by new codes of law, largely derived from the Western world. In the Ottoman Empire in the 1850s and 1860s, for example, the Commercial Code, the Penal Code, the Code of Commercial Procedure, and the Code of Maritime Commerce were all based on French models. But when the Ottoman reformers came to the law of obligations – contract, tort, etc. – they debated whether again to turn to European law or to compile a comparable code derived from Islamic sources.

Eventually the latter view prevailed. So the resultant code, commonly known as the *Majalla*, completed in 1876, was compiled from the rulings of a selection of Sunni jurists – although all these opinions had received some form of recognition from the Hanafi school. The *Majalla* was thus of immense jurisprudential significance. For the first time in history, a code of law based firmly on principles derived from the *Shari'a* was enacted by the authority of the state. And for the first time, again, a compilation was made of provisions of heterogeneous origin, selected on the broad principle of their suitability to modern life, rather than their established precedent in one particular school. Moreover, all these new codes were administered in secular courts by personnel trained in modern law schools. It was only family law that continued to be applied in the age-old way in the *Shari'a* courts, uncodified and unreformed.

The second change was less obvious, but equally important. In 1915, the position of Muslim wives, sometimes tying them – even in impossible circumstances – to their husbands under the dominant Hanafi rules, virtually compelled the Sultan to intervene even in matters of family law. So he issued two imperial decrees permitting wives to request a judicial dissolution of marriage in certain circumstances sanctified by one or another of the Sunnian schools. Once this dyke had been opened, the tide came in very fast indeed. In 1917 the Ottoman Law of Family Rights was promulgated, based on an extended application of these principles.

In one Muslim country after another, much the same happened. In 'British India' the new secular codes were based on the Common Law of England, rather than the Civil Law of France. Here both secular law and the uncodified family law of different religious communities were administered by the same courts. In Turkey, by contrast, the *Shari'a* was abolished and European codes, only slightly adapted, adopted in its place.

In Saudi Arabia, on the other hand, the *Shari'a* remains dominant – though even there statutory regulations began to proliferate. Most Muslim countries, however, now have largely secular codes in all except family law – which must, they insist, remain distinctively Islamic. And even this has been codified – in whole or in part – in a way which makes it more suitable for modern life. In countries such as Somalia and the People's Democratic Republic of Yemen, the presence of Marxist influence in such codes is sometimes plain to see.

I AM A MUSLIM

I had my first lessons in religion – Islam – on my mother's lap, and learnt to utter a few verses from the *Qur'an* by heart. Her recitations of the *Qur'an* in the early hours of the morning left a lasting impression on me, which resounds in my ears to this day whenever I remember her. I lost my father when I was barely one year old, and my young mother had a hard time bringing up a family of six children, hence she sought refuge in religion and prayers, and took special care in our religious education. The verses she memorized carry us through in our daily prayers all our life.

During my youth and working life I was not a particularly devout Muslim. My religion has become much more important following my retirement. Part of this rekindled interest is undoubtedly influenced by my association with fellow Muslims. Even so, I wouldn't call myself a strict follower of the faith. I shun some of the practices and puritanical teachings of the so-called 'fundamentalists'. I pray daily, but wouldn't like to be coerced into religious rituals. Rather, I find comfort and solace in praying to Allah in solitude. Although praying in congregations can be inspiring, I sometimes find it too repetitive and ritualistic.

I have a family with two grown-up children, both born in the West. Being raised in a Western society made a significant difference in their upbringing. In particular, compared with my upbringing in India, they had minimal religious teaching. This concerns me, as I feel responsible for alienating them from their faith. I now believe that religious education is an essential part in moulding the character of a person, irrespective of the religion they decide to follow. The moral and religious aspects of life have become all the more important in the present-day world, where families struggle to stay together, and societies seem to be going through a period of upheaval. My wife and I are, therefore, taking extra care with our grandchildren, making sure they receive basic lessons in religious and moral education.

A few years ago I performed the *Hajj* pilgrimage with my family, which has left another lasting impression on me. The annual *Hajj* is a once-in-a-lifetime occasion for Muslims to meet fellow pilgrims from all over the world. It is an experience that tests one's patience, tolerance, and physical endurance. It also inspired a sense of fellow feeling for others.

A mosque is supposed to be a place for prayers and social contact. Unfortunately, I find there is little scope to talk with, and enquire about, others; the only other way to socialize with fellow Muslims is at private parties or weddings.

Muslims have very few religious festivals, the main two being after Ramadan and Bakrid (*'Id-al-Adha*), and young and old, rich and poor alike meet to celebrate these with great fervour. My recollection of *'Id* (*Eid*) celebrations in childhood is one of rejoicing and excitement, as well as days of preparations. We all dressed in our new clothes and visited friends and relations. I remember there being plenty of delicious food, which was prepared and exchanged. The best part for the children was collecting money from the elders. and then all visiting the cinema house. Everybody knew everybody else in the town, and it was important to visit them to make up any differences. It was a time of renewing ties and friendships. Unfortunately, I find there is little community life in this country. It is probably this feeling of isolation that impels us to our religion.

Although my religion is not so important to me, at times of trouble my thoughts go automatically towards religion. A feeling of helplessness makes me submit to God Almighty. I feel my religion is my personal affair, and I don't like the intervention of a third person; but I do regard the prophet Muhammad as a good role model, who has left marvellous examples of compassion, piety, simplicity, and honesty. There is no walk of life for which he has not left guidance. Although I pray daily, I only read the scriptures occasionally.

Because the *Qur'an* is in Arabic, which I hardly understand, I read translations, as well as various interpretations and commentaries.

I get comfort in submission to Allah, and thank Him for His bounty, my good health, the air we breathe, the water we drink, the sunshine, and the seasons we enjoy without our asking or paying for it. If living in a secular society means not recognizing these gifts of God, then I don't want to live in such a society. I would much rather be a religious person.

As a religious person, I observe certain food regulations. Islam has strict guidelines about what to eat and what not to eat. For example, it forbids the consumption of any intoxicating drinks. I wear Western clothes for convenience and climatic reasons, and I think it is everyone's right to wear and eat what they want. That said, I think it is good for people to dress in a way that reflects their distinctive culture. Otherwise this world becomes a monotonous and boring place to live in.

I'm not a strict follower of Islam, yet our family life is very much influenced by our faith. We follow our religion in matters relating to marriage, birth, and death. My wife performs prayers five times a day, and recites the *Qur'an* daily. My son also attends the mosque once a week, work permitting. However, living in a Western society it is not always possible to meet the requirement that a Muslim should pray five times a day. Again, there is no fixed day for our festivals and sometimes they fall on a working day, which can present difficulties. For example, during the month of Ramadan, a Muslim is supposed to fast from daybreak to sunset. Because this may mean sixteen or seventeen hours of fasting, depending on the season, it becomes very strenuous for a working person. Hence, there are limitations to following our religion in the strictest terms.

Mohammad A. Khan

Thus the present picture is very different from that of the past. Whereas the once-dominant *Shari'a* is now, for the most part, confined to family law, the current tendency is to produce civil codes that incorporate principles derived from Islamic law alongside those of an alien origin. A few countries have, even more recently, begun to introduce some Islamic criminal sanctions and economic practices — a clear evidence of a resurgence of Islamic fundamentalism. In most Muslim countries, moreover, the law — whatever its origin — has been codified by legislative enactments. Thus the authority of the law, once implicit and transcendent, is now, in most countries, constitutional, resting on the will of the people as expressed by their executive or legislature.

NORMAN ANDERSON

CHAPTER 48

Islam in the Modern World

 The story of the Islamic world from 1700 has often been described in terms of the 'decline of Islam' confronted by the 'rise of the West', or the struggle between a vanishing 'tradition' and a triumphant 'modernity.' This is now rejected as an over-simplified picture.

RIVAL CAMPS

The increasing political corruption and military weakness of the once powerful imperial structures of the Ottomans of Turkey, the Safavids of Iran, and the Mughals of India was paralleled throughout the eighteenth century by the economic expansion of the British, French, and Dutch empires. Economic penetration alone, however, had little immediate impact upon Muslim religious developments, which were directed at the social and moral reconstruction of Islamic societies, and a reorientation of the Sufi tradition. Sunni revival movements arose out of local conditions, while ideas of reform were disseminated by traditional means, such as the annual pilgrimage to Mecca. Indeed the holy cities of Mecca and Medina were centres of study visited by scholars from as far afield as India and Morocco.

Two outstanding – but contrasting – figures were the Indian Sufi, Shah Wali Allah (1702–62) of Delhi, and the puritan Arab, Muhammad ibn Abd al-Wahhab (1703–92). Although each stressed the *Qur'an* and the Prophet's *sunna* (model example) as binding sources for faith and law, and each rejected the blind imitation of generations of medieval legal scholarship, Wali Allah accepted the possible vision of an immanent God, while Abd al-Wahhab emphasized the transcendence of the One Unique – and unknowable – God. Their influence has come down to the present.

MODERNIZERS

By the end of World War I, the three Muslim empires lay dismembered, and European colonial powers occupied, or directly influenced, the entire Muslim world. 'Modernity', understood as a cluster of social, political, economic and cultural institutions and values, was a transformation historically originating in Europe and North America. In the European overseas dominions, Muslims experienced modernity within a power relationship between themselves and their colonial masters, which ensured their responses to it would differ significantly. Specifically, Muslims experienced Europe's power not as secular, but as Christian power. While Muslims welcomed the material benefits of science and technology, they remained ambivalent to modern values, such as democracy, and hostile to missionary propaganda against the core of their faith. In places such as India, Algeria, and Palestine, the retreat from colonial rule down to the 1960s left much suffering and bitterness in its wake. Not surprisingly, modern Muslim reformers of the late nineteenth and twentieth centuries found it difficult to embrace either social change as secularization, or the marginalization of religion away from concerns for political, economic, or social problems.

Two early major Sunni modernist reformers were the Indian Sayyid Ahmad Khan (1817–98) and the Egyptian Muhammad 'Abduh (1845–1905), both of whom received a more or less traditional education, had an early relationship with Sufi spirituality, and later gained first-hand experience of Europe, influences which informed their efforts at social reform focused upon education and the need to modernize Islam. They held that, rather than interpreting the *Qur'an* in terms of the Prophetic Traditions (*Hadith*), revelation could be understood solely in its own terms, implicitly proposing that every Muslim could search scripture's meaning for him/herself. The banner of all modernist thought was *surah* 13:12: 'God does not alter what is in a people until they alter what is in themselves.' Rather than adhere literally to the past, Muslims must shape their future in the public interest, in order to deal with the dramatic new circumstances of the modern era. Religious debate and controversy has continued through the twentieth century to the present day.

THE RADICALS

The aim of more radical reformers was to Islamize modernity, rather than modernize Islam. Two key radicals who helped to shape movements sometimes called 'fundamentalist' or 'Islamist' were the Indian/Pakistani Abu al-Ala Maududi (1903–79) and the Egyptian Sayyid Qutb (1906–66), both of whom believed deeply that Muslims should conduct their entire lives according to God's law. Their work also provided a strident, if not trenchant, critique of secular Western societies. A similar impulse moved Ayatollah Khomeini's revolution in Iran in 1979. Radicals became the chief target of secularists who formed the backbone of the new political elites of the new Muslim nation states following independence from colonial powers. Underlying these controversies is a contest over rival claims of authority to interpret the foundational religious sources. Some secularists even attempted to justify the separation of religion from politics by appealing to the Prophet's model community in Medina.

BEYOND 9/11

Over the past quarter of a century, Western observers and governments have noted the phenomenon of a 'resurgent Islam'. The tragic events of 11 September 2001 seemed to some to confirm fears of a 'clash of civilizations'. In this perception, two important factors have been overlooked. First, discussions among Muslim leaders worldwide, conservatives included, expressed long-held concern over the dangers of mounting religious extremism within the community, well aware that their own agendas

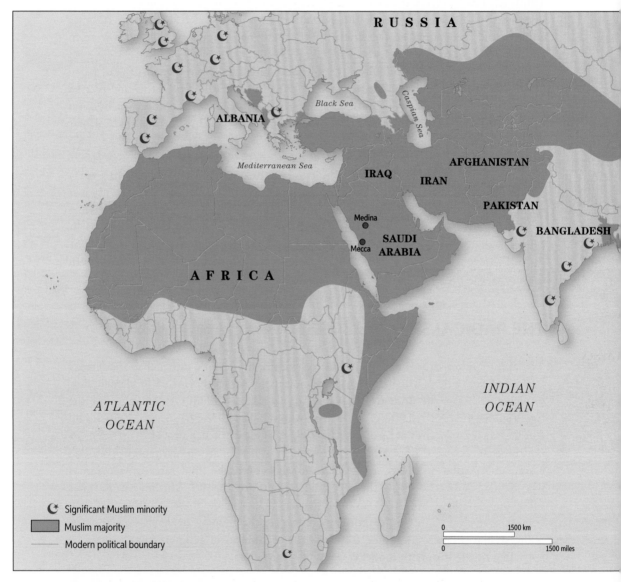

The Islamic World Today

were in danger of being hijacked by a minority. Second, extremists have articulated in religious terms current social-political problems that plague their own and other Muslim societies. Such problems include the corruption of, and repression by, regimes closely supported by Western governments, some of whose policies are widely regarded as perpetrating injustices upon Muslim peoples in areas such as Palestine, Chechnya, Afghanistan, Algeria, Iraq, and Bosnia. Effective resolution of such conflicts would help to undermine solutions proposed by extremist religious groups, and give moderate Muslim voices a forum for debate with often equally immoderate and unrepentant secularist power holders.

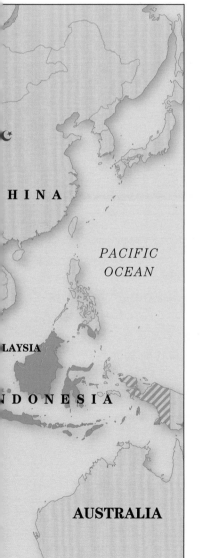

WOMEN AND MEN

In this multifaceted debate a growing contribution is to be expected from Muslim women. The individual's sense of the broader Muslim community is strong; men and women pray as equals in the eyes of God, and the contribution of each to community life is accepted equally by God: 'I will deny no man or woman among you the reward of their labours' (The *Qur'an*, *surah* 3:195). Whereas the spiritual equality of men and women has been traditionally agreed upon, questions of patriarchal power and social equality have been hotly contested for more than a century. Modernist thinkers, male and female — challenged by radicals, both male and female — have sought to reduce male privilege in the family, for example, by arguing that the *Qur'an*'s true intent supported monogamous marriage, not polygyny; by raising the marriage age, and thereby abolishing union with, or between, children; by restricting the male right of divorce, and increasing the grounds upon which women may seek divorce. Yet the overall goal of change is still to preserve a harmonious and stable family life, contributing to the greater good of the community, with the relationship of its parts — men, women, and children — based upon equity. It is part of the contest over who may 'speak for God' in interpreting the divine message. Female scholars and laywomen, albeit slowly and quietly today, are insisting their voices be heard too. As the future unfolds, observers should be more attentive to what Muslims, men and women, say as well as do.

DAVID WAINES

QUESTIONS

1. Why is Muhammad so important in Islam?

2. Explain the role in Islam of traditions from other religions.

3. How and why do Sunni and Shi'a Muslims differ in their view of the succession to Muhammad?

4. Explain how decisions in *Shari'a*, the Muslim legal system, are reached.

5. How does Muslim doctrine on the *Qur'an* demonstrate its huge importance to Islam?

6. What is Sufism, and why is it inappropriate to refer to it as a 'sect' of Islam?

7. Explain *tawhid*, the Muslim doctrine of monotheism.

8. How far do the Five Pillars reflect Islam as the religion of a united community?

9. Why is Mecca so important to Islam?

10. Why do some Muslims today believe their religion to be incompatible with Western secularism?

FURTHER READING

Armstrong, Karen, *Islam: A Short History*. London: Phoenix, 2001.

Aslan, Reza, *No God but God: The Origins, Evolution, and Future of Islam*. New York: Random House, 2006.

Coulson, N. G., *A History of Islamic Law*. Edinburgh: Edinburgh University Press, 1964.

Esposito, John, ed., *The Oxford Encyclopedia of the Modern Islamic World*. New York: Oxford University Press, 1995.

Hilldenbrand, Robert, *Islamic Art and Architecture*. London: Thames and Hudson, 1998.

Nasr, Seyyed Hossein. *The Garden of Truth: The Vision and Promise of Sufism, Islam's Mystical Tradition*. New York: HarperOne, 2008.

Peters, Francis E., *A Reader on Classical Islam*. Princeton: Princeton University Press, 1994.

Qureshi, Emran, and Michael A. Sells, eds, *The New Crusades: Constructing the Muslim Enemy*. New York: Columbia, 2003.

Watt, W. Montgomery, *Islamic Philosophy and Theology*. Edinburgh: Edinburgh University Press, 1962.

PART 10
SIKHISM

SUMMARY

Of the world's major religions, Sikhism is one of the youngest. Around 1500, Nanak, the religion's founder, is said to have been transformed by God while bathing, and emerged with the words 'There is no Hindu, there is no Muslim' – a simple creed which formed the basis for Sikhism. Reflecting this idea, Sikh scripture begins by emphasizing the unity of God and his creation. Accordingly, believers are encouraged to accept all religious traditions, and to treat all humanity with equal respect – radical notions in sixteenth century Punjab, riven by conflict between Hindus and Muslims, and dominated by the social restrictions of the caste system. *Karma* and the cycle of life – *chaurasi* – are important in Sikhism: in order to escape the punishment of rebirth, one must aspire to the Guru's example. This is not achieved by asceticism, however, since the Guru was a married man, who fulfilled his obligations to both family and community. After Nanak, a line of ten Gurus, who consolidated his legacy, led Sikhism. During this period, Sikhism's primary scripture, the *Adi Granth*, was compiled, from the work of the first five Gurus. In the era of the tenth – and last – Guru, the *Adi Granth* was itself instituted as a Guru, while the *Khalsa*, the community of the initiated, was founded.

Sikhism's early development was in a Muslim kingdom. In time, Sikhs would establish their own short-lived state; but during the nineteenth and twentieth centuries had to exist under British rule, and then within the largely Hindu secular Indian republic. In the late nineteenth century, the Sikh reform movement emerged, to reassert the religion's distinct identity, which many feared was being lost. The last decades of the twentieth century saw the rise of a Sikh-Punjabi nationalist movement, which inevitably resulted in significant conflict with the Indian state, most notably during the 1980s. A significant and vocal diaspora community meanwhile has grown in the West, as a result of post-war migration.

CHAPTER 49

A Historical Overview

The history of Sikhism has always been closely linked to the Punjab, the land of its origins, because of its situation in the north-west of the Indian subcontinent, always the first region of the fertile northern plains to be exposed to successive conquests by invaders crossing the great mountain boundaries through such routes as the Khyber Pass. The first such cultural inroads recorded were those of the Aryan tribes in the Vedic period, which initiated the beginnings of the Hindu tradition. The last were the invasions mounted by Muslim sultans from Afghanistan and Central Asia from early in the first millennium CE, which resulted not only in the establishment of centuries of Muslim rule over the Punjab, but also in the presence of substantial numbers of Muslims in Punjabi society, largely the product of peaceful conversion.

When Sikhism first emerged, some five hundred years ago, it appeared in a society already religiously divided. It would be quite misleading to think of Sikhism as a mechanical combination of Hindu and Muslim elements, since from its beginnings it has been self-defined as a new and independent third way. Equally, its evolution needs to be understood as a complex process of the ongoing relationship, within the Punjab and beyond, of a vigorous minority community to the two numerically larger traditions of Hinduism and Islam.

GURU NANAK

Nanak (1469–1539) is revered by all branches of the religion as the defining first Guru of the *Sikhs* (Punjabi for 'disciples'). He was by birth a Hindu of the Khatri caste – professionals with strong hereditary links to the administration – and his father was a village accountant. Nanak himself was married with a family, and had a career as an administrator working for a local Muslim nobleman. His mission began when he was around the age of thirty, with a transforming experience of the divine reality, granted to him when he entered the river to bathe. Mysteriously hidden from the view of his companions, he emerged after three days, uttering

> *Great Guru whose encounter brought the Lord to mind!*
>
> *With his teaching as their salve, these eyes survey the world.*
>
> *Attached to the other, some traders left the Lord and roamed.*
>
> *How few have realized the Guru is the boat,*
>
> *Which delivers those he favours safe across.*
>
> Adi Granth 470.

the words 'There is no Hindu, there is no Muslim,' taken as the inaugurating formula of the new religion. Nanak then embarked upon an extended series of travels, before returning later in his life to the Punjab, where he established a settled community of the first Sikhs.

Guru Nanak's teachings are embodied in his verses, hymns, and longer poetical works, which now form a substantial collection at the heart of the Sikh scriptures. In their broad thrust, these teachings are similar in content to those of other North Indian teachers of the medieval period from lower castes, such as Kabir (1440–1518) and Ravidas. They all preached that salvation was dependent upon devotion not to a divine incarnation, such as Krishna, but to the undifferentiated Formless One; and that to observe caste practices and Brahmanical authority was as futile for those who wished to be saved as obedience to the alternatives promulgated by Islam. But the subsequent, successful, independent development of Sikhism itself shows that Nanak was much more than just another teacher in this dissenting tradition of medieval Hinduism, called *nirgun bhakti* (devotion to the Formless).

Nanak's hymns combine a remarkable beauty and power of poetic expression with a distinctive coherence and ability for

Gurudwara Bangla Sahib, the most prominent Sikh gurdwara in Delhi, associated with the eighth Guru, Har Krishan, was first built in 1783.

systematic exposition, which is perhaps to be related to his professional background. Their contents embrace repeated praise of the divine order presided over and permeated by its creator, the one and only Immortal Being (*Akal Purakh*), with a penetrating analysis of the human condition, which is condemned through egotistical self-will (*haumai*, literally 'I-me') to the mechanical succession of suffering, and endless rebirths in blind unawareness of that order. In place of the false claims to offer true guidance offered by the religious specialists of the day, whether Brahmans, yogis, or Muslim clerics, Nanak sets out his own prescription for human salvation: the necessity of inner transformation through listening to the voice of the True Guru within the heart, and meditating with love upon the Divine Name. Only thus may freedom from self be gained, and escape from the cycle of transmigration be achieved, so that the liberated soul may at last join the company of saints in their eternal singing of praises at the court of the Immortal Being.

There is, however, nothing automatic about access to the path of salvation that Nanak describes. His hymns repeatedly emphasize that a righteous life is no guarantee of salvation, since the coming of the inner True Guru to any given individual depends on the favour of the Immortal Being. For this to happen, it is equally a necessary condition that the individual should have prepared him or herself for the True Guru's coming by living properly. Such a life does not entail the practice of elaborate rituals, or extreme asceticism, which are both frequently stated to be quite pointless. What is important is rather the discipline of living a normal life in this world, practising loving meditation on the divine reality, and supporting others through an honest existence, as summed up in the triple formula of 'the Name, giving, and keeping clean' (*nam dan isnan*).

THE LATER GURUS

As has been repeatedly demonstrated, the successful establishment of a religion depends not just upon the teachings of its founder, but also upon how the community created by them is subsequently organized. Besides being a teacher of outstanding force and insight, Guru Nanak was evidently a most capable organizer of his followers. He laid the foundations of some of the defining practices of the subsequent Sikh tradition, notably the establishment of daily offices of prayer (*nitnem*) and the practice of congregational assembly to hear the hymns of the Guru. Although married with two sons, Guru Nanak went outside his family to select a disciple to succeed him as the second Guru of the Sikh community, or *Panth* (path, way).

From the time of Guru Nanak's death, the Sikh Panth was led by a line of living Gurus, until the death of the tenth Guru in 1708. While rejection of the Hindu caste hierarchy was symbolically reinforced by the third Guru, Amar Das — through the institution of the *langar*, the temple kitchen offering food to all irrespective of caste — all the Gurus were from the same Khatri caste as Nanak; and from the fifth Guru onwards the succession became hereditary within a single family. Initially the centre of the community shifted with each Guru, until Guru Arjan founded the great temple at Amritsar known as the Golden Temple (*Harimandir*), which since its inauguration in 1604 has been the focal point of Sikhism.

At the same time, Guru Arjan undertook a project of still greater importance, in providing a unifying object of devotion for the Sikh Panth, through his codification of the Sikh scriptures, issued with the Guru's authority as the *Adi Granth* (original book). This is an enormous hymnal, filling 1,430 pages in the standard modern edition, and having a central place in the ritual of the Sikh temples, or *gurdwara* (gate of the Guru). Besides the compositions of Guru Nanak, the *Adi Granth* also contains those of the next four Gurus — who each used the same poetic name 'Nanak', in keeping with the belief that the transmission of the

THE TEN GURUS

Guru Nanak (1469–1539)
founder of Sikhism
Guru Angad (1539–52)
Guru Amar Das (1552–74)
Guru Ram Das (1574–81)
Guru Arjan (1581–1606)
Guru Hargobind (1606–44)
Guru Har Rai (1644–61)
Guru Har Krishan (1661–64)
Guru Tegh Bahadur (1664–75)
Guru Gobind Singh (1675–1708)

SIKHISM TIMELINE

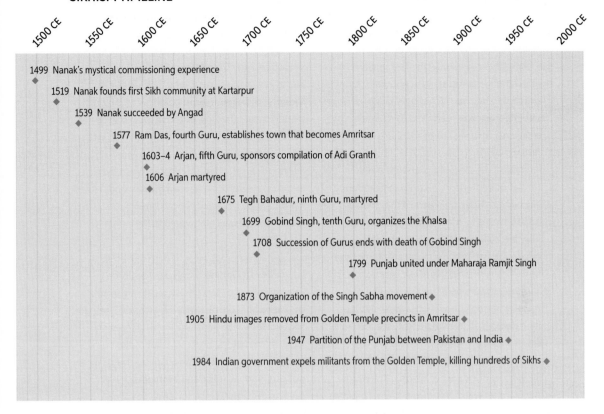

1500 CE   1550 CE   1600 CE   1650 CE   1700 CE   1750 CE   1800 CE   1850 CE   1900 CE   1950 CE   2000 CE

1499 Nanak's mystical commissioning experience

1519 Nanak founds first Sikh community at Kartarpur

1539 Nanak succeeded by Angad

1577 Ram Das, fourth Guru, establishes town that becomes Amritsar

1603–4 Arjan, fifth Guru, sponsors compilation of Adi Granth

1606 Arjan martyred

1675 Tegh Bahadur, ninth Guru, martyred

1699 Gobind Singh, tenth Guru, organizes the Khalsa

1708 Succession of Gurus ends with death of Gobind Singh

1799 Punjab united under Maharaja Ramjit Singh

1873 Organization of the Singh Sabha movement

1905 Hindu images removed from Golden Temple precincts in Amritsar

1947 Partition of the Punjab between Pakistan and India

1984 Indian government expels militants from the Golden Temple, killing hundreds of Sikhs

light of the guruship blended them into a seamless line of 'light blended into light' (*joti jot samai*). Guru Arjan himself is the largest single contributor, accounting for about one third of the whole. Its contents also include hymns by non-Sikh authors, such as Kabir and Ravidas, and the Muslim Farid, collectively referred to as 'devotees' (*bhagats*). The language of most of the scripture is a mixture of Old Punjabi and Old Hindi, written in the special Sikh script, *Gurmukhi*. The elaborate arrangement of several thousand hymns, itself an outstanding achievement of editorship, is not primarily by author, but by the mode (*raga*) in which they are to be sung. While no other early Sikh literature has the same canonical authority as the *Adi Granth*, popular devotion has always been fostered by the prose hagiographies of Guru Nanak – called *janamsakhis* (birth-witnesses) – which were first produced during this period.

GURU GOBIND SINGH AND THE *KHALSA*

The Panth grew significantly in numbers and membership during the time of the early Gurus, which overlapped the reign of the great Mughal emperor Akbar (1542–1605). But the strategic location of the Punjab inevitably embroiled the Gurus in imperial

THE *KHALSA*

On *Baisakhi* day in 1699, the tenth Guru founded the *Khalsa*, the community of initiated (*amritdhari*) Sikhs. The nucleus of this dynamic community is popularly known as the five beloved ones (*panj-piare*), who volunteered their readiness to sacrifice their lives for the sake of the Guru on that historic day.

Thereupon the Guru prepared *amrit* ('water of immortality') – popularly known as *khande di pahul* ('water of the double-edged sword') – for the initiation ceremony. The five volunteers, who belonged to different caste groups, drank *amrit* from the same bowl, signifying their entry into the casteless fraternity of the *Khalsa*. The next most important innovation was to change their names. All five volunteers, like the Guru, had traditional Hindu names before the initiation ceremony. Now they were given a new corporate name: 'Singh'. Afterwards, the Guru received *amrit* from the *panj-piare*, and changed his name from Gobind Rai to Gobind Singh. He also admitted women into the *Khalsa*, who after the initiation received the name 'Kaur'.

According to tradition, Guru Gobind Singh prescribed a new code of discipline for members of the *Khalsa*, which includes the wearing of five emblems, collectively known as *panj kakke* (five ks), because each begins with the letter '*kakka*' of the Gurmukhi script:

kes – uncut hair
kangha – a small wooden comb worn in hair
kirpan – a sword, nowadays a small one
kacha – a pair of knee-length breeches
kara – a steel bracelet worn on the right wrist

It is believed Gobind Singh also declared that members of the *Khalsa* must not smoke or chew tobacco, or consume alcohol. They should not eat meat slaughtered according to Muslim custom, and must not molest a Muslim woman. Although a turban (*pag*) is not one of the prescribed emblems, it has far greater significance for Sikhs than any other head-covering. A male Sikh is required to wear the turban in public as a symbol of commitment to Sikh ideals.

---

politics, and Guru Arjan became the first Sikh martyr, when Akbar's less tolerant successor ordered his execution. During the seventeenth century, the Panth expanded from its initial, largely professional and commercial, membership, to embrace increasing numbers of Sikhs from the Jat farming caste. At the same time, an increasingly militant policy was reflected in the proclamation under Arjan's son, Guru Hargobind, of claims to secular (*miri*) as well as spiritual authority (*piri*). Continuing conflict with the Mughals came to a further head with the execution in Delhi of the ninth Guru, Tegh Bahadur.

This led to a radical new formation of the community under the martyred leader's son, Guru Gobind Singh, the tenth and last Guru. Guru Gobind consciously adopted the role of a ruler, as well as that of guru, in his court at Anandpur, in the Punjab. His most important innovation was the re-establishment of the Guru's authority over the Panth, through the foundation of a new order called the *Khalsa*, the Guru's elite. While the Sikh Panth has always continued to contain many followers of Nanak and the gurus who choose not to become baptized members of the *Khalsa*, it is the latter who have led the Panth since the time of the last Guru. Gobind Singh's own sons were all killed in the course of his struggles against the forces of the Mughal emperor Aurangzeb (1618–1707), and he was himself killed by a Muslim assassin. After his death, the line of living Gurus came to an end, and their authority was henceforth vested in the scripture, expanded by the addition of Guru Tegh Bahadur's hymns to Guru Arjan's collection, an d since revered as the *Guru Granth Sahib.*

> *Surrounded, with no choice, in turn*
> *I too attacked with bow and gun.*
> *When matters pass all other means,*
> *It is allowed to take up arms.*
>
> *Dasam Granth* 1391.

Compositions by Guru Gobind Singh, some of which form part of the daily liturgy, and many more by others associated with him, were assembled in another volume of lesser canonical status, the *Dasam Granth* (Book of the Tenth One). A further influential set of extra-canonical Sikh religious literature also came into being at around this time, in the form of the *Rahitnamas*, simple manuals prescribing various rules of conduct (*rahit*) for the Sikhs of the *Khalsa*.

During the eighteenth century, the Punjab was fought over between the declining Mughal Empire and new Muslim invaders from Afghanistan. This was the heroic age of the Sikh Panth, which was organized into local guerrilla bands, who mounted a spirited resistance to both sets of Muslim armies, and who even in defeat are remembered for their glorious acts of martyrdom (*shahidi*). Led and manned by the Jat Sikhs, who had now become the dominant group in the community, the *Khalsa* forces achieved complete political success with the capture of Lahore, the provincial capital, which became the centre of a powerful Sikh kingdom under Maharaja Ranjit Singh (1799–1839), whose generous patronage is responsible for the splendid appearance of many of the great Sikh temples today. But Ranjit Singh's weaker successors proved unable to resist the pressure of the British, who, after two hard-fought wars, finally incorporated the Punjab into their Indian Empire in 1849.

CHRISTOPHER SHACKLE

CHAPTER 50

Sacred Writings

Sikh scripture emerged under the leadership of human Gurus, and culminated in having ultimate authority within the Sikh tradition.

SRI GURU GRANTH SAHIB

The principal scripture of the Sikhs is the *Adi Granth*, the eternal book, or original collection of compositions in book form. In everyday Sikh usage, the *Adi Granth* is reverentially referred to as the *Sri Guru Granth Sahib*, which implies affirmation of faith in the scripture as Guru. The words *Sri* (Sir) and *Sahib* (Lord) are honorific titles, indicating the highest authority accorded to the scripture. The *Adi Granth* opens with the basic creed (*Mul Mantra*), affirming the fundamentals of the Sikh faith. It begins with the phrase '*Ek Onkar*' (one God), signifying the oneness and unity of God, and affirms that the Supreme Being, or God, is 'One without a second'.

The *Adi Granth* was compiled by the fifth Guru, Arjan, in 1604, and contains the compositions of the first five Sikh Gurus, alongside the writings of Muslim and Hindu saints of the medieval period, some of whom belonged to the lowest caste group (*Shudra*). The entire collection is recorded in *Gurmukhi* script, which is also used for modern Punjabi. Because of its association with the Gurus and the scripture, *Gurmukhi* acquired a sacred status within the Sikh community.

The contents of the *Adi Granth* are respectfully referred to as *bani* (voice) and as *gurbani* (utterance of the Guru). Guru Nanak affirms the divine origin of the *bani*: 'As the *bani* of the Lord comes to me so do I proclaim its knowledge' (*Adi Granth* 722). The Guru is, in a primary sense, the 'voice' of God. Guru Nanak clarifies the distinction between the Divine Guru and the human Guru: he regarded himself as the minstrel (*dhadi*) of God (*Akal Purakh*), who openly proclaimed the glory of the divine Word (*Shabad*).

The process of identification of the *bani* with the Guru (God) began with Guru Nanak and was extended by his successors. For example, the third Guru, Amar Das, proclaimed: 'Love the *bani* of the Guru. It is our support in all places and it is bestowed by the Creator himself' (*Adi Granth* 1335). Similarly, the fourth Guru, Ram Das, says: 'The *bani* is the Guru, and the Guru the *bani*, and the nectar (*amrit*) permeates all souls ...' (*Adi Granth* 982). The scripture concludes with Guru Arjan's hymn *Mundavani* (seal) which summarizes the essence of Sikh faith: 'In the platter are placed three things, truth, contentment, and wisdom, as well as the nectar of the Lord's Name [*amrit-nam*], the support of all.'

The *Adi Granth*, on its completion, was accorded the utmost sacred and authoritative status in 1604 when it was installed by Guru Arjan in the newly built Golden Temple (*Harimandir*) at Amritsar. Guru Arjan says: 'The book [*Adi Granth*] is the abode of the Supreme Lord.' From the time of Guru Nanak, the Sikh community began to use the *gurbani* in devotional singing (*shabad kirtan*) as part of congregational worship. Currently the original copy of the *Adi Granth* is in the possession of the Sodhi family at Kartarpur, Punjab.

The tenth Guru, Gobind Singh, terminated the line of human Gurus by bestowing guruship on the *Adi Granth*, to which he had added the compositions of his father, the ninth Guru, Tegh Bahadur. Since then, the *Adi Granth* has been revered as a human Guru, and is respectfully addressed as the *Sri Guru Granth Sahib*. It is placed on a high platform, under a canopy, and a ritual fan (*chauri*) is waved over it while a service is in progress. The presence of the *Guru Granth Sahib* is regarded as mandatory on almost all ceremonial and domestic occasions, such as weddings, initiation ceremonies, and naming ceremonies.

The *Dasam Granth* is the second scriptural book of the Sikhs, containing the compositions of the tenth Guru, Gobind Singh, and other poets, collected by Mani Singh after the death of Gobind Singh, and completed in 1734. The *Dasam Granth* is not installed in all *gurdwaras*, but is found at the two historic *gurdwaras* of Hazoor Sahib and Patna Sahib, popularly called *Takhat* (Throne of the Immortal Being), two of the five centres of temporal authority in Sikh society. Some of its compositions are recited during the preparation of *amrit* (water used for the initiation ceremony) and other acts of worship.

Bhai Gurdas was the scribe who wrote out the *Adi Granth*, under the direction of Guru Arjan. The collection of his writings is called *varan* (ballads), popularly known as 'the key to the *Adi Granth*', and normally sung and quoted by Sikh musicians and preachers at the *gurdwaras*.

SEWA SINGH KALSI

Guru Nanak on the Divine Name

If I could live for millions and millions of years, and if the air was my food and drink,

if I lived in a cave and never saw either the sun or the moon, and if I never slept, even in dreams

– even so, I could not estimate Your Value. How can I describe the Greatness of Your Name?

The True Lord, the Formless One, is Himself in His Own Place.

I have heard, over and over again, and so I tell the tale; as it pleases You, Lord, please instill within me the yearning for You.

If I was slashed and cut into pieces, and put into the mill and ground into flour,

burnt by all-consuming fire and mixed with ashes

– even then, I could not estimate Your Value. How can I describe the Greatness of Your Name?

If I was a bird, soaring and flying through hundreds of heavens,

and if I was invisible, neither eating nor drinking anything

– even so, I could not estimate Your Value. How can I describe the Greatness of Your Name?

Siri Ragu 2, Adi Granth 14–15.

CHAPTER 51

Beliefs

The central teaching in Sikhism is belief in the oneness of God: Sikh scripture begins with the phrase '*Ek Onkar*' (one God). All people — irrespective of caste, creed, colour, and sex — emanated from one divine source. Sikh Gurus have used a number of terms from Islamic and Hindu traditions for God, including Allah, Qadir, Karim, and Paar Brahma.

The diversity in God's creation is perceived as a divine gift, with all religious traditions regarded as capable of enriching the spiritual and cultural lives of their believers. According to Sikh teaching, all human groups evolved and developed their modes of worship and religious institutions within the context of their social environment. Reflecting on the essence and universality of religious truth, the tenth Guru, Gobind Singh, wrote:

> *Recognize all humankind, whether Muslim or Hindu as one. The same God is the Creator and Nourisher of all. Recognize no distinction among them. The temple and the mosque are the same. So are Hindu worship and Muslim prayer. Human beings are all one.*

> (*Dasam Granth*)

The nature of God is clearly manifested in Guru Nanak's first composition, the basic creed popularly known as the *Mul Mantra*, and in his first utterance, 'There is no Hindu, there is no Muslim.' The opening phrase of the *Mul Mantra* summarizes the fundamental belief of the Sikhs: the words '*Ek*' (one) and '*Onkar*' (God) emphasize the oneness of God. God is also believed to be the creator, from whom the universe has emanated. God is beyond the qualities of male and female; they are attributes of the creation, not the creator. Nanak says: 'The wise and beauteous Being is neither a man nor a woman nor a bird' (*Adi Granth* 1010).

> *Firstly God created light and then by his omnipotence, made all human beings. If we emanate from the same divine light, how can we say some are born higher than others? O, men, my brethren, stray ye not in doubt. Creation is in the Creator and the Creator is in Creation. He is fully filling all places.*
>
> *Adi Granth* 1349–50

As God is believed to be *ajuni*, he/she does not experience birth or die. God's having no gender further signifies the unity and equality of humankind.

Sikhism is strictly monotheistic: belief in God's incarnation and worship of idols is strongly disapproved of. Since God is without any form, colour, mark, or lineage, he/she cannot be installed as an idol. God is regarded as eternal truth (*ad sach*), without beginning and end, whereas everything else in this universe — including the sun, moon, stars, and earth — will perish. The notion of permanence applies only to God, who will remain divine truth forever.

HUKAM (DIVINE ORDER)

The term *hukam* (order, command) entered the Sikh/Punjabi vocabulary from Arabic. In Islam, God is perceived as one who gives orders, a commander (*Hakam*). In Sikhism, *hukam* is perceived as the divine order; everything in this universe is believed to be working according to God's *hukam*. The Sikh gurus used the concept of *hukam* extensively in their compositions to describe the nature of creation, the universe, and human life. Nanak refers to *hukam* as the divine hand behind the functioning of the universe, as well as behind the daily lives of human beings.

Although human beings are unique in God's creation, alone endowed with the ability to discriminate between good and evil, the most significant aspects of human existence, such as birth and death, are beyond their control. Human life (*manas janam*) is a divine gift; both birth and death occur according to *hukam*. At Sikh funerals, death is explained as eternal reality; it occurs according to the *Alahi Hukam* (divine order, Allah's order). Therefore, mortals must submit to God's will, without any doubt or questioning. Guru Nanak reflects on the concept of *hukam* by posing the question, 'How may a man purify himself? ... This is brought about by living in accordance with God's command or will' (*Hukam Adi Granth* 2).

The concept of *hukam* raises a fundamental question. Are mortals helpless creatures in God's kingdom? Sikh teachings reject this view, and proclaim that all human beings are endowed with the ability to determine their own destiny. If someone commits evil deeds, he or she will suffer accordingly: that which one sows, that one shall reap. Ultimately, falsehood and evil will be destroyed, and truth prevail. For the attainment of truth, one needs to engage in righteous deeds.

MUKTI (SPIRITUAL LIBERATION)

The word *mukti* is the Punjabi version of the Sanskrit term *moksha* (to be free from, to release), denoting the final release, or spiritual liberation, of the soul from human existence, leading to merging with the Supreme Soul (*Parmatma*). According to the Sikh teaching, the soul (*atma*) is immortal, while the body in which it resides is perishable. After death, the body is cremated, and the *atma* either merges with the Supreme Soul, or passes from one form of life to another, depending upon one's *karma* in this world. As a religious concept, the term *karma* (literally: deeds, actions) denotes one's preordained destiny. Although Sikhs believe in the doctrine of *karma*, they do not regard human beings as helpless creatures. The notion of *jivan-mukta* (see below) transcends the limitations of *karma*, and transforms it into a dynamic force.

For the cycle of birth and death, the Sikh Gurus used the term *awagaun*, based on the doctrine of *karma* and the transmigration of souls. According to traditional Hindu belief, there are 8,400,000 forms of existence before one is reborn as a human being. Those who are sinful, and engage in evil-doing, keep going through the cycle of birth and death regarded as the most degrading state: *narak* (hell). At a Sikh funeral, the officiant recites the final prayer (*antam-ardas*) invoking God's forgiveness for the departed soul, and saving him or her from *awagaun*.

To avoid the ultimate punishment of *chaurasi* (cycle of birth and death), Sikhs are required to conduct themselves according to the teachings of the Sikh Gurus, working towards becoming Guru-oriented (*gursikh*), rather than self-oriented (*manmukh*). A Sikh is taught to live as an honest householder, a true believer in the oneness of God and the equality of humankind, while earning a living by honest means (*kirat karna*), and sharing with others (*vand chhakna*).

A Sikh who succeeds in attaining the status of *gursikh* is called *jivan-mukta*, liberated from worldly temptations such as lust (*kaam*), anger (*krodh*), greed (*lobh*), attachment (*moh*), and false pride or ego (*ahankar*). Another attribute of a *jivan-mukta* is his or her faith in *gurbani* to earn *mukti* now rather than after death. A *gursikh* transforms into a *jivan-mukta* by leading a life of detachment from worldly temptations, while actively engaged in the social and cultural enrichment of society, or *seva* (voluntary service). A *jivan-mukta* Sikh is like a lotus that remains clean, despite living in muddy water.

DHARMSAL (PRACTICE OF RIGHTEOUSNESS)

The term *dharmsal* is composed of *dharm* (religious, moral, and social obligations) and *sal* (a place of abode). Guru Nanak describes the earth as *dharmsal* (a place to practise righteousness), established by God within the universe. In this *dharmsal*, human life is regarded as the highest and most precious form, as well as a divine gift. The earth, and everything in it, is believed to carry the divine stamp.

> *In pride, man is overtaken by fear. In utter commotion he passes his life. Pride is a great malady because of which, he dies, is reborn and continues coming and going.*
>
> Adi Granth 592

According to Sikh teaching, Sikhs are not passive spectators, or recluses, in this world; they are expected to be active participants in human affairs, and Guru-oriented (*gursikh*). The concept of *dharmsal* implies faith in the oneness of God, and in the equality of humankind. Guru Nanak reprimanded Hindu ascetics (*yogis*) who advocated the path of renunciation, abdicating their social obligations. Apart from Har Krishan, who died aged eight, all the Sikh gurus were married men, who demonstrated their faith in their adherence to the householder's state (*grihsth-ashrama-dharma*). For a Sikh, there is no place for the renunciation of society.

GURPARSAD (GRACE AND BLESSING)

The term *gurparsad* is composed of *gur* (from *guru*) and *parsad* (Sanskrit for grace, blessing), which is also applied to the sanctified food offered to the congregation at the culmination of a Sikh service. *Gurparsad* is the last word of the *Mul Mantra*, standing for the eternal Guru (God), and affirms Sikh belief, and the way God can be realized. The Sikh Gurus used several terms to elaborate the concept of *gurparsad*, such as *karam* (Arabic), *mehar* and *nadar* (Persian), and *kirpa* (Sanskrit). It is believed that everyone's destiny is preordained, according to his or her *karma*, and ultimately one is responsible for its consequences. Guru Nanak says, 'Through grace is reached the Door of The Divine' (*Adi Granth* 145), and that, as one spark of fire can burn huge amounts of firewood, so acts of devotion and love of God may annul the consequences of bad *karma*. The Sikh Gurus repeatedly affirm that divine grace is the fruit of sincere devotion to God.

Two elderly Sikhs at the Gurudwara Bangla Sahib, Delhi. Note their long turbans and distinctive metal bangles.

THE *MUL MANTRA*

Ek Onkar	There is one God	*Ajuni*	beyond the cycle of birth and death
Satnam	eternal truth is his/her name	*Saibham*	self-created, self-existent
Karta Purakh	Creator of all things	*Gurparsad*	known by the grace of the Guru.
Nirbhau	without fear		
Nirvair	without enmity	*Guru Granth Sahib* 1	
Akal Murat	timeless, immortal, never incarnated		

NAMSIMRAN (MEDITATING ON GOD'S NAME)

The concept of *nam* (name) is one of the key doctrines in Sikhism, symbolizing the eternal truth, or God. In everyday usage, the term *namsimran* is applied to the discipline of daily meditation undertaken by devout Sikhs, during which it is common practice to use a rosary, often repeating the words *Waheyguru* and *Satnam*. Many Sikhs participate in *namsimran* sessions organized at *gurdwaras*.

The Sikh Gurus used the concept of *nam* to affirm their faith in the omnipresence of God, and impressed upon their disciples the necessity of the discipline of *namsimran*. They assert that *nam* is the creator of everything; through nam comes all wisdom and light; *nam* extends to all creation; there is no place where *nam* is not.

SEWA SINGH KALSI

CHAPTER 52

Worship and Festivals

In popular Sikh usage, the act of worship means reading from the scripture and reciting a selection of hymns (*path-karna*). In individual or congregational worship the central focus is on the utterances of the Gurus in the *Adi Granth* (*gurbani*). Sikh festivals, which are both religious and cultural celebrations, fall into two categories: *gurpurb*, an anniversary when a Guru is remembered, and *mela*, a fair. The most popular melas are *Baisakhi*, *Diwali*, and *Hola*.

INDIVIDUAL WORSHIP

The pattern of individual worship is prescribed in the Sikh code of discipline (*Rehat Maryada*), published in 1951. The daily routine (*nitnem*) comprises texts from the *Adi Granth* and rules for personal cleanliness. A Sikh should rise early and take a bath, then recite the hymns of *Japji*, *Jap*, and *Ten Sawayyas*. At sunset he or she should recite the hymn of *Rahiras*, and before going to bed recite the hymn of *Sohila* and the prayer *ardas* (petition).

Worship can be undertaken anywhere in peace and quiet, and most Sikh households have a collection of hymns normally recited during worship (*gutka*), wrapped in cloth and kept in a safe place. Many devout Sikhs also have a copy of the *Guru Granth Sahib* at home, respectfully kept in a special room, usually located on the top floor. Although any building where a copy of the *Guru Granth Sahib* is installed qualifies to be called a *gurdwara*, a family *gurdwara* is strictly a private shrine, not open to the general public.

CONGREGATIONAL WORSHIP

Congregational worship takes place at the *gurdwara*. There is no fixed day, but in the diaspora most services take place on a Sunday. The term *gurdwara* is composed of *guru* (denoting the *Guru Granth Sahib*) and *dwara* (gate or house), and is attributed to the sixth Guru, Hargobind, who is believed to have built *gurdwaras* at sites associated with his predecessors. During the period of the first five Gurus, a Sikh place of worship was known as a *dharmsala*. According to tradition, Guru Nanak established the first at Kartarpur, as a place where a congregation (*sangat*) of men and women of all caste groups would gather for communal worship and hymn-singing (*shabad kirtan*), followed by a communal meal (*langar*). The institutions of *sangat*, *shabad kirtan*, and *langar* emerged as distinguishing features of the Sikh tradition.

Historic *gurdwaras* have been built on sites linked to important events in the development of Sikhism: for example, Gurdwara Kesgarh at Anandpur, where the tenth Guru, Gobind Singh, established the *Khalsa* in 1699; and Gurdwara Sis Ganj in Delhi, built where the ninth Guru, Tegh Bahadur, was beheaded by the Mughal authorities. Community-based *gurdwaras* are autonomous institutions, established by local Sikh communities, and run by locally elected management committees, which are answerable only to their local *sangat*.

A similar pattern of service is observed at all *gurdwaras*, beginning with the recital and singing of *Asa di var* in the morning, followed by more hymn-singing from scripture. The service concludes with the recital of *ardas* by the *granthi* (reader of the scripture), while members of the *sangat* stand silently with folded hands. After the *ardas*, a randomly chosen hymn from the scripture is read out to the congregation, called *hukam-nama* (divine order for the day). The service ends with the distribution of sanctified food (*karah parshad*) to members of the congregation, symbolizing Sikh belief in the equality of humankind.

The way a Sikh expresses his or her reverence for the scripture might create the impression that the Sikhs are idol worshippers: for example, when a Sikh enters the congregational hall, he or she approaches the *Adi Granth*, makes an offering, and bows. In fact, the devotee is showing devotion towards the teachings of the Gurus, *Guru Granth Sahib*.

GURPURBS

The term *gurpurb* is made up of *gu* (short for *guru*) and *purb* (a sacred or auspicious day). Four main *gurpurbs* are celebrated by Sikhs throughout the world:
- The birthday of Guru Nanak: 26 November
- The birthday of Guru Gobind Singh: 5 January
- The martyrdom anniversary of Guru Arjan: 16 June
- The martyrdom anniversary of Guru Tegh Bahadur: 24 November

In India, *gurpurbs* are celebrated by carrying the *Guru Granth Sahib* in processions around towns and villages. In villages, the scripture is placed in a decorated palanquin (*palki*), and the procession is led by five initiated (*amritdhari*) Sikhs carrying swords, symbolizing the 'five beloved ones' initiated by the tenth Guru in 1699.

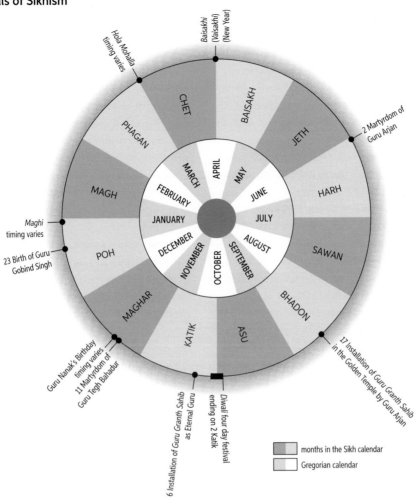

The diagram shows the following festival markers around the Sikh calendar wheel:
- Baisakhi (Vaisakhi) (New Year)
- Hola Mohalla timing varies
- 2 Martyrdom of Guru Arjan
- 17 Installation of Guru Granth Sahib in the Golden Temple by Guru Arjan
- Diwali four day festival ending on 2 Katik
- 6 Installation of Guru Granth Sahib as Eternal Guru
- 11 Martyrdom of Guru Tegh Bahadur
- Guru Nanak's Birthday timing varies
- 23 Birth of Guru Gobind Singh
- Maghi timing varies

Sikh calendar months: CHET, BAISAKH, JETH, HARH, SAWAN, BHADON, ASU, KATIK, MAGHAR, POH, MAGH, PHAGAN

Gregorian months: MARCH, APRIL, MAY, JUNE, JULY, AUGUST, SEPTEMBER, OCTOBER, NOVEMBER, DECEMBER, JANUARY, FEBRUARY

Legend:
- months in the Sikh calendar
- Gregorian calendar

BAISAKHI

The festival of *Baisakhi* is celebrated on the first day of the month of *Baisakh* in the Punjabi calendar, and nowadays has a special importance for the Sikhs as it marks the birthday of the *Khalsa*. In Punjab, farmers begin harvesting the wheat crop after the *Baisakhi* celebrations. Apart from religious ceremonies, a number of cultural activities are organized, such as *kabadi*, football, hockey, and wrestling. Traditional *Bhangra* dancing, when dancers dress up in colourful Punjabi costumes, is the climax of the celebrations.

I AM A SIKH

I was born in a Sikh village called Talhan, in the state of Punjab, India. It had its own large temple (*gurdwara*).

Every year, the residents of the village and the surrounding areas celebrated the important religious festivals and took part in processions, and with the other children I joined in. My early nurturing in Sikh traditions took place within my family and this village community. I knew the basic beliefs of Sikhism at a very young age.

In 1968 my family moved to Leeds, England. I was only nine, and this was quite an experience for all of us. None of us could speak English. We found it hard to socialize, and everything around us felt very different. We were fortunate to have a very helpful English family next door. They had two daughters the same age as myself. We used to play together, and their father took me to school on my first day, because my parents could not speak English. This helped us settle in at our local primary school, and made us feel at home in Leeds. At school, we began to learn English. We were very keen and worked hard, attending extra English classes for Asian children. We made lots of friends. At that time there was only one *gurdwara* in Leeds – simply called 'the Sikh temple'. Although it was a three-mile walk from our house, we attended regularly on Sundays. I also attended Punjabi classes there.

Attending the *gurdwara* on a regular basis for prayers, in the presence of the congregation, and listening to hymn-singing (*shabad kirtan*), helped me understand the meaning of 'the oneness of God'. I began to take part in voluntary help (*seva*) in the community kitchen (*langar*). Food is served to everyone attending, including visitors from other faiths and backgrounds. Importantly, all are served the same meal, as this shows equality.

Soon after we arrived in Leeds, my elder brother and I had a haircut. In our new surroundings, we were embarrassed to have long hair. When I moved to secondary school, I met a young Sikh who wore a turban. I was impressed, and soon began to grow my hair again and wear a turban. Although I am not an 'initiated Sikh', I wear a turban to identify myself as a follower. I also wear a steel bracelet (*kara*) on my right wrist. My middle name is Singh, a name given to all male Sikhs by the tenth Guru. I do not cut my hair or trim my beard, and do not drink or smoke, both of which are against Sikh teachings.

My religious discipline is based on Sikh teachings, central to which is the belief that there is only one God. My daily commitments include meditation on God's name (*nam japna*), sharing with others (*vand chhakna*), voluntary service (*seva*), and earning my living honestly (*kirat karna*). These are most important for every Sikh. Every morning before breakfast I say the morning prayer, the *Mul Mantra*. My mother taught me this when I was young, and since she passed away – more than twenty years ago – I have said it daily. I regularly participate in religious activities and festivals at the *gurdwara*, such as *Baisakhi, Diwali* and other celebrations. These bring the community and families together, enabling the younger generation, including my children, to learn more about Sikhism.

Gradually, my involvement at the *gurdwara* has increased, as has my commitment to helping others. As Sikhs, we take part in the activities of Leeds Concord multi-faith fellowship. Recently my youngest daughter lit the candles at the Peace Service, on behalf of the Sikh community. I regularly contribute towards Sikh activities, including donations towards the upkeep of the *gurdwara* and the community kitchen (*langar*). My job as a Technical Liaison Officer involves a lot of travelling. I come into contact with people of different backgrounds and faiths, and with my turban, beard and so on, I openly display my commitment to my faith. I enjoy my work and, as I do it, I apply my faith's teaching about equality and truthful living (*kirat karna*).

My wife came from India in 1983 and, having completed postgraduate studies, became a primary school teacher in Leeds. Because of my cultural tradition, I had an arranged marriage, conducted at the gurdwara in the presence of the Sikh holy book (*Guru Granth Sahib*) and the congregation. Verses from the *Guru Granth Sahib* were read out and sung by the priest. Not only did I marry a person of the same religion, but we also bring up our three children within the faith. Both my wife's and my own influence on the children has encouraged them to speak Punjabi as well as English, and to attend the gurdwara on a regular basis. I hope that, by learning the value of prayer, by understanding the importance of helping and respecting others, and by learning the Gurus' teachings, my children will follow me in the faith and commit their lives to God.

As a family, we have visited India. As well as seeing the tourist attractions, we visited many gurdwaras in the Punjab and Delhi. Our visit to the famous Golden Temple at Amritsar was most exciting, and gave me a greater understanding of my religious tradition.

I have enjoyed music from an early age, particularly shabad kirtan. I can listen to shabad kirtan in the morning before going to work, as well as in the evening. I find this very helpful in my quest to learn more about the Sikh faith. It is also helpful for my children. However, we don't listen to religious music alone. We also enjoy traditional Indian music, folk music, and bhangra dancing.

I think the teachings of the Sikh faith have made me a better person. I thank God, who has given me so much and, in return, I want to give back to God as much of myself as I can, by committing myself to the Sikh faith.

Resham Singh Bhogal

HOLA

Hola takes its name from the traditional Hindu festival of *Holi*, which is celebrated by communal singing, dancing, and throwing colours on people, irrespective of caste, gender, and status. Guru Gobind Singh disapproved of the *Holi* festival, regarding it as wasteful and degrading. He summoned his followers to Anandpur to celebrate the festival of *Holi* differently: instead of merrymaking, he organized mock battles between two groups of Sikh volunteers, and trained them in martial arts, thereby giving them a new purpose in life. The title of the festival was changed to *Hola*, and the tradition of martial arts remains associated with it.

DIWALI

Diwali is one of the traditional festivals of India, popularly known as the festival of lights; its origin is traced to the homecoming of Lord Rama from exile. Hindus illuminate their homes and temples, and exchange gifts of sweets with friends and relatives. The festival has another significance for Sikhs: it is associated with the release of the sixth Guru, Hargobind, from the Gwalior Fort, where he was imprisoned by the Mughal emperor Jahangir. The Guru's arrival in Amritsar was celebrated by the illumination of the city by his followers. Nowadays, special *Diwali* services are conducted at the *gurdwaras*, celebrating the release of Guru Hargobind, and affirming a distinct Sikh identity. *Gurdwaras* and private houses are decorated with candles, and firework displays are organized. The tradition of illuminating the Golden Temple (*Harimandir*) marks the climax of the *Diwali* festivities.

SANGRAND

Pool, or sarovar, at the Sikh Gurudwara Bangla Sahib, Delhi, India, whose water is considered holy.

The first day of every month in the Hindu lunar calendar is called *Sangrand*, from the Sanskrit word *sangkrant*, denoting the entrance of the sun into a new sign of the Zodiac. In Sikhism, it is observed in a special service (*diwan*) at the *gurdwara*, with the name of the new month ritually announced from scripture. Guru Arjan composed the 'hymn of twelve months' (*Bara Maha*), each of its twelve parts illustrating a stage of life and the journey of the soul, while directing the Sikhs to conform to the prescribed code of discipline each month. Before setting off to work on this festival day, Sikhs visit the *gurdwara* to invoke divine grace for the well-being of their family and the whole of humankind. Listening to the recital of the name of the new month is perceived as a meritorious boon. The festival of *Baisakhi* occurs at *Sangrand* in the month of *Baisakh* (usually 14 April) and the ceremony of replacing the old covering of the flagpole with a new one (*Nishan Sahib*) takes place at the *gurdwaras* on this day.

SEWA SINGH KALSI

CHAPTER 53

Sikhism Today

The evolution of Sikhism has remained closely involved with political and social developments in the Punjab, throughout a century of British rule, and since 1947 in independent India. Like many other Asian religions, Sikhism first experienced the challenges of modernity at the same time as those of nineteenth-century European colonialism. A Sikh reform movement proved remarkably successful in articulating for much of the twentieth century a reinforced Sikhism, which survived the community's traumatic experience of the partition of Punjab between India and Pakistan in 1947. More recent decades, however, have been marked by tensions between the politicized expression of Sikhism, which grew out of the reform movement, and an Indian political leadership increasingly identified with Hindu majoritarianism. The same period also saw the establishment of substantial Sikh diasporas in Britain and North America, where the challenges of adapting Sikhism to the very different circumstances of the international, twenty-first century, English-speaking world are most acutely faced.

SIKH REFORM

In the heyday of colonial rule, in the later nineteenth century, the leaders of all sections of Indian society, including the Sikhs, had to confront the linked implications of British political dominance and their dominant Victorian world view, with its strongly Christian emphasis. A path of total resistance to modernity was chosen by a few, such as Baba Ram Singh (1816–84), but his self-proclamation as Guru confined his support to the Namdhari Sikh sect which he founded.

The mainstream leadership realized, however, that a more complex process of accommodation to the new order was required for the successful survival of the Sikh community. The Sikhs' distinct religious identity was seen to be doubly threatened: by the dismantling of state-supported Sikh political institutions after the British conquest of Ranjit Singh's kingdom, and by the threat of assimilation into a resurgent Hinduism. The latter threat was forcefully articulated in the Punjab by the modernist Arya Samaj organization, founded by Dayananda Sarasvati (1824–83), whose doctrine of all truth being found in the *Vedas* was found offensively dismissive of the teachings of the Sikh Gurus.

To combat these challenges, a number of reformist associations (*Singh Sabhas*) were founded in the main cities of the Punjab. Through these associations, and making full use of the new communication systems established by the colonial state, a number of gifted lay leaders, often honoured with the title *Bhai* (Brother), came to formulate a redefinition of Sikhism which has remained the dominant orthodoxy to the present day. Like most reformers, the *Singh Sabha* activists saw the contemporary plight of Sikhism as the consequence of a falling away from the pristine ideals of an earlier age. They diagnosed an increasing reversion to Hinduism in both religious and social practice as the cause of what had gone wrong, and preached the necessity of a return to the glorious age of the Gurus, marked by uncompromising monotheism, and the adoption of a simple and devout lifestyle untainted by superstition. The title of the most famous of many tracts through which their message was disseminated, 'We are not Hindus' (*Ham Hindu Nahin*, 1898), by Bhai Kahn Singh Nabha (1867–1938), points to the cornerstone of the reformists' programme, their strenuous efforts to distinguish the Sikhs of the *Khalsa* as a community quite separate from its Hindu origins and traditionally close ties with Hinduism.

The reformists often justified their definition of Sikhism in relation to Hinduism by an analogy of the relation betweens between Protestantism and Roman Catholicism. Fitting well with imperial policies of 'divide and rule', it found particular favour with the British, as a way of ensuring the separate loyalty of their Sikh troops, who were recruited as a reliable minority, out of all proportion to their numbers in the population – and army regulations specified strict adherence to *Khalsa* practice in the Sikh regiments. At the same time, a remarkable cultural transformation was effected within the Sikh community itself, through the literary and scholarly activity of leading reformers such as Bhai Vir Singh (1872–1957). Developing Punjabi in the Gurmukhi script as a vehicle for modern communication, they produced new editions of the scriptures with extensive commentaries, and an impressive body of creative writing, which often drew upon the mythic power of Sikh history to drive home the reformist message.

SIKH POLITICAL ACTIVISM

By the end of World War I, the reformists had given the Sikhs the confidence and coherence to engage with the nationalist politics of the late colonial period. A new activist phase was launched with the *Akali* movement, established to push through the transfer of control of the major *gurdwaras* from their hereditary guardians, who administered their vast endowments, often for private profit. A programme of mass demonstrations, producing violent conflicts and fresh martyrs for the cause, eventually resulted in government sanction for the Sikh *Gurdwaras* Act of 1925, which gave control of the great *gurdwaras* of the Punjab to an elected committee of male Sikhs, the Shiromani Gurdwara Prabandhak Committee (SGPC), which became the single most important voice within Sikhism, and through its resources now supports the *Akali Dal*, the main Sikh political party. The British refused Sikh women the right to become members; however, since Indian independence in 1947, women have been elected, even to the prestigious post of secretary and president.

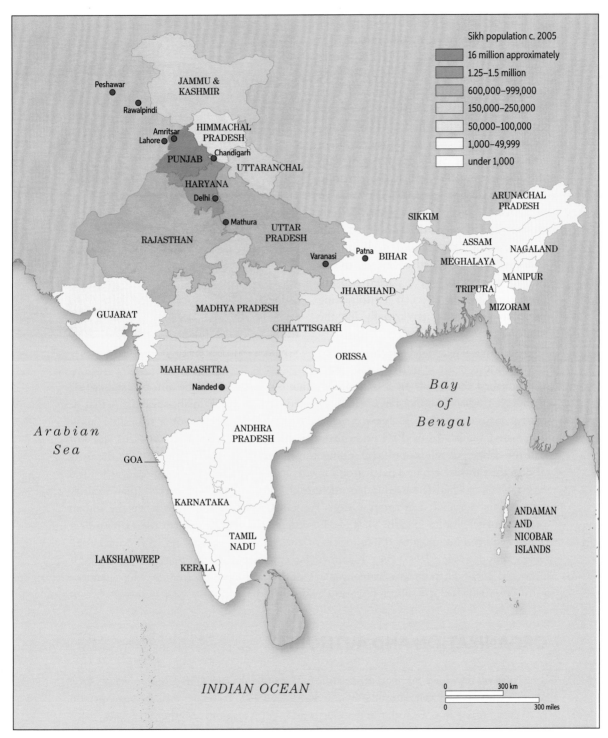

Sikh population c. 2005

	16 million approximately
	1.25–1.5 million
	600,000–999,000
	150,000–250,000
	50,000–100,000
	1,000–49,999
	under 1,000

Peshawar
Rawalpindi
JAMMU & KASHMIR
HIMMACHAL PRADESH
Amritsar
Lahore
Chandigarh
PUNJAB
UTTARANCHAL
HARYANA
Delhi
ARUNACHAL PRADESH
SIKKIM
Mathura
RAJASTHAN
UTTAR PRADESH
Varanasi
Patna
BIHAR
ASSAM
NAGALAND
MEGHALAYA
MANIPUR
JHARKHAND
TRIPURA
MIZORAM
GUJARAT
MADHYA PRADESH
CHHATTISGARH
ORISSA
MAHARASHTRA
Nanded
Bay of Bengal
Arabian Sea
ANDHRA PRADESH
GOA
ANDAMAN AND NICOBAR ISLANDS
KARNATAKA
TAMIL NADU
LAKSHADWEEP
KERALA
INDIAN OCEAN

0   300 km
0   300 miles

Sikhism in India Today

For the next decades, the leaders' chief energies were devoted to the pursuit of a political settlement that would guarantee the position of Sikhs as a distinctive ethno-religious minority. The approach of Indian independence was marked by increasing polarization between Hindus and Muslims. With no realistic chance of achieving their own country, the Sikhs' lot was cast with the Hindus in 1947, when the partition of the Punjab between India and Pakistan was effected, at the cost of massive ethnic cleansing. Although this uprooted half the community that found itself on the Pakistan side, its resettlement in Indian Punjab in place of the departed Muslim population had the effect of consolidating the Sikh population territorially for the first time.

Young Sikhs at a national gathering in Italy, 2011.

From this base, and building on Sikh identification with Punjabi, the *Akali Dal* launched the *Punjabi Suba*, or Punjabi State campaign, with the aim of establishing within the Indian Union a linguistically-defined state with a Punjabi-speaking – that is, Sikh – majority. Although this was achieved with the separation of a truncated Sikh-dominated Punjab from the Hindu-majority state of Haryana in 1966, this did not halt the dangerous religio-political momentum that had been set in motion. By the early 1980s, the Punjab became a battleground, with armed Sikh activists, inspired by the ideal of establishing Khalistan as an independent Sikh country, opposed by the Indian security forces. This culminated in the notorious events of 1984 at Amritsar, when the Indian prime minister, Indira Gandhi (1917–84), ordered the army to storm the *Harimandir* – which had been occupied by the followers of the charismatic young preacher Sant Jarnail Singh Bhindranvale (1947–84). Her own later assassination by her Sikh bodyguards provoked anti-Sikh pogroms in many parts of India, killing thousands. The separatist cause eventually lost the support of most Sikhs in India.

ORGANIZATION AND AUTHORITY

The rules of reformed Sikhism are set out in the official *Guide to the Sikh Way of Life* (*Rehat Maryada*), first issued as a pamphlet by the SGPC in 1945. It defines a Sikh as any person
* whose faith is in one God, the ten Gurus and their teaching, and the *Adi Granth*
* believes in the necessity and importance of initiation (*amrit*)
* does not adhere to any other religion.

Sikhism is a religion without priests, so authority in the larger *gurdwaras* rests with the lay committees which run them, not with the 'keepers of the scripture' (*granthis*) whom they employ.

THE SIKH DIASPORAS

The necessarily rather rigid redefinitions of Sikhism first formulated by the *Singh Sabha* leaders in the late nineteenth century are beginning to be perceived as in need of adjustment, to meet the changed circumstances of the twenty-first century. With the failure of the long pursuit of solutions through political means in India, there are signs that the chief impetus for such a reformulation may come from the increasingly confident and well-established diaspora communities now settled for over a generation in Britain, Canada, and the USA, totalling about one million, and even numerically significant in relation to the fifteen million Indian Sikhs.

The Sikh diasporas remain closely linked to the Punjab, through family ties, the rituals of the *gurdwara* and the great Sikh festivals (*gurpurbs*), and regular pilgrimages to the great shrines associated with the Gurus. But they are also directly exposed to their Western environments, and relatively free from the constraints felt within an increasingly Hindu-dominated India, encouraging the emergence of a new intellectual leadership, based within Western universities and using English rather than Punjabi as its prime medium of expression.

Several emerging trends may be signalled as pointers. A new critical attention is being given to sensitive topics, notably the study of the formation of the scripture, and the interpretation of key mythic episodes of Sikh history, such as the foundation of the *Khalsa*. There is also a revaluation of the importance of other traditions within Sikhism that were marginalized by the triumph of the reformed *Khalsa*, to whom the SGPC *Rehat Maryada* almost exclusively refers, neglecting the many who follow the teachings of Guru Nanak and his successors, but do not observe the full *Khalsa* discipline. And women's voices are starting to be articulated in a religious tradition that has been so powerfully dominated by the bearded male presence. These and other trends have yet to coalesce; but it seems certain that traditional authority will become subject to increasing challenges, as Sikhism – like all other religions – grapples with an ever-changing modern world.

CHRISTOPHER SHACKLE

QUESTIONS

1. Explain the role of Guru Nanak's example in Sikhism.

2. Why does Sikhism reject asceticism?

3. Why is the *Adi Granth* so revered?

4. Why does Sikhism reject the caste system?

5. How have Hinduism and Islam influenced Sikhism?

6. How do Sikhs believe they can overcome *chaurasi* (the cycle of death and rebirth)?

7. How far was the Tenth Guru responsible for shaping Sikhism?

8. Explain the importance of the *Khalsa* in Sikhism.

9. What factors are responsible for the tension between Sikhism and the Indian state in recent decades?

10. How important is the *Rehat Maryada* to the development of Sikhism in recent decades?

FURTHER READING

Brown, Kerry, *Sikh Art and Literature*. London: Routledge, 1999.

Fenech, Louis E., *Martyrdom in the Sikh Tradition: Playing the Game of Love*. Delhi: Oxford University Press, 2000.

McLeod, W. H., *Historical Dictionary of Sikhism*. Lanham, MD: Scarecrow Press, 1995.

McLeod, W. H., *Sikhism*. London: Penguin, 1997.

Nat, J. S., *The Sikhs of the Punjab*. Cambridge: Cambridge University Press, 2008.

O'Connell, Joseph T., Milton Israel, and Willard G. Oxtoby, eds., *Sikh History and Religion in the Twentieth Century*. Toronto: University of Toronto Centre for South Asian Studies, 1988.

Shackle, Christopher, ed., *Sikh Religion, Culture and Ethnicity*. Richmond, Surrey: Curzon, 2001.

Singh, Patwant, *The Sikhs*. New York: Knopf, 2000.

PART 11
RELIGIONS IN TODAY'S WORLD

SUMMARY

Throughout the modern period there has been speculation about the collapse of religious belief and rumours of the death of God. Modernity, it has been said, inevitably entails secularization. The progress of the sciences in particular leaves little room for traditional religious belief. However, while it is true that there has been, and continues to be, a haemorrhaging of people from mainstream churches, religion is still alive and well in today's world. Indeed, it is experiencing robust health in the non-Western world where faiths such as Islam and Christianity flourish. In the Western world, while many are disillusioned with traditional religious institutions, authorities and hierarchies, and have even abandoned religious belief altogether, growing numbers are finding spiritual fulfilment elsewhere. Some believe without feeling the need to belong to an institution. Others turn to the increasing number of new religions and alternative spiritualities on offer. Yet others, particularly since the 1960s, have been attracted to Eastern traditions, such as Hinduism and Buddhism. More typical of believers in today's world are those who, influenced by postmodern, consumer-oriented, religiously plural cultures, 'pick and mix' from a range of traditions, beliefs and philosophies.

CHAPTER 54

New Religious Movements

The term 'New Religious Movements' (NRMs) covers a variety of religious organizations that have emerged in recent times, commonly referred to as 'cults'. The term 'cult' is inappropriate, being pejorative and lacking a clear definition. Some scholars have defined a new religion as an organization that has arrived in the West since World War II, while others regard 'new' as spanning the last 150 years. NRMs are a global, not merely a Western, phenomenon: there are some 10,000 NRMs in Africa alone, around 3000 in the USA, and 500–600 in Britain. There are an estimated 31 million followers in Japan.

NRMs tend to fall outside mainstream religion, sometimes because of doctrinal disputes, at times because of controversial practices. The mass deaths of followers of the Peoples Temple in Jonestown, Guyana (1978), and of David Koresh and the Branch Davidians in Waco, Texas (1993), and the deaths of members of the Solar Temple in Switzerland and Canada (1994), the UFO religion Heaven's Gate in California (1997), and the Movement for the Restoration of the Ten Commandments of God in Uganda (2000), and Aum Shinrikyo's sarin gas attack on the passengers of the Tokyo underground, killing twelve and injuring many others (1995), reinforced the perception that NRMs are violent, although such incidents are rare.

THE BAHÁ'Í

Sayyid 'Ali Muhammad, born in Shiraz, Persia (modern-day Iran) in 1819, claimed to be a messenger of God, and called himself the Báb, meaning 'the gate', preparing the way for a greater messenger. His new movement caused a stir, and he was executed in 1850. Mirza Husayn 'Ali Nuri (1817–92), now took the name Bahá'u'lláh, and founded the Bahá'í faith. In 1853, Bahá'u'lláh moved to Baghdad, where in 1863 he claimed to be the bearer of a new message from God, built on previous world religions, and destined to take humanity to the next stage of development: world unity. Bahá'u'lláh was subsequently exiled to Akko (Acre), Israel, where he died in 1892. His shrine, just outside Akko, is the holiest site for Bahá'ís, and the world centre of the Bahá'í faith is nearby. By the early twenty-first century there were more than 5 million Bahá'ís living in more than 230 countries, with the largest community in India and large communities in Latin America, Africa, and South-East Asia.

CHRISTIAN-RELATED NRMs

The Mormon Tabernacle, Temple Square, Salt Lake City, Utah, USA.

Nineteenth-century NRMs in the West were predominantly Christian. William Miller (1782–1849), an early proponent of Adventism, proclaimed that Christ's second coming was imminent. He named 1843, and subsequently 1844, as the year of Christ's return; his followers' disillusionment in 1844 became known as the 'Great Disappointment'. His ideas were nonetheless influential. Ellen G. White (1827–1915), who founded the Seventh-day Adventists in 1861, taught that Jesus had returned, but that his presence was invisible.

Charles Taze Russell (1852–1916), who co-founded Zion's Watch Tower Tract Society in 1881, also taught the doctrine of Christ's 'invisible presence', although the Jehovah's Witnesses, as Russell's successor, Joseph Franklin Rutherford (1869–1942), named them in 1931, now regard 1914 as the date of this event.

The Church of Jesus Christ of Latter-day Saints (the 'Mormons') claims a new revelation, afforded to Joseph Smith Jr (1805–44), its founder-leader. The angel Moroni reportedly lent him a set of gold plates, from which he translated *The Book of Mormon* (1830), which tells of Jesus Christ preaching in the USA after his resurrection. Smith was murdered in 1844, after which Brigham Young (1801–77) took over the leadership and led the 'saints' to the Great Salt Lake in Utah, where they set up their headquarters.

Another significant movement was New Thought, or Higher Thought, which promoted the concept that Infinite Intelligence – or God – is everywhere, and emphasized health improvement through mental 'affirmations'. These ideas influenced Mary Baker Eddy's (1821–1910) Christian Science and also the Hopkins Metaphysical Association, set up by Emma Curtis Hopkins (1849–1925) in 1887. Some of Hopkins' students set up their own organizations, the best known of which is the Unity School of Christianity, or Unity Church, founded in Kansas City, Missouri in 1889.

Contact with spirits constituted a further strand. Modern spiritualism can be traced back to 'rappings' heard by the Fox sisters of Hydesville, New York, in 1848, although spiritualist churches emphasize healing as much as contact with the departed. Helena P. Blavatsky (1831–91), one of the founders of the Theosophical Society, claimed contact with a number of 'Ascended Masters', advanced spiritual beings who once lived on earth. Ascended Masters – sometimes called the 'Great White Brotherhood' – feature in other organizations, such as the Rosicrucians and the Church Universal and Triumphant, and also in the New Age 'channelling' movement.

NRMs IN THE 1960s AND 1970s

A new wave of NRMs occurred in the 1960s. Bible-based and charismatic, the 'Jesus Movement', or 'Jesus People', gained momentum within the youth counter-culture of that period, sometimes involving communal living and sharing of possessions. Converts had often previously been on drugs, and the Love Family, or Church of Jesus Christ at Armageddon, founded by Paul Erdman (b. 1940) in 1968, encouraged their use.

Of the communal groups, the best known are The Family International (TFI), previously known as the Children of God, or COG, and The Holy Spirit Association for the Unification of World Christianity, or Unification Church (UC). Founded by David Brandt Berg (also known as 'Moses David', 1919–94), COG espoused Protestant fundamentalism, but became controversial for its 'flirty fishing' – or 'FFing' – the offer of sex to seekers, mainly by female members.

Although offering an interpretation of the Bible, the Unification Church presents a new revelation, claimed by founder-leader Sun Myung Moon (1920–2012). Moon taught that Jesus was unable fully to accomplish his messianic mission, which was to marry and beget sinless children. Sun Myung Moon and his wife Hak Ja Han Moon are jointly regarded as the new messiahs, and members can be grafted into their restored family through a Blessing ceremony – the 'mass wedding'.

> *Emperors, kings and presidents ... have declared to all heaven and earth that Reverend Sun Myung Moon is none other than humanity's saviour, messiah, returning Lord, and true parent.*
>
> Sun Myung Moon

INDIAN-DERIVED NRMs

The first Hindu *swami* (world-renouncer) to visit the West was Ramakrishna's pupil Swami Vivekananda (1863–1902), who spoke at the World's Parliament of Religions in Chicago in 1893, and founded the Vedanta Society in New York in 1894. Several

other gurus also travelled to the West, notably
Paramahansa Yogananda (1893–1952), founder

Hare Krishna members on an American sidewalk.

of the Self-Realization Fellowship in 1920; Meher Baba (1894–1969), who in 1954 declared he was the Avatar of the age; the Maharishi Mahesh Yogi (1918–2008), who developed the Transcendental Meditation (™) technique and acted as guru to the Beatles; Sri Chinmoy (1931–2007), who promoted 'inner peace'; Swami A. C. Bhaktivedanta Praphupada (1896–1977), founder of the International Society for Krishna Consciousness (ISKCON), better known as the 'Hare Krishna' movement[1]; and Prem Pal Singh Rawat (b. 1957, formerly known as Guru Maharaj Ji), leader of the Elan Vital movement and its predecessor, the Divine Light Mission (DLM).

Although Satya Sai Baba (1926–2011) never visited the West, he was well known as a miracle-worker, and his followers averred that he could materialize objects such as

---

1 The 'Hare Krishna' mantra was introduced by the ecstatic teacher Chaitanya Mahaprabhu (1486–1534), and the movement focuses on the Hindu deity Lord Krishna.

rings and watches. Followers made pilgrimages to his two ashrams in India to receive *darshan*: Sai Baba claimed to be the reincarnation of Sai Baba of Shirdi (d. 1918), an avatar, spiritual saint, and miracle worker. Less well known, but equally important, is Dada Lekhraj (1876–1969), who founded Brahma Kumaris, a movement aiming to improve the status of women, led by his female disciples following his death. Celibacy is encouraged and Raja Yoga – a mental practice aimed at uniting the soul with the divine – is taught.

Bhagavan Shri Rajneesh (1931–90), later known as Osho, was born into a Jain family in India, but taught an idiosyncratic form of Zen Buddhism. In the 1970s, members dressed in orange or red clothes and became popularly known as the 'orange people'. His teachings rejected authority, and extolled sexual freedom and materialism. In 1981 Rajneesh moved to Oregon, USA, and set up his own 'enlightened city', known as Rajneeshpuram. Following conflict with local residents, Osho was arrested in 1985 and the community disbanded, though the Osho organization survives.

BUDDHIST NRMs

After arriving in the USA in 1897, D. T. Suzuki (1870–1966) wrote prolifically on Zen. The 1960s US youth counter-culture took the Zen notion of the 'Buddha within' to mean personal licentiousness, and this anarchic counter-cultural version of Zen is sometimes known as 'Beat Zen', after the 'Beatniks' of the late 1950s. Buddhist NRMs derive from various traditions.

The Vipassana movement promotes a Theravada meditative practice aimed at seeing reality's true nature. Vipassana is an ancient practice, revived in Myanmar (Burma) and Thailand during the twentieth century, but its modern expression is taught to Western laypeople and to women.

Innovative forms of Tibetan Buddhism include the New Kadampa Tradition (NKT), founded by Geshe Kelsang Gyatso (b. 1931), which became controversial because of a ritual practice known as Dorje Shugden, opposed by the Dalai Lama.

The Soka Gakkai International (SGI), founded in 1930, derives its teachings from the Japanese teacher Nichiren (1222–82) and his favoured scripture, the *Lotus Sutra*. SGI members regularly chant the mantra *nam myoho renge kyo* — literally 'Homage to the ineffable law of the lotus teaching' – which is believed to have immense power, yielding material pragmatic benefits as well as spiritual ones.

The Friends of the Western Buddhist Order (FWBO) seek to develop a new form of Buddhism for Westerners. Founded by the Venerable Sangharakshita (Dennis Lingwood, b. 1925), it emphasizes 'right livelihood' – the fifth point of the Buddha's Eightfold Path – rather than the monastic practice of seeking alms from lay supporters.

Engaged Buddhism is based on the teachings of Thich Nhat Hanh (b. 1926), a Zen monk from Vietnam, and emphasizes active involvement in social and political issues.

BLACK POWER MOVEMENTS AND WHITE ISLAM

Some NRMs have originated from black communities.

Originating in Jamaica, the Rastafarians were initially a Black Power movement supported by the descendants of slaves. They interpreted the Bible's teachings as pointing to Ethiopia, where they believed Emperor Haile Selassie (1891–1975) was their messiah, who would herald a return to Africa. Following Haile Selassie's death, such ideas have been reappraised, and a variety of expectations now exists.

Malcolm X in 1962.

Other Black Power movements drew on Islam. The Nation of Islam (NOI) was originally a black supremacist organization, established in the 1930s, and later led by Elijah Muhammad (Elijah Poole, 1897–1975). Malcolm X (Malcolm Little, 1925–65) joined but left in 1964, having reconsidered NOI's racism.

The white population's interest in Islam tends to focus on Sufism, originally introduced to the USA in 1910 by Inayat Khan (1882–1927), and made popular by the writings of Idries Shah (1924–96).

UFO RELIGIONS

Unidentified Flying Objects (UFOs) have gained significance for a number of spiritual seekers, and the resulting organizations have come to be collectively known as 'UFO religions'. Typically, they hold that the gods are extra-terrestrials, who communicate with key individuals.

The earliest UFO religion in the West was the Aetherius Society, established by George King (1919–97) in 1954 or 1955. Better known is the Raëlian Movement, whose enthusiasm for modern technology includes promoting human cloning, which they believe is the key to personal immortality. Western UFO religions are often Bible-based; Raël (Claude Vorilhon, b. 1946) contends that spaceships are frequently alluded to in Judaeo-Christian scripture, for example the chariots of Elijah and Ezekiel.

HUMAN POTENTIAL MOVEMENT

Although sometimes classified as a UFO religion, the Church of Scientology is unusual in having no obvious spiritual ancestry. Science fiction writer L. Ron Hubbard (1911–86) gained prominence in 1950 with his best-selling self-improvement classic *Dianetics: The Modern Science of Mental Health*. Dianetics claims to rid the 'thetan' (the self) of harmful 'engrams' (records of unpleasant past experiences) that impede the mind. Once these are removed, the practitioner is regarded as 'clear' and can proceed to the various levels of 'Operating Thetan', which are disclosed only to authorized students.

Scientology is one of several groups that form part of the Human Potential Movement (HPM), an umbrella term for organizations claiming to offer enhanced quality of life. Werner Erhard (b. 1935), founder of Erhard Seminar Training (est — now Landmark Forum) previously studied Scientology, but other groups have no such influence: for example Silva Method, PSI Mind Development, and the School of Economic Science (SES), which is influenced by Advaita Vedanta.

The Human Potential Movement is a loosely defined cluster of groups and ideas, which merges into the equally nebulous New Age Movement (NAM), characterized by eclecticism, an optimism about human nature, and a disenchantment with organized religion.

From the 1980s the NRM climate changed and few new religions emerged. Falun Gong is the major significant one: founded in 1992 in China by Li Hongzhi (b. 1951), it offers a set of physical exercises similar to *tai ch'i*, with a path to becoming a Buddha. Other changes in NRMs include less community living, less proselytizing, less media attention, and greater institutionalization. Many NRMs have learned from past indiscretions and changed some controversial practices.

GEORGE D. CHRYSSIDES

CHAPTER 55

Secularization and Sacralization

'Secularization' names the process whereby religion declines in significance in personal life and/or society. By contrast, 'sacralization' (or 'de-secularization') names the process whereby religion grows in significance in personal life and/or society. There is normally – though not inevitably – a link between the level of significance which religion holds in personal life and in society.

SECULARIZATION AND SACRALIZATION IN THE WEST

Levels of secularization or sacralization are normally measured in terms of the numbers of active participants in religious institutions such as churches. By this measure, most Western societies have experienced secularization since the late nineteenth century, and the process has accelerated dramatically since the mid-1960s. In Sweden, for example, churchgoing is now down to just 4 per cent of the population. Rates of secularization vary by country, however, as well as by institution. Levels of congregational participation are higher in the USA than in most European countries, and in most places 'liberal' or 'mainline' denominations (both Catholic and Protestant) have declin ed faster than any other forms of Christianity.

Secularization has been more evident at the social than the personal level. The important social functions once performed by the churches in Western societies have gradually diminished, as the modern state and secular agencies have taken over responsibility for politics, education, welfare, and so on. At the national level, some modern states instigated a formal separation between church and state; and at the local level, the status and importance of the church and the clergy also diminished. In cultural terms too, Christianity has ceased to be a dominant force, being forced to compete with alternative sources and systems of meaning. At the personal level, however, religion still retains widespread allegiance. Whilst religious behaviours such as church attendance have declined, religious belief and self-identification remain high. In the 2011 census for England and Wales, for example, 59 per cent of the population identified themselves as 'Christian', whilst 96 per cent in the USA still affirm belief in God.

When personal 'Christian' belief is interrogated, however, it is often found to be 'nominal' – without accompanying commitment to churchgoing or any other form of active Christian involvement. In recent decades there has also been a noticeable shift away from a commitment to 'religion' towards a commitment to 'spirituality', and away from belief in a theistic God 'out there' towards belief in a more immanent 'Spirit'. In other words, as well as witnessing a decline in traditional religion, the late twentieth century appears to have witnessed the rise of new, more immanent, and 'holistic' forms of spirituality, which have more to do with the cultivation of unique subjective life than conformity to God-given norms. In this sense both secularization (of traditional religion) and sacralization (of new forms of spirituality) seem to be taking place simultaneously.

SECULARIZATION AND SACRALIZATION OUTSIDE THE WEST

If we move beyond the West to the rest of the world, we find evidence of sacralization of a rather different sort, namely the resurgence of traditional forms of religion. Nearly all the so-called 'world religions', including Hinduism and Buddhism, have experienced some revitalization since the 1970s, but the most dramatic growth has been enjoyed by resurgent Islam (sometimes called Islamism) and charismatic Christianity (sometimes called Pentecostalism). Journalists often bracket all these developments together, in speaking of the rise of 'fundamentalism', but the term is misleading insofar as it obscures important differences between different forms of religious revival.

Outside the West, religious resurgence is most evident in post-colonial regions, and sacralization is often bound up with the assertion of new, 'independent' identities. In the case of resurgent Islam, these identities are importantly national and pan-national, with Islam helping 'the Muslim world' establish itself over and against the cultural and economic encroachments of the West. In the case of charismatic Christianity, religion is more often mobilized at the personal and local level, where it helps individuals to establish, defend, and strengthen their identities by harnessing the power of God as Holy Spirit. In conditions of poverty, hardship, and social dislocation, these religions also have important roles to play in providing much-needed support – material, social, and spiritual.

REASONS FOR SECULARIZATION

The reasons for secularization and sacralization in the modern world are hotly debated. To date, sociologists of religion have devoted far more energy to developing theories of secularization than sacralization, mainly because the former process has been of longer duration and had greater impact in Western societies.

> *The fate of our times is characterized by rationalization and intellectualization and, above all, by the 'disenchantment of the world'. Precisely the ultimate and most sublime values have retreated from public life either into the transcendental realm of mystic life or into the brotherliness of direct and personal human relations.*
>
> Max Weber,
> *Science as a Vocation* (1919).

Five main varieties of 'secularization theory' may be distinguished, depending on which process of modernization each identifies as the salient cause:

1. Theories which focus on *differentiation* argue that religion has lost significance as the process of 'functional' or 'structural' differentiation has separated functions in modern society into specialist spheres – politics, education, the law, and so on – each of which seeks to become autonomous from religion.

2. Theories which focus on *rationalization* single out the process by which modern society becomes rationalized, bureaucratized, and 'scientific' in its modes of operation as responsible for the 'disenchantment' and 'demystification' of the world.

3. Theories which focus on *pluralization* argue that beliefs are plausible when everybody one knows holds them, but become less plausible when one becomes aware that other people believe different things. The gradual pluralization of modern society therefore renders traditional belief implausible – unless it is able to sustain itself within a bounded subculture.

4. Theories which focus on *individualization* suggest that the process by which authority is internalized is damaging to religion, since the latter seeks to have authority over people, rather than let them make their own choices.

5. Theories which focus on *societalization* maintain that religion flourishes at the level of the local community, and therefore argue that the process by which wider – particularly national – society becomes more important than local societies is destructive of religion.

Although these different theories are often regarded as competitive, they may also be treated as mutually compatible, since each singles out a different aspect of the general process of modernization as responsible for secularization. In practice, therefore, they may work better in combination than in isolation. There is also a good deal more work to be done in testing these theories, to determine their power in relation to specific instances of secularization – whether by investigating historically the ways in which particular institutions have secularized, or by researching empirically the reasons why individuals drop out of religion.

CAUSES OF SACRALIZATION

Whilst there are no established 'theories of sacralization', it is possible to make some general observations about the conditions under which religion seems to do well.

Religions do best, it seems, when they are allied with dominant political and economic power – for example, the spread of Christianity from late antiquity to the Middle Ages – or when they allow peoples to resist such power – for example, the success of religion in Northern Ireland or Poland. In both circumstances religions have much to offer by way of social unity, cohesion, and strength of purpose.

But religions also do well when they offer empowerment, not at the social, but at the personal level. Historically, this is evident in the highly varied manifestations of religion that are often classified – or dismissed – as 'magic'. In the latter, individuals attempt to harness sacred power to their own ends, often for healing or prosperity. Established religions and their representatives inevitably object to 'magic', not least because it threatens their monopoly over the sacred.

In late modern capitalist contexts, we see another instance of religion growing because of what it has to offer by way of personal empowerment in the growth of 'spirituality'. Current socio-economic as well as cultural conditions encourage a 'turn to the self', in which secure structures and given roles fall away, and individuals are required to fend for themselves in the modern economy. Rather than falling back on what is 'given', individuals have to create and recreate themselves in order to survive and flourish. In this situation, it

I AM A RASTAFARIAN

I am a writer called Benjamin Zephaniah. My full name is Benjamin Obadiah Iqbal Zephaniah. For me, this is significant because it reflects the Muslim and Judeo-Christian religious traditions. Like the hair of Lord Shiva, the Hindu god, my hair is matted in 'dreadlocks' (or *jata*). I also practise Tibetan meditation. What religion am I? In a sense I am all of the above. But ask me what I am and I will tell you that I am a Rastafarian.

It is impossible for me to speak about Rastafarianism without talking about politics. After all, Ras Tafari was the original name of Haile Selassie I (1891–1975), the last emperor of Ethiopia. It is also impossible to talk about Rastafarianism without referring to the fact that I am black. That said, you don't have to be political or black to be a Rastafarian.

My full conversion to the faith happened when I was seventeen years old. It was a matter of life, death, and freedom. In the mid-1970s I was one of the many forgotten, unemployed, first-generation black youths who roamed the streets of London, unable to see a future, and carrying a feeling of hopelessness. Not only did we have a hopeless future, we were also told that we had a past that started with slavery. The education we were receiving seemed to suggest that black people were incapable of controlling their own destiny. Suddenly Rastafari changed all that. Here was a faith and a movement that pointed to the long, and often glorious, past of black people. It gave me pride in being black and, most importantly, it taught me that there is nothing wrong with seeing God through black spectacles – from the perspective of a black person.

I stopped walking the streets with my head held down. My head was held high, and there was a spring in my step. I now knew that my roots went back much further than Jamaica, and I started to look towards Africa. Rastafarians recognize Africa as the home of humanity, Ethiopia as its capital, and Haile Selassie as being directly in the line of Solomon. All this symbolism helped me to stand on my own feet. But most importantly, I was made aware that I could find Jah (as Rastafarians refer to God) by looking inwards. I learnt how to read any of the many holy books, or any scientific book, and apply my own intelligence. I learnt that rituals may be of some use, but that there is a way to find a direct line to Jah through meditation and inner peace. I was no longer concerned with understanding the world, I was now able to 'overstand' it. For the Rastafarian, to overstand is to apply your mind to a subject, and discern a greater meaning than the obvious one. Again, in seeking to understand a person, one overstands when one truly empathizes with that person. In other words, overstanding goes beyond basic understanding.

Rastafari is a form of black liberation theology. Although we say that we shall be liberated in heaven, Rastafarians insist that we must also be liberated here on earth. Rastafarian liberation theology has no party manifesto. It is not political in that sense. Rather, it is about social responsibility; and, if that means speaking out about the misuse of power in society, then so be it. I see it as my duty to take a stand, and to help those who are struggling to help themselves. Rastafari has given purpose to my writing. I am a scribe of Rastafari, bearing witness and is not surprising to find that 'religion' gives way to new forms of 'spirituality' that offer the healing, enhancement, and cultivation of unique subjective lives. God is no longer seen as a being to be obeyed, but as a power, energy, or Spirit that can be harnessed to the task of 'becoming all that I can be'. Under these conditions, personal growth becomes identified with spiritual growth, and the sacred finds a new role in societies that had often been expected to become wholly secular.

LINDA WOODHEAD

writing the third testament. I am full of this sense of purpose. In interviews I have no problem answering that often asked question, 'What is the poet's role in society?' The number of books I sell, or my popularity, is of little importance to me. Making sure that what I write is written is far more important. Having said that, I do not believe that it is our job to preach. Rastafarians are not out to convert people, which is why I and many other Rasta writers don't write Rasta poetry. Rather, it is poetry about the world; poetry for the body and the soul; poetry for every body and every soul. I have found my role in life, and I am perfectly content with it. I have no great ambitions. My only ambition would be to do what I do better, and do more of it.

Many Rastafarians live in communes. However, while it is certainly good and pleasant for brethren to dwell together in unity, this is not always possible. I do not live in a commune. Although it would be very difficult for me to live a communal life, fortunately Rastafari has taught me to be at ease with my 'self' and not to fear silence, darkness, or solitude. Although I work for and celebrate the community, and value my relationship with others, there is also a great sense of liberation in not relying on the congregation to find strength. Nor do I feel the need for a building as a centre of worship. Jah is always with me. To be precise, Jah is part of me. So I have no real need to look outward for Jah. To find and worship Jah, I must look within.

I used to be very critical of Rastafarians who had children that did not wear dreadlocks, and worse still of those who did not raise their children as Rastas.

I thought that if mummy and daddy were Rastas, baby should follow. But I have come to realize that it is up to me (the parent) to live a good life and be a good example to my child. My child should freely want to become a Rasta because of what he sees in me. I have found my spiritual path, and my personal relationship with Jah means a lot to me. So if my child does not become a Rastafarian, but is nevertheless influenced positively by me, I still feel that I have done well before Jah – I am still doing the work of Jah.

When it comes to religious practice, I focus on compassion, which I extend to every living thing. This means there are many practices I won't take part in. I am opposed to violence and war – except in self-defence – and the manufacture of arms. I will have nothing to do with a trade that relies on the unfair exploitation of workers or forced labour. I am also a vegan. Not only will I not eat animals – I will not even wear leather products, unless there are no alternatives. To do so, I believe, would spoil my meditation, and disturb my communion with Jah. Although I do understand that there is a time to reap and a time to sow, a time to heal and a time to kill, and so on, Jah tells me that such a time is not now. When I feel that every animal is my friend, I find that I have a direct connection with the earth, nature, and even that most abstract of things called 'the universe'. I have learned that to have a direct relationship with Jah and with creation makes for a contented guy who is at ease with his 'self'.

Benjamin Zephaniah

CHAPTER 56

Religion and Globalization

At first blush, one could be forgiven for imagining that globalization might simply be destructive of religion, or that religion would resist globalization. Are not religions bound up with ancient tradition, timeless ritual, and local experience? And doesn't 'globalization' suggest cutting-edge economies, jet-setting travellers, and instant communication by internet or smart phone?

Well, yes and no. Religious tradition does not necessarily imply looking only backwards. And the global world of fast food and transnational corporations cannot shake off religion like yesterday's fashions. For instance, the so-called Islamism that produced the attacks on the USA in September 2001 and then spawned the Islamic State is both planted in the past and has hopes for the future. It uses weaponized planes, cars vans, and social media to achieve its goals.

More broadly, we can safely say that religious activity is both a cause and effect of globalization. Among other things, missionary movements and religious territorial expansion fostered early forms of globalization. At the same time, globalization is both corrosive of, and a carrier for, religions. The multiplicity of media messages may unsettle notions of 'truth'. But online religious resources have caught on in a big way too, offering new modes of religious engagement. Thus we cannot grasp globalization without considering its religious dimensions; and we cannot reflect intelligently on religion today without considering its globalizing aspects.

These big words — religion and globalization — are notoriously difficult to define. Rather than a neat capsule of meaning, each is more like a menu or agenda. 'Religion' and 'globalization' give us an idea of what kinds of dishes we're about to eat, or what kind of topics will engage the discussion. We will start by sampling some aspects of globalization, and then suggest some ways in which religion may be understood in fresh ways in a globalized world.

GRASPING GLOBALIZATION

To many, globalization is primarily an economic process, typified by corporations, such as Microsoft, Apple, Google or Amazon that operate everywhere. These corporations not only exist as global enterprises, but also supply the means of operating over

Microsoft office in Germany.

vast distances: the world, for them, has become 'one place' for inventing, manufacturing, analyzing data, and selling. This is made possible by both rapid transport and — crucially — new communications media: these are the means of globalization, of making the world one place.

Simultaneously, though, these businesses have to acknowledge localities. Microsoft's and Amazon's headquarters are situated in Washington State, USA, and their products often have to be modified for local use. Languages differ, and so do climates and cultures. Not everyone speaks English or has air-conditioning. Such considerations indicate a demand for products suitable for distinct parts of the world. Corporations such as Microsoft have to be 'glocal' — both global and local.

Similarly, religious activities are increasingly globalized. The internet has become a key means of shrinking distances that previously separated different segments of the same religious groups. Anglican Christians in the global North, for instance, have become acutely aware of the more numerous dioceses in the global South, especially in Africa, as southern membership has mushroomed in contrast with drastic depletion in the North. Northern churches are learning from the experiences of the South, often using new means of contact. As well, every religion now has a diaspora — group members scattered well beyond their original place of activity — and Muslim, Jewish, Christian, Sikh, and Hindu diasporas can keep in touch using new technologies. In this sense, globalization draws people closer.

JIHAD v. McWORLD

Churchgoers outside Hillsong Church,
Sydney, Australia at Christmas.

But globalization is paradoxical: the same forces that
seem to unite also divide. Those with great promise may also present dire threat. Take
Bangalore, South India. In the 'new economy' world of globalization, Bangalore is the
'Silicon Plateau' of shiny high-tech offices, a booming software industry, and affluent
consumers in new shopping malls. But the surrounding state of Karnataka, including
Bangalore, is predominantly rural, with high poverty rates. Landless labourers are forced
to seek work in the city, so that the proportion of poor people living in huts with no
services is growing faster than in other Indian cities – in fact, fewer services are available,
precisely because they are overused by the sprawling science and technology parks.

A key paradox of globalization is seen in political theorist Benjamin Barber's neat phrase,
'Jihad v McWorld'. The fact that you can buy Big Macs anywhere reminds us that one
fast-food company has managed to bring its products to the most remote regions. Here,
globalization seems to mean 'the world as one brand'. But along with the sameness comes
difference. The more the world is remade in the image of big corporations, the more people
want to stress their distinctive identities and particular styles and tastes. Barber's point is
that the two cannot be separated; they feed on each other, or are in tension with each other.
Indeed, his phrase recalls the basic theme of religion and globalization. If McWorld offers a
homogeneous diet of beef-in-bread, Jihad warns of scattered scuffles of holy war.

A SHORT INTRODUCTION TO WORLD RELIGIONS

CULTURE CLASH

The resurgence of jihad led some, such as political scientist Samuel Huntingdon, to caution about a 'clash of civilizations' overtaking the new global world. One could say that this helpfully highlights the vital role of religions in globalization. But there is a danger of tarring all with the same brush – 'religions produce violence' – or, worse, suggesting that some religions are characterized by their worst elements, while others may be considered as basically beneficent, but with eccentric margins. The truth is that the main world religions have many manifestations, and Muslims are no happier to be lumped with Islamists than Christians with Appalachian snake-handlers or Jews with the 'fundamentalists' of Gush Emunim.

WORLD RELIGIONS TODAY			
Religions	Percentage of population	Population	Annual growth rate
Christian	32.29	2,229,951,315	1.2%
Muslim	22.90	1,581,765,792	1.9%
Hindu	13.88	958,695,903	1.2%
Non-religious	13.58	937,904,918	0.7%
Buddhist	6.92	478,164,008	1.3%
Chinese	5.94	409,917,596	0.0%
Other	0.85	58,613,020	0.8%
Sikh	0.35	23,990,543	1.4%
Jew	0.21	14,523,554	0.3%
Bahá'í	0.09	6,181,049	0.9%

Religions with a growth rate of over 1.2% are increasing faster than the world's population.

If we explore one icon of globalization, the internet, we soon find both mainstream and fundamentalist religion in cyberspace. Helpful resources from major religious organizations are available – including, curiously, re-published classics of sacred or devotional literature – as well as signs of serious spirituality and engaged faith. But strident hate-filled fundamentalist sites also abound – and these sometimes even wage cyberwar against each other – including sabotaging each other's sites! The new technologies that foster globalization may be shaped for many purposes. Outcomes are not inevitable, nor can anything be predicted simply by referring to globalization or the internet.

One can say, however, that today's fundamentalisms are produced by globalization and the cultural forces at work in its wake. Wherever one voice threatens to dominate, others will assert themselves. And wherever a babel of voices is heard, someone will issue a call back to the 'one true faith'. If this was once so with Western TV-based media, how much more is it now true of the plethora of online videos, images, and texts. Many strident voices may now be heard, rubbing salt in the wounds of decades of neglect and humiliation. So it is no surprise that, for instance, some North African and Middle Eastern countries see a future only in the past, in a revival of old verities and strict laws. In this case, religious renewal is a response to globalization. In today's West, too, there is growing nostalgia for an idealized past, often also with a religious halo.

HOPEFUL OUTCOMES

Seen both ways, the religion-and-globalization theme will not fade fast. In fact, if this analysis is correct, it will continue to be a crucial arena of activity and site of struggle for the foreseeable future. The challenge is one that must be met, if the global world is to be one worth living in. As yet, there are precious few signs that powerful corporations

I AM A SPIRITUAL SEEKER

My name is Helen Serdiville; I have been married for twenty-five years; I have a son of twenty-three, who is a trainee commercial lawyer, and a daughter of twenty-one, who is a retail manager. I have my own business in the field of accounts and business services. I do not fit into any religious category completely.

From an early age, I had strong spiritual feelings that were self-discovered, not taught by any religious denomination. Having been brought up in a divided Roman Catholic/Protestant family, I decided that, although I had been baptized a Roman Catholic, I would make my own mind up when I felt the need.

We lived out of town, in a rural area, when I was young. Always conscious of a powerful inner sense in God, I felt surrounded by him in the earth, trees, rivers, and the wind itself. As an only child, I was wrapped up in the seasons and the elements, and found inner happiness in the beautiful world that God has given us. In my dreams – or, some would say, astral adventures – I would soar above the world, and visit places and people at will. It was not until I was about eleven that I realized not everyone could do this. What I believed to be normal set me apart from my friends, and made me realize I saw the world differently from the way they did.

Now, as an adult, my spirituality has two sides to it. At least that is how it might appear to an observer. When I married my husband, I accepted his Roman Catholic faith, and over the years have found it to be a 'comfort blanket' in times of need or sorrow. I draw upon the community of the church, recognize the strength of the family of God, and value the communal spirit of worshipping with others. A Sunday homily provides

helpful insights into the meaning of the Bible, and the ongoing love that God has for us. I also find the act of confession and contrition within Catholicism a cleansing process that provides renewal for my soul. The traditional church is, therefore, my 'public religious face', that I present to the world.

On the other hand, my private faith is one of spiritual searching. On the outside I say traditional prayers to God which are heartfelt and genuine. But in my inner private meditation, I delve back in time, beyond the confines of the church and the words written and formulated by men – and most were men! I look back to the creator, to the source of all life; I search for God. I long to draw upon the divine love to help me become what I am destined to be. I want to understand and accept the path chosen for me. I want God to make me a better person. I want to live continually in the presence of the divine. Every day I try to find some quiet time when I can meditate. This can be anywhere at any time. Sometimes, even at work, I will take a few minutes, if I am on my own. I close my eyes and go 'inwards' to my special place, and cut out the distractions of everyday life. I may need calming if the day is stressful, or just a moment to 'touch the spirit within' for a feeling of comfort in a mad world. My meditation also has another purpose – namely self-healing – which can be both spiritual and physical. I believe that the human spirit, or life force, is connected to God and, moreover, that God is able and willing to heal the soul and mend the body.

I look for guidance. Although I do not consciously have a specific 'spirit guide', I feel there is a guardian or once-sovereign states will take the lead in shaping the global for humane ends; which leaves a — perhaps paradoxical — role for religious voices to let themselves be heard again. But they will have to become clearer about how they contribute to a world of respect, trusting relationships, and mutual care. A reading of recent history shows how quickly religious smorgasbords sour, so those voices will have to acknowledge their particularities.

For example, Christianity has too often allowed itself to become blinkered, belligerent, and bigoted — but this is not the whole story. In the twenty-first century, opportunities are open to show what contribution authentic spirituality might make to the messy everyday realities of a globalizing world. While some Muslims have resisted the world of Disney and Nike as decadent, all too many Christians have embraced consumerism without even noticing. For, while large corporations tend to direct globalization, they cannot do so without persuading the world's citizens to believe in consumerism as the route to contentment. And that, as we have seen, helps to widen the rich/poor gap, and fuel fundamentalisms.

Positively, then, Christians could revisit the gospels to find there a story to live by. This story roots humans not just in the world of forests, oceans, and cities, but as spiritual beings with material experience and real relationships. It seeks not merely to know 'who I am' but who is the other, and how should I treat her? And it sees human contentment not as an outcome of gadgets and gizmos, but from a genuine commitment to justice and to care. This perspective would oppose neither enjoyment of life's good things nor the development of the world as one place. But it would be a globalization from below, in which Gaza ceases to be an open prison, Syrian refugees are welcomed, and Bangalore's poor have a place; where hostility gives way to healing.

DAVID LYON

---

angel that watches over me. Indeed, at times of great stress or sadness, I have been fortunate to have experienced 'spiritual cleansing' and empowerment in the form of light and colour that enters my body and gives me inner calm and peace. This experience helps me to face the future with a different outlook altogether. I feel my faith transcends cultural barriers and draws elements from many religions. I have heard this described as 'spiritual shopping' and – to a large extent – that is how I see my spiritual path. The stock on the shelves of the spiritual supermarket is extensive and varied and I want to make as much use of it as I can.

As part of my spiritual beliefs, the subject of reincarnation figures strongly. As a child I always knew – before I had even heard the term for it – that I had had a previous life. I often thought to myself, 'I already knew that from before.' And it was often said to me that I was 'an old soul'. I believe that the time spent in this life paves our way for a life ultimately in the presence of God. Through many lives, we progress spiritually and draw nearer to God.

Ultimately, I believe that, although many religious people may be spiritual, those who have a deep spirituality of their own do not need to embrace traditional religion at all. Seeking spiritual enlightenment allows our souls to soar, to escape the confines of our cerebral prison, and to search for our own truth in the light of God's love.

Helen Serdiville

CHAPTER 57

Religion and Politics

From the eighteenth century, 'Western' nations have witnessed attempts to confine religion to the realm of private belief and practice, tolerated in as much as the religious commitment of individuals and groups does not impact upon the public, and therefore political, domain. As a result, a general perception has arisen that religion and politics should not mix; they belong to different spheres of human interest and activity, while an all-pervasive secularist agenda has dictated how public life should be organized and what constitutes its primary concerns. The consequent separation of church (the custodian of the sacred) and state (the political community) is a specifically Western and modern idea, stemming more from secular philosophy than from any particular religious understanding.

Nonetheless, it is difficult historically to see 'politics' and 'religion' as entirely distinct entities. In animist and tribal religions, cultic practice was intended to ensure the welfare of the group. Roman religious practice was, in part, expressed in emperor worship, while Greek religion expected citizens to undertake the civic aspects of ceremonial and sacrifice, all in pursuit of the common good. Such considerations can be discerned in subsequent history, where religion and politics have maintained a complex – if increasingly ambivalent – relationship.

SEPARATE CONCERNS

'Religion' and 'politics' have separate but related interests. Religions generally claim to answer metaphysical and existential questions, and expose human beings either to the divine call or to transcendence of the world and its concerns. Religions usually posit eternal and binding values that assist in interpreting the why and wherefore of the universe. They provide principles, morals, and laws that their adherents are to follow, but which offer little direct and pragmatic advice concerning how to respond to the exigencies of modern life. As a result, religions tend to influence politics through the teaching of certain pedagogues, through individuals as they follow their vocation in political life, or through those who would subvert existing structures, rather than by providing a blueprint for social life or the political economy.

Politics, however, is basically the way in which society is organized in order to make social life possible. Its concerns tend to be immediate, even when short-term action constitutes a policy for the establishment of long-term goals. Despite its pragmatism, often diluted by dogmatic concerns, politics remains a branch of ethics, because it is vulnerable to abuse. Political organizations can be oppressive and brutal, necessitating a commitment to commonly held values of goodness, justice, and virtue. As religious teaching often provides the source for understanding these principles, a close relationship between religion and politics can be considered almost inevitable. This is evident in the doctrine and practice of the world's three major monotheistic faiths, as demonstrated in the following brief and general accounts.

JUDAISM

Judaism emerged out of the biblical history of a chosen people and promised land. The Hebrew people had a specifically religious identity: they were Yahweh's elect people, whose life, socially and individually, was to reflect Yahweh's Torah (law). The result was a political identity that was indelibly linked to religious belief and practice. While officially secular, the modern state of Israel contains many who wish to see the theological understanding of land and people enshrined in political institutions. Some, such as the Gush Emunim (Bloc of the Faithful), have seen the expansion of Israel's territory as the fulfilment of biblical promises, while some rabbis have been keen to confirm the Jewish status as a chosen people, and thus beneficiaries of certain privileges and rights. Nevertheless, others resident within it, such as members of Neturei Karta (Guardians of the City), see the modern state of Israel as a sacrilegious human trespass on the divine prerogative. For them, it is God, not human beings, who will restore the nation of Israel.

CHRISTIANITY

From its inception, Christianity differentiated between religious and political authority, partly because of its emergence as a weak and vulnerable social group, partly because of ambiguity in the interpretation of Jesus' injunction to 'Give to Caesar what is Caesar's, and to God what is God's' (Matthew 22:21), and partly because of the influence of the Emperor Constantine and the role of the church following the collapse of the Roman Empire. The Augustinian and Magisterial Reformation traditions have asserted that believers belong to two states or cities: the sacred city, which has its home in heaven, and the earthly city, which is ruled over by princes and governments. However, this is not strictly the separation of the secular and the sacred, because the state – the earthly city – is ruled by those whose vocation under God is to govern, and whose rule must consequently conform to the divine will. In Christian thought, politics is both the legitimate concern of each believer, to act and live in a way pleasing to God, and the specific task of keeping the peace under God's law. Part of the church's task is to prick the state's conscience, but the assumption that the state is governed by Christians committed to act as stewards belongs to the medieval conception of Christendom far more than to contemporary secular, multicultural, religiously plural societies.

ISLAM

Islam knows no separation between the sacred and the secular. All aspects of human life are to be drawn under the direct influence of the law of Allah, to which the only response is obedience. In its traditional forms, Islam views political leadership as a succession descending from the Prophet, practised by those who are selected as caliphs (Sunni) or imams (Shia). These leaders implement Shari'a law, but are expected to seek Shura, or consultation with those under their governance. In all Islamic traditions the need to rebuke the unjust ruler remains a primary responsibility, though — as in other religious systems — this is more difficult to achieve in practice than to uphold in theory. Nevertheless, the obedient life, in all its aspects, individual and social, spiritual and civic, internal and external, should express the divine will. As a result, there is no value in the separation of religion and spirituality, on the one hand, from politics and social practice on the other.

RELIGION AND POLITICS

Religions have historically exercised a potent influence on politics. The relationship of church and state, primarily through the established Church of England and its privileged status in parliament, influences British society to the present day, though in the twenty-first century this is more implicit than explicit. The Puritan founders of the USA inspired a later generation, influenced by deistic and rationalistic traditions, to exalt freedom, choice, and individual conscience as basic rights, even in matters of religion. Hindu traditions played an important role in forging an Indian political identity, prior to that country's independence in 1947. Pakistan was founded in the same year, as an Islamic state, and, over time, has attempted to modernize, while also upholding Shari'a law. Buddhism was an important factor in anti-colonialist movements in Myanmar, while liberation theology assisted many in Latin America in opposing unsatisfactory secular regimes — although poverty remains at significant levels on the subcontinent. All these examples hold a common view of religion in its various guises as exercising a liberating influence, influencing politics for the better, and challenging corruption and injustice.

POLITICIZATION

From the mid-twentieth century, a renewed association developed between religion and politics, resulting from disillusionment with secular values and dissatisfaction with policies of modernization. Hindu traditions became a significant force in Indian politics, particularly manifest in the Bharatiya Janata Party (BJP) and its association of land, religion, and national identity. In Thailand and Sri Lanka, the prima facie other-worldly and pacifist convictions of Buddhism seemed to be set aside as particular groups on occasion embraced violence in order to preserve a political system congenial to their own survival. Although from the time of the sixth Guru, Hargobind (1595–1644), Sikhism has maintained that state and religion are natural allies, it has emerged as a political force in India, particularly following the declaration of the Sikh state, Khalistan, in 1986. In the USA, Christians have exercised a political influence through organizations such as the Moral Majority and the Christian Coalition, as they opposed the liberalization of US society and its abandonment of what they saw as core Christian values, especially regarding the family unit and procreation.

FUNDAMENTALISM

Much of this renewed political interaction can be attributed to the rise of religious fundamentalism, which achieved its first institutional expression when the Iranian revolution of 1979 swept the Shah from power and installed the Ayatollah Khomeini as national leader. Islamic militancy increased throughout the 1970s, and following this takeover became a far more potent force in the Middle East and Africa, reaching an infamous expression in the Taliban regime in Afghanistan. The attack on the World Trade Center, New York, on 11 September 2001 ('9/11'), perpetrated by al-Qaeda against what was perceived to be the corrupting influence of the West, has had far-reaching consequences. The 'war on terror' initiated by the US government and its allies largely failed in its goal of establishing Western-style (and inevitably secular) democracies in the Middle East, facing instead the rise of so-called 'Islamic State', which in 2014 declared a worldwide caliphate from its base in Syria and Iraq.

Some have seen the inspiration for Islamic State in the ultra-conservative Salafi, or Wahhabist, tradition, which traces its history to an eighteenth-century Islamic jurist, Muhammad ibn 'Abd al-Wahhab (1703–92), who campaigned to restore pure monotheistic worship instead of popular, but idolatrous, practices. The movement gained potency through its political pact with the House of Saud and the support given to its teaching by successive governments in Saudi Arabia. Others have seen the work of Sayyid Qutb (1906–66) as justifying Islamic State's aggression towards those considered to be enemies of Islam, both those belonging to the Muslim faith and those who do not. Either way, while radical Islamic movements such as Islamic Jihad and al-Qaeda appear to have considered violence to be a modus operandi, for Islamic State it has been a modus vivendi. Its prominence on the world stage is largely the result of the threat it poses to the West, especially through direct acts of terror and attempts to control oil reserves. Possibly Boko Haram, based in Nigeria, and active in Chad, Niger, and Cameroon, fully encapsulates this violent reaction against Western influence (its name can be translated as 'Western education is forbidden'). Aligned with Islamic State, this group was declared the deadliest terrorist group in the world in 2015, having killed more than 20,000 people and displaced a further two million.

Perhaps more than any other religion, Islam has been criticized for its political associations, and the willingness of its most militant followers to take extreme measures to achieve their goals. As a result, the concern of many that religion and politics had too close an association has, in the twenty-first century, given way to the fear that religion, at least in some of its forms, has too close an association with terrorism.

Responses to fundamentalism

The response to this situation has been mixed. In France, since 2004 a ban has been placed on the wearing of religious symbols in state schools, and since April 2011 a ban on concealment of the face in public, whether by mask, helmet, balaclava, niqab, or burqa. In the UK, the Racial and Religious Hatred Act (2006) attempted to prevent prejudicial and violent acts against religious groups, which increased particularly against the Muslim population after 9/11. This act's definition of 'religious hatred' as 'hatred against a group of persons defined by reference to religious belief or lack of religious belief' led some to allege that the Bible and the Qur'an were thus rendered illegal documents, while others worried about freedom of speech, especially in the context of comedy and satire. Such policies are at best paradoxical, involving the state's direct intrusion into what it previously considered to be private belief and practice. The right of the state to dictate the extent of religious expression appeared to be upheld when the European Court of Human Rights agreed with the French government's argument that the ban on the veil was based on a particular idea of what social life and acceptable public engagement might mean. The suppression of religious symbols has stemmed from a dubious sense that shared secular values can lead to a common sense of national identity that can properly be imposed on citizens regardless of their personal convictions.

Removing militant Islamic graffiti in Indonesia.

A SHORT INTRODUCTION TO WORLD RELIGIONS

In the USA, the apparent failure of President Jimmy Carter (b. 1924) to deal effectively with the crisis that saw fifty-two diplomats held hostage in Tehran for 444 days after the ascent to power of the Ayatollah Khomeini became a catalyst which saw evangelical Christians transfer allegiance from the Democrat to the Republican cause. Conservative Christianity has aligned itself with conservative politics, especially the reduction in welfare spending, reactionary approaches to perceived attacks on the traditional family such as rights for homosexuals or access to abortion, promotion of the right of individuals to defend themselves or carry arms, support for the state of Israel, and strong – even aggressive – foreign policy when US interests are perceived to be jeopardized. The alignment of conservative Christianity with right-wing politics has influenced a number of presidential campaigns, resulting in a significant impact on contemporary global politics.

Government and religion

Historically, religion has related to politics in several ways. Governments and subversive groups can claim direct religious inspiration for their policies and initiate a theocracy where the state is governed by a priestly caste; religion can hold a theological view of political institutions, where the state and its organs are divinely ordained to maintain order; religion can act as the political conscience of a society, with religious institutions criticizing political policy and calling for action when those policies are perceived as contradicting eternal values; religion can oppose the political status quo for being too compromising. In the West, governments have often sought to appropriate religious conviction in order to promote the social good, though 'religion' is often homogenized, and, when religious commitment overrides any sense of a shared national identity or common humanity, it is rarely understood. Nevertheless, in all instances, the association of religion and politics holds the potential to do both good and harm – the latter being most prominent when religious practitioners fail to live up to the highest ideals of their own creed.

ROBERT POPE

CHAPTER 58

Women and Religion

WOMEN AND WORLD RELIGIONS

The dominance of men in society and religious structures appears almost universal, across the globe and from the beginning of recorded human history. While there are a few important exceptions amongst traditional African religions, for example, all of the so-called 'world religions' have evolved in patriarchal cultures. It is predominantly men who have formulated their religious beliefs, recorded, transmitted, and interpreted religious texts, created and led institutions, controlled rituals and worship, and, importantly, written the histories of their traditions. There are recorded instances where women have played prominent roles in these traditions, but these are isolated, and usually exist as anomalies alongside a mainstream culture where only men are the educated decision-makers. So in Islam, all accepted legal rulings have been made by men; in Buddhism, the most senior nun must defer to the most junior monk; and in Hinduism, the Brahmanic priesthood (like the traditional Christian priesthood and Orthodox Jewish rabbinate) has been the sole preserve of men. This male dominance of religious institutions, which for the most part continues until this day, went largely unchallenged until the latter half of the twentieth century.

In Europe and North America – 'the West' – it could be said that the successes of the movement for women's equality have been in spite of religious traditions rather than because of them. Societal change in this regard has come, albeit very slowly, as a result of a predominantly secular women's movement. This movement has been aided by the loosening of women's confinement within the domestic sphere, brought about by industrialization, war, the availability of contraception, and increased access to education for women. Religious structures have generally functioned as a conservative force in society, upholding traditional roles for women and men. In those instances where greater equality has been granted to women within religious institutions, the change has usually been vigorously resisted, as with the Anglican Communion's decision to include female priests and bishops. Within traditional religions, views on gender are often underpinned theologically by texts and teachings about the God-willed or 'natural' order of things, meaning that change will only take place as a result of considerable scholarly and theological effort.

WOMEN AND THE STUDY OF WORLD RELIGIONS

The Western study of 'world religions' has its roots in Orientalism, the study of non-Christian cultures and religions, which developed in tandem with the colonial enterprise to 'the Orient' in the eighteenth and nineteenth centuries. At that time, very few women were highly educated or had the opportunity to travel, and therefore the discipline consisted for the most part of male scholars studying male-dominated traditions, generally oblivious to the missing voices and experiences of women. Moreover 'religion', for these early pioneers, was viewed through a thoroughly Christian lens: they were concerned primarily with texts, theological beliefs (as opposed to practice), and the structures of authority. Women, by and large, had no prominent role in any of these, and so Orientalist scholars found no cause to question their androcentric presuppositions. Forms of religion, such as Shamanism, where women were more prominent were dismissed as magic or superstition. In those few instances where women were implicated in the object of inquiry, women's voices were still not heard. A case in point can be found in the nineteenth-century British debates around the Hindu practice of sati – the ritual burning of a Hindu widow on her deceased husband's funeral pyre — a practice abolished by the British in 1829. This debate was not informed by the experiences of women, but instead endeavoured to establish whether the practice was sanctioned by the authoritative Vedic texts.

These Orientalist scholars assumed themselves to be involved in a scientific, objective study of other religions, as is evident in the classic text, F. Max Müller's Introduction to the Science of Religion (1882). However, the notion that it is possible to engage in an objective study of anything was increasingly called into question during the twentieth century. Critical theory highlighted the inevitable influence of bias on all the choices made by the scholar, conscious and unconscious. Orientalism, from which the supposedly position-neutral discipline of 'Religious Studies' had evolved, was exposed as a form of colonialism (see Edward Said's Orientalism, 1978). With the increase in the number of women at universities, and the rise of feminist thought in the 1970s, 1980s, and 1990s, female scholars increasingly exposed the male bias (androcentrism) in evidence in the discipline of Religious Studies, as well as in theological scholarship and in religious traditions themselves. As renowned feminist scholar Carol P. Christ remarked: 'We are slowly beginning to realise that the religious lives of one-half of humanity have never adequately been studied.'

FEMINISM AND THE STUDY OF RELIGIOUS TRADITIONS

Feminist and gender-critical approaches, which have developed since the 'second wave' feminism of the 1960s, have been slow to make inroads into the domains of theology and religious studies. This is in part due to the potentially huge implications of such scholarship, both for the study of religion and for the religious traditions themselves. They call into question what counts as religion, the methods adopted, the content to be explored, and the validity of firmly-held religious narratives. The percentage of scholars in religious studies and theology adopting gender-critical approaches is low, as is that of feminist scholars from other disciplines who see religion as an essential aspect of their study. Yet those engaged in gender-critical studies of religion have produced some of the most exciting and ground-breaking work in their field in the last forty years. Many have also pioneered an approach that breaks down the distinction between theology and religious studies, and have been important drivers behind the development of interreligious and comparative studies. Although feminist studies are still most developed within, or with reference to, Christianity and Judaism, by the 1980s feminist studies of religious traditions had extended to include Eastern traditions too.

FEMINIST SCHOLARS OF RELIGION: REFORMISTS AND REVOLUTIONARIES

Those who have engaged in a feminist study of religion can be broadly divided into two categories – 'revolutionaries' and 'reformists' – though these terms have also been resisted. On the one hand are those who believe traditional religions are fundamentally and inescapably patriarchal, and therefore to be abandoned. The revolutionaries, largely from Christian and Jewish backgrounds, have focused on the male imagery of the biblical God as beyond reform, as in Mary Daly's *Beyond God the Father* (1973), for example. These scholars often move on to explore non-traditional, minority, or 'heretical' sources, or New Religious Movements, which can perhaps better express and embody the equality and importance of women, often through a focus on goddess spirituality. (See, for example, Carol P. Christ's *Rebirth of the Goddess*, 1997.)

One the other hand there are those who argue that it is the message of liberation that is basic, or essential, to the tradition, and that this has been overlaid by the patriarchal culture within which the tradition emerged. They point to elements within the tradition which, they argue, show real potential for reform, such as important female figures and non-canonical texts that have hitherto been obscured, as well as re-interpretations of traditional texts and teachings. It has been argued, for example, that the Buddha, Jesus, Muhammad, and Guru Nanak (the founding figures of Buddhism, Christianity, Islam, and Sikhism respectively) were all radical in according greater roles and/or rights to women than were afforded to them in their time. Feminist exegesis of scriptures has been particularly important within Judaism, Christianity, and Islam, where they play a central and authoritative role within the tradition. Studies of classic texts has been less critical for reformers within Buddhism, Hinduism, and the Chinese traditions. Across all these traditions, many feminist scholars have also shifted their attention to religious practice, recognizing that it is in the realm of ritual and religion as an everyday activity that women are perhaps best seen as having agency in their religious lives.

GENDER STUDIES AND RELIGION

Some see feminist discourse as unable to tackle the gender inequality in religion and in the study of religion which it has successfully identified. Feminist discourse has at times been accused of championing the interests of white, Western, middle-class, educated, straight women, without recognition of all those women whose voices have been denied or simply assumed.

Some African-American scholars, arguing that white feminists have too often been blind to the ways in which race and class informed and shaped women's experiences of oppression, have preferred to describe themselves as 'womanist' rather than feminist. Many Muslim women do not identify with the label 'feminist', associating it with the imposition of distinctly Western values and norms. They have attempted to define a distinctive 'Islamic Feminism', or chosen to eschew the term all together. These scholars point out, for example, that Western feminists have often rushed to critique practices such as arranged marriage and dress codes that require modesty as damaging products of a patriarchal system, without taking time to listen to women who argue for the benefits of these practices for women.

Turning to the future, it seems more scholars may be comfortable under the umbrella of 'Gender Studies', which is thoroughly post-colonial in its outlook, as defined by leading feminist scholar of religion Ursula King. Gender Studies also has the potential to reach out beyond the perception that the issues involved are 'women's issues'. Gender studies has been primarily focused on women because of their historical voicelessness, but King stresses that it is important to consider not only the construction of femininity, but also that of masculinity, within religious traditions. (See, for example, deSondy's ground-breaking work, exploring the construction of masculinity in Islam.) It is within this broader conception of Gender Studies that gender-critical scholars of religion stand to make the biggest impact in their fields.

MAGDALEN LAMBKIN

QUESTIONS

1. What factors do you think explain the growth of new religious movements (NRMs) since the late nineteenth century?

2. Why is engagement with political issues so important in the Bahá'í faith?

3. What factors explain the decline of traditional religion in the West?

4. What factors explain the growth of religion outside the West in recent years?

5. Can religion and politics ever be entirely separated?

6. How has globalization shaped religion since the late twentieth century?

7. 'Fundamentally, religion and modern secularism are incompatible.' Discuss this statement with reference to at least three religious traditions.

8. How does the unique experience of women shape the study of religion and religious experience?

FURTHER READING

Castelli, E. A. ed., *Women, Gender, Religion: A Reader. New York: Palgrave, 2001*

Chang, Maria Hsia, *Falun Gong: The End of Days*. New Haven, CT: Yale University Press, 2004.

Chryssides, George D., *A Reader in New Religious Movements: Readings in the Study of New Religious Movements*, London: Continuum, 2006

Dawkins, Richard, *The God Delusion*. New York: Houghton Mifflin, 2006.

Heelas, Paul, The New Age Movement: Celebrating the Self and the Sacralization of Modernity. Oxford and Cambridge, MA: Blackwell, 1996.

Sutcliffe, Stephen J., *Children of the New Age: A History of Alternative Spirituality*. New York: Taylor and Francis, 2002.

Smith, Peter, *A Concise Encyclopedia of the Bahá'í Faith*. Oxford, UK: Oneworld Publications, 2000.

York, Michael. The Emerging Network: A Sociology of the New Age and Neo-Pagan Movement. Lanhan, MD: Rowan & Littlefield, 1995.

FURTHER READING ON WORLD RELIGIONS

Bowker, John, ed., *Oxford Dictionary of World Religions*. Oxford: Oxford University Press, 1997.

Eliade, Mircea, ed., *The Encyclopedia of Religion*. 16 vols. New York: Macmillan, 1987.

Oxtoby, Willard G., and Alan F. Segal, A Concise Introduction to World Religions, Don Mills, Canada: Oxford University Press, 2007.

Smart, Ninian, ed., *Atlas of the World's Religions*. Oxford: Oxford University Press, 1987.

Smith, Jonathan Z., ed., *The HarperCollins Dictionary of Religion*. New York: HarperSanFrancisco, 1995.

Woodhead, Linda ed., Religions in the Modern World. London and New York: Routledge 2002.

Rapid Fact-Finder

This fact-finder was written by Angela Tilby and John-David Yule, revised and expanded by Christopher Partridge in 2005, and further revised and expanded for this new edition.

The terms include some that do not appear in this book. These are common terms included to give additional information to readers.

Words printed in small capitals indicate cross-reference.

A

'Abbasid dynasty (750–1258 CE) The second great Islamic dynasty, and third caliphate, which ruled from Baghdad.

Abhidhamma Pitaka THERAVADA Buddhist scripture on techniques of mind-training. The aim is to eliminate the idea of the self.

Abraham, Isaac, and Jacob The three PATRIARCHS who are continually remembered in the Jewish liturgy as the original recipients of God's promise and blessing.

Absolute, The Term for GOD or the divine often preferred by those who conceive of God predominantly in abstract or impersonal terms.

Abu Bakr MUHAMMAD's father-in-law and traditionally his earliest convert. He was elected CALIPH after the PROPHET's death and ruled for two years, fighting tribes who were trying to break away from the Islamic community.

Adi Granth Sacred book of Sikhism. It is regarded as the eternal GURU for the SIKH community. It is the central focus of the Sikh home and of the GURDWARA.

Adonai *see* YHWH.

Advaita ('non-dualism') The monist (*see* MONISM) doctrine of SHANKARA, that all reality is fundamentally one and divine.

Æsir Plural of '*as*', meaning 'god'. The collective noun used in Norse literature for the pantheon of deities.

African Independent Churches African churches which have risen in the past 100 years and offer a synthesis of CHRISTIANITY with traditional INDIGENOUS RELIGIONS.

Afterlife Any form of conscious existence after the death of the body.

Agadah/Aggadah A moral or devotional Jewish teaching derived from the midrashic exposition of a Hebrew text (*see* MIDRASH).

Agape Greek word for 'love' that has come to express the Christian understanding of God's love which does not depend on any worthiness or attractiveness of the object of his love.

Agni Indian fire god of Vedic times (*see* Vedas). As sacrificial fire, Agni mediates between gods and people and is especially concerned with order and ritual.

Ahimsa Indian virtue of non-violence. It usually applies to abstention from harming any living creature and hence to vegetarianism. The doctrine was developed in JAINISM, BUDDHISM, and some HINDU sects.

Ahmadiyya sect Offshoot of ISLAM founded in India by Mirza Ghulam Ahmad (died 1908), who is believed to be the MESSIAH, the Shi'a MAHDI. The sect denies the authority of the 'ULAMA', IJMA', and JIHAD.

Ahriman *see* ANGRA MAINYU.

Ahura Mazda/Ahrmazd ('wise lord') ZOROASTER's name for God. He demands ethical and ritual purity and he judges human souls after death.

Akhenaten Name adopted by Amenophis IV, king of Egypt c. 1353–1335 BCE, in honour of ATEN ('the sun disc'), whose cult he promoted to the exclusion of all others in a short-lived reform of Egyptian religion.

Akiva, Rabbi (c. 50–135 CE) Jewish teacher who developed the MISHNAH method of repetitive transmission of teachings.

Albigensians The Cathars of southern France who flourished in the late twelfth and early thirteenth centuries.

Alchemy Mystical science of chemical manipulation which seeks to change base metals into gold, find the universal cure for illness, and discover the secret of immortality. Its study passed from Hellenistic Egypt through the Arabs to medieval Europe.

Al-Ghazali (1058–1111 CE) Orthodox Muslim legal expert who renounced his post and became a Sufi (*see* Sufism). He attacked the incursions of Greek thought into Islam and defended the teaching of the Qur'an.

Al-Hallaj (died 922 CE) Sufi MYSTIC who was crucified because of his confession 'I am the real,' which was taken as a claim to divinity.

'Ali Cousin and son-in-law of MUHAMMAD. SUNNI Muslims claim he was elected fourth CALIPH in 656 CE; Shias that he was the first Imam, and that he and his descendants are Muhammad's rightful successors.

Allah The Muslim name for God. Allah is one; there are no other gods.

All-India Muslim League Organization founded in 1906 CE to promote the interests and political aspirations of Indian Muslims.

Almsgiving The giving of free gifts, usually of money, to the poor. In Islam it is obligatory (*see* zakah). In Theravada Buddhism the lay community is linked to the sangha by their provision of food for the monks, which is collected on a daily almsround.

Alternative spiritualities One of the more significant developments in particularly Western religious adherence has been the emergence of private, non-institutional forms of belief and practice known as 'alternative spiritualities'.

Amida *see* AMITABHA.

Amidah ('standing') The principal Jewish daily prayer, also known as the Eighteen Benedictions, recited standing.

Amitabha ('infinite light') Celestial Buddha worshipped in China and Japan (where his name is Amida). He is believed to live in a 'pure land' in the far west where those faithful to him go after death (*see* JODO SHINSHU; NEMBUTSU; PURE LAND BUDDHISM).

Amritsar Site of the Golden Temple, the holiest shrine of the SIKH religion, completed by Arjan, the fifth GURU.

Analects One of the four books of the so-called Confucian canon. It contains the essence of CONFUCIUS's teaching.

Ananda One of the most prominent members of the BUDDHA's SANGHA. Traditionally he was the Buddha's cousin and many of the sayings are addressed to him, including the words of comfort shortly before the Buddha's death.

Anatta/Anatman Meaning 'not-self', a Buddhist term indicating that there is no permanent self or ego. *Anatta* is one of the three characteristics of existence.

Ancestor veneration The practice in INDIGENOUS RELIGIONS of making offerings to the spirits of the dead and expecting to communicate with them through DREAMS.

Angels Spiritual beings who in JUDAISM and CHRISTIANITY act as the messengers of GOD. They have two primary functions: to worship God, and to support and encourage human beings.

Anglican churches Worldwide groupings of churches which

recognize the primacy among equals of the Archbishop of Canterbury.

Angra Mainyu/Ahriman The chief spirit who is opposed to AHURA MAZDA in Zoroastrian belief. His nature is violent and destructive.

Anicca/Anitya Buddhist term for the impermanence and changeability which characterizes all existence.

Animism A term formerly used to describe pre-literary religions.

Anthroposophy Spiritual system invented by Rudolf STEINER. It stresses the threefold nature of humanity as physical, etheric, and astral body.

Anu The sky god of ancient Sumerian religion and high god of the Sumerian pantheon. He had little to do with human affairs and delegated his authority to ENLIL.

Anubis Jackal-headed god of ancient Egypt who conducted souls to judgment and weighed them in the great balance.

Aphrodite Greek goddess of love and patroness of beauty and sexual attractiveness. Her cult was imported from the Near East.

Apocalyptic Genre of writing in CHRISTIANITY and JUDAISM, concerned with hidden truths, pointing to the ultimate triumph of faith and the judgment of nations. Daniel and Revelation are examples in the BIBLE.

Apocrypha Historical and wisdom writings found in the Greek version of the Hebrew scriptures but excluded from the canon of the HEBREW BIBLE. The Roman Catholic Church and Eastern Orthodox churches accept its authority,

but Protestant churches distinguish it from inspired SCRIPTURE.

Apollo A major god of both Greeks and Romans, though Greek in origin. He is sometimes seen as the sun and is the patron of the arts (especially music), or prophecy, of divination, and of medicine.

Apostle (1) 'One who is sent', name for the twelve original followers of JESUS OF NAZARETH, also PAUL. The 'apostolic age' is a time of great authority for the Christian CHURCH. (2) Title of MUHAMMAD.

Apostles' Creed A statement of faith used by Western Christian churches and often repeated in services. Introduced during the reign of Charlemagne (c. 742–814). (*See* CREED.)

Aquinas, Thomas (1225–74 CE) Dominican theologian and philosopher whose teachings form the basis of official Roman Catholic theology..

Archetypes Term invented by C. G. JUNG to describe the concepts held in common by different people at different times and in different places.

Arianism Fourth-century Christian heresy of Arius, who denied the divinity of Christ, claiming that the Son of God was created and not eternal. It was condemned at the Council of Nicea in 325 CE but flourished until the Council of Constantinople in 381 CE. (*See* ECUMENICAL COUNCILS.)

Aristotle (384–322 BCE) Greek philosopher and scientist who taught on every branch of knowledge valued in his time. His work was rediscovered in the Middle Ages and laid the basis for the theology of Thomas AQUINAS and for the HUMANISM of the Renaissance.

Ark (1) Israelite religious artefact, probably in the form of a portable miniature temple, which was carried into battle as evidence of the presence of God (*see* YHWH).
(2) A cupboard in the wall of a synagogue that faces Jerusalem, where the handwritten parchment scrolls of the Torah are kept.

Artemis Greek goddess and patroness of virginity, hunting, archery, and wild animals. She was also the protector of the newly born and the bringer of death to women.

Arthur Legendary hero of Celtic Britain who may have originated as a Romano-British chieftain. His legends were gradually worked into a coherent Christian framework in which he became the medieval ideal of a Christian king.

Aryan Word describing the Caucasian people who invaded India around 2000 BCE and who gradually imposed their language and culture upon the earlier inhabitants.

Asceticism Austere practices designed to lead to the control of the body and the senses. These may include FASTING and MEDITATION, the renunciation of possessions, and the pursuit of solitude.

Asgard The home of the gods in Norse religion. It is a mountainous region rising out of Midgard.

Ashkenazim One of the two main cultural groups in Judaism which emerged in the Middle Ages. Their tradition is from Palestinian Jewry and they live in Central, Northern, and Eastern Europe.

Ashram In Indian religion, a hermitage or monastery. It has come to denote a communal house for devotees of a GURU.

Astral plane The intermediate world, according to THEOSOPHY and SPIRITUALISM, to which the human consciousness passes at death.

Astrology The study of the influence of the stars on the character and destiny of human beings.

Aten The sun in ancient Egyptian religion. In the reforms of AKHENATEN he was worshipped as the one true God.

Athanasius (296–373 CE) Bishop of Alexandria who strongly resisted the teachings of ARIANISM and developed the Christian doctrines of the INCARNATION and the TRINITY.

Athena One of the great Greek goddesses of Mount OLYMPUS who sprang fully armed from the head of her father, ZEUS. She is the patroness of war, of the city of Athens, and of many crafts and skills.

Atman Sanskrit word meaning soul or self. The Upanishads teach that *atman* is identical to brahman, i.e. the soul is one with the divine.

Atonement (1) Ritual act which restores harmony between the human and the divine when it has been broken by SIN or impurity. (2) In CHRISTIANITY, reconciliation between God and humanity required because of the absolute holiness of God and the sinfulness of men and women. As human beings are incapable of achieving atonement, it is a work of God's GRACE, through the death of Jesus Christ, for human sin.

Atonement, Day of *see* YOM KIPPUR.

Augustine (354–430 CE) BISHOP of Hippo in North Africa who was converted to CHRISTIANITY from the teaching

of the MANICHAEANS. He stressed the absolute GRACE of God in men and women's SALVATION and the depravity of human beings through ORIGINAL SIN.

Augustus Title of the first Roman emperor, formerly known as Octavian, who ruled 31 BCE–14 CE. While he was still alive he was declared a god and after his death he was worshipped throughout the Empire.

Austerity Ascetic practice in which one exercises self-restraint or denial, for example, the restriction of food during a fast.

Avalokiteshvara ('regarder of the cries of the earth') Celestial BUDDHA worshipped by Tibetans and in Korea, Japan, and China. The DALAI LAMA is believed to be an emanation of him. This Buddha is known under male and female forms and is depicted with a thousand arms.

Avalon Celtic island of immortality replete with miraculous apple trees. Here the hero ARTHUR was taken to recover from his mortal wounds.

Avatar ('one who descends') In popular HINDUISM, Lord VISHNU appears on earth at intervals to assert ancient values and destroy illusion. The main tradition refers to ten descents, nine of which have already happened. KRISHNA is the most famous *avatar*. Some modern cults claim to worship a living *avatar*.

Averroes *see* IBN RUSHD.

Avesta The scriptures of Zoroastrianism. It includes the *Gathas*, a series of poems reminiscent of the hymns of the Vedas, which may go back to Zoroaster himself.

Ayatollah ('sign of God') Term for a great MUJTAHID who has authority in the SHI'A MUSLIM community.

Ayn Sof *see* EIN SOF.

Aztec new fire ceremony Ritual which took place at the end of every AZTEC cycle of fifty-two years. It was performed at night on a volcanic hill visible from many parts of the valley of Mexico.

Aztecs An indigenous people whose empire in central Mexico flourished from the late twelfth century CE until the coming of the conquistador Hernando Cortes in 1519. Their religion centred around a sacred calendar and featured human sacrifice in which the heart torn from a living victim was offered to the gods. (*See also* HUITZILOPOCHTLI; QUETZALCOATL; TEZCATLIPOCA; TLALOC; XIPE TOTEC; XIUHTECUHTLI.)

B

Baal Divinity of ancient Canaanite or Phoenician fertility religion. The name means 'lord'.

Baal Shem Tov (1698–1760 CE) Jewish MYSTIC who founded the movement of HASIDISM. His original name was Israel ben Eliezer.

Babism *see* BAHÁ'Í FAITH.

Babylonian epic of creation The story of the god MARDUK's fight with the primordial ocean.

Bahá'í faith A religious movement that arose out of the Persian Islamic Babi sect, led by the 'Báb' ('gate', 1819–50).

Balder The son of ODIN and FRIGG, the wisest and most beautiful of the Norse gods. He was killed by the wiles of LOKI but could not be restored to ASGARD because Loki refused to weep for him.

Baptism The SACRAMENT of entry into the Christian CHURCH (1). By washing in water in the name of the TRINITY. In the case of infants, promises are made on behalf of the child for later CONFIRMATION.

Baptist churches Protestant churches emphasizing the BAPTISM of adult believers by total immersion.

Bar Mitzvah ('Son of the Commandment') Ceremony by which Jewish boys, at the age of thirteen, accept the positive commandments of JUDAISM and are counted as adult members of the community.

Bat Mitzvah ('Daughter of the Commandment') Ceremony, mainly in non-ORTHODOX communities, by which Jewish girls, at the age of twelve, accept the positive commandments of Judaism and are counted as adult members of the community.

Barth, Karl (1886–1968 CE) Swiss Calvinist theologian who reacted against Liberal Protestantism in theology and declared theology's central theme to be the WORD OF GOD.

Beautiful names of God Ninety-nine names which characterize the will of ALLAH in ISLAM.

Beltane Celtic spring festival and origin of May Day. The name means 'shining fire' and it is likely that sacred fires were lit for the people to dance around, encouraging the growth of the summer sun.

Benares/Varanasi/Kashi The most holy city of HINDUISM, situated on the banks of the GANGES. It is a centre for the worship of SHIVA and attracts a million pilgrims every year.

Benedict (c. 480–550 CE) Monk and reformer who wrote a Rule of monastic life which has been followed by MONKS and NUNS of the Western church ever since.

Bhagavad Gita ('song of the lord') A section of the MAHABHARATA in the form of a battlefield dialogue between the warrior prince Arjuna and KRISHNA, disguised as his charioteer.

Bhagavan/Bhagwan Indian title meaning 'lord' or 'worshipful'. It is frequently used of VISHNU. It is also a title of honour used by devotees of holy men.

Bhagavan Shree Rajneesh (1931–90 CE) Indian spiritual teacher and philosopher who founded his own ASHRAM at Pune (Poona) in India.

Bhajana An Indian song or HYMN in praise of God usually sung communally at devotional gatherings and accompanied by musical instruments.

Bhakti Love of, or devotion to, God. It is one of the Hindu paths to union with God (*see* yoga).

Bible The book of CHRISTIANITY, comprising the Hebrew OLD TESTAMENT and the NEW TESTAMENT which, Christians believe, together form a unified message of God's SALVATION.

Bishop The most senior order of ministry in the Christian CHURCH (1) with authority to ordain PRIESTS (2). Many REFORMED CHURCHES do not have bishops.

Black stone Sacred object set in the wall of the Ka'ba sanctuary in Mecca. During the rites of pilgrimage (*see* HAJJ) the faithful try to kiss or touch the stone.

Blavatsky, Helena Petrovna (1831–91 CE) Founder in 1875 of the Theosophical Society (*see* Theosophy), who

claimed to have received the 'ancient wisdom' after seven years in Tibet being taught by various Mahatmas.

Bodhi In various schools of BUDDHISM, 'awakening', or 'perfect wisdom', or 'supreme ENLIGHTENMENT' (1).

Bodhidharma Traditionally the first teacher of Ch'an Buddhism who moved from southern India to China in c. 520 CE.

Bodhisattva In Mahayana Buddhism a saint or semi-divine being who has voluntarily renounced NIRVANA in order to help others to salvation. In popular devotion *bodhisattvas* are worshipped as symbols of compassion.

Bon/Bön A branch of Tibetan VAJRAYANA.

Book of Mormon Sacred SCRIPTURE of MORMONISM which was revealed to Joseph SMITH. The Mormons regard it as the completion of the biblical revelation.

Book of the Dead Name given to various collections of spells, often illustrated, buried with the dead of ancient Egypt to assist their souls through the judgment.

Book of Shadows A term used in contemporary WICCA of the book in which rituals, invocations, and spells are recorded.

Booths/Tabernacles/Sukkot Jewish festival marking the end of the harvest. Branch- or straw-covered booths remind JEWS of God's protection during their forty-year journey through the wilderness.

Brahma The creator god of HINDUISM. With VISHNU and SHIVA, BRAHMA belongs to the TRIMURTI of classical HINDU thought.

Brahman In HINDUISM, the divine, absolute reality.

Brahmins *see* CASTE SYSTEM.

Breviary Liturgical book containing instructions for the recitation of daily services as followed by the Christian clergy, MONKS and NUNS of the Western church, with the proper hymns, psalms, and lessons for each service.

Brighid Celtic goddess of poetry, prophecy, learning, and healing. The Romans associated her Gaulish equivalent with Minerva. She was absorbed into Irish Christianity as St Brighid, whose feast day coincides with a Celtic spring festival.

Buber, Martin (1878–1965 CE) Austrian–Jewish theologian whose religious roots were in HASIDISM.

Buddha ('the one who has awakened'/'enlightened one') (1) Siddhartha GUATAMA, a sage of the SHAKYA tribe who lived in India in around the sixth century BCE, the founder of BUDDHISM.
(2) Any human being or celestial figure who has reached ENLIGHTENMENT (1).

Buddhaghosa Buddhist writer of the fifth century CE who wrote many commentaries on the scriptures and one original work, *The Path of Purification*.

Buddha image Representation of the BUDDHA used in all forms of BUDDHISM. The Buddha is most commonly portrayed in the LOTUS POSTURE, but there are also versions of him standing or lying on one side. The various postures and position of the hands symbolize the defeat of evil, the achieving of ENLIGHTENMENT, the preaching of the DHAMMA, and the final NIRVANA.

Buddhism The religion which developed from the teaching of

the BUDDHA and which spread from India into south-east Asia, later expanding into northern Asia, China and Japan. The two principal divisions are the THERAVADA (HINAYANA) and the MAHAYANA.

Butsudan A Japanese domestic altar to the BUDDHA which contains images or objects of worship and memorial tablets to ancestors.

C

Caliph ('deputy' or 'representative') Title of the leaders of the MUSLIM community after the death of MUHAMMAD. The first three caliphs ruled from MEDINA; the UMMAYADS from Damascus, and the 'ABBASIDS from Baghdad.

Calvin, John (1509–64 CE) French theologian who organized the REFORMATION from Geneva. He emphasized justification by faith and the sole authority of the BIBLE and in particular that each person's eternal destiny was decided irrevocably by God and only those destined for salvation would come to faith.

Cao Dai Religious and political movement which started in southern Vietnam around 1920. Firmly nationalistic, its teachings are a mixture of BUDDHISM and TAOISM.

Cardinal Member of a college of ordained high officials in the ROMAN CATHOLIC Church who, since 1059, have elected the POPE. Cardinals are appointed by the pope.

Cargo cults Term used for new religious movements of Melanesia and New Guinea which imitate European ritual in the hope of thereby receiving European-type material wealth

– 'cargo'. They look for the arrival of a MESSIAH who will banish illness and distribute the cargo among the people.

Caste system The division of a society into groups reflecting and defining the division of labour. In Hinduism, caste is traditionally seen as the creation of Brahma, each caste emerging symbolically from different parts of his body.

Catechism (1) Instruction on Christian faith; for example, instruction in question and answer form given to those preparing for BAPTISM or CONFIRMATION. (2) A popular manual of Christian doctrine.

Catechumen Candidate in training for Christian BAPTISM.

Cathars Members of a medieval heretical Christian sect which flourished in Germany, France, and Italy before their suppression in the thirteenth century. (*See also* ALBIGENSIANS.)

Catholicism CHRISTIANITY as practised by those who emphasize a continuous historical tradition of faith and practice from the time of the APOSTLES (1) to the present day.

Celts Population group occupying much of Central and Western Europe during the first millennium BCE. They worshipped the mother goddess and various local and tribal deities. Evidence suggests that they practised human sacrifice. Their priests were the Druids. *See* DRUIDRY.

Cernunnos ('the horned one') Celtic horned god associated with the earth and fertility, and protector of the animal kingdom.

Chac Rain god of the MAYA (3). He is portrayed as an old man with a long nose and weeping eyes.

Chakras According to Indian thought and many contemporary alternative spiritualities, there are seven (sometimes six) chakras (meaning 'wheels') or spiritual energy centres located in the human body. The chakras are sometimes called 'lotus centres'.

Chant Type of singing in which many syllables are sung on a single note or a repeated short musical phrase. Many religions use chanting in worship. Jews and Christians chant the PSALMS; Buddhists and others their own sacred SCRIPTURES. The repetitive nature of chanting can aid MEDITATION.

Characteristics of existence In the BUDDHA's teaching all existence is marked by the three characteristics: ANATTA; ANICCA; DUKKHA.

Charismatic movement Renewal movement in Catholic and Protestant churches stressing the work and manifestation of the HOLY SPIRIT in the life of the church and of the individual believer.

Chela In Indian religion, a disciple, student, or follower of a GURU.

Chi In Chinese thought, chi is a universal energy, which manifests in the negative and positive polarities of *yin* and *yang*. The manipulation of chi is central to a form of Chinese yoga known as Chi Gung (Chi Gong, Quigong, Chi Kung) to some forms of acupuncture and martial arts, such as t'ai chi.

Chinvat bridge The bridge of judgment in the teaching of ZOROASTER.

Chorten *see* STUPA.

Christ Greek word for MESSIAH. First applied to JESUS OF NAZARETH by his followers, who believed him to fulfil the hopes of ISRAEL, it later became more a proper name of Jesus than a title.

Christadelphians Christian sect founded by John Thomas (1805–71 CE) in the USA, which claims to have returned to the beliefs and practices of the original DISCIPLES. They reject the doctrines of the TRINITY and INCARNATION and have no ordained ministry.

Christian Follower of JESUS OF NAZARETH, the CHRIST, a member of the Christian CHURCH (1).

Christianity Religion based on the teachings of JESUS OF NAZARETH, the CHRIST, and the significance of his life, death, and RESURRECTION.

Christian Science Christian sect founded in the USA by Mary Baker EDDY in 1866. It began with a small group fathered 'to reinstate primitive Christianity and its lost element of healing'.

Christmas The festival of the birth of CHRIST celebrated in Western Christendom on 25 December (not necessarily the date believed to be the actual date of his birth).

Christology Teaching about the nature of the person of CHRIST.

Chuang Tzu Chinese Taoist teacher who lived in the fourth and third centuries BCE. He commended a way of life according to nature which disregarded the conventions of CONFUCIANISM.

Chu Hsi (1130–1200 CE) Chinese philosopher who expounded a system rather similar to that of PLATO.

Church (1) The community of all CHRISTIANS, seen in the NEW TESTAMENT as the 'body of Christ', of which he is the head. (2) Building used for Christian WORSHIP. (3) A local group, organized section, or 'denomination' of the church (1).

Circumcision The cutting off of the prepuce in males or the internal labia in females as a religious rite. It is widely practised in traditional African religion, either shortly after birth or at puberty. In JUDAISM boys are circumcised at eight days of age in commemoration of ABRAHAM's COVENANT with God. Circumcision is also practised in ISLAM.

Civil religion Religion as a system of beliefs, symbols, and practices which legitimate the authority of a society's institutions and bind people together in the public sphere.

Conciliar process The decision making of the CHURCH through the resolutions of specially convened councils or synods in which the will of CHRIST is revealed to the gathered body.

Confirmation Christian rite involving the laying on of hands on those who have been baptized, with prayer for the gift of, or strengthening by, the HOLY SPIRIT. It is often the sign of becoming a communicant member of the CHURCH (1). In Orthodox churches it is performed at BAPTISM.

Confucianism The system of social ethics taught by CONFUCIUS and given imperial recognition in China in the second century CE.

Confucius/K'ung Fu-tzu (551–479 BCE) Chinese civil servant and administrator who became known as a teacher, opening his classes to everyone regardless of wealth or class. His teachings, especially the idea of LI, became the basis of a system of social ethics which greatly influenced Chinese society after his death.

Congregationalists *see* INDEPENDENTS.

Conservative Judaism Movement which tries to stand midway between Orthodox and PROGRESSIVE JUDAISM. It claims to accept the Talmudic tradition (*see* TALMUD) but to interpret the TORAH in the light of modern needs.

Conversion A moral or spiritual change of direction, or the adoption of religious beliefs not previously held.

Coptic Church The Church of Egypt, a more or less tolerated minority in Egypt since the coming of ISLAM in 642 CE. The Church is 'monophysite', i.e. it rejects the teaching about the INCARNATION OF CHRIST agreed at the ECUMENICAL COUNCIL of Chalcedon.

Corroboree Ceremony of the Australian Aboriginals comprising festive and warlike folk dances.

Cosmology (1) The study of the nature of the cosmos. (2) In religion, cosmologies concern the relationship between the divine and the natural world. This relationship is usually described in MYTHS or stories of how God or the gods had brought the world, humanity, and particular peoples into existence and how they continue to relate to them.

Councils of the Church *see* ECUMENICAL COUNCILS.

Counter-Reformation The revival and reform of the Roman Catholic Church as a reaction to the REFORMATION. Its reforms included those of the Council of Trent (1562–63 CE).

Covenant A bargain or agreement. In JUDAISM the chief reference is to that made with MOSES at SINAI: GOD, having liberated his people from Egypt, promises them the land of ISRAEL and his blessing and protection as long as they keep the TORAH. The term is also used of God's special relationship with the house of DAVID. With the defeat of the Kingdom of Judah in 586 BCE, Jeremiah's prophecy of a new covenant written on the people's hearts came into its own. In the Christian NEW TESTAMENT the sacrificial death of JESUS OF NAZARETH marks the sealing of a new covenant between God and the new Israel, the Christian CHURCH, which completes and fulfils the old covenant.

Cranmer, Thomas (1489–1556 CE) Archbishop of Canterbury under Henry VIII who helped overthrow papal authority in England and created a new order of English worship in his *Book of Common Prayer* of 1549 and 1552.

Creation The act of GOD by which the universe came into being. Hence also refers to the universe itself. In JUDAISM, CHRISTIANITY, and ISLAM creation is usually thought of as being *ex nihilo*, from out of nothing that existed before. In HINDUISM it is believed that the universe has been outpoured from God and will contract into him at the end of the age.

Creation myth A story that explains the divine origins of a particular people, a place or the whole world. In some INDIGENOUS RELIGIONS and ancient religions it is ritually re-enacted at the beginning of each year.

Creation Spirituality Initiated in 1977 by the Dominican theologian Matthew Fox (b. 1940), it is highly critical of traditional CHRISTIANITY, which is described as the 'Fall–Redemption' tradition, emphasizing original sin and the fundamental badness of humanity and the created order.

Creed Formal statement of religious belief. In CHRISTIANITY, the two creeds used most commonly today are the APOSTLES' CREED and the NICENE CREED.

Crusades The military expeditions undertaken by Christian armies from Europe from the eleventh to the fourteenth centuries intended to liberate the Holy Land from ISLAM.

Cybele Phrygian MOTHER GODDESS whose ecstatic rites included a bath in the blood of a sacrificial bull. Her cult spread to Greece in the fifth century BCE and to Rome in around 210 BCE.

Cynic Follower of the eccentric Greek philosopher Diogenes (c. 400–325 BCE) who taught that people should seek the most natural and easy way of life, ignoring conventions.

D

Dakhma Persian term for the TOWER OF SILENCE of ZOROASTRIANISM.

Dalai Lama Former religious and secular leader of Tibet, widely held to be the reincarnation of AVALOKITESHVARA.

Daruma Japanese name for BODHIDHARMA. It is also the name of a doll used by Japanese children which resembles Daruma.

Dasara An Indian festival usually celebrated in October.

Dastur Parsi priest who is responsible for the rituals of the FIRE TEMPLES and wears a white turban.

David King of the Israelite tribes around 1000–962 BCE who united them and extended their territory. He was a musician and poet, to whom a number of psalms in the BIBLE are ascribed. The belief is common to JUDAISM and CHRISTIANITY that the MESSIAH would be a descendant of David.

Deacon Junior minister in the Christian CHURCH. The word means 'servant' and the deacon's functions originally included the distribution of ALMS to the poor.

Dead Sea Scrolls Sacred writings of a breakaway Jewish sect which were discovered in 1947 at Qumran on the western shore of the Dead Sea. Many scholars identify the sect with the ESSENES.

Death of God theology Radical American movement of the 1960s seeking to reconstruct Christianity on the basis of atheism.

Deists Followers of a movement for natural religion which flourished in seventeenth-century England. They rejected the idea of revelation and held that the Creator did not interfere in the workings of the universe.

Delphic Oracle Most authoritative source of prophecy and political advice in Ancient Greece. Run by the priests of APOLLO, its prophet was a woman, the Pythia ('pythoness'), who uttered her oracles in a state of induced frenzy.

Demeter Greek goddess of fertility and growth. Worshipped throughout the Greek world, she was identified with the Egyptian ISIS, the Phrygian CYBELE, and the Roman Ceres as the MOTHER GODDESS.

Demiurge Term used in GNOSTICISM to describe the creator god, seen as wilful, passionate, and ignorant.

Demonology Teaching about the demonic and all forms of personified evil.

Dervish Islamic MYSTIC belonging to one of the orders which induce ecstasy by movement, dance, and the recitation of the names of God.

Devadatta Cousin of the BUDDHA, and one of his earliest disciples. In some texts he is in conflict with the Buddha and leads a schismatic movement.

Devil Term generally used to describe an evil spirit. In CHRISTIANITY the devil (SATAN) is the personification of evil who is permitted to tempt and accuse human beings within the overall providence of God.

Dhamma The teaching of the BUDDHA – his analysis of existence expressed in the FOUR NOBLE TRUTHS and his cure as outlined in the NOBLE EIGHTFOLD PATH. Dhamma is sometimes represented as an eight-spoked wheel. (*See also* DHARMA.)

Dhammapada One of the best-known texts of the PALI CANON expounding the essence of THERAVADA Buddhist teachings. It encourages Buddhist disciples to achieve their own salvation, relying on no external saviour or authority.

Dharma In HINDUISM, cosmic order, the law of existence, right conduct. Also, in BUDDHISM, the teaching of the BUDDHA (*see* DHAMMA).

Diana Italian goddess who was associated with wooded places, women, childbirth, and the moon. She became identified with the Greek ARTEMIS.

Diaspora (I) The geographical spread of a people who share a common culture. (2) The term was originally used to describe the spread of the Jewish nation, the dispersion from the land of ISRAEL.

Dietary laws Rules about food and drink that are characteristic of a particular religion. Thus JUDAISM prohibits the simultaneous preparation or eating of milk and meat products, bans totally the eating of, for example, pork and shellfish, and regulates the ritual slaughter of other animals for meat. ISLAM proscribes pork and alcohol. JAINISM bans all animal products.

Digambara ('sky-clad') Member of a major sect of JAINS who followed MAHAVIRA in believing in the virtue of total nudity. Numerous in the warm south of India, they tend to wear robes in public.

Dionysus Greek god of wine and of liberation, a dying and rising god identified with OSIRIS. His cult probably came from Thrace or Phrygia. In the late Hellenistic world (*see* HELLENISM) the cult of Dionysus became an important MYSTERY RELIGION.

Disciple Followers of a religious leader or teaching. In CHRISTIANITY it refers to the original followers of Jesus in the NEW TESTAMENT and is widened to include all Christian 'followers' throughout history.

Divali *see* DIWALI.

Divination The art of the DIVINER.

Divine kingship The belief that kings and queens are descended from the gods and rule with their authority. The ritual purity of the divine king guarantees the community's welfare.

Diviner One who tells the future either by reading the signs of nature in the weather, stars, or the flight of birds, or by the manipulation of objects such as sticks, stones, bones, or playing cards. An important figure in ancient Roman religion, Chinese religion, and many INDIGENOUS RELIGIONS (*see* I CHING; TAROT CARDS).

Divinities Name given to minor gods or spirits in INDIGENOUS RELIGIONS who rule over an area of the world or some human activity – e.g. storms, war, farming, marriage.

Diwali Festival of light celebrated by HINDUS, JAINS, and SIKHS. For Hindus it marks the return of RAMA from exile and his reunion with SITA as told in the RAMAYANA. For Jains it is the beginning of a new ritual and commercial year and celebrates Mahavira's transcendence to MOKSHA and the enlightenment of his disciple Gautama. For Sikhs it is a commemoration of the release from prison of the sixth GURU and his return to the city of Amritsar.

Doctrine A religious teaching or belief which is taught and upheld within a particular religious community.

Dravidian Word describing the pre-Aryan civilization based in the Indus valley. It was overturned by Aryan invaders around 2000 BCE. Today Dravidian peoples inhabit southern India.

Dreams One of the chief sources of revelation to the individual in INDIGENOUS RELIGIONS. Dreams may contain warnings or commands or promises of blessing.

Dreamtime In Australian INDIGENOUS RELIGION, the mythical period in which, according to Aboriginal tradition, ancestral beings moved across the face of the earth forming its physical features.

Druidry (I) The priestly caste of Celtic society. It is likely that they presided at sacrifices, made and enforced legal decisions, and passed on the traditions of learning, magic, healing, and ritual. (2) Since the late eighteenth century, in Wales and Cornwall, self-identified Druids, many of whom were Christian, established national philanthropic and cultural events. (3) In the twentieth century there was a revival of specifically Pagan Druidry.

Dualism (I) The belief that reality has a fundamentally twofold nature. Opposed to MONISM it describes the belief that there is a radical distinction between God and the created world. (2) The belief that there are two fundamentally opposed principles: one of good, the other of evil. This moral dualism is the basis of ZOROASTRIANISM. (3) The belief that the mind and the body are fundamentally different yet act in parallel.

Duat *see* TUAT.

Dukkha Buddhist term for unsatisfactoriness or suffering. Birth, illness, decay, death, and REBIRTH are symptoms of a restless and continuous 'coming-to-be' which marks all existence as *dukkha*.

Durga ('the inaccessible') In Hindu tradition, the consort of SHIVA in one of her terrifying forms.

Dussehra *see* DASARA.

E

Easter The festival of the RESURRECTION of CHRIST, the greatest and oldest festival of the Christian CHURCH (I). Its date is fixed according to the paschal full moon and varies from year to year.

Eastern Orthodox churches Family of self-governing churches looking to the Ecumenical PATRIARCH, the Patriarch of Constantinople, as a symbol of leadership. (*See also* GREAT SCHISM.)

Ecclesiology Teaching about the church.

Eco-feminism A movement which seeks spiritual enlightenment through a synthesis of feminism with concern for the environment.

Ecumenical councils Assemblies of Christian BISHOPS whose decisions were considered binding throughout the Christian church. These ended with the GREAT SCHISM, though the Roman Catholic Church has continued to assemble councils into the twentieth century.

Ecumenical movement Movement for the recovery of unity among the Christian Churches. It dates from the Edinburgh 'World Missionary Conference' of 1910 and today focuses in the WORLD COUNCIL OF CHURCHES.

Eddy, Mary Baker (1821–1910 CE) American spiritual teacher and founder of CHRISTIAN SCIENCE. She believed that orthodox CHRISTIANITY had repressed CHRIST's teaching and practice of spiritual healing and that healing was not miraculous but a natural expression of the divine will. She founded the First Church of Christ Scientist in Boston in 1879.

Eid *see* 'ID AL-'ADHA, 'ID AL-FITR.

Ein Sof Name for God used in Jewish MYSTICISM, in particular in the KABBALAH, meaning the

endless, the absolute infinite whose essence is unrevealed and unknowable.

El Great god and 'creator of creation' among the Canaanite and Phoenician peoples.

Elder An officer of the church in the PRESBYTERIAN and INDEPENDENT CHURCHES.

Election God's choice of ISRAEL to be his people as expressed in the COVENANT at Mount SINAI and manifested in the gift of the land of Israel. In JUDAISM the election of the Jews carries responsibility. They are to bear witness to the reality of God in the world by keeping the TORAH. In Christian theology, the concept is widened to include GENTILE converts to CHRISTIANITY who spiritually inherit the promises made to the PATRIARCHS and to MOSES.

Eleusinian Mysteries MYSTERY RELIGION of DEMETER, centred at Eleusis near Athens.

Eliezer, Israel ben *see* BAAL SHEM TOV.

Elohim Plural form of the Canaanite word for a divinity (*see* DIVINITIES), usually translated 'God' and used as a name of God by the HEBREWS (*see also* EL).

Elysium Paradise of Greek religion. It was held to be either far away across the sea, or a section of the underworld ruled not by HADES, but by Kronos, one of the ancient Titan race.

Emperor, Japanese Since the reign of the legendary JIMMU TENNO the emperors of Japan claimed divine descent from Amaterasu Omikami. SHINTO thus became an expression of imperial power and nationalism.

Enki The water god of ancient Sumerian religion.

Enlightenment (1) Full spiritual awakening. (2) In BUDDHISM, the realization of the truth of all existence which was achieved by the BUDDHA in his meditation at Bodh Gaya. Enlightenment or final enlightenment also refers to the passing into NIRVANA of anyone who follows the Buddha's way and attains release from the cycle of birth and REBIRTH. (*See also* BODHI.) (3) Eighteenth-century European movement of philosophy and science which stressed the supremacy of reason over revelation and tradition.

Enlil The wind god in ancient Sumerian belief. He persuaded the other gods to plan the destruction of humankind in a great flood.

Epic of Gilgamesh Babylonian poem, the earliest versions of which date to the eighteenth century BCE. It tells the story of Gilgamesh's vain quest for the secret of immortality and includes the BABYLONIAN FLOOD STORY.

Epicureanism Philosophical school founded by Epicurus (341–270 BCE) and holding an atomic theory of the universe. It teaches that the gods are irrelevant to human life, the chief end of which is happiness.

Epistle (1) Letter in the NEW TESTAMENT to a Christian community or individual usually from one of the APOSTLES.
(2) Letter on doctrine or practice addressed to a Christian community in post-apostolic times.

Eros Greek god of love, Cupid to the Romans, the son of APHRODITE. In the Christian era 'cupids' became angelic beings symbolizing divine benevolence and compassion.

Eschatology Teaching about the 'last things'. In Christianity this includes discussion of the end of the present world order, the SECOND COMING/PAROUSIA, the final judgment, PURGATORY, HEAVEN, and HELL.

Esoteric Word meaning 'inner', suggesting something (e.g. a knowledge or a teaching) that is available only for the specially initiated and secret from outsiders and perhaps even from ordinary believers.

Essenes Jewish group which withdrew to live a monastic life in the Dead Sea area during the Roman period. Many scholars believe the DEAD SEA SCROLLS were the scriptures of an Essene community.

Eucharist ('thanksgiving') The central act of Christian worship instituted by CHRIST on the night before his death. It involves sharing bread and wine which are sacramentally associated with the body and blood of Christ. (*See* SACRAMENT.)

Evangelicals CHRISTIANS of all denominations who emphasize the centrality of the BIBLE, justification by faith, and the need for personal conversion. In Germany and Switzerland, the term refers to members of the Lutheran as opposed to the Calvinist churches.

Evangelism The preaching of the Christian GOSPEL to the unconverted.

Exile (1) The period between 597 BCE and around 538 BCE when leading JEWS from the former Jewish kingdoms were held in captivity in Babylon. (2) The condition of Jewish life in the DIASPORA, away from the land of ISRAEL.

Exodus The flight of the people of ISRAEL from Egypt under the leadership of MOSES.

Exorcism Removal of sin or evil, particularly an evil spirit in possession of someone, by prayer or ritual action.

Ezra Scribe of the Babylonian EXILE who was sent with a royal warrant from the Persian king to reform religion in JERUSALEM.

F

Faith Attitude of belief, in trust and commitment to a divine being or a religious teaching. It can also refer to the beliefs of a religion, 'the faith', which is passed on from teachers to believers.

Fall of Jerusalem The capture of JERUSALEM and the final destruction of the TEMPLE OF JERUSALEM by the Roman general Titus in 70 CE at the end of a revolt which broke out in 66 CE.

Family Federation for World Peace and Unification Another name for the Holy Spirit Association for the Unification of World Christianity, commonly known as The Unification Church, or, after the name of the founder, the Moonies.

Fasting Total or partial abstinence from food, undertaken as a religious discipline. In INDIGENOUS RELIGIONS it is often a preparation for a ceremony of INITIATION. In JUDAISM and CHRISTIANITY it is a sign of mourning or repentance for SIN. It is also more generally used as a means of gaining clarity of vision and mystical insight.

Fatwa An authoritative legal declaration or religious opinion made by a Muslim scholar, or MUFTI, applying SHARI'A to a particular situation.

Fellowship The common life of Christians marked by unity and mutual love, a creation of the HOLY SPIRIT.

Feminist theology A movement developed first in the USA which uses the experience of being female in a male-dominated society as a basis for critical reflection on Christian thought, tradition, and practice.

Feng Shui Literally translated as 'wind' and 'water', it is the Chinese art of living in harmony with one's environment in order to ensure happiness and prosperity. It emerged during the Han dynasty (206 BCE– 220 CE) and, by the twelfth century, had been developing into the quasi-science of geomancy. Feng shui is used to make wise decisions about the location of buildings, furniture, and gardens, all of which are believed to contribute to human well-being.

Fire sermon One of the BUDDHA's most famous sermons traditionally preached at Gaya to 1000 fire-worshipping ascetics.

Fire temples Parsi temples where the sacred fire of AHURA MAZDA is kept continually burning. (*See* DASTUR; PARSIS.)

Five pillars of Islam Five duties binding upon every Muslim and signifying commitment to Islam. They are: the SHAHADAH (the Islamic creed); SALAH (ritual prayer); SAWM (fasting in the month of RAMADAN); ZAKAH (almsgiving); and HAJJ (undertaking the pilgrimage to MECCA).

Five precepts Ethical restraints for Buddhists, who are to refrain from: taking life, stealing, wrong sexual relations, wrong use of speech, drugs and intoxicants.

Five relationships The codification and application of CONFUCIUS's teaching to the five basic relationships of human life. These are father and son; older brother and younger brother; husband and wife; elder and younger; ruler and subject. The stress is on reciprocity and Confucius believed that such correct behaviour would weld society in 'the way of heaven'.

Four noble truths The BUDDHA's analysis of the problem of existence – a four-stage summary of his teaching: (1) all that exists is unsatisfactory; (2) the cause of unsatisfactoriness (DUKKHA) is craving (TANHA); (3) unsatisfactoriness ends when craving ends; (4) craving can be ended by practising the NOBLE EIGHTFOLD PATH.

Four rightly guided caliphs SUNNI ISLAM accepts ABU BAKR, 'UMAR, 'UTHMAN and 'ALI as legitimate successors to MUHAMMAD.

Four stages of life HINDU outline of a man's ideal spiritual life.

Francis of Assisi (1182–1226 CE) Founder of the Franciscan monastic order who lived by a simple rule of life, rejecting possessions, ministering to the sick and having a special concern for nature.

Freemasonry Originally a religious brotherhood of English masons founded in the twelfth century. In the sixteenth century it spread to the European mainland where in Roman Catholic countries it became associated with Deism (*see* DEISTS). In the UK and USA today it is a semi-secret society which retains certain mystical symbols and ceremonies. Members are committed to a belief in GOD as 'the great architect of the universe', symbolized by an eye.

Frey Norse god of beauty with power over rain and sunshine and the fertility of the earth.

Freyja Norse goddess and sister of FREY; her name means 'lady'. She is patroness of love and sorcery and drives a chariot pulled by cats.

Friends, Society of *see* QUAKERS.

Frigg Chief of the Norse goddesses and wife of ODIN; the goddess of love and fertility. She knows the fates of people but cannot avert destiny.

Fundamentalism The doctrine that the BIBLE is verbally inspired and therefore inerrant and infallible on all matters of doctrine and history. The bases of fundamentalism were set out in twelve volumes, *The Fundamentals*, published between 1910 and 1915.

G

Gabriel (1) An archangel named in both the Old and New Testaments. In the Gospel of Luke he foretells the births of John the Baptist and Jesus. (2) In ISLAM Gabriel (Jibril) is associated with the 'faithful spirit' by whom the QUR'AN was revealed to MUHAMMAD. Jibril also transported Muhammad from MECCA to JERUSALEM and from there to the throne of God during the NIGHT JOURNEY.

Gaia Greek name for MOTHER GODDESS, now revived by the hypothesis originated by J. E. Lovelock according to which all living beings on earth are part of a single living organism.

Gandhi (1869–1948 CE) Leader of the Indian independence movement and the greatest spiritual and political figure of modern India. Disowning violence, he advocated political change through non-violent resistance.

Ganesha Elephant-headed god much loved in popular HINDUISM, especially in western India. He is the god of good beginnings and is a symbol for luck and wealth in business and daily life.

Ganges The holy river of India whose waters are sacred for all HINDUS. Pilgrims wash away evil in its waters and the ashes of the dead are thrown into it.

Gautama/Gotama Family name of the BUDDHA. Legend depicts him as a great prince born into a royal household.

Gemara Part of the Jewish TALMUD that takes the form of a series of rabbinical commentaries on the MISHNAH.

Genius (1) In occult religion, a guardian spirit or familiar. (2) In Roman religion, the spirit of a man, giving rise to his maleness.

Gentile Person who is not a JEW.

Ghat ('holy place') In HINDU use, a word which can refer to a range of hills, a ritual bathing place, or a cremation ground.

Ghost dance A dance which sprang out of a religious movement of the 1870s among Native Americans.

Glossolalia Expression in unknown tongues by people in a heightened spiritual or emotional state. In the Christian CHURCH (1) it is used to express WORSHIP to GOD and prophetic messages, in other religions to express a state of religious ecstasy.

Gnosticism Movement of ESOTERIC teachings rivalling, borrowing from and contradicting early CHRISTIANITY. Gnostic sects

were based on MYTHS which described the creation of the world by a deluded DEMIURGE and taught a way of salvation through *gnosis*, 'knowledge' of one's true divine self.

Gobind Singh, Guru (1666–1708 CE) The tenth GURU of the Sikh community. He formalized the Sikh religion, requiring Sikhs to adopt a distinctive name and dress.

God (1) The creator and sustainer of the universe; the absolute being on whom all that is depends. (2) A being with divine power and attributes; a deity, a major DIVINITY.

Goddess (1) Female form of god.
(2) The supreme being conceived as female as in some modern Pagan religious movements. Worshippers of the Goddess claim that they are continuing the ancient religion of the MOTHER GODDESS who was a personification of nature.

Good Friday The Friday before EASTER, in CHRISTIANITY, kept by the CHURCH (1) as a holy day, sometimes including FASTING, penance, and witness, in memory of the crucifixion of Jesus CHRIST.

Gospel (1) One of the four accounts of the 'good news' about Jesus in the NEW TESTAMENT. (2) The Christian message, proclamation of 'good news', referring especially to Jesus' teaching about the KINGDOM OF GOD and to the preaching of the CHURCH about Jesus. (3) The ritual reading of a set portion from the Gospels (1) in the context of the EUCHARIST. (4) A partial account of the life and teaching of Jesus, usually ascribed to

a New Testament figure but rejected by the Church as heretical.

Gospel of Thomas Syriac text of a collection of sayings of Jesus discovered at Nag Hammadi in Egypt in 1947.

Gotama *see* GAUTAMA.

Grace (1) Unmerited favour, especially in the divine salvation of the unworthy. An essential concept in CHRISTIANITY, where it is contrasted with merit, Christians believe that nobody receives SALVATION because he or she deserves it but only by God's grace. (2) A prayer or blessing before a meal.

Great Schism The SCHISM declared in 1054 CE between the Eastern and Western Christian churches resulting from disagreements over the pope's claim to supremacy, and the doctrine of the HOLY SPIRIT.

Gregory of Nyssa (c. 330–395 CE) Christian theologian who helped develop the doctrine of the TRINITY and expounded the BIBLE as a spiritual path leading to the perfect contemplation of God.

Ground of Being Phrase used by German-US theologian Paul Tillich (1886–1965 CE) to describe GOD. It stresses the immanence of God as depth or ground rather than his transcendence as creator.

Gurdjieff, George Ivanovich (1873–1949 CE) Spiritual teacher whose book *Meetings with Remarkable Men* relates his search for wisdom.

Gurdwara SIKH temple and meeting place, consisting of a worship area which houses the GURU GRANTH SAHIB, and a cooking and eating area, the *langar*, for the meal which ends Sikh worship.

Guru ('teacher') A spiritual teacher or guide who, in Indian religion, awakens a disciple to a realization of his or her own divine nature. In SIKH religion it refers to the ten teachers, from Guru NANAK to Guru GOBINDH SINGH, who ruled the community.

Guru Granth Sahib *see* ADI GRANTH.

H

Hades (1) Greek god of the dead and ruler of the UNDERWORLD. Because it was considered unlucky to speak his name, he is often referred to as Pluto (the 'rich'). (2) Greek name for the underworld, the abode of the dead. In the Septuagint version of the HEBREW BIBLE it translates *sheol*. In Christian usage it is sometimes used for the interim abode of the departed as distinguished from HELL, the abode of the damned.

Hadith Traditions of MUHAMMAD's words and actions, many of which complement or elucidate the directions of the QUR'AN.

Hagadah/Haggadah Prayer-book used by Jews on the eve of PASSOVER for the SEDER ritual.

Hajj Pilgrimage to MECCA which is one of the FIVE PILLARS OF ISLAM and which MUSLIMS are obliged to make at least once in a lifetime. On arrival at Mecca, pilgrims make seven anticlockwise circuits of the KA'BA and, if possible, kiss the BLACK STONE.

Halakhah (from HEBREW verb 'to walk') A legal teaching based on the midrashic exposition of a Hebrew text (*see* MIDRASH).

Hamartiology Teaching about sin.

Hammurabi (eighteenth century BCE) Mesopotamian ruler who produced a law code laying down punishments for various transgressions and enunciating principles for the conduct of business and social life.

Hanukkah ('dedication') Eight-day Jewish festival marked by the lighting of ritual candles which celebrates the rededication of the TEMPLE OF JERUSALEM by JUDAS MACCABEUS in 164 BCE.

Hanuman Monkey-god of popular HINDUISM. In the RAMAYANA he led a monkey army against a host of demons.

Hara-Kiri The Japanese traditional practice of ritual suicide among the warrior classes.

Hare Krishna Mantra used by devotees of KRISHNA to induce ecstatic union with the divine. (*See also* INTERNATIONAL SOCIETY FOR KRISHNA CONSCIOUSNESS.)

Hasidim ('the pious') Followers of BAAL SHEM TOV, who taught a new kind of HASIDISM in the eighteenth century CE.

Hasidism Jewish mystical movement with roots in the KABBALAH which arose in the eighteenth century in response to the teachings of BAAL SHEM TOV. It stressed the presence of God in everyday life and the value of prayer.

Heathenism Also referred to as 'The Northern Tradition' or 'Asatru' ('faith in the deities'), Heathenism is a form of contemporary Paganism which focuses on Anglo-Saxon, Norse, and Germanic traditions. Popular Heathen teachings include belief that this world, MIDGARD/Middle Earth, is one of nine linked by the 'World Tree', YGGDRASIL. There are two groups of deities, the ÆSIR and the VANIR. A popular form of

Heathenism is Odinism, the spirituality of which focuses on the Norse god ODIN.

Heaven (I) The realm of God or of the gods. (2) In CHRISTIANITY the dwelling place of God and the ultimate home of the saved, regarded both as a place and a state.

Hebrew (I) A member of the Semitic tribes which emerged as the people of ISRAEL. (2) The (Semitic) language of the ancient people of Israel, of the HEBREW BIBLE, and of the modern state of Israel.

Hebrew Bible The Jewish SCRIPTURES which comprise the Books of the Law (*see* TORAH), the PROPHETS, and the WRITINGS.

Heimdall White god and watcher of the gods in Norse religion.

Hecate An earth goddess who probably originated in Asia Minor. A popular deity in contemporary Paganism.

Hell Realm where the wicked go after death. In CHRISTIANITY, it is total separation from God. Most religions describe a place or a condition for the wicked following death. ZOROASTRIANISM, JUDAISM, and ISLAM all describe such a state following divine judgment after death. Even religions which have a doctrine of reincarnation, such as Buddhism and Hinduism, include teachings about hells (although belief in reincarnation makes them quite different from the teachings of Christianity and Islam).

Hellenism The adoption of the Greek language, culture, philosophy, and ideas, particularly around the Mediterranean, from the time of Alexander the Great (356–323 BCE).

Hera Greek goddess, the wife of ZEUS and queen of heaven.

Heresy The denial of a defined doctrine of the Christian faith. The word means 'chosen thing' and refers to the heretic's preference for an individual option over the consensus of the CHURCH (I).

Hermes Greek messenger god and son of Zeus, protector of travellers, bringer of luck, and god of thieves and merchants.

Hermeticism Mystical movement based on a collection of Egyptian scriptures from the first to third centuries CE.

Herzl, Theodor (1860–1904 CE) Leader of the Zionist movement (*see* ZIONISM).

Hesiod Greek poet, probably of the eighth century BCE, whose THEOGONY sought to draw together the ancestries of the Greek gods, understanding creation in terms of procreation.

High Priest Traditional head of the Jewish priesthood and organizer of TEMPLE worship. His function was to enter the Holy of Holies and offer sacrifice on the DAY OF ATONEMENT.

Hijrah ('going forth') The migration of MUHAMMAD from MECCA to MEDINA in 622 CE. The MUSLIM calendar, the *Hijri* calendar, counts years 'after *Hijrah*'.

Hillel Pharisaic Jewish teacher of the first century CE. He was known for his humane and lenient interpretations of the TORAH.

Hinayana ('lesser vehicle') Buddhist term used to indicate the doctrine of salvation for oneself alone, in contrast to MAHAYANA. Most Buddhists of south-east Asia prefer the term THERAVADA to describe this school of BUDDHISM.

Hindu Word used by Arabs to describe people living beyond the Indus Valley. Today it refers generally to people practising Indian religion who are neither Muslim, Sikh, Parsi, nor Jain, and also to their religion, Hinduism.

Hinduism A term coined by Europeans for a religious tradition and social system that emerged in India. It is an umbrella term for an enormous range of beliefs and practices, from the worship of local village deities to the thought of a great philosopher such as Shankara.

Hoa Hao Offshoot of the Vietnamese CAO DAI movement. It is Buddhist-based and has been strongly nationalistic.

Holi HINDU spring festival which celebrates the love of KRISHNA and RADHA.

Holiness The sacred power, strangeness, and otherness of the divine. In the BIBLE and the QUR'AN the term has moral implications and refers to God's purity and righteousness as well as to that which invokes awe.

Holocaust (from the Latin BIBLE's word for 'whole burnt offering') The name given to Hitler's extermination of six million Jews in the Nazi death camps in Europe from 1941–45. The Holocaust is also referred to by many Jews as the *Shoah* (catastrophe).

Holy Communion Name widely used by Anglicans and some Protestants for the Christian EUCHARIST.

Holy Spirit The third person of the Christian TRINITY. The Holy Spirit is the source of faith and new life in the believer and the church, giving 'spiritual gifts', guidance, and holiness.

Holy Spirit Association for the Unification of World Christianity *see* FAMILY FEDERATION FOR WORLD PEACE AND UNIFICATION.

Homer Author of the Greek epics the *Iliad* and the *Odyssey*, which date from between the tenth and eighth centuries BCE.

Honen (1133–1212 CE) Japanese teacher of PURE LAND BUDDHISM.

Horus Egyptian hawk-headed sky god, associated with the king.

House churches/New churches Networks of charismatic, non-denominational churches which started in the 1960s. Members claim they are restoring the conditions of the primitive church, which met for worship in members' houses.

Hsün-tzu Chinese Confucian scholar of the third century BCE who blended the philosophies CONFUCIANISM and TAOISM.

Huaca Any of the multitude of DIVINITIES recognized by the INCAS; also, an Inca holy place, shrine, or temple.

Huiracocha *see* VIRACOCHA.

Huitzilopochtli AZTEC god of war and the sun. His name means 'hummingbird wizard' and he was perpetually at war with darkness and night.

Hui Yuan *see* PURE LAND BUDDHISM.

Humanism Way of life based on the belief that what is good for human beings is the highest good.

Hus, Jan (1374–1415 CE) Bohemian reformer who denounced the worldliness of the clergy.

Hymn A sacred song sung in the context of communal worship; a PSALM of communal praise. Hymns are particularly important in Christian and

Sikh worship and in the gatherings of the Hindu BHAKTI cults (*see* BHAJANA).

I

I Ching/Book of Changes One of the five classics of Chinese literature which was originally attributed to CONFUCIUS but is now thought to be much earlier.

Ibn Rushd (1126–98 CE) MUSLIM philosopher, known in the West as AVERROES, who was greatly influenced by PLATO and ARISTOTLE.

Icon A likeness of a divine figure or SAINT painted on wood or inland in mosaic and used in public or private devotion.

'Id al-'Adha The great festival of the MUSLIM year, commemorating Ibrahim's preparedness to sacrifice his son, Isma'el.

'Id al-Fitr The MUSLIM feast which ends the fasting month of RAMADAN.

Ijma' The consensus of opinion of the MUSLIM community.

Ijtihad A way for the Islamic community to develop its law to deal with new situations. It is a ruling given by one MUSLIM teacher, rather than by general consensus (*see* IJMA').

Imam Meaning 'model' or 'example', the term refers to three types of leader within Islam. (1) The leader of ritual prayer in the local community. (2) Used in a more exalted sense, the term refers to leaders of particular Islamic schools of thought. Similarly, it is an honorific title given to great Islamic scholars (e.g. AL-GHAZALI). (3) It has a special significance in the Shi'ite community. The term refers to a unique intercessor with exceptional spiritual authority,

knowledge, and charisma. Imams are agents of divine illumination, indispensable for understanding the relevance of divine revelation for the contemporary community.

Immortals Various beings who live in the Realm of Great Purity, according to the teachings of TAOISM

Inanna The MOTHER GODDESS as worshipped in ancient Sumer.

Inca The divine king who ruled over the INCAS.

Incarnation (1) The Christian doctrine that GOD became human in Jesus CHRIST, so possessing both human and divine natures. (2) A term sometimes used for the HINDU doctrine of the AVATAR.

Incas Empire centred on Cuzco in modern Peru from around 1100 CE until the Spanish conquest (1532 CE).

Incense Sweet-smelling smoke used in worship, made by burning certain aromatic substances.

Inclusive language A response to feminism which tries to eradicate the assumption in speech and writing that maleness is more normally human than femaleness.

Independence, Day of Jewish festival of thanksgiving on the anniversary of the birth of the state of ISRAEL (4).

Independents/ Congregationalists CHRISTIANS who uphold the authority and independence of each local church, claiming this system to be the earliest form of church order.

Index of prohibited books The official list of books which members of the Roman Catholic Church are forbidden to possess or read, first issued in 1557.

Indigenous religions The preferred term for religions which are sometimes referred to as 'primal', 'tribal', 'traditional', 'primitive', and 'non-/pre-literate' religions. Contemporary indigenous religions include Native American religion and Australian Aboriginal religion.

Indra ARYAN god of war and storm. There are 200 hymns to him in the RIG VEDA (*see* VEDAS).

Indulgence The remission by the Christian church of a period of correction in PURGATORY. The sale of indulgences by unscrupulous 'pardoners' was one of the abuses which led to the REFORMATION.

Initiation Ceremony marking coming of age, or entry into adult membership of a community. It is also used of the secret ceremonies surrounding membership of the MYSTERY RELIGIONS. (*See also* CONFIRMATION; NAVJOTE; RITES OF PASSAGE; SACRED THREAD CEREMONY.)

Inquisition Papal office for identifying heretics, founded by Pope Gregory IX and staffed by the Franciscan and Dominican religious orders.

Intercession Prayer offered on behalf of others by a believer on earth or by a SAINT in HEAVEN. In CHRISTIANITY, supremely the work of CHRIST, who intercedes for men and women before GOD.

International Society for Krishna Consciousness (ISKCON) Founded in 1965 by A. C. Bhaktivedanta Swami Prabhupada (1896–1977), and popularly known as the Hare Krishna movement.

Inti The SUN GOD of the INCAS.

Ishtar Babylonian goddess, mother, and wife of TAMMUZ

and associated with the fertility rites of death and resurrection. Worshipped in various forms all over the Ancient Near East, she was known as Astarte to the Phoenicians and as Ashtoreth to the Hebrews.

Isis Great Egyptian goddess of motherhood and fertility. The sister and wife of OSIRIS, she restored him to life after he was murdered by SETH.

Isis cult MYSTERY RELIGION based on the MYTH of ISIS and OSIRIS which became particularly popular in the Roman world from the first century CE.

Islam (infinitive of the Arabic verb 'to submit') Teachings derived from the QUR'AN, which is the revelation to MUHAMMAD, a religion of submission to the will of Allah. (*See also* ALLAH; MECCA; MUSLIM; FIVE PILLARS; SUNNI; SHIA.)

Isma'ilis A group of SHI'A Muslims who accept the legitimacy of Ismail and his son as the sixth and seventh Imams (*see also* MAHDI; TWELVERS).

Israel (1) Name given by GOD to Jacob the patriarch and hence to his descendants, the 'people of Israel'. (2) The land promised by God to Abram (ABRAHAM) in the early traditions of JUDAISM. (3) The Northern Kingdom of Israel which seceded from Solomon's kingdom in 922 BCE and was destroyed by the Assyrians in 722 BCE. (4) The modern state of Israel, founded in Palestine as a Jewish state in 1948 CE.

Izanagi The sky god in SHINTO, and the father of Amaterasu. With his consort, Izanami, he created the islands of Japan.

J

Jade Emperor The supreme divinity in TAOISM, who came into prominence about the tenth century CE. He presided over life and death and kept account of human actions.

Jahannam MUSLIM name for HELL which is frequently mentioned in the QUR'AN as a place of scorching fire and black smoke.

Jain ('one who has conquered') A follower of the religion known as JAINISM.

Jainism Religion of India that derives its name from Jina (conqueror). This term (and the related term Tirthankara) is used of a religious teacher who is believed to have attained enlightenment and omniscience. The most recent Jina was MAHAVIRA, who is regarded as the founder of Jainism. Early in its history Jainism separated into two main sects: DIGAMBARA Jainism and SHVETAMBARA Jainism. (*See also* DIGAMBARA; JINA, JIVA; MAHAVIRA; PARSVA; SHVETAMBARA.)

Janus Roman god of beginnings whose name derives from *janua*, 'entrance' or 'gate'. He is portrayed with a two-faced head, facing both ways.

Jarovit Slavic war god.

Jehovah *see* YHWH.

Jehovah's Witnesses Christian sect founded in the 1870s by C. T. RUSSELL. It propagates its own version of the BIBLE (The New World Translation), which it regards as inspired and inerrant, and stresses the imminent return of CHRIST.

Jerome (c. 342–420 CE) Translator of the BIBLE into Latin (the 'Vulgate' version). He wrote many commentaries on the text.

Jerusalem Fortified city captured by DAVID in the c.

1000 BCE which became the capital and principal sanctuary for the people of ISRAEL. It has remained the focus of Jewish religious aspirations and ideals. It is a holy city for CHRISTIANS because of its association with the passion, death, and RESURRECTION of JESUS OF NAZARETH. For MUSLIMS it is the holiest city after MECCA. The MOSQUE of the Dome of the Rock stands over the site of Muhammad's NIGHT JOURNEY.

Jesus of Nazareth Teacher, prophet, and worker of miracles in first-century Palestine and founder of Christianity. He taught the coming of the KINGDOM OF GOD with forgiveness and new life for all who believed.

Jew (1) A person who is regarded as a member of the Jewish race. (2) A person who identifies with JUDAISM, the religion of the Jews.

Jihad ('striving') A much-misunderstood concept, jihad is the relentless fight against worldliness.

Jimmu Tenno Traditionally the first Japanese EMPEROR, who began his reign in 660 BCE.

Jinas Also called 'Tirthankaras' ('ford-makers'), *Jinas* ('conquerors') are Jain religious teachers who have attained enlightenment and omniscience by conquering SAMSARA (the continuous cycle of birth, death, and rebirth to which those with KARMA are bound).

Jinja The SHINTO sanctuary. They vary in size from roadside shrines to beautifully located halls surrounded by trees and entered through traditional arched gateways (*see* TORII).

Jinn Spiritual creatures in Islamic belief who are made of smokeless flame.

Jiva A soul or 'life monad' according to JAIN belief. Jivas

are infinite and omniscient but in this world KARMA weighs them down into a material existence.

Jodo Japanese name for PURE LAND BUDDHISM.

Jodo Shinshu ('True Pure Land Sect') A refinement of PURE LAND BUDDHISM founded by SHINRAN.

Johanan ben Zakkai Creator of the academic SANHEDRIN in Jamnia after the FALL OF JERUSALEM in 70 CE.

Judah HaNasi ('The Prince', 135–217 CE) Leader of the academic Jewish SANHEDRIN in Galilee. He was responsible for compiling the MISHNAH.

Judaism The religion that developed from the religion of ancient ISRAEL and has been practised ever since by the JEWS. It is an ethical MONOTHEISM based on the revelation of GOD to MOSES on Mount SINAI and his giving of the Law (*see* TORAH).

Judas Maccabeus (d. 160 BCE) Jewish revolutionary who opposed the Hellenizing Seleucid emperor Antiochus Epiphanes, who had set up an image of Olympian ZEUS in the TEMPLE OF JERUSALEM. Though he achieved religious freedom, he failed to establish a free Jewish state.

Judgment The divine assessment of individuals and the settling of their destinies, a notion found in many religions. Christianity teaches that judgment is based on the individual's response to Christ.

Jumis Latvian harvest god.

Jung, C. G. (Carl Gustav) (1875–1961 CE) Swiss psychiatrist who invented the theory of ARCHETYPES. He investigated the significance of MYTHS, symbols, and DREAMS, and found in them evidence for a 'collective unconscious' which was at the root of religion.

Juno Roman goddess, counterpart of the Greek HERA, and wife of JUPITER.

Jupiter/Jove Principal god of the Romans, identified with the Greek ZEUS.

K

Ka The guardian spirit of each individual which, according to Egyptian belief, survived death and lived on in the next world, where it was reunited with *ba*, breath.

Ka'ba ('cube') The sanctuary in MECCA to which all MUSLIMS turn in prayer. Set in its eastern corner is the BLACK STONE.

Kabbalah Jewish mystical tradition which flourished in the teaching of two schools: the practical school based in Germany which concentrated in prayer and MEDITATION; the speculative school in Provence and Spain in the thirteenth and fourteenth centuries.

Kabir (c. 1440–1518) Indian poet and hymn writer who influenced the development of early Sikhism. He attempted a synthesis of ISLAM and HINDUISM, rejecting the CASTE SYSTEM and CIRCUMCISION, but teaching the love of God, rebirth, and liberation.

Kali Consort of the HINDU god SHIVA, and both the goddess of destruction and the Great Mother, giver of life.

Kalki In HINDU tradition, the last AVATAR of VISHNU who will descend on a white horse, with a sword, to kill the wicked and bring the world to an end.

Kami Powers of nature which are venerated in SHINTO. They are beneficent spirits who help in the processes of fertility and growth.

Kamma PALI word for KARMA.

Karaites ('readers of scripture') Heretical Jewish school of the eighth century CE which denied the validity of the TALMUD and the oral tradition. They held to a literalist view of the TORAH.

Karma SANSKRIT word for work or action. In Indian belief every action has inevitable consequences which attach themselves to the doer requiring reward or punishment. Karma is thus the moral law of cause and effect.

Karo, Joseph (1488–1575 CE) Jewish legal teacher and MYSTIC.

Kashrut The code in JUDAISM according to which food is ritually clean or unclean. It refers particularly to meat, which must be slaughtered so as to ensure the minimum of pain and the draining off of blood.

Kashi *see* BENARES.

Khalsa Originally the militant community of SIKHS organized by Guru GOBIND SINGH in 1699 CE. Now it is the society of fully committed adult members of the Sikh community.

Khandha *see* SKHANDHA.

Kharijites MUSLIM party of seceders from 'ALI, the fourth CALIPH. They opposed the UMMAYAD DYNASTY, believing that the succession should be based on a democratic vote. They were puritans strongly critical of the moral laxity that developed as Ummayad power increased.

Khnum Creator god of ancient Egypt.

Kingdom of God The rule of God on earth. In JUDAISM God is king of the universe, the sole creator and ruler. The kingdom will be brought by the MESSIAH and will include the restoration of ISRAEL. In CHRISTIANITY, JESUS OF NAZARETH proclaimed

the arrival of the kingdom in himself. Christians share in the kingdom now, and it will be completed and fulfilled at his SECOND COMING.

Kitab-i-Aqdas Meaning 'the most holy book', this is one of the most important works of Bahá'u'lláh. It contains most of the laws and many social ordinances of Bahá'u'lláh.

Kitab-i-Iqan Meaning 'the book of certitude', this is one of the most important works of Bahá'u'lláh. It addresses a range of theological questions and provides interpretations of the BIBLE and the QUR'AN.

Koan Technique used in RINZAI ZEN to bring about SATORI.

Kojiki SHINTO scripture which is the oldest book in the Japanese language, though it is written using Chinese characters.

Koko Spirits of dead ancestors in the popular cults of the Zuñi people of northern Mexico.

Kol Nidrei *see* YOM KIPPUR.

Kook, Abraham Isaac Rabbi (1868–1935 CE) First Chief Rabbi of the Holy Land.

Koran *see* QUR'AN.

Kotel *see* WESTERN WALL.

Krishna The eighth incarnation of VISHNU according to HINDU tradition. Though of noble birth, he was brought up as a cowherd. Eventually he obtained his inheritance and ruled in justice. He is also the main character in the BHAGAVAD GITA, where he appears disguised as the charioteer of Prince Arjuna.

Krishnamurti, Jiddhu (1895–1986) Indian spiritual teacher who was brought up by a leading Theosophist, Mrs Annie Besant, who proclaimed him as a World Teacher.

Kshatriya *see* CASTE SYSTEM.

Kuan-yin Chinese name for the great BODHISATTVA AVALOKITESHVARA, especially when thought of in female form.

Kukai (774–835 CE) Japanese Buddhist teacher who tried to reconcile BUDDHISM with SHINTO. He is sometimes regarded as a manifestation of the Buddha VAIROCANA.

Kundalini Energy that is coiled like a serpent at the base of the spine according to TANTRISM. When awakened by YOGA it leaps up the spine to the brain giving an experience of union and liberation re-enacting the sexual union of SHIVA and SHAKTI.

L

Laity (from Greek *laos*, 'people') The non-ordained members of a religious community (*see* ORDINATION), or those with no specialist religious function.

Lakshmi Lord VISHNU's consort. She appears in the *Rig Veda* (*see* VEDAS) as good fortune. She is involved in Vishnu's descents to earth as an AVATAR. Some associate her with SITA and RADHA, the consorts of RAMA and KRISHNA.

Lama Tibetan religious leader, a title formerly applied only to abbots, but later used of any monk. Lamas have been credited with magical powers which are said to be attained through years of arduous training.

Lao-tzu Traditionally the author of the TAO TE CHING and a contemporary of CONFUCIUS.

Lares Roman agricultural spirits who were worshipped at crossroads and in the home as household gods.

Latter-Day Saints, Church of Jesus Christ of see MORMONISM; SMITH, JOSEPH.

Lent In CHRISTIANITY, a forty-day period of FASTING and penitence before EASTER, originally a period of training and examination for those who were baptized at Easter.

Ley lines Straight geological lines of spiritual force which some adherents of NEW AGE RELIGIONS believe were discovered and used in the NEOLITHIC PERIOD.

Li CONFUCIUS's concept of propriety or reverence which he believed should direct all relationships between members of society.

Libation The RITUAL outpouring of drink as an offering to DIVINITIES or ancestor spirits.

Liberation Theology Originating in Latin America, associates SALVATION with the political liberation of oppressed peoples.

Limbo According to Roman Catholic doctrine, the dwelling place of souls (e.g. of unbaptized children) excluded from HEAVEN but not subjected to HELL or PURGATORY.

Liturgy ('public service') (I) Any regular prescribed service of the Christian Church. (2) The EUCHARIST, especially in ORTHODOXY.

Logos Greek for word or principle. In STOICISM it identified the principle of reason, immanent in nature.

Loki The opponent of the ÆSIR in Norse mythology who is bent on their downfall and the overthrow of the world order.

Lord's Supper Name for the Christian EUCHARIST favoured by the Protestant reformers who saw the Eucharist primarily as a memorial of CHRIST's death.

Lotus Type of water lily, a Buddhist symbol of ENLIGHTENMENT.

Lotus posture Style of sitting upright and cross-legged, used as a position for MEDITATION in Hindu and Buddhist practice.

Lotus Sutra MAHAYANA Buddhist scripture in the form of a sermon preached by the BUDDHA (I) to a vast throng of gods, demons, rulers, and cosmic powers. It contains the essence of Mahayana teachings on the eternity of the Buddha, the universal capacity for Buddhahood, and the compassion and power of the BODHISATTVAS

Lucretius (c. 100–55 BCE) Roman poet and philosopher who expounded the materialist and rationalist doctrines of EPICUREANISM in his poem 'De rerum natura' ('On the nature of things').

Lugh (Irish: 'The Shining One'; Welsh: Lleu) Most honoured of the Celtic gods, a war god, the patron of commerce and moneymaking, and prototype of human beings.

Luria, Isaac (CE 1514–72) Jewish teacher from Spain who developed the Kabbalistic teachings of the Zohar (see KABBALAH).

Luther, Martin (1483–1546 CE) Founder of the German REFORMATION. He held that people could only be justified before God by faith in JESUS CHRIST, not by any 'works' of religion.

Lutheran churches Important churches in Scandinavia, other parts of Western Europe, and the USA. They value theological study and emphasize the weekly sermons.

M

Maccabees The family and supporters of JUDAS MACCABEUS. They were the forerunners of the ZEALOTS in fighting a holy war against alien rulers.

Madhva (1197–1276 CE) Indian philosopher who founded a dualist school (see DUALISM) in opposition to the MONISM of SHANKARA.

Magi Priestly class of ancient Persia who at first opposed the spread of ZOROASTER's teachings.

Magic The manipulation of natural or supernatural forced by SPELLS and RITUALS for good or harmful ends.

Mahabharata One of the two great epics of the HINDU scriptures compiled by the third or second century BCE. Ascribed to the sage Vyasa, it tells of the war between two families, the Kauravas and the Pandus.

Maharishi Mahesh Yogi see TRANSCENDENTAL MEDITATION.

Mahatma SANSKRIT title of great respect or veneration meaning 'great soul'.

Mahatma Gandhi see GANDHI.

Mahavira Great JAIN teacher who traditionally lived 599–527 BCE, though this is disputed. He abolished the distinctions of the CASTE SYSTEM and tried to spread his teaching among the Brahmins.

Mahayana ('large/great vehicle') The form of BUDDHISM practised in Nepal, China, Tibet, Korea, and Japan. Mahayana accepts more scriptures than THERAVADA, and has developed various forms of popular devotion based on the doctrine of the BODHISATTVAS.

Mahdi 'The guided one' who according to SHI'A teaching will come at the end of the world. The Mahdi is identified with Muhammad al-Mahdi who disappeared in 880 CE and is believed to be hidden until his reappearance.

Maimonides, Moses (1135–1204 CE) Jewish philosopher who lived in Spain and later Egypt and attempted a synthesis of Aristotelian and biblical teaching.

Maitreya The Buddha-to-be, or the next BUDDHA to appear on earth according to MAHAYANA teachings.

Mana Polynesian word for the invisible spiritual power which permeates all things. It has been adopted as a general term in the study of INDIGENOUS RELIGIONS.

Mandaeans Members of a Gnostic sect teaching redemption through a divine saviour who has lived on earth and defeated the powers of darkness.

Mandala A visual aid in the form of a series of coloured concentric circles used in BUDDHISM and HINDUISM. Concentration on the mandala enables the disciple to see himself in relation to the Buddha's compassion and thus to achieve ENLIGHTENMENT.

Manichaeans Followers of Mani (around 216–276 CE), a Persian teacher whose strict ascetic system was designed to release the divine spark trapped in every person by the wiles of SATAN.

Manitou Name used by the Algonquin Indians of North America to refer to spiritual powers.

Mantra A symbolic sound causing an internal vibration which helps to concentrate the mind and aids self-realization, e.g. the repeated syllable 'om', and in Tibetan Buddhism the phrase OM MANI PADME HUM. A mantra is sometimes given by a spiritual teacher to a disciple as an INITIATION.

Mara In BUDDHISM, the evil one, temptation.

Marduk Babylonian deity who superseded the Sumerian god ENLIL. He was addressed as Bel, the Supreme Lord.

Marriage, sacred A religious rite involving real or simulated sexual intercourse which represents the marriage of earth and sky in the fertilization of the soil and the growth of the crops.

Mars Roman war god, regarded second only to JUPITER.

Martyr ('witness') Title originally applied to Christians who died rather than renounce their faith during times of persecution. Now a term applied to anyone who dies for a religious belief.

Mary, the mother of Jesus Because of her role in the divine plan of salvation, Mary is honoured by all Christians and venerated by Roman Catholic and Eastern Orthodox Christians.

Masoretes A group of Jewish scholars from the Babylonian and Palestinian schools who from the seventh to the eleventh centuries CE supplied the text of the HEBREW BIBLE with vowel points and divided it up into sentences and paragraphs.

Mass Name for the Christian EUCHARIST derived from the words of dismissal.

Matsuri Japanese name for a solemn celebration intended to invoke worship of the SHINTO gods and obedience to their moral will.

Maya (1) Illusion or deception in HINDU thought. *Maya* is concerned with the diverse phenomenal world perceived

by the senses. It is the trick of *maya* to convince people that this is all that exists and thus blind them to the reality of BRAHMAN and the oneness of existence. (2) Legendary mother of the BUDDHA (1). (3) People of an ancient Central American empire which spread from Yucatan to El Salvador. Mayan civilization was at its height around 300–900 CE and was finally broken up by the Spaniards in the sixteenth century.

Mecca Holy city of Islam, in Saudi Arabia, the birthplace of MUHAMMAD, and later the base for his MUSLIM state after its conquest in 630 CE. Pilgrimage to Mecca, HAJJ, is one of the FIVE PILLARS OF ISLAM and all Muslims are required to face Mecca to perform ritual prayer five times a day.

Medicine man *see* WITCH DOCTOR.

Medina Formerly Yathrib, city 100 miles/169 km north of MECCA, the political base for MUHAMMAD from 622 CE until his conquest of Mecca.

Meditation Deep and continuous reflection, practised in many religions with a variety of aims, e.g. to attain self-realization or, in theistic religions, to attain union with the divine will.

Medium One who is possessed by the spirit of a dead person or a DIVINITY and, losing his or her individual identity, becomes the mouthpiece for the other's utterance.

Megaliths Large stone monuments dating from the late NEOLITHIC PERIOD. They mark burial mounds and temples and may have served as a calendar of times and seasons.

Meher Baba (1894–1969 CE) Indian spiritual leader, regarded by his followers as an AVATAR.

Mencius (b. 371 BCE) Confucian teacher who expanded and developed CONFUCIUS's teachings.

Mendelssohn, Moses (1729–86 CE) German Jewish rationalist philosopher who taught that the three central propositions of JUDAISM are: the existence of God; providence; the immortality of the soul.

Mercury Roman messenger god, identified with the Greek HERMES.

Merit In BUDDHISM the fruit of good actions which can be devoted to the welfare of other beings.

Merlin Bard and magician in the romances of the CELTS, later the mentor of ARTHUR. He has become a popular figure in some forms of contemporary Pagan spirituality.

Messiah ('anointed one') A HEBREW word referring to the person chosen by God to be king. (1) After the end of the Israelite monarchy it came to refer to a figure who would restore ISRAEL, gathering the tribes together and ushering in the KINGDOM OF GOD. (2) In the Christian NEW TESTAMENT, JESUS OF NAZARETH is described by messianic titles, e.g. messiah, CHRIST, 'the King', 'the One who Comes'.

Methodist churches Churches deriving from those which joined the Methodist Conference, first established in 1784 by John WESLEY. They are now spread worldwide, promoting EVANGELISM and social concern.

Mezuzah ('doorpost') Parchment (often cased) and inscribed with the SHEMA placed on the door frame of a Jewish house.

Middle Way The BUDDHA's description of his teaching as a

mean between the extremes of sensuality and asceticism. It is designed to lead to NIRVANA.

Midgard/Middle Earth The home of human beings according to Norse cosmology. Midgard is the middle of the nine worlds. It is now part of contemporary HEATHEN belief.

Midrash A method of exposition of HEBREW texts designed to reveal the inner meaning of the TORAH.

Mihrab Semi-circular recess in the wall of a MOSQUE which indicates the direction of the holy city MECCA, which is the direction for MUSLIM prayer.

Mimir In Norse mythology, the fount of wisdom who guards the well of knowledge at the root of YGGDRASIL.

Minaret (from the Arabic for lighthouse) A tower attached to a MOSQUE from which the call to prayer, *adhan*, is broadcast to the MUSLIM community.

Mindfulness Buddhist method of contemplative analysis.

Ming Chinese emperor (first century CE) of the Han dynasty who, according to tradition, introduced Buddhist scriptures from north-west India.

Minister (1) A lay or ordained Christian who has been authorized to perform spiritual functions (ministries, literally 'service') in the CHURCH. (2) General title for any member of the clergy, especially those of Protestant denominations.

Minoan religion Religion of the Bronze Age civilization of Crete. The Minoans probably worshipped the MOTHER GODDESS and reverenced SACRED SNAKES and SACRED BULLS.

Miracle An event which appears to defy rational explanation and is attributed to divine intervention.

Mishnah A compilation of Jewish oral teachings undertaken by Rabbi JUDAH HANASI in around 200 CE. It quickly became second in authority only to the HEBREW BIBLE and formed the basis of the TALMUD.

Missal Liturgical book containing all that is said or sung throughout the year at the celebration of the MASS.

Mission The outreach of a religion to the unconverted.

Missionaries Those who propagate a religious faith among people of a different faith. BUDDHISM and CHRISTIANITY have been the most notable missionary religions.

Mithra Originally a god of the Indo-Iranians, he was worshipped in the Hindu VEDAS as Mitra and was an important figure in ZOROASTRIANISM, where he was particularly associated with ideas on judgment and the priesthood. To the Romans he was the god Mithras of MITHRAISM. (*See also* SOL INVICTUS.)

Mithraeum In MITHRAISM a cave-like sanctuary housing a statue of MITHRA slaying the bull.

Mithraism Religion of MITHRA which flourished throughout the early Roman empire. Popular among soldiers, it stressed courage and endurance. (*See also* SOL INVICTUS.)

Moderator MINISTER of the PRESBYTERIAN CHURCH appointed to constitute and preside over one of the courts that govern the life of the church.

Mohammed *see* MUHAMMAD.

Moksha SANSKRIT word meaning liberation from the cycle of birth, death, and rebirth. Permanent spiritual perfection experienced by an enlightened soul after the physical body has died.

Monism The belief that there is only one basic reality in spite of the appearance and experience of diversity.

Monk A member of a male religious community living under vows which usually include poverty, chastity, and the wearing of a distinctive form of dress. Monastic orders are found in Christianity, Buddhism, Hinduism, and Jainism. The Buddhist monk is a member of a SANGHA. (*See also* BENEDICT.)

Monotheism The belief that there is one supreme GOD who contains all the attributes and characteristics of divinity.

Moon, Sun Myung (1920–2012) Korean engineer, businessman, and founder of the FAMILY FEDERATION FOR WORLD PEACE AND UNIFICATION.

Moonies *see* FAMILY FEDERATION FOR WORLD PEACE AND UNIFICATION.

Moravians Protestant pietist Christians continuing the simple ideals of an earlier, mid-fifteenth century group, 'The Bohemian Brethren' or Unity of the Brethren.

Mormonism Unorthodox Christian sect founded in 1830 CE in the USA on the basis of the visionary experiences of Joseph SMITH. The Mormon Church, officially the 'Church of Jesus Christ of Latter-day Saints', has about 14 million members, half of them in the USA and Canada.

Moroni *see* SMITH, JOSEPH.

Moses The father of JUDAISM who received the TORAH from God on Mount SINAI, having led the people of ISRAEL out of captivity in Egypt. The first five books of the Hebrew BIBLE are traditionally ascribed to him.

Mosque MUSLIM place of public worship, consisting usually of an outer courtyard for ablutions and a large unfurnished inner area where Muslims kneel, sit, or prostrate themselves in worship.

Mother goddess/Great Mother The personification of nature and the natural processes of fertility and growth connected with the earth. Worship of a mother goddess was universal in the Ancient Near East, Asia, and Europe (*see* CYBELE, DEMETER, INANNA, ISHTAR, ISIS). Her worship continues in HINDUISM, where the consorts of SHIVA (DURGA, KALI, PARVATI) have some of her characteristics. There is some revival of her worship in feminism, ECO-FEMINISM, and among adherents to the GAIA hypothesis and practitioners of WITCHCRAFT.

Muezzin Person who calls the MUSLIM faithful to prayer.

Mufti A canon lawyer in ISLAM who gives formal legal advice on questions brought to him in accordance with the QUR'AN, the SUNNAH, and the law schools.

Muhammad (c. 570–632 CE) Prophet and apostle of ISLAM, the final messenger of God whose message, the QUR'AN, sums up and completes the previous revelations to the Jews and Christians.

Muharram A commemoration by Shi'ite MUSLIMS (*see* SHI'A) of the murder of Hussein ibn 'Ali, Muhammad's grandson.

Mujtahid MUSLIM teacher who gives a ruling, legal decision, or deduction on the basis of his own learning or authority (*see* IJTIHAD).

Mullah An Arabic word which means a 'teacher' or 'scholar' – an exponent of the sacred law of ISLAM.

Muslim 'One who submits' to the will of God, a follower of ISLAM.

Muslim brotherhood Egyptian organization founded in 1928 CE by Hasan al-Banna. The brotherhood was influential after World War II and worked against ZIONISM and Westernization. It is active in Egypt and many other Middle Eastern and North African countries.

Mystery religions Cults based on ancient MYTHS which flourished in Greece, in Rome and throughout the Roman empire. Initiates went through a dramatic and secret ceremony in which they identified with the divinity at the centre of the myth and experienced salvation and the assurance of immortality.

Mystic One who seeks direct personal experience of the divine and may use PRAYER, MEDITATION or various ascetic practices to concentrate the attention.

Mysticism The search for direct personal experience of the divine. There is a distinction between seeing mysticism as leading to identification with GOD (as is common in HINDUISM) and as leading to a union with God's love and will (as in ISLAM, JUDAISM, and CHRISTIANITY).

Myth A sacred story which originates and circulates within a particular community. Some myths explain puzzling physical phenomena or customs, institutions and practices whose origin in the community would otherwise be mysterious. (*See also* CREATION MYTH.)

N

Nagarjuna (c. 150–250 CE) MAHAYANA Buddhist philosopher who taught that the truth of reality was void or emptiness.

Nakayama Miki (1798–1887 CE) Founder of the Japanese religion TENRIKYO.

Namu Myoho Renge Kyo Formula coined by NICHIREN as the essential truth of the LOTUS SUTRA.

Nanak, Guru (1469–1539 CE) Indian religious teacher and founder of the SIKH religion. He intended to reconcile HINDUS and MUSLIMS and travelled widely preaching a monotheistic faith (*see* MONOTHEISM) which was influenced by BHAKTI and SUFISM.

Native American Church Religious organization of Native Americans founded in the 1880s. It teaches a synthesis of native religion and Christianity.

Nature spirits Spirits of trees, hills, rivers, plants, and animals which are acknowledged with prayers and offerings in most INDIGENOUS RELIGIONS.

Near-death experience Visionary sequence of events occasionally reported by those resuscitated. Features include a sensation of being OUT OF BODY, a journey down a long tunnel, the appearance of a being of light who is sometimes identified as CHRIST or an ANGEL, and a flashback of one's past life.

Nembutsu ('Hail to the BUDDHA AMIDA') The formula of faith taught by the Japanese Buddhist teacher HONEN.

Nemesis Greek goddess who personified the retribution due to evil deeds. Her vengeance was regarded to be inevitable and exact.

Nemeton 'Sacred place' in Celtic religion, usually an enclosed woodland grove.

Neolithic period The New Stone Age, from about 10,000 BCE until the Early Bronze Age.

Neo-Platonism Religious and philosophical movement from the third to the sixth centuries CE. It used the teachings of PLATO as a basis for ascetic practices and mystical experience.

Neptune Italian water god who became associated with POSEIDON and acquired his mythology.

Nestorianism CHRISTIAN HERESY that claimed that two separate persons, human and divine, existed in the incarnate CHRIST (as opposed to the orthodox view that God assumed human nature as one person in Christ). Although condemned in 431 CE it continued to flourish in Persia.

New Age With roots in particularly Theosophy, the term refers to alternative spiritualities which emerged in the mid-1960s principally on the west coast of the USA and spread throughout North America and Europe. The movements are characterized by a concern to realize the spiritual potential of the individual self, which is often believed to be divine.

New religion There is a scholarly debate over the precise definition of a 'new' religion. Some scholars limit the definition to those religions that have emerged since 1945 (i.e. since the end of World War II) or, indeed, even later (i.e. since 1960).

New Testament The second division of the Christian Bible, comprising the GOSPELS, the Acts of the Apostles, the Revelation of John, and various EPISTLES.

New Year, Jewish *see* ROSH HASHANAH.

Nibbana PALI word for NIRVANA.

Nicene Creed The fullest version of the orthodox Christian CREED, compiled to counter Christological heresies in the fourth century.

Nichiren (1222–1282 CE) Japanese Buddhist reformer who taught that the LOTUS SUTRA contained the ultimate truth and that it could be compressed into a sacred formula: NAMU MYOHO RENGE KYO.

Night Journey The journey of MUHAMMAD from the temple in MECCA to the TEMPLE OF JERUSALEM, which is described in the QUR'AN.

Nihongi SHINTO scripture which contains the Japanese CREATION MYTH and legends of the gods.

Ninigi The son of Amaterasu in SHINTO belief. At a time of chaos in heaven Amaterasu sent him down to rule the islands of Japan, making him the first Japanese EMPEROR.

Nirvana In BUDDHISM, the state when DUKKHA ceases because the flames of desire are no longer fuelled. It is a state of unconditioned-ness and uncompounded-ness beyond any form of known or imagined existence.

Nkulukulu ('the old, old one') Zulu name for God.

Noble Eightfold Path In BUDDHISM, the way to extinguish desire by adopting right views; right resolves; right speech; right action; right livelihood; right effort; right mindfulness; right concentration/meditation.

Non-realism Movement arising from DEATH OF GOD theology which claims that religious doctrines refer only to human sources of value and do not refer to objective reality.

Norns The Fates of Norse religion. The names of the three norns mean Past, Present, and Future.

Numen In Roman religion, the divine power suffusing nature. From this concept Rudolf Otto developed the idea that the root of religion was a sense of holy power. This he termed the 'numinous'.

Nun A member of a religious community of women, as found in CHRISTIANITY, BUDDHISM, HINDUISM, and JAINISM. Nuns live under vows usually including poverty, and chastity and often wear a distinctive form of dress. (*See also* BENEDICT.)

Nut The sky goddess of Egyptian mythology whose body is lined with stars.

O

Obeah Religious and magical practices of the West Indies which are usually of West African origin. (*See also* VOODOO.)

Occult Teachings, arts, and practices that are concerned with what is hidden and mysterious, as with WITCHCRAFT, ALCHEMY, and DIVINATION.

Odin Chief of the Norse gods. Variants of his name include Woden (Anglo-Saxon) and Wotan (German).

Odinism *see* HEATHENISM.

Ohrmazd *see* AHURA MAZDA.

Old Catholic churches A group of national churches which have separated from Rome.

Old Testament The HEBREW BIBLE as the first division of the Christian BIBLE.

Olympus, Mount The highest mountain in Greece (9572 feet/2917m), held to be the home of the twelve greatest Greek gods under the leadership of ZEUS.

Om mani padme hum ('the jewel in the LOTUS') Tibetan mantra whose six syllables are held to correspond to the six worlds of Tibetan Buddhist teaching: om, 'gods'; ma, 'anti-gods'; ni, 'humans'; pad, 'animals'; mi, 'hungry ghosts'; hum, 'hell'.

Omnipotence All-powerful.

Omniscience All-knowing. Simultaneous knowledge of all things.

Ordination Rite in the Christian CHURCH by which chosen individuals are authorized as MINISTERS of the Word of God and the SACRAMENTS. In BUDDHISM the term denotes entry into the SANGHA.

Origen (c. 184–c. 254 CE) Theologian who tried to present biblical CHRISTIANITY using the ideas of HELLENISM.

Original sin The SIN of Adam and Eve, the first human beings, in eating from the forbidden tree in the Garden of Eden, expressing independence from God. In Christian teaching the inevitable consequence is seen as separation from God; human creatures inherit Adam and Eve's 'fallen' state, resulting in the need for SALVATION.

Orphism Religious movement which began in Thrace and flourished in the sixth century BCE. It taught a way of

liberation through ASCETICISM and held also a doctrine of REINCARNATION.

Orthodox Judaism Traditional JUDAISM which is Talmudic (*see* TALMUD) in belief and practice, and the largest of the modern groupings .

Orthodoxy CHRISTIANITY as practised by the Eastern Churches after the GREAT SCHISM. Orthodox Christians are found mostly in Eastern Europe, the Balkan States, and Russia.

Osiris Egyptian vegetation god, the force behind the cycle of growth and decay. As a symbol of death and resurrection, Osiris became associated with life after death and the judgment of individual souls.

Ottoman Empire (1453–1918 CE) The empire of the Ottoman Turks who were converted to ISLAM. It stretched from the Middle East to the Balkans and at its height to the frontiers of Austria. The empire went into slow decline in the eighteenth century and its religious life stagnated.

Out-of-body experience Sensation of separation of the self from the body occasionally reported in mystical or drug-induced trance, or as part of a NEAR-DEATH EXPERIENCE.

P

Pachacamac Leader of the gods in the religion of the INCAS.

Pachamama MOTHER GODDESS in the INDIGENOUS RELIGION of the Andes.

Pagan/Paganism The word 'pagan' (derived from the Latin term *pagus*, which literally means 'from the countryside' or 'rural') was first used in a general religious sense by the

early Christians to describe the non-Christian gentile religions. It is now generally used to refer to a broad range of nature-venerating religious traditions.

Pagoda A Buddhist building in south-east Asia built over Buddhist RELICS and often characterized by a series of superimposed spires.

Palaeolithic period ('Old Stone Age') The prehistoric age covering from around 2.6 million years ago to c. 10,000 BCE.

Pali Vernacular language of northern India in the BUDDHA's time, and hence the language of early BUDDHISM and the THERAVADA SCRIPTURES.

Pali Canon The basic Buddhist SCRIPTURES – the only scriptures valid among THERAVADA Buddhists. Traditionally the collection began soon after the BUDDHA's death when his followers met to receive the TIPITAKA/TRIPITAKA or 'three baskets' of his teaching.

Pan Arcadian fertility god, patron of shepherds and herdsmen, usually portrayed with goat's horns and legs.

Panchen Lama Title given to one of the leading abbots of TIBETAN BUDDHISM, whose authority paralleled that of the DALAI LAMA, though its emphasis was more on spiritual matters.

Pantheism The belief that all reality is in essence divine.

Parousia *see* SECOND COMING.

Parsis Descendants of the ancient Zoroastrian Persians (*see* ZOROASTRIANISM) living in India, mostly near Mumbai (Bombay). They practise an ethical MONOTHEISM with a RITUAL life that expresses the purity of AHURA MAZDA.

Parsva Important figure in JAINISM. Born a prince around

850 BCE he renounced his throne and became an ascetic, finally gaining omniscience.

Parvati ('mountaineer') Consort of SHIVA, in HINDU mythology, like Shiva both beautiful and terrifying.

Passover Seven-day Jewish spring festival marking the deliverance from Egypt (*see* EXODUS). Since Talmudic times (*see* TALMUD) the festival has begun with a service in the home where unleavened bread, wine, and bitter herbs symbolize the joys and sorrows of the Exodus.

Patriarch (1) 'Father-figure'; especially in family and community; in JUDAISM and CHRISTIANITY, refers to the founders of the faith such as ABRAHAM, ISAAC, AND JACOB. (2) Head of one of the EASTERN ORTHODOX churches.

Paul APOSTLE of CHRISTIANITY who established new churches throughout Asia Minor and Macedonia. Originally a PHARISEE, he was converted by a vision of CHRIST on the road to Damascus. He wrote several New Testament EPISTLES.

Penates Spirits or gods who protected the Roman household and family and were guardians over the household stores.

Pentateuch *see* TORAH (1).

Pentecost (1) Hellenistic name for Jewish harvest festival, fifty-two days after PASSOVER. More usually called *Shavuot* or the Festival of Weeks. (2) Christian festival marking the coming of the HOLY SPIRIT upon the APOSTLES fifty days after EASTER.

Pentecostal churches Churches which have formed from a renewal movement which started in the USA in the early 1900s. They teach the experience of 'baptism in the

Holy Spirit' which shows itself in speaking in tongues (*see* GLOSSOLALIA) and other 'spiritual gifts'.

Perkons/Perkunas/Perun Supreme god of ancient Russia, particularly associated with thunder and lightning.

Peter Apostle and close follower of JESUS OF NAZARETH, from whom he received the name Peter, meaning 'rock' in Greek. He held a position of leadership among the early apostles.

Pharaoh In the BIBLE, the title of the king of Egypt. The reigning king was identified with the god HORUS, and was held to be responsible for the fertility of the land.

Pharisees Jewish anti-nationalistic party that emerged in the time of the MACCABEES. They believed that God was universal and taught the individuality of the soul and the RESURRECTION.

Philo of Alexandria (c. 25 BCE–40 CE) Jewish philosopher who tried to reconcile Greek philosophy with the Hebrew scriptures.

Philosophy of religion The branch of philosophy which investigates religious experience considering its origin, context, and value.

Phylacteries *see* TEPHILLIN.

Pilgrimage A journey to a holy place, undertaken as a commemoration of a past event, as a celebration, or as an act of penance (*see also* HAJJ). The goal might be a natural feature such as a sacred river or mountain, or the location of a MIRACLE, revelation, or THEOPHANY, or the tomb of a hero or SAINT.

Pilgrim Fathers Puritan Christian group who left England for America in the Mayflower in 1620 CE and founded the colony of Plymouth, Massachusetts.

Plato (c. 427–347 BCE) Greek philosopher and pupil of SOCRATES. He taught the theory of Forms or Ideas, which are eternal prototypes of the phenomena encountered in ordinary experience.

PL Kyodan ('Perfect Liberty Association') One of the NEW RELIGIONS of Japan, founded in 1924 It is based on SHINTO but accepts KARMA from Buddhism and teaches that the ancestors have an influence on the lives of believers.

Plotinus (c. 205–69 CE) Philosopher and author of NEO-PLATONISM whose speculations influenced early Christianity.

Polytheism The belief in and worship of a variety of gods, who rule over various aspects of the world and life.

Pontifex High priest of Roman religion and member of a guild of priests whose president was the *pontifex maximus*. From the fifth century CE the title was applied to Christian BISHOPS, usually the POPE.

Pontius Pilate Roman procurator of the province of Judea 26–36 CE under whose authority JESUS OF NAZARETH was crucified.

Pope BISHOP of Rome, Vicar of CHRIST, and head of the ROMAN CATHOLIC Church, regarded as the successor of PETER.

Poseidon Greek god of the seas and waters, usually presented as a tall bearded figure carrying a trident.

Prayer The offering of worship, requests, confessions, or other communication to God or gods publicly or privately, with or without words; often a religious obligation.

Prayer wheels Wheels and cylinders used by Buddhists in Tibet and northern India.

Prehistoric religion RELIGIONS dating from the period before the development of writing.

Presbyter ('elder') Term for a Christian minister used in the NEW TESTAMENT interchangeably with BISHOP. Later it was held that the authority of the presbyter (from which comes 'PRIEST') derived from the bishop.

Presbyterian churches REFORMED CHURCHES whose teachings and order of worship reflect Calvinism. They are governed by a pyramid of elected, representative courts.

Priest (1) One authorized to perform priestly functions including mediation between God or gods and humanity, the offerings of SACRIFICE and the performance of RITUAL in many religions. (2) A Christian MINISTER, the term deriving from PRESBYTER.

Progressive Judaism Term covering the Liberal and Reform movements which emerged in JUDAISM in nineteenth-century Europe.

Propaganda Sacred Congregation for the Propagation of the Faith, a ROMAN CATHOLIC body concerned with MISSION in non-Christian countries. It dates from the COUNTER-REFORMATION, and is now known as the Congregation for the Evangelization of Peoples.

Prophet One who speaks for or as a mouthpiece of God or a god. (1) The Old Testament prophets were social and religious reformers of ISRAEL (3) and Judah and of the people of God in EXILE. They proclaimed God's prospective judgment of Israel; they recalled the people to obedience to God, some offering a hope of a future vindication. (2) In ISLAM the Prophet is MUHAMMAD, who brings the word and judgment of God to final utterance.

Prophets, The The second division of the HEBREW BIBLE, including the histories and the prophetic books.

Protestantism Christian faith and order as based on the principles of the REFORMATION. It emphasizes the sole authority of the BIBLE; justification by faith; the priesthood of all believers.

Psalm A sacred song or poem. The Book of Psalms in the BIBLE provides the basis for much Jewish and Christian worship.

Ptah The chief god of Memphis in ancient Egypt, usually depicted bearded, in mummified shape, and carrying three sceptres.

Puja ('reverence') Refers to temple and domestic worship in BUDDHISM and HINDUISM, and to the keeping of rites and ceremonies prescribed by the Brahmins (*see* CASTE SYSTEM).

Puranas A vast corpus of sacred writings (c. 350–950 CE), which include mythologies of Hindu deities and AVATARS of VISHNU, the origins of the cosmos, and of humanity, pilgrimage, ritual, law codes, caste obligations, and so on.

Pure Land Buddhism Buddhist sect founded by a Chinese monk, Hui-Yuan (334–416 CE) who was called the First Patriarch of Pure Land Buddhism. It is characterized by faith in the BODHISATTVA AMITABHA, the creator of a 'pure land' in the west. Through faith his devotees hoped to be transported there after death.

Purgatory In Roman Catholic teaching, the temporary state of punishment and purification for the dead before their admission to heaven.

Purim ('lots') Joyful Jewish festival celebrating the story of Esther, wife of the Persian king Xerxes, who defeated the anti-Jewish plot of the king's steward, Haman.

Pyramid Type of Egyptian royal tomb, usually tapering to the top from a square base, constructed between about 2630 and 1640 BCE. Pyramid-shaped structures are also found in Mesoamerica.

Pythagoras (c. 570–500 BCE) Greek philosopher, musician, and mathematician who taught that number was the basis of reality and that mathematics offered insight into the invisible world.

Q

Quakers Members of the Religious Society of Friends, deriving from a puritan group which formed around George Fox in the 1650s. They have no SACRAMENTS and no ordained ministry. Instead authority derives from the 'inner light of the living Christ' in each believer.

Quetzalcoatl Mythological figure in MAYA and AZTEC religion. He may have been a king of a pre-Aztec civilization.

Qur'an The central sacred text in Islam – the Muslim holy scripture. Muslims believe the Qur'an, meaning 'recitation', was revealed to the PROPHET MUHAMMAD, piecemeal, by God via Jibril (Gabriel) and is written in Arabic.

R

Ra see RE

Rabbi ('my master') Jewish religious teacher and interpreter of the TORAH. In modern JUDAISM he or she is a minister to the community, a preacher, and a leader of SYNAGOGUE worship.

Rabbinic Judaism The religion of the RABBIS who – beginning from the second centruy CE – expanded the interpretation of the TALMUD and produced authoritative codes of laws, responses, views, and judgments, mostly in the form of correspondence with particular communities.

Radha In HINDUISM, friend and love of the god VISHNU as his AVATAR KRISHNA.

Radhakrishnan, Sarvepalli (1888–1975 CE) Indian philosopher who became vice-president and then president of India.

Radical Theology Term sometimes used for theology committed to left-wing politics or for theology that tends towards NON-REALISM.

Ragnarök The doom of the Norse gods, the end of the world order.

Rama The seventh incarnation of VISHNU according to HINDU tradition. He is the epitome of righteousness and moral virtue.

Ramadan Islamic lunar month in which MUSLIMS are obliged to fast from food and water between sunrise and sunset.

Ramakrishna (1834–86 CE) Hindu Brahmin (see CASTE SYSTEM) who taught that all religions are paths to the same goal. He laid the foundation of Hindu universalism.

Ramakrishna Mission Indian religious order founded in 1897 by VIVEKANANDA. Its aims are to teach VEDANTA and to care for the sick and needy.

Ramanuja (d. 1137 CE) Indian philosopher who opposed SHANKARA's stress on the oneness of being and denied that the divine lord belonged to a lower order of reality.

Ramayana One of the two great epics of the HINDU scriptures compiled in the second or first century BCE.

Rammohan Roy (1772–1833 CE) HINDU reformer who founded the Brahmo Samaj, an ethical organization with monotheistic tendencies, in opposition to the idolatry of popular devotion.

Rastafarianism Religious and political movement centred in the Caribbean. It is a cult of Ras Tafari, better known as Haile Selassie (1892–1975 CE), Emperor of Ethiopia (1930–74).

Re Sun god and supreme god of the religion of ancient Egypt.

Rebirth Buddhist modification of REINCARNATION in the light of the ANATTA teaching.

Redemption God's saving work of buying back or recovering what is his. In JUDAISM it refers to the restoration of ISRAEL; in CHRISTIANITY to the ransoming of sinners from the power of SIN and death.

Red Hats Unreformed branch of TIBETAN BUDDHISM whose practices owe much to the former Tibetan religion of BON, or BÖN.

Reformation The movement within Western CHRISTIANITY between the fourteenth and the seventeenth centuries which led to the separation of the Protestant churches from Rome.

Reformed churches Churches which inherit the Calvinist Protestant tradition, including PRESBYTERIANS, INDEPENDENTS, Calvinistic METHODISTS, and CONGREGATIONALISTS.

Reiki The term is often translated as 'Universal Life Force Energy'. It is a method of spiritual healing founded in Japan by Mikao Usui (1865–1926).

Reincarnation The belief that individual souls survive death and are reborn to live again in a different body, thus passing through a series of lives. Held in pre-ARYAN India, the belief is associated with the doctrine of KARMA.

Relics Bones or remains of SAINTS, venerated and accredited with miraculous powers in many religions.

Religion (from Latin *religare*, 'to tie something tightly') A system of belief and worship, held by a community who may express its religion through shared MYTHS, DOCTRINES, ethical teachings, RITUALS, or the remembrance of special experiences.

Renunciation Giving up ownership of material possessions. In some religions, such as Buddhism, renunciation extends to psychological detachment from material possessions, including one's own body.

Restorationism Movement to restore the CHURCH to a pristine state in which the KINGDOM OF GOD is established through a charismatically ordained ministry. Restorationists see themselves as EVANGELICALS and Pentecostalists, but with a new edge to their commitment.

Resurrection (1) The Christian belief that JESUS OF NAZARETH was raised from death by God the Father who thus vindicated him as MESSIAH and revealed his defeat of death and SIN. (2) The raising of all the dead for JUDGMENT as taught in JUDAISM, CHRISTIANITY, and ISLAM.

Rinzai Zen School of ZEN which employs startling techniques (e.g. KOANS) to induce SATORI.

Rissho Kosei Kai An offshoot of the Reiyukai movement which is spreading the teachings of NICHIREN Buddhism beyond the boundaries of Japan.

Rita The cosmic order as understood in the Hindu VEDAS.

Rites of passage Religious ceremonies which mark the transition from one state of life to another. In many religions these transitional periods are felt to be dangerous and to require spiritual protection. Examples include birth rites, INITIATION rites, marriage rites, and funeral rites.

Ritual Religious ceremonial performed according to a set pattern of words, movements, and symbolic actions. Rituals may involve the dramatic re-enactment of ancient MYTHS featuring gods and heroes, performed to ensure the welfare of the community.

Roma The personification of the city of Rome, worshipped by the Romans as a goddess.

Roman Catholic Catholic CHRISTIAN who recognizes the authority of the POPE, the Bishop of Rome.

Rosh Hashanah The Jewish New Year, celebrated as the anniversary of creation.

Rosicrucianism Mystical system founded in seventeenth-century Germany and based on an account of a secret brotherhood founded

'to improve mankind by the discovery of the true philosophy'.

Rugievit Slavic god with seven faces from the island of Rügen.

Rumi, Jalal al-Din (d. 1273 CE) Sufi MYSTIC and poet, author of the *Mathnavi*, and founder of a DERVISH order.

Russell, C. T. (Charles Taze) (1852–1916 CE) US Bible scholar who started a periodical called *Zion's Watchtower* after being influenced by speculation about the return of CHRIST. This grew into the JEHOVAH'S WITNESSES movement.

Russian Orthodox Church The principal church of Russia since 988 CE.

S

Saadia Ben Joseph (892–940 CE) Head of the Jewish academy at Susa in Babylon. He defended the cause of RABBINIC JUDAISM against the KARAITES and the doctrine of the oneness of God against the Christian TRINITY.

Sabbath (*Shabbat*) Jewish day of worship and rest lasting from Friday sunset to Saturday sunset.

Sacrament 'an outward and visible sign of an inward and spiritual grace' (Book of Common Prayer). REFORMED CHURCHES count only BAPTISM and the EUCHARIST as sacraments, both being instituted by CHRIST. Roman Catholic and Orthodox Churches add CONFIRMATION, marriage, ORDINATION, penance, and extreme unction (the anointing of the sick).

Sacred Thread ceremony INITIATION ceremony performed on HINDU and BUDDHIST boys. A sacred thread is placed around the neck indicating that

the boy is one of the twice-born and has entered the first stage of life.

Sacrifice The ritual offering of animal or vegetable life to establish communion between humans and a god or gods.

Sadducees Aristocratic Jewish party which emerged in the times of the MACCABEES. They rejected the oral law and late doctrines like the RESURRECTION.

Sai Baba (1926–2011 CE) Spiritual teacher from south India regarded by his followers as an AVATAR.

Saint (1) Holy person or dead hero of faith venerated by believers on earth and held to be a channel of divine blessing. The Protestant reformers rejected the practice of devotion to saints. (2) In the NEW TESTAMENT and some Protestant churches, a term for any believer.

Salafiyya Puritan Sunni Islamic party which emerged in nineteenth-century Egypt. It accepted the authority only of the QUR'AN and the SUNNAH and rejected the 'ULAMA'. In time it grew closer to the WAHHABI MOVEMENT.

Salah Islamic ritual prayer which is carried out five times a day, facing MECCA and using ritual movements to accompany the words. One of the FIVE PILLARS OF ISLAM.

Salvation (1) In the BIBLE, deliverance of God's people from their enemies, and especially from SIN and its consequences, death and HELL, hence also the whole process of forgiveness, new life, and final glorification for the believer. (2) In Eastern religions, release from the changing material world to identification with the ABSOLUTE.

Samhain Celtic festival marking the beginning of winter, celebrated on 1 November with feasting and carousals.

Samsara ('stream of existence') Sanskrit word which refers to the cycle of birth and death followed by rebirth as applied both to individuals and to the universe itself.

Sanctuary A place consecrated to a god, a holy place, a place of divine refuge and protection. Also, the holiest part of a sacred place or building. Historically, in some cultures, a holy place where pursued criminals or victims were guaranteed safety.

Sangha Community of Buddhist MONKS which started with the BUDDHA's first disciples.

Sanhedrin Jewish supreme council of seventy which organized religious life during the period of independence following the revolt of the MACCABEES.

Sannyasi ('one who renounces') The last of the Hindu FOUR STAGES OF LIFE.

Sanskrit The language of the ARYAN peoples and of the Hindu scriptures. It is an Indo-European language related to Latin, Greek, and Persian.

Sarasvati In HINDUISM, the goddess of truth and consort of BRAHMA, the Creator.

Satan In the BIBLE, the personification of evil and identified with the DEVIL.

Satanism Sometimes referred to as 'devil-worship'.

Satguru (1) In SIKHISM, GOD, the true and eternal GURU. (2) In popular HINDUISM a term for a revered teacher such as SAI BABA.

Satori ENLIGHTENMENT in ZEN BUDDHISM.

Saturnalia Roman festival of Saturn, a mythical king of Rome and father of the god JUPITER, which began on 17 December. A time of banquets and present-giving, some of its characteristics were transferred to the festival of CHRISTMAS.

Sawm *see* FIVE PILLARS OF ISLAM.

Schism A deliberate division or split between Christians that disrupts the unity of the CHURCH.

Scribes Officials who organized the religious life of the Jewish community after the EXILE of 586 BCE. They regulated the observance of the SABBATH, communal prayer, and fasting and were the interpreters of the Law.

Scripture Writings which are believed to be divinely inspired or especially authoritative within a particular religious community.

Sebek Egyptian god associated with water and death.

Second Coming/Parousia The personal second coming of CHRIST which, Christians believe, will be a time of judgment and the inauguration of the KINGDOM OF GOD in its fullness.

Sect A group, usually religious, which has separated itself from an established tradition, claiming to teach and practise a truer form of the faith from which it has separated itself. For example, the JEHOVAH'S WITNESSES and the SEVENTH-DAY ADVENTISTS are sectarian Christian organizations.

Sefirot According to the teachings of Jewish Kabbalistic MYSTICISM (*see* KABBALAH), the potencies and attributes by which God acts and makes himself known.

Sephardim One of the two main cultural groups in JUDAISM which emerged during the Middle Ages. Sephardic Jews lived in Spain and Portugal and their traditions go back to Babylonian Jewry.

Serapis State god of Ptolemaic Egypt whose worship spread throughout the Mediterranean.

Seth The evil brother of OSIRIS in Egyptian mythology. He became the god of war, storms, deserts, and disorder.

Seven Precepts of the Sons of Noah The obligations placed on all men and women, regardless of race or faith, according to Jewish teaching. They comprise abstinence from idolatry, blasphemy, incest, murder, theft, the eating of living flesh, and the implementation of justice.

Seventh-Day Adventists Christian sect which emerged from a number of nineteenth-century groups stressing the imminent return of CHRIST. They observe Saturday as the Sabbath, accept the BIBLE as infallible, and require a lifestyle of strict temperance.

Shabbat *see* SABBATH.

Shahadah *La ilaha illa Allah*. The first four words of the MUSLIM confession of faith, 'There is no god but God', which continues 'and MUHAMMAD is his prophet'. To accept this creed is to be a Muslim. It is the first of the FIVE PILLARS OF ISLAM.

Shaivism Worship of the Hindu god SHIVA and his family. It is particularly strong in southern India and appeals to extreme ascetics.

Shakti ('energy', 'power') A feminine word, particularly associated with SHIVA and his consorts (*see* DURGA; KALI; PARVATI).

Shakyamuni ('The wise man of the SHAKYAS') One of the names of the BUDDHA.

Shakyas Tribe to which the BUDDHA's family belonged.

Shaman (1) An ecstatic priest-magician among the Tungu people of Siberia. (2) By extension, a similar figure in other INDIGENOUS RELIGIONS and ancient religions.

Shamash Babylonian sun god and lord of justice who rewards honesty and loyalty and brings retribution on the wicked.

Shammai *see* HILLEL.

Shankara (788–820 CE) The best-known exponent of classical HINDU philosophy.

Shari'a ('path') Body of law for the MUSLIM community which derives from the QUR'AN, the SUNNAH, and other sources, the legitimacy of which is debated in the different schools of law.

Shavuot *see* WEEKS, PENTECOST.

Shaykh/Sheikh/Shaikh (1) An Arab tribal leader. (2) Sufi spiritual teacher (*see* SUFISM), somewhat analogous to the Hindu GURU.

Shekhinah The presence or manifestation of God as described in the TARGUMS and later Jewish writings. It came to refer to the indwelling of God in creation.

Shema The Jewish confession of faith, recited in the morning and evening service. '*Shema*' is the opening word in HEBREW of the confession: 'Hear, O Israel, the Lord our God, the Lord is One …'

Shi'a/Shi'ites A minority group in ISLAM, comprising 15 per cent of MUSLIMS. They reject the first three CALIPHS, believing 'ALI to be MUHAMMAD's true successor

and first IMAM. The Shi'a live mostly in Iraq, Iran, Lebanon, Pakistan, and India.

Shingon 'True Word' sect of Japanese Buddhism founded in the ninth century CE and characterized by a complex sacramental and magical ritual which may have been influenced by TANTRISM and by indigenous SHINTO practices.

Shinran (1173–1263 CE) Disciple of HONEN and founder of the Japanese Buddhist sect JODO SHINSHU.

Shinto The indigenous nature religion of Japan which has provided a focus for nationalistic aspirations. (*See also* EMPEROR, JAPANESE; IZANAGI; JIMMU TENNO; JINJA; KAMI; KOJIKI; MATSURI; NIHONGI; NINIGI.)

Shirk ('association') In ISLAM the greatest sin, that of ascribing equals to God. (*See also* TAWHID.)

Shiva One of the great gods of HINDU devotion. He is a god of contrasts, presiding over creation and destruction, fertility and asceticism, good, and evil. His symbol is a phallus-shaped pillar denoting procreation.

Shoah *see* HOLOCAUST.

Shotoku, Prince Japanese ruler who introduced BUDDHISM as the state religion.

Shudras *see* CASTE SYSTEM.

Shulhan Aruch *see* KARO, JOSEPH.

Shvetambara ('white-clad') Member of a major JAIN sect who rejected the DIGAMBARA stress on the virtues of nudity.

Siddhartha Personal name of GAUTAMA the BUDDHA.

Sikh ('disciple') Follower of the Sikh religion which developed in the fifteenth century CE in northern India as a synthesis of ISLAM and

Hinduism. (*See also* ADI GRANTH; GOBINDH SINGH; GURDWARA; KABIR; KHALSA; NANAK; SINGH.)

Sin (1) An action which breaks a divine law. (2) The state of rebellion against God which, in Christian teaching, has been the human condition since the Fall of Adam and Eve and their expulsion from the Garden of Eden.

Sin Babylonian moon-god and guardian of the city of Ur.

Sinai, Mount Mountain in the south of the Sinai peninsula where, according to tradition, God revealed himself to MOSES and gave him the Ten Commandments.

Singh Surname used by SIKHS when they become a member of the KHALSA.

Sinkyo Traditional religion of Korea.

Sita Consort of RAMA in Hindu tradition.

Skandha/Khandha Term referring to the five factors which compound human personality according to Buddhist teaching. They are form, sense perception, consciousness, intellectual power, and discrimination.

Skilful means Buddhist practice of compassion in sharing the DHAMMA with the unenlightened.

Smith, Joseph (1805–44 CE) Founder of MORMONISM who claimed to be the recipient of a divine revelation to the former inhabitants of America in the form of golden plates inscribed in ancient languages.

Socrates (469–399 BCE) Greek philosopher and teacher and mentor of PLATO.

Soka Gakkai 'Value-creating society' of lay members of

the Japanese Buddhist sect NICHIREN, founded in 1930 in a wave of new cults.

Sol Invictus ('unconquered sun') A name for MITHRA.

Soma The juice of the Indian *soma* plant, which may have been fermented or had hallucinogenic properties. It was drunk by gods and men in the VEDAS, and regarded as a mediating god with power over all plants and as a conveyor of immortality.

Son of Man Title used by Jesus Christ to refer to himself, traditionally used to describe Christ's humanity.

Sorcerer A practitioner of harmful MAGIC. In INDIGENOUS RELIGIONS sorcerers are sometimes believed to be able to kill others through magic.

Soteriology Teaching about SALVATION.

Soto Zen School of ZEN Buddhism which teaches a gradual and gentle way to SATORI.

Soul (1) The immortal element of an individual man or woman which survives the death of the body in most religious teachings. (2) A human being when regarded as a spiritual being.

Spell A formula of words with or without accompanying RITUAL actions which is believed to have the power to manipulate natural or supernatural forces for good or evil ends.

Spiritualism Any religious system or practice which has the object of establishing communication with the dead. Most modern spiritualist churches derive from a movement which grew up in mid-nineteenth-century America. Spiritualists seek to

communicate with the dead through such means as table-turning and automatic writing.

Steiner, Rudolf (1861–1925 CE) Founder of ANTHROPOSOPHY. He originally followed THEOSOPHY and ROSICRUCIANISM, but broke with these groups and developed his mystical ideas into an educational, ecological, and medical programme for spiritual progress.

Stoicism Philosophical school founded by Zeno of Citium (c. 335–263 BCE) and named after the porch or *stoa* where he taught in Athens. Stoics believed that the world order reflected the divine intelligence – the LOGOS which was present in all creation. Human beings could attain virtue – harmony with the universe – by learning self-sufficiency and behaving with courage and self-control.

Stonehenge Megalithic monument (*see* MEGALITHS) on Salisbury Plain, England.

Stupa Tibetan Buddhist shrine, found by roadsides, in fields, and at gateways. It is shaped as a pointed dome, often with a spire crescent and disc at the top, and built on a square base.

Subud Spiritual teaching of the Javanese Muslim teacher Pak Subuh (1901–87 CE). It emphasizes submission to the Life Force through a course of spiritual training designed to open up the individual to the reality of God.

Sufism Islamic mystical movement that gained prominence in the eighth century CE as a reaction to the worldliness of the UMMAYAD DYNASTY. Sufis claimed direct experience of ALLAH through ascetic practices.

Sukkot *see* BOOTHS.

Sundance Four-day ceremony which grew up among Native

Americans Plains in the 1870s as a reaction against white attempts to break up the traditions and beliefs of the people. The ceremony was crushed by the US army.

Sun God In the INCA religion, the creator of Manco Capac, the first Inca, and father to all the Inca rulers.

Sunnah ('trodden path') The source of authority in Islamic lawmaking which is second only to the QUR'AN.

Sunni The majority group in ISLAM, comprising about 85 per cent of MUSLIMS. They accept the authority of the FOUR RIGHTLY GUIDED CALIPHS and the developing process of lawmaking guided by the community's legal experts. Sunni Muslims live in the Arab states in North, West, and East Africa, and in India and Indonesia.

Sutta Pitaka An important collection of THERAVADA Buddhist SCRIPTURES.

Suzuki, Daisetz T. (1870–1966 CE) Japanese ZEN scholar who played a major part in introducing Zen Buddhism to the Western world.

Swami General term for a HINDU holy man or member of a religious order.

Swaminarayan (1781–1830 CE) Gujarati preacher and founder of a popular sect which attracted Sikh and Hindu followers.

Swedenborg, Emmanuel (1688–1772 CE) Swedish scientist who became a MYSTIC and visionary. He taught a kind of pantheistic THEOSOPHY (*see* PANTHEISM) centred on Jesus Christ. He founded the New Church.

Synagogue Jewish meeting place for worship and study. Synagogues grew out of the

TORAH schools of the SCRIBES during the EXILE. After the destruction of the TEMPLE OF JERUSALEM (70 CE), synagogues became the centres of Jewish life.

Syncretism The growing together of two or more religions making a new development in religion which contains some of the beliefs and practices of both.

T

Tabernacles, Festival of *see* BOOTHS.

Taboo Polynesian word applied to an object, place, or person which is prohibited because of its holy or dangerous character.

T'ai Chi (1) The 'Transcendent Absolute' or 'Great Ultimate' which is the underlying cause and unity of all things in early Chinese Taoist and later neo-Confucian thought. It is the nearest equivalent to GOD in Chinese thought. (2) The name of a martial art often practised as a form of spiritual development.

Tallit Jewish prayer-shawl fringed at the four corners and used during morning prayer, SHABBAT, and Jewish festivals.

Talmud The written interpretation and development of the HEBREW scriptures. There are two versions: the Palestinian, compiled while the Jews were under duress from the Christian Church, and the Babylonian which is more detailed and complete.

Tammuz Babylonian/Syrian fertility deity. A young god who, in mythology, died and was resurrected after the pattern of the Egyptian OSIRIS.

Tanha ('craving') The main cause of suffering as analyzed by the BUDDHA in the FOUR NOBLE TRUTHS.

Tantrism Tibetan Buddhist practices which aim at direct experience of the enlightened self through symbols, visual images, repetition of sounds, prescribed movements, breath control, and ritualized sexual intercourse.

Tao ('way') In TAOISM, the underlying principle of reality.

Taoism Chinese philosophy outlined in the TAO TE CHING. Its aim is to achieve harmony with all that is by pursuing inaction and effortlessness. Taoism gradually evolved an elaborate mythological system and incorporated notions of spirit possession, ALCHEMY, and DIVINATION.

Tao te ching Chinese religious work compiled in the fourth century BCE and ascribed to LAO-TZU.

Targum A (usually) Aramaic translation of a HEBREW scripture reading. The translator was expected to make a free interpretation.

Tarot cards Deck of seventy-eight cards marked with various symbolic figures which are shuffled and dealt as a form of DIVINATION.

Tat tvam asi ('you are that') Phrase from the UPANISHADS which expresses the claim that BRAHMAN, the divine power sustaining the universe, and ATMAN, the soul, are one.

Tawhid ('asserting oneness') The essential MUSLIM doctrine of the unity of God.

Tephillin/Tefillin ('phylacteries') Small boxes containing scriptural texts written on parchment, worn by JEWS (2) on the head and arm during prayer.

Temple Building designed for WORSHIP of God or gods, usually containing a SANCTUARY or holy place where SACRIFICE may be offered.

Temple of Heaven Great Chinese temple in Peking where the Chinese emperors received the mandate of heaven (*see* T'IEN) to rule over the Chinese people.

Temple of Jerusalem/Holy Temple TEMPLE first built by Solomon on a site bequeathed by DAVID. This temple was destroyed in 586 BCE. The second temple was dedicated in 515 BCE. It was desecrated by the Hellenistic Seleucid king Antiochus Epiphanes but rededicated by JUDAS MACCABEUS. Rebuilding was begun under Herod the Great in 20 BCE. The temple was virtually completed in 62 CE, but destroyed by Titus in 70 CE.

Ten Gurus In SIKHISM GURU NANAK and his nine successors who are seen as sharing the same essential insights into the nature of God.

Tendai Japanese Buddhist sect based on a former Chinese sect T'ien-t'ai, and founded in the ninth century CE. Tendai was an attempt at a synthesis between MAHAYANA teachings which stressed MEDITATION and those that stressed devotion.

Tengri The supreme god of the Mongols. Also a collective name for gods.

Tenrikyo 'Religion of Heavenly Wisdom' founded in Japan by NAKAYAMA MIKI, and based at the city of Tenri.

Tetragrammaton *see* YHWH.

Tezcatlipoca ('that which causes the Black Mirror to shine') AZTEC god of night and the north, a magician, symbolized by a jaguar.

Theism The belief in one supreme GOD who is both TRANSCENDENT and involved in the workings of the universe.

Theocracy ('divine government') Term describing a state which is constituted on the basis of divine law. It is an important concept in ISLAM, where it is sometimes believed that the law of the land should be identical with the SHARI'A. The regime of CALVIN in Geneva was also theocratic.

Theodicy The defence of God as both good and omnipotent, which accounts for the existence of suffering and evil. The term was coined in 1710 by Gottfried Leibniz.

Theology (1) A systematic formulation of belief made by or on behalf of a particular individual or CHURCH or other body of believers. (2) The critical study of RELIGION, particularly CHRISTIANITY, with regard to its origins, SCRIPTURES and other texts, DOCTRINES, ethics, history, and practices.

Theophany A divine appearance, revelation, or manifestation, usually inducing awe and terror in those who witness it. Examples are the appearance of God to MOSES on Mount SINAI amidst thunder, lightning, smoke, and trumpet blasts; the appearance of KRISHNA in his divine form, 'like a thousand suns', as described in the BHAGAVAD GITA.

Theosophy A term applied to various mystical movements but which refers particularly to the principles of the Theosophical Society founded by Madame BLAVATSKY in 1875. These comprise a blend of Hindu, Buddhist, and Christian ideas, together with particular stress on REINCARNATION, immortality, and the presence of GOD in all things.

Theravada ('the doctrine of the elders') The form of BUDDHISM practised in Sri Lanka, Myanmar (Burma), Thailand, Cambodia, and Laos, which sticks firmly to the teachings of the VINAYA PITAKA and rejects the doctrine of the BODHISATTVAS.

Thirteen Principles Articles of Jewish faith formulated by Moses MAIMONIDES in the twelfth century CE.

Thomas, John *see* CHRISTADELPHIANS.

Thor Norse god of thunder and lightning.

Thoth Ibis-headed Egyptian god, patron of writing and counting, who recorded the weighing of souls in the judgment after death.

Three Body doctrine MAHAYANA Buddhist teaching that the BUDDHA exists in three aspects.

Three refuges Brief dedication used by Buddhists and traditionally given by the Buddha himself: 'I go to the Buddha for refuge; I go to the Dhamma for refuge; I go to the Sangha for refuge.'

Thunderbird A totem (*see* TOTEMISM) found widely among Native Americans of North America.

Tibetan Book of the Dead Book of instructions and preparations for death and rites to be performed for the dying.

Tibetan Buddhism/Vajrayana A mixture of BUDDHISM, TANTRISM, and the ancient Bön religion of Tibet. The two main groups are the RED HATS and the YELLOW HATS.

T'ien ('heaven') Chinese term sometimes used for the supreme GOD.

Tipitaka The 'three baskets' of the BUDDHA's teaching, the canon of SCRIPTURE for THERAVADA Buddhists, comprising the VINAYA PITAKA, the SUTTA PITAKA, and the ABHDHAMMA PITAKA.

Tirthankaras *see* JINA.

Tlaloc AZTEC god of rain and vegetation.

Tongues, Speaking in *see* GLOSSOLALIA.

Torah (1) The five books of the Law (the PENTATEUCH) revealed to Moses; the first division of the HEBREW BIBLE. (2) 'The teaching', the correct response of ISRAEL to God, outlined in the rules for purity and social justice. (3) The cosmological principle of order which embraces moral and religious instruction as well as the physical ordering of the universe by God.

Torii Gateway to a SHINTO shrine which consists of two vertical posts supporting two horizontal bars, the higher of which is often curved at each end towards the sky.

Totemism (from a Native American word meaning 'relative') The belief in some INDIGENOUS RELIGIONS that particular animals or sometimes plants or other objects have a special relationship with the tribal group and act as its guardians.

Totem poles Tall decorated posts, found especially among Native Americans, which display tribal relationships with ancestors and guardian spirits.

Towers of Silence Parsi mounds used for the disposal of corpses.

Transcendent That which is above or beyond common human experience or knowledge.

Transcendental Meditation/ TM MEDITATION technique taught by Maharishi Mahesh Yogi which has flourished in the West since the 1960s.

Transfiguration The occasion of CHRIST's appearance in glory to three of his disciples during his earthly ministry. It is celebrated as a feast in the Eastern Churches and by many in the West.

Transmigration of souls The belief held by some Hindus that souls are detached from their bodies at death and are attached to other human, animal, or vegetable bodies.

Trimurti The three principal deities in HINDUISM – BRAHMA, VISHNU, and SHIVA, who are believed to control the three activities – creation, preservation, and destruction – inherent in the created cosmos.

Trinity Christian doctrine of GOD as three Persons, equally God: the Father, the Son, and the HOLY SPIRIT, constituting the divine unity.

Tripitaka (1) Sanskrit spelling of the (Pali) word TIPITAKA. (2) The SCRIPTURES of THERAVADA BUDDHISM, which include translations of THERAVADA texts, SANSKRIT MAHAYANA texts, and some Chinese additions and commentaries. Also called the San-tsang.

Triple gem The BUDDHA as teacher, the DHAMMA as his teaching, and the SANGHA as the community who live by his teaching. The 'triple gem' is the core of the Buddhist faith.

Tuat/Duat The other world in Egyptian mythology.

Twelvers The majority group among SHI'A Muslims who hold that the twelfth IMAM, Muhammad al-Mahdi, will reappear as the MAHDI on the last day. (*See also* ISMA'ILIS.)

Tyr The oldest of the Norse gods. Originally a sky god like ZEUS or VARUNA, his attributes were taken over by ODIN.

U

UFO ('unidentified flying object') The subject matter for many speculative groups since the 1950s. Members consider the spiritual and practical significances of UFO sightings.

'Ulama' The doctors of the law in ISLAM. They are the interpreters of the SHARI'A and the upholders of Islamic orthodoxy.

'Umar Caliph after the death of ABU BAKR, 634–644 CE. His rule was a period of dramatic expansion for ISLAM, into Mesopotamia, Persia, and Lower Egypt.

Ummayad dynasty (661–750 CE) The Islamic dynasty based on the Meccan family Ummaya. The caliphate was based in Damascus. Under the Ummayads ISLAM spread through North Africa to Spain and as far east as the Indus.

Ummah The MUSLIM community; those who have received God's revelation through MUHAMMAD and live in submission to it.

Underworld The abode of spirits after the death of the body. In many religions the underworld is a shadowy half-real place presided over by a god of death. (*See also* HADES; HELL; TUAT.)

Unification Church *see* FAMILY FEDERATION FOR WORLD PEACE AND UNIFICATION.

Unitarianism Dissenting movement which spread in Britain, Poland, and Hungary from the sixteenth century. Unitarians reject the Christian doctrines of the TRINITY and INCARNATION and defend a reason-based ethical THEISM.

Untouchables Indians who belong to no caste (*see* CASTE SYSTEM) and are therefore banished from normal social life.

Upanishads The last books of the Indian VEDAS which were written in SANSKRIT between 800 and 400 BCE. They develop the concept of BRAHMAN as the holy power released in sacrifice to the point where it becomes the underlying reality of the universe. The soul, ATMAN, is identified with the holy power, Brahman.

'Uthmān ibn 'Affān Son-in-law of MUHAMMAD who succeeded 'UMAR as caliph in 644 CE. Under his caliphate the final authoritative version of the QUR'AN was produced.

V

Vairocana A title for the sun in ancient HINDU mythology. In MAHAYANA Buddhism, it became a title for one of the great Buddhas.

Vaishnavism Worship of, or devotion to, the Hindu god VISHNU. Devotees regard him as the sole deity, of whom other gods are mere aspects.

Vaishyas *see* CASTE SYSTEM.

Vajrayana ('diamond vehicle') An expression sometimes used for Tibetan Buddhism, a form of MAHAYANA Buddhism which has distinctive doctrines and practices.

Valhalla ('hall of the slain') The part of ASGARD in Norse mythology reserved for dead heroes waiting for the final battle RAGNARÖK. The dead heroes spent their time drinking, playing games, and fighting.

Valkyries ('choosers of the slain') Female servants of ODIN in Norse mythology who choose which side is to have victory in battle and which warriors are to die. They conduct the dead to VALHALLA and wait on them with food and drink.

Vampyr/vampire Spirit of a dead person in Slavic folklore who lives by sucking the blood of the living.

Vanir ('shining ones') Divine beings of Norse mythology who at first fought with the ÆSIR and later allied with them and came to live in ASGARD.

Varanasi *see* BENARES.

Varuna Indian sky god of the Vedic period (*see* VEDAS). He produced the cosmic order and was seen as a heavenly ruler and lawgiver as well as a moral guardian of the earth.

Vatican Councils The first was convened by POPE PIUS IX in 1869–70 CE. It resulted in the dogma of Papal Infallibility. The second (1962–65 CE) was called by John XXIII. It led to a modernization of Roman Catholic worship and improved relations with other churches.

Vedanta (1) 'The end of the VEDAS'. A name for the UPANISHADS, which close the period of HINDU revelation. (2) Indian philosophy based on the teachings of SHANKARA. Its basic tenet is that only BRAHMAN, the Absolute, is fully real.

Vedas Scriptures which express the religion of the ARYAN people of India. They comprise HYMNS, instructions for RITUAL, and cosmological speculations. There are four divisions: *Rig Veda*, hymns to the Aryan gods who are personifications of natural forces; *Sama Veda*, verses selected for chanting (*see* CHANT); *Yajur Veda*, prose

instructions on matters of ritual; *Atharva Veda*, rites and SPELLS in verse, especially concerned with curing illness.

Venus Roman goddess of love, identified with APHRODITE.

Vesta Roman goddess of the hearth and protectress of domestic life.

Vestments Special garments worn by the Christian clergy during liturgical services (*see* LITURGY).

Vinaya Pitaka One of the oldest Buddhist scriptures, consisting of the rules of discipline for the SANGHA, and related commentaries.

Viracocha/Huiracocha The uncreated creator-god in the religion of the INCAS.

Vishnu In HINDUISM, the divine as preserver and life-giver, the creator of the cosmos. He and SHIVA are the two great gods of Hindu devotion.

Vivekananda (1863–1902) Follower of RAMAKRISHNA and founder of the RAMAKRISHNA MISSION in 1897.

Voodoo Religion of estimated 75 per cent of the people of Haiti, as well as others in the West Indies and parts of South America. Voodoo is highly syncretistic. West African DIVINITIES are worshipped, often as Christian SAINTS, and their sanctuaries closed during the Christian season of LENT.

W

Wahhabi movement Puritanical SUNNI ISLAM movement founded by Muhammad ibn 'Abd al-Wahhab of Arabia (1703–92 CE). The movement has revived in the twentieth century and is the dominant religious influence in Saudi Arabia.

Wailing Wall *see* WESTERN WALL.

Wandering On In Buddhist thought the continual cycle by which the KARMA of past actions causes the coming-to-be of new mental and physical states which in turn produce more karma and further phases of existence.

Wandjina Spirit beings of the Australian Aboriginal DREAMTIME who are believed to have left their shadows on rock and cave walls in paintings and engravings.

Weeks/Shavuot Jewish feast celebrated seven weeks after PASSOVER. It has become associated with the giving of the Ten Commandments on Mount SINAI. Also known as PENTECOST.

Werewolf Human being who has been transformed into a wolf in Slavic folk tradition.

Wesley, John (1703–91 CE) Founder of the METHODIST movement. He travelled through Britain on horseback preaching the 'new birth'.

Western Wall/Wailing Wall/Kotel Site in JERUSALEM used by JEWS to lament the FALL OF JERUSALEM and the continuing suffering of the Jews and to pray for restoration. It is believed to be part of the original Herod's Temple, the only part left standing after the destruction of 70 CE.

Wicca Also called 'the Old Religion', 'witchcraft', 'wisecraft', or simply 'the Craft', the term is taken from the Anglo-Saxon *wicce*, meaning 'witch' or 'wise woman'.

Witch doctor/Medicine man A healer in INDIGENOUS RELIGIONS. The terms are rarely used today as they are felt to have misleading connotations.

Word of God Christian term for the BIBLE, or part of it.

World Council of Churches Body including many Protestant and Orthodox churches, first constituted at Amsterdam in 1948 (*see* CONCILIAR PROCESS, ECUMENICAL MOVEMENT).

World Fellowship of Buddhists Society founded in 1950 in Ceylon (Sri Lanka) by G. P. Malalasekera to bring together Buddhists of all traditions and nations.

Worship Reverence or homage to God or a god which may involve PRAYER, SACRIFICE, RITUALS, singing, dancing, or chanting.

Wovoka (1856–1932 CE) Paiute Native American PROPHET and MYSTIC who, reacting against white domination, urged his followers to live in peace, fighting the whites through the power of the GHOST DANCE.

Wrath The righteous anger of God against SIN.

Writings The third and final division of the HEBREW BIBLE, comprising the Wisdom literature (such as Job and Proverbs), the Psalms, the later histories, and other material.

Wyclif, John (c. 1320–84) English religious reformer. He and his associates translated the Vulgate (Latin) into English.

X

Xipe Totec ('the flayed one') In Mexican mythology, the god of the west and of agriculture, who skinned himself like the maize.

Xiuhtecuhtli ('turquoise lord') The ancient Mexican fire god.

Y

Yahweh *see* YHWH.

Yama In the VEDAS the primordial man who crosses through death and becomes immortal. He is therefore god of death who judges men and consigns them to heaven or hell.

Yasna The form of public worship in ancient ZOROASTRIANISM, elements of which are retained by the PARSIS.

Yellow Hats Reformed branch of TIBETAN BUDDHISM whose leader is the DALAI LAMA.

Yggdrasil The great ash tree which unifies the creation according to Norse mythology. Its three roots reach ASGARD, MIDGARD, and Niflheim, the UNDERWORLD.

YHWH The 'tetragrammaton', the sacred name of the God of ISRAEL which was revealed to Moses. The name means 'I am'. It could not be spoken and the Hebrew '*Adonai*' ('the Lord') was substituted when the scriptures were read aloud.

Yin and Yang The polarity of energies in Chinese philosophy. *Yang* is masculine, dynamic, bright, and good; *yin* is feminine, passive, dark, and bad.

Yoga A way to union with GOD in HINDU philosophy. It also forms one of the six classical systems of Indian thought. Traditionally there are eight stages of yoga: restraint, discipline, posture, breathing, detachment, concentration, meditation, and trance.

Yogi Indian holy man who has reached ENLIGHTENMENT through yogic practices (*see* YOGA). (*See also* TRANSCENDENTAL MEDITATION.)

Yom Kippur/Day of Atonement Jewish day of FASTING and repentance, the most solemn day of the Jewish year.

Z

Zaddiq/Zadik Jewish teacher in the later Hasidism

Zakah A 'poor tax' charged at the rate of 2.5% of a person's total income for the year, in ISLAM.

Zarathushtra *see* ZOROASTER.

Za-Zen Japanese term for the form of MEDITATION practised in ZEN monasteries.

Zealots Jewish nationalistic party in Roman times who believed that the Roman presence was a defilement of the land and a flouting of TORAH.

Zen Japanese Buddhist movement which developed from the Chinese Ch'an school in the twelfth century CE. Zen aims at harmony in living and uses secular arts such as tea-making and calligraphy to develop effortless skills.

Zeus Supreme ruler of the Greek gods. Sometimes the name Zeus stood simply for God, as supreme deity.

Zevi, Shabbetai (1628–76 CE) Kabbalistic RABBI from Smyrna who became the centre of a messianic movement which spread throughout the Jewish world (*see* KABBALAH).

Ziggurat Ancient Babylonian TEMPLE in the form of a tower rising from a broad base to a narrow top.

Zionism The movement to establish a national and permanent homeland for Jews.

Zohar Most important writing of the Jewish KABBALAH.

Zombie Term used in Haiti and South America for the 'living dead'.

Zoroaster/Zarathushtra Prophet and founder of ZOROASTRIANISM. He lived in Persia, possibly as early as 1200 BCE.

Zoroastrianism The religion of ancient Persia, founded by ZOROASTER, possibly related to the Vedic religion of India (*see* VEDAS).

Zurvanism Zoroastrian heresy according to which an absolute being called Zurvan ('time') was the origin of good and evil.

Index

Numbers in **bold type** indicate pages with illustrations.

Picture Acknowledgments

Dreamstime: pp. 13, 21, 36, 46, 48, 53, 88, 92, 94, 108, 122, 129, 161, 169, 174, 176, 179, 223, 243, 277, 276, 280, 291, 326, 331, 333, 335, 343

Illustrated London News: p. 3

Israel Government Tourist Office: p. 213

Photolink: pp. iii, 9, 84, 85, 95, 105, 120, 127, 235, 241, 242, 256, 259, 288

Pixabay: pp. 261, 344, 352,

Tim Dowley Associates: pp. 16, 99, 206, 250, 273, 305, 315, 322